Nothing stays forever.
藤崎 竜

I can take time off three times a year, at New Year's, Golden Week and Obon, because that's when double issues come out. I look forward to it and make plans, but when I try to spend time according to my plans, I get more tired than when I'm working.

The best way to spend my holidays seems to be to take it easy.

Ryu Fujisaki

封神演義

Ryu Fujisaki's *Worlds* came in second place for the prestigious 40th Tezuka Award. His *Psycho +*, *Wāqwāq* and *Hoshin Engi* have all run in *Weekly Shonen Jump* magazine, and the *Hoshin Engi* anime is available on DVD in Japan and North America. A lover of science fiction, literature and history, Fujisaki has made *Hoshin Engi* a mix of genres that truly showcases his amazing art and imagination.

HOSHIN ENGI VOL. 20
SHONEN JUMP Manga Edition

STORY AND ART BY RYU FUJISAKI

Based on the novel *Hoshin Engi*, translated by Tsutomu Ano,
published by Kodansha Bunko

Translation & Adaptation/Tomo Kimura
Touch-up Art & Lettering/HudsonYards
Design/Matt Hinrichs
Editor/Jonathan Tarbox

VP, Production/Alvin Lu
VP, Sales & Product Marketing/Gonzalo Ferreyra
VP, Creative/Linda Espinosa
Publisher/Hyoe Narita

Printed in Canada

Published by VIZ Media, LLC
P.O. Box 77010
San Francisco, CA 94107

10 9 8 7 6 5 4 3 2 1
First printing, September 2010

HOSHIN ENGI

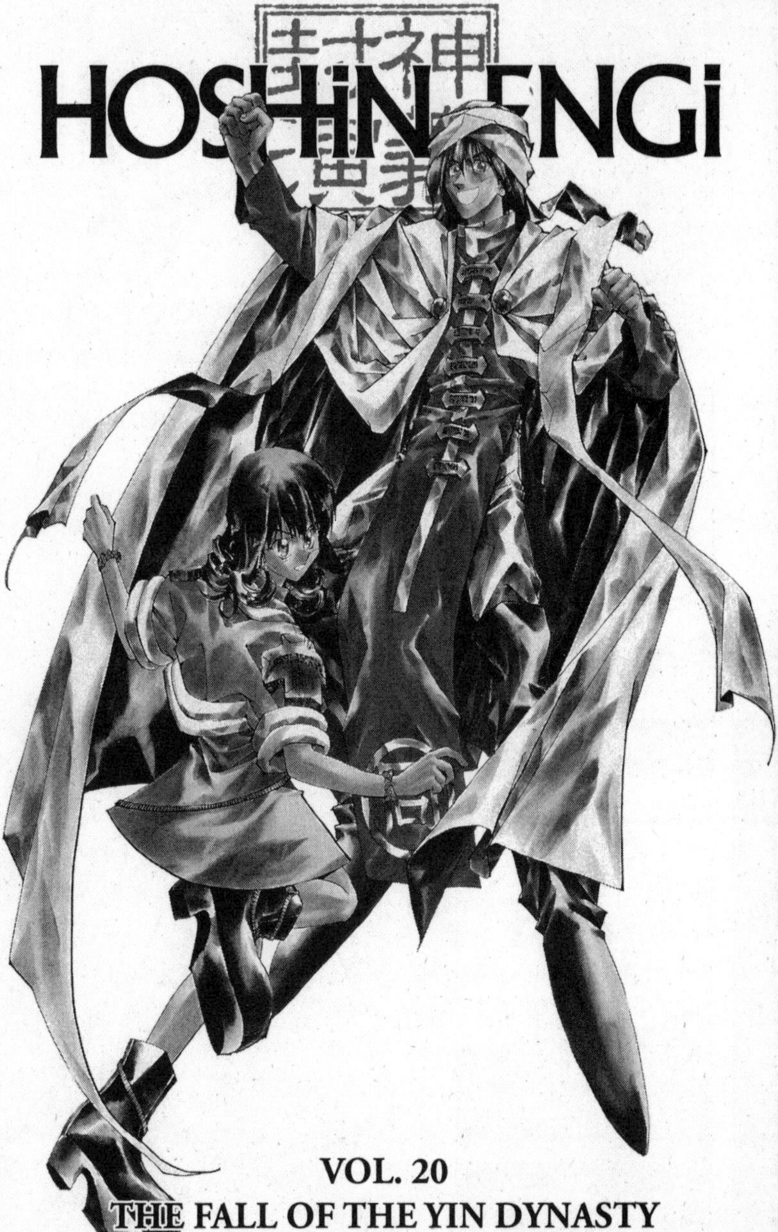

VOL. 20

THE FALL OF THE YIN DYNASTY

STORY AND ART BY RYU FUJISAKI

THE CHARACTERS

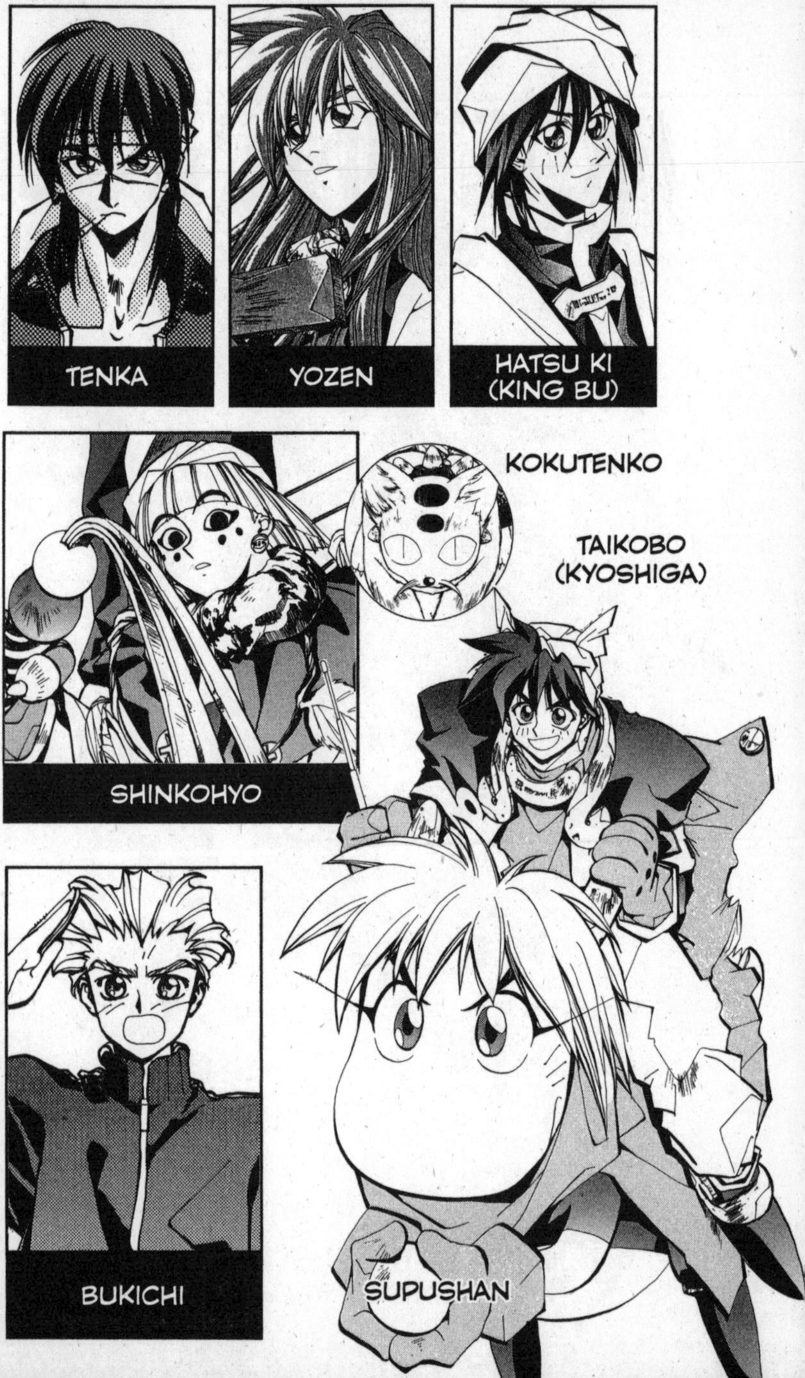
TENKA
YOZEN
HATSU KI
(KING BU)
KOKUTENKO
TAIKOBO
(KYOSHIGA)
SHINKOHYO
BUKICHI
SUPUSHAN

KING CHU

JOKA

DAKKI

OKIJIN

KOKIBI

The Story Thus Far

Ancient China, over 3,000 years ago. It is the era of the Yin Dynasty.

After King Chu, the emperor, married the beautiful Dakki, the good king was no longer himself and became an unmanly and foolish ruler. Dakki, a *Sennyo* with a wicked heart, took control of Yin, and the country fell into chaos.

To save the human world, the Hoshin Project was put into action. The project will seal evil Sennin and Doshi into the Shinkai and cause Seihakuko Sho Ki to set up a new dynasty to replace Yin. Taikobo, who was chosen to execute this project, acts to install Sho Ki's heir Hatsu Ki as the next king.

Taikobo and his comrades suffer huge casualties in the intense battles, but in the end they manage to defeat their enemies. After defeating Bunchu, they finally reach Bokuya, the final guard station before Choka, the royal capital of Yin. There, Taikobo and his comrades must battle against the monarch King Chu, who is Dakki's strongest minion. When King Chu sees his people cower in fear at their king who has turned into a monster, his loneliness makes him sane again.

VOL. 20
THE FALL OF THE YIN DYNASTY

CONTENTS

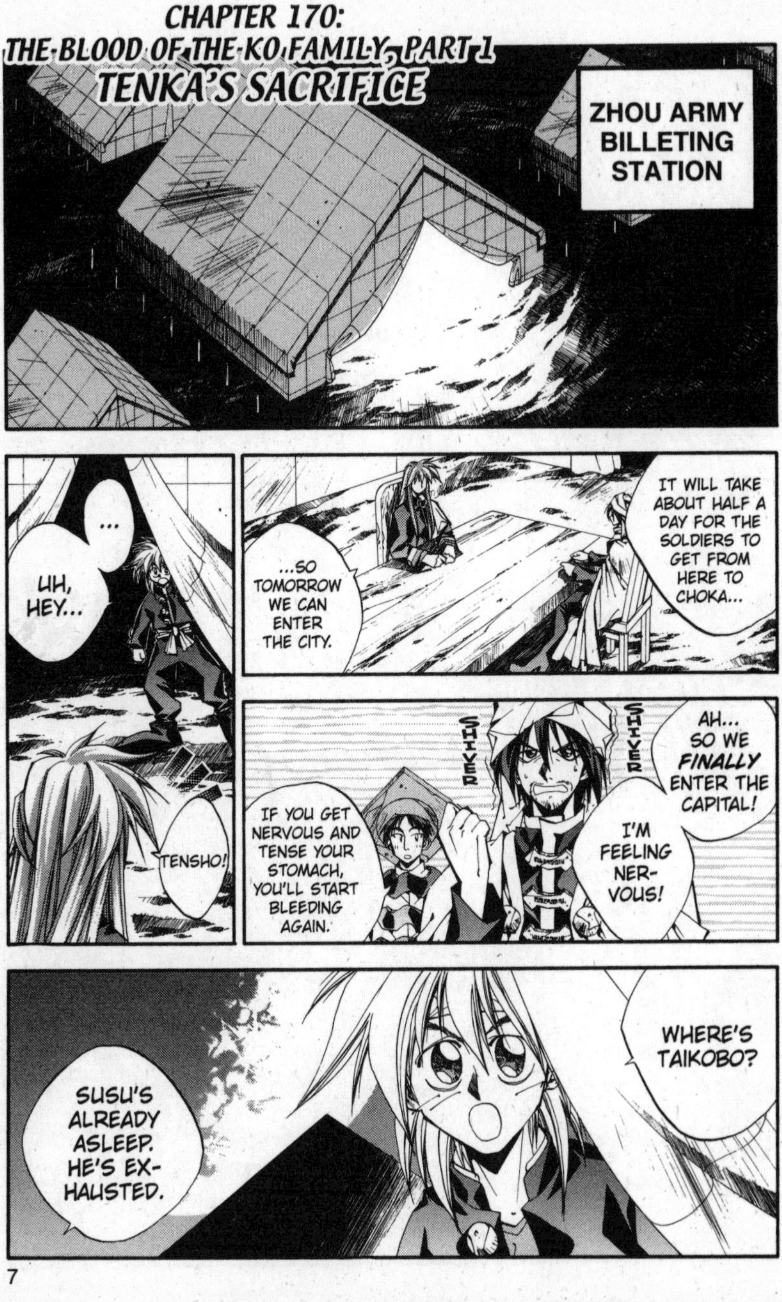
CHAPTER 170:
THE BLOOD OF THE KO FAMILY, PART 1
TENKA'S SACRIFICE
ZHOU ARMY BILLETING STATION
IT WILL TAKE ABOUT HALF A DAY FOR THE SOLDIERS TO GET FROM HERE TO CHOKA...
...SO TOMORROW WE CAN ENTER THE CITY.
SHIVER
SHIVER
AH... SO WE *FINALLY* ENTER THE CAPITAL!
I'M FEELING NER-VOUS!
IF YOU GET NERVOUS AND TENSE YOUR STOMACH, YOU'LL START BLEEDING AGAIN.
...
UH, HEY...
TENSHO!
WHERE'S TAIKOBO?
SUSU'S ALREADY ASLEEP. HE'S EX-HAUSTED.

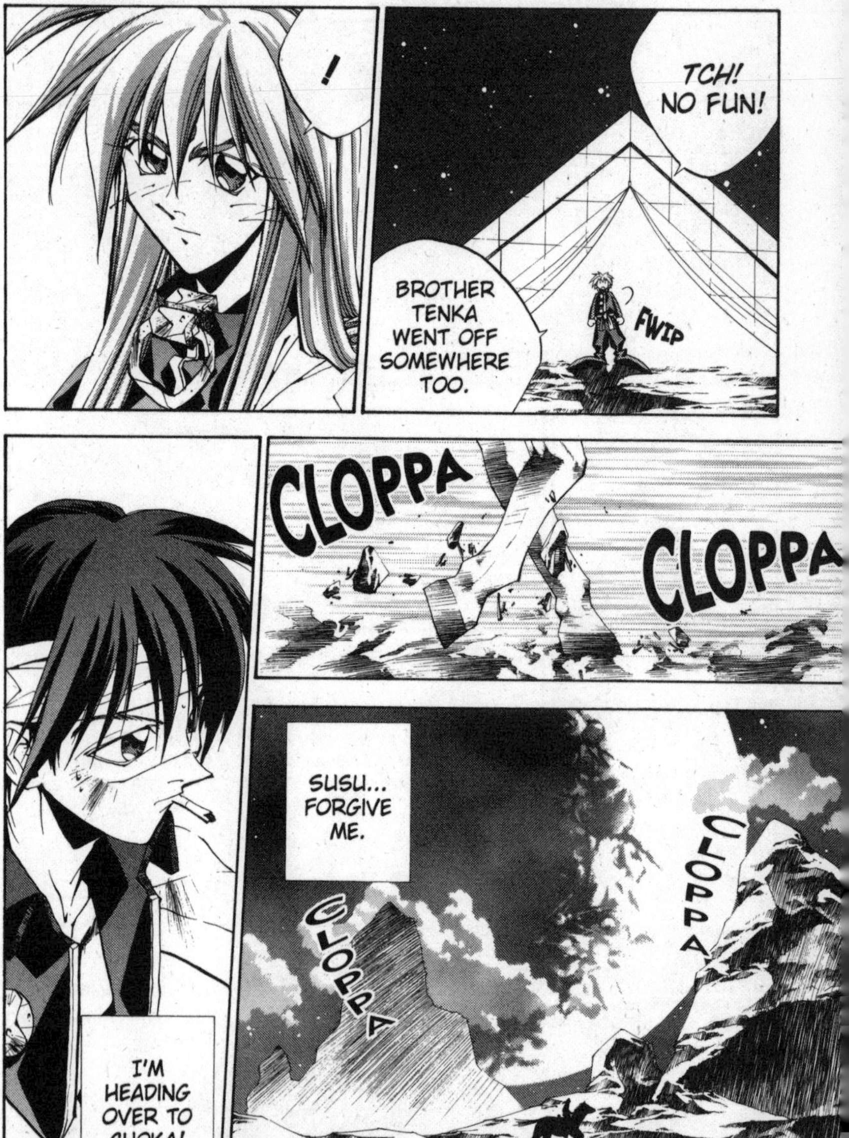
TCH! NO FUN!
BROTHER TENKA WENT OFF SOMEWHERE TOO.
FWIP
!
CLOPPA
CLOPPA
SUSU... FORGIVE ME.
CLOPPA
CLOPPA
I'M HEADING OVER TO CHOKA!

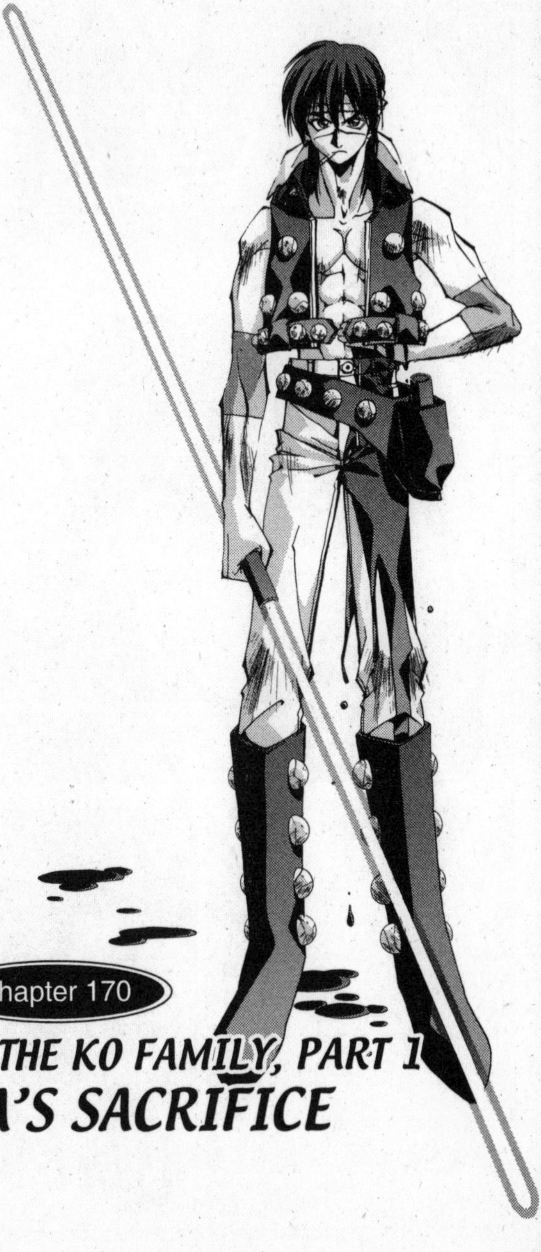

Chapter 170

THE BLOOD OF THE KO FAMILY, PART 1
TENKA'S SACRIFICE

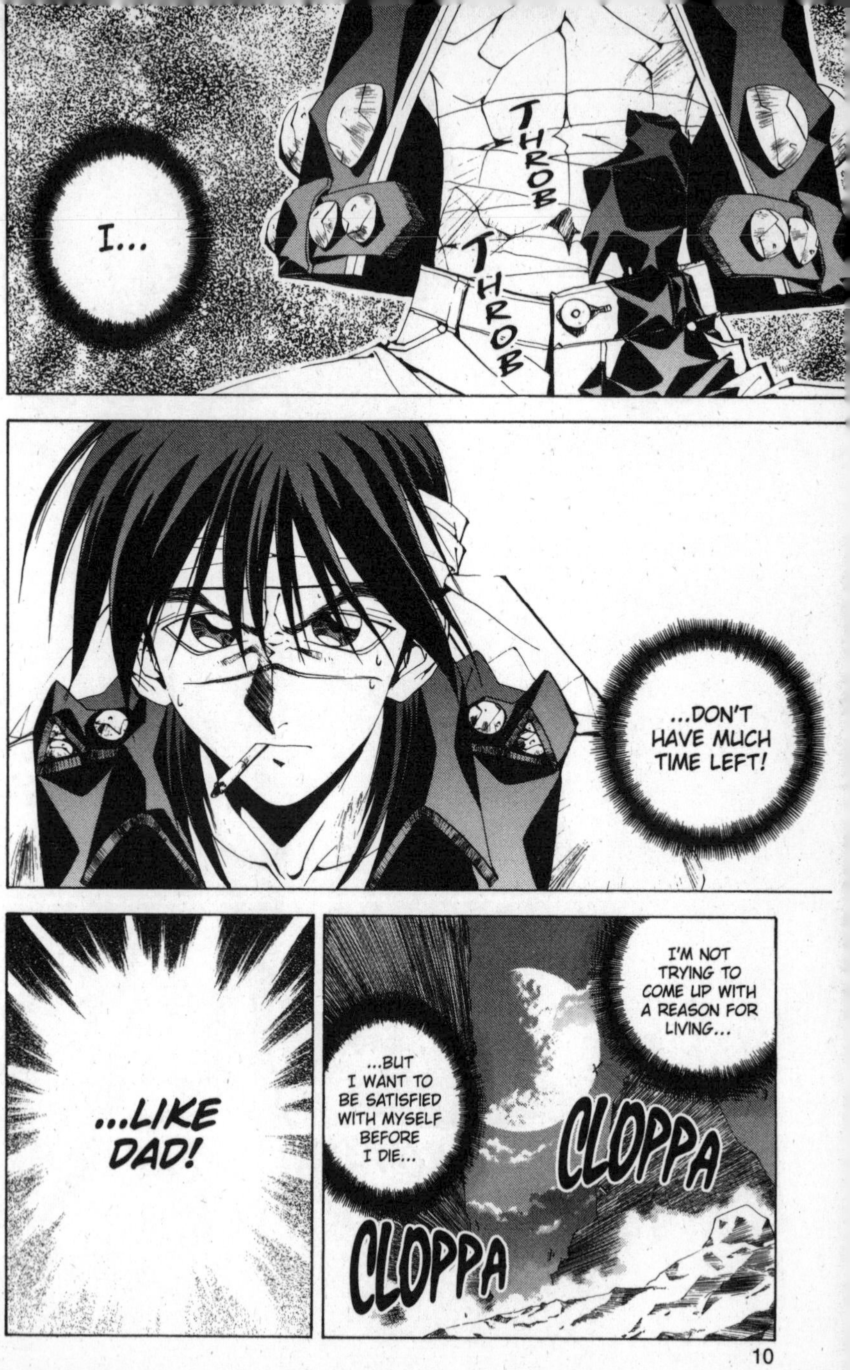
THROB
THROB
I...
...DON'T HAVE MUCH TIME LEFT!
I'M NOT TRYING TO COME UP WITH A REASON FOR LIVING...
...BUT I WANT TO BE SATISFIED WITH MYSELF BEFORE I DIE...
CLOPPA
CLOPPA
...LIKE DAD!

READ THIS WAY

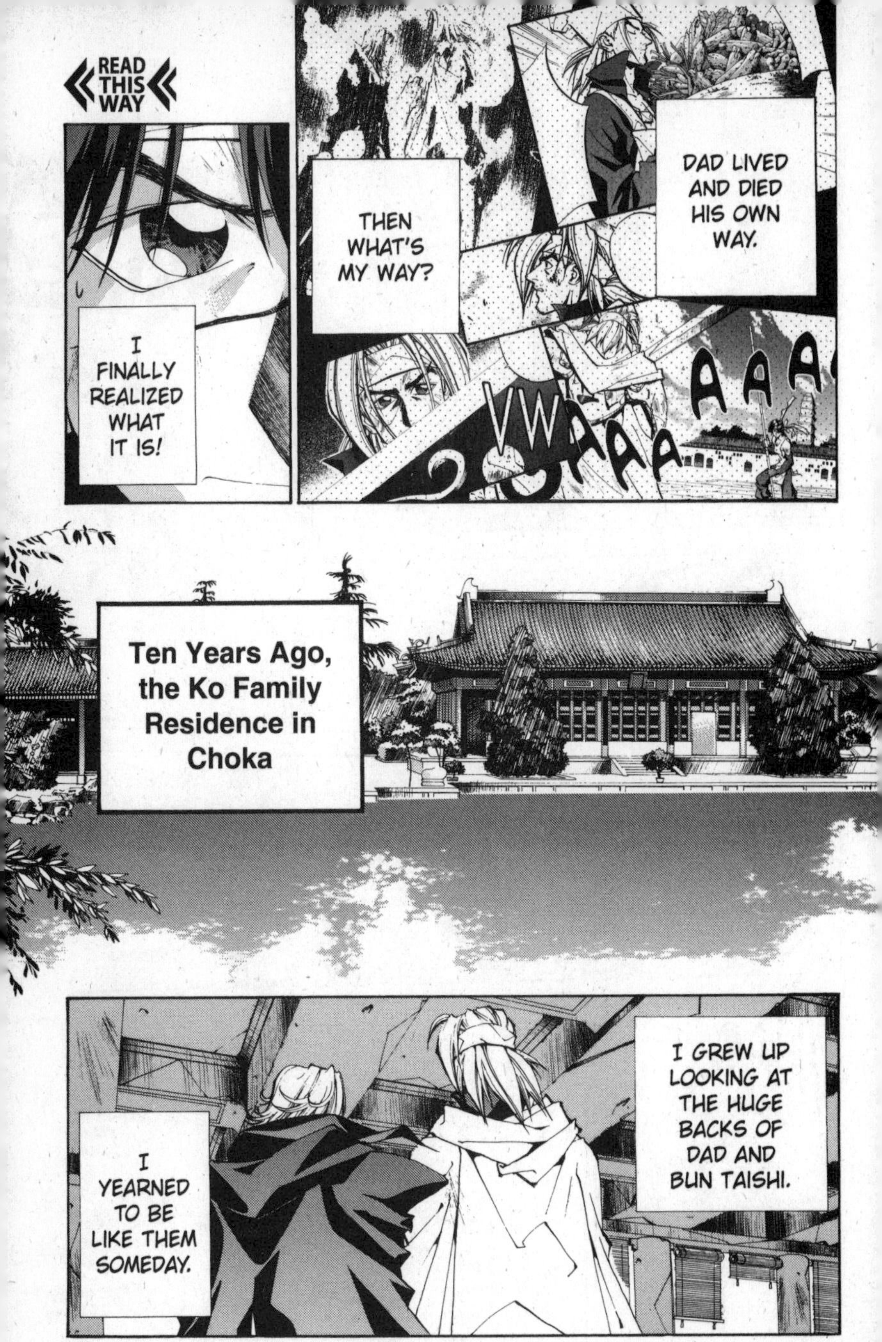
DAD LIVED AND DIED HIS OWN WAY.
THEN WHAT'S MY WAY?
VWAAAAAAAAA
I FINALLY REALIZED WHAT IT IS!
Ten Years Ago, the Ko Family Residence in Choka
I GREW UP LOOKING AT THE HUGE BACKS OF DAD AND BUN TAISHI.
I YEARNED TO BE LIKE THEM SOMEDAY.

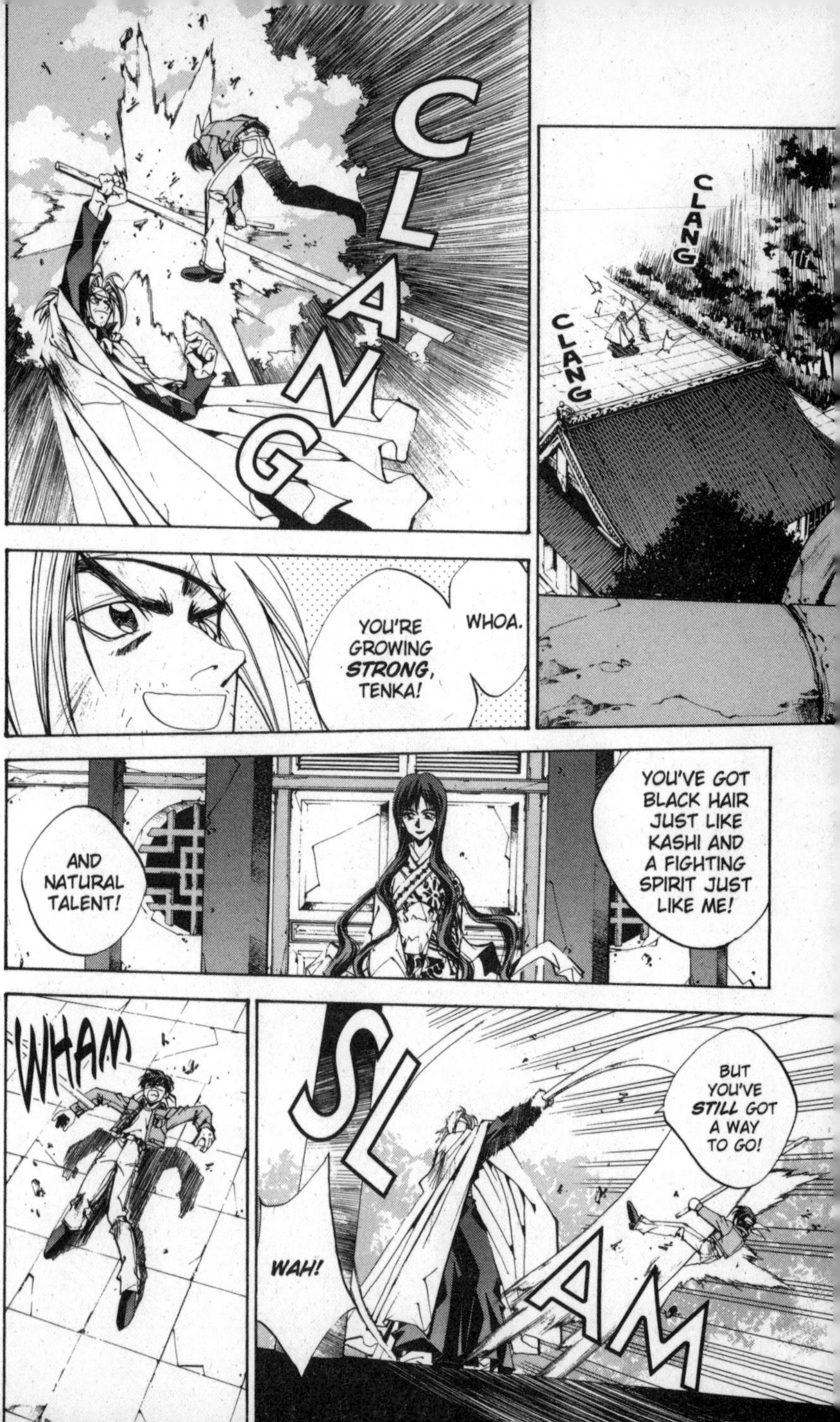
CLANG
CLANG
CLANG
WHOA.
YOU'RE GROWING STRONG, TENKA!
YOU'VE GOT BLACK HAIR JUST LIKE KASHI AND A FIGHTING SPIRIT JUST LIKE ME!
AND NATURAL TALENT!
BUT YOU'VE STILL GOT A WAY TO GO!
SLAM
WAH!
WHAM

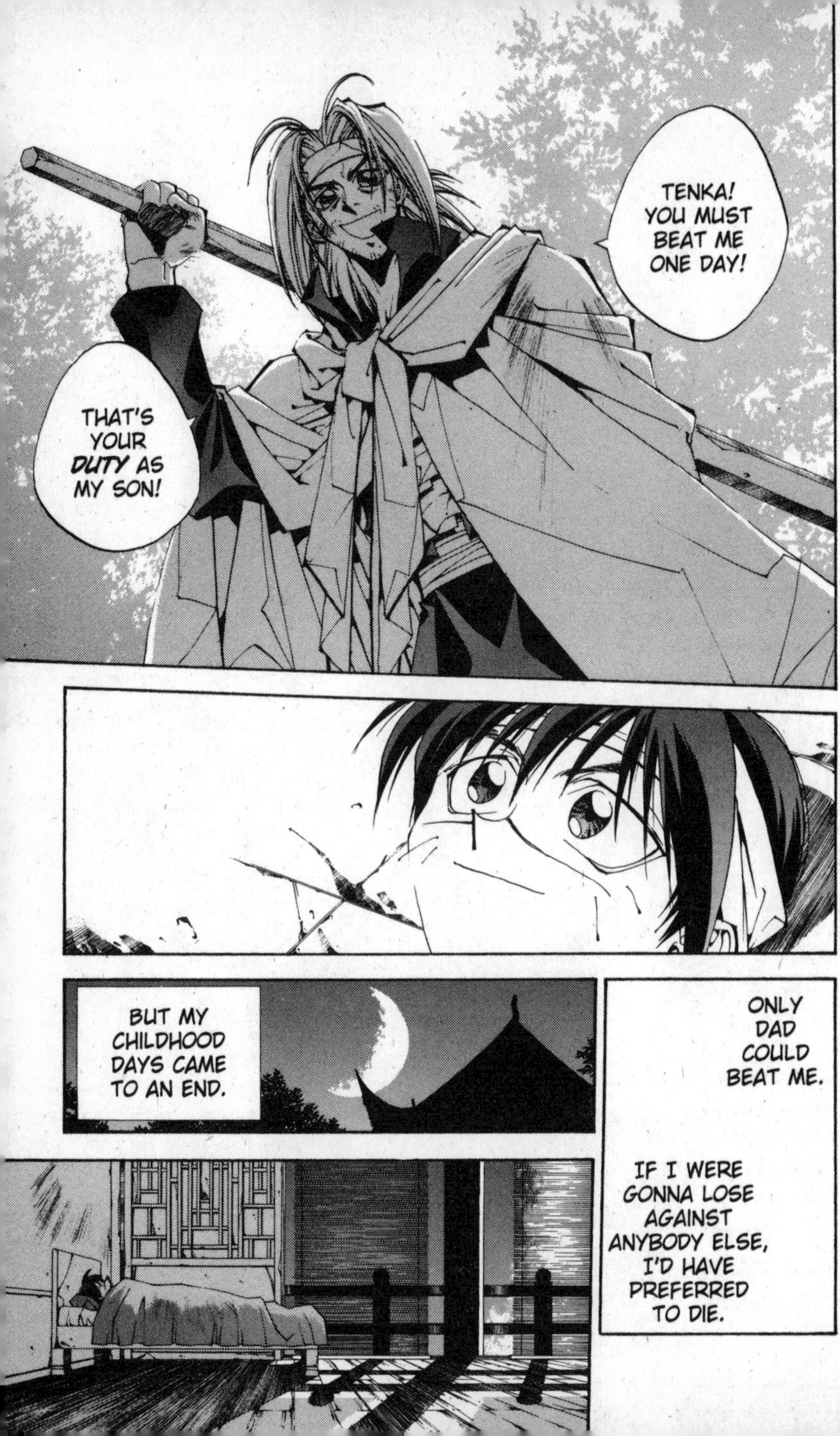
TENKA! YOU MUST BEAT ME ONE DAY!
THAT'S YOUR *DUTY* AS MY SON!
ONLY DAD COULD BEAT ME.
BUT MY CHILDHOOD DAYS CAME TO AN END.
IF I WERE GONNA LOSE AGAINST ANYBODY ELSE, I'D HAVE PREFERRED TO DIE.

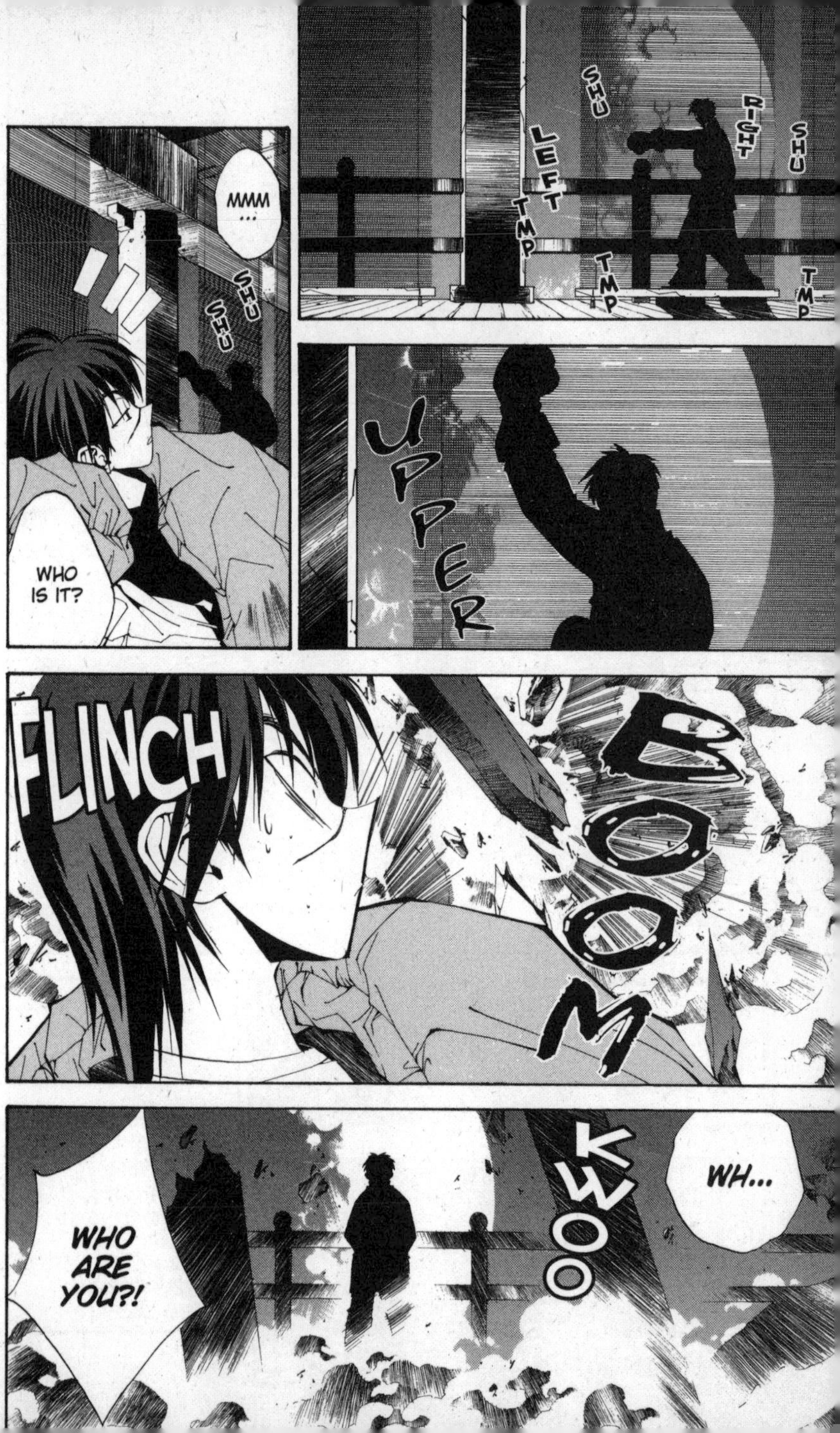
SHU
LEFT
RIGHT
SHU
TMP
TMP
TMP
UPPER
MMM...
SHU
SHU
WHO IS IT?
BOOM
FLINCH
WH...
KWOO
WHO ARE YOU?!

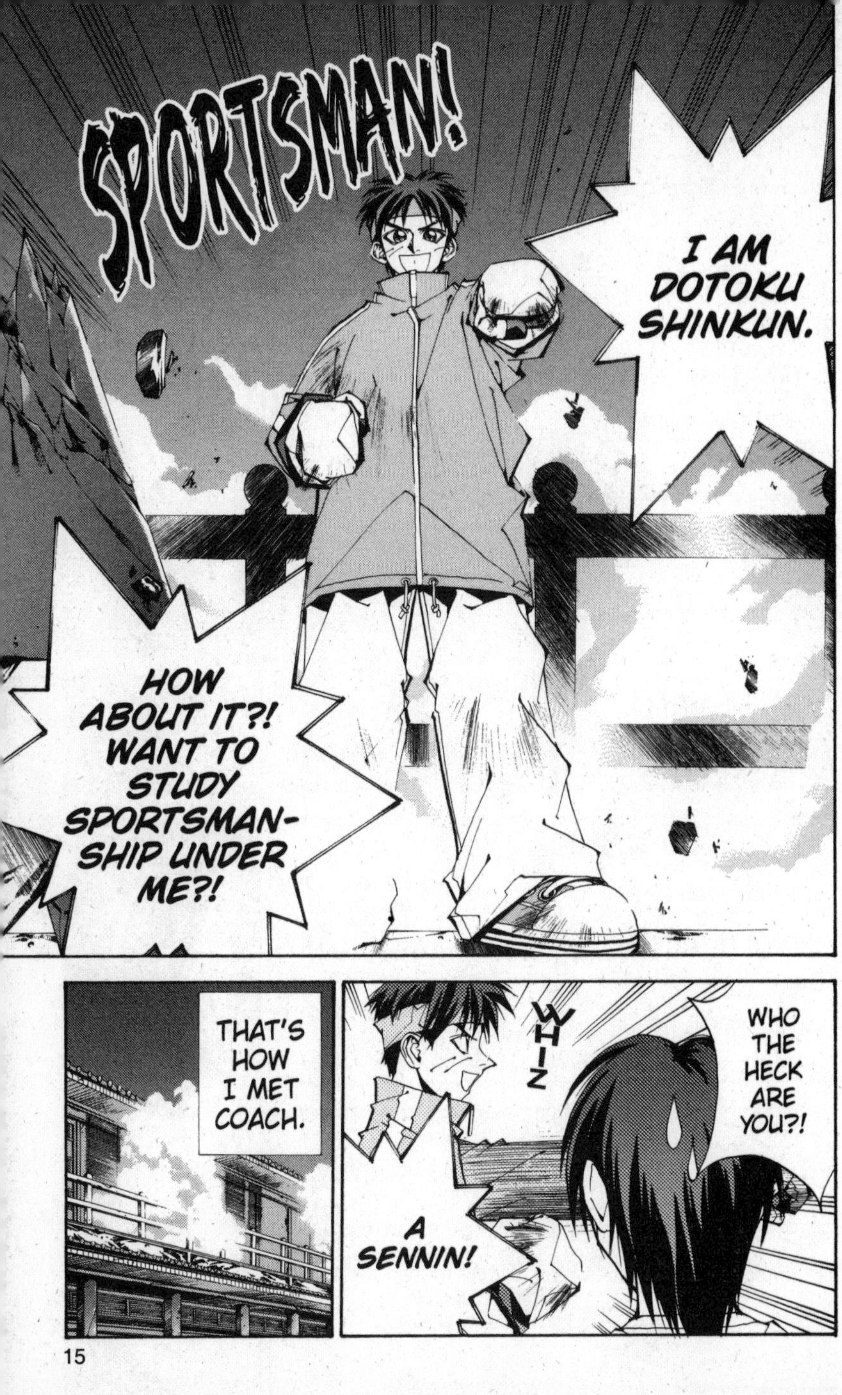
SPORTSMAN!
I AM DOTOKU SHINKUN.
HOW ABOUT IT?! WANT TO STUDY SPORTSMANSHIP UNDER ME?!
WHIZ
WHO THE HECK ARE YOU?!
A SENNIN!
THAT'S HOW I MET COACH.

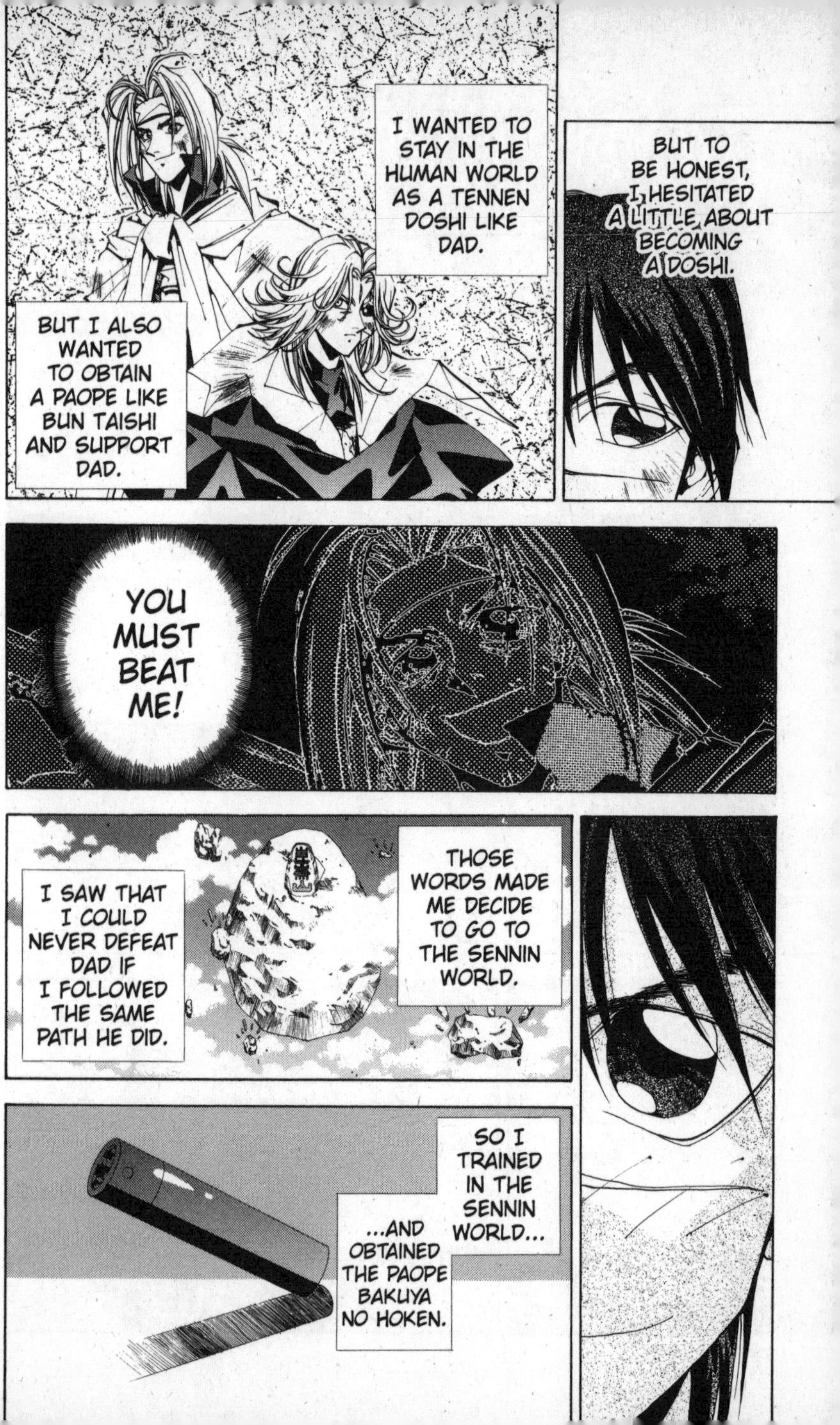
BUT TO BE HONEST, I HESITATED A LITTLE ABOUT BECOMING A DOSHI.
I WANTED TO STAY IN THE HUMAN WORLD AS A TENNEN DOSHI LIKE DAD.
BUT I ALSO WANTED TO OBTAIN A PAOPE LIKE BUN TAISHI AND SUPPORT DAD.
YOU MUST BEAT ME!
THOSE WORDS MADE ME DECIDE TO GO TO THE SENNIN WORLD.
I SAW THAT I COULD NEVER DEFEAT DAD IF I FOLLOWED THE SAME PATH HE DID.
SO I TRAINED IN THE SENNIN WORLD...
...AND OBTAINED THE PAOPE BAKUYA NO HOKEN.

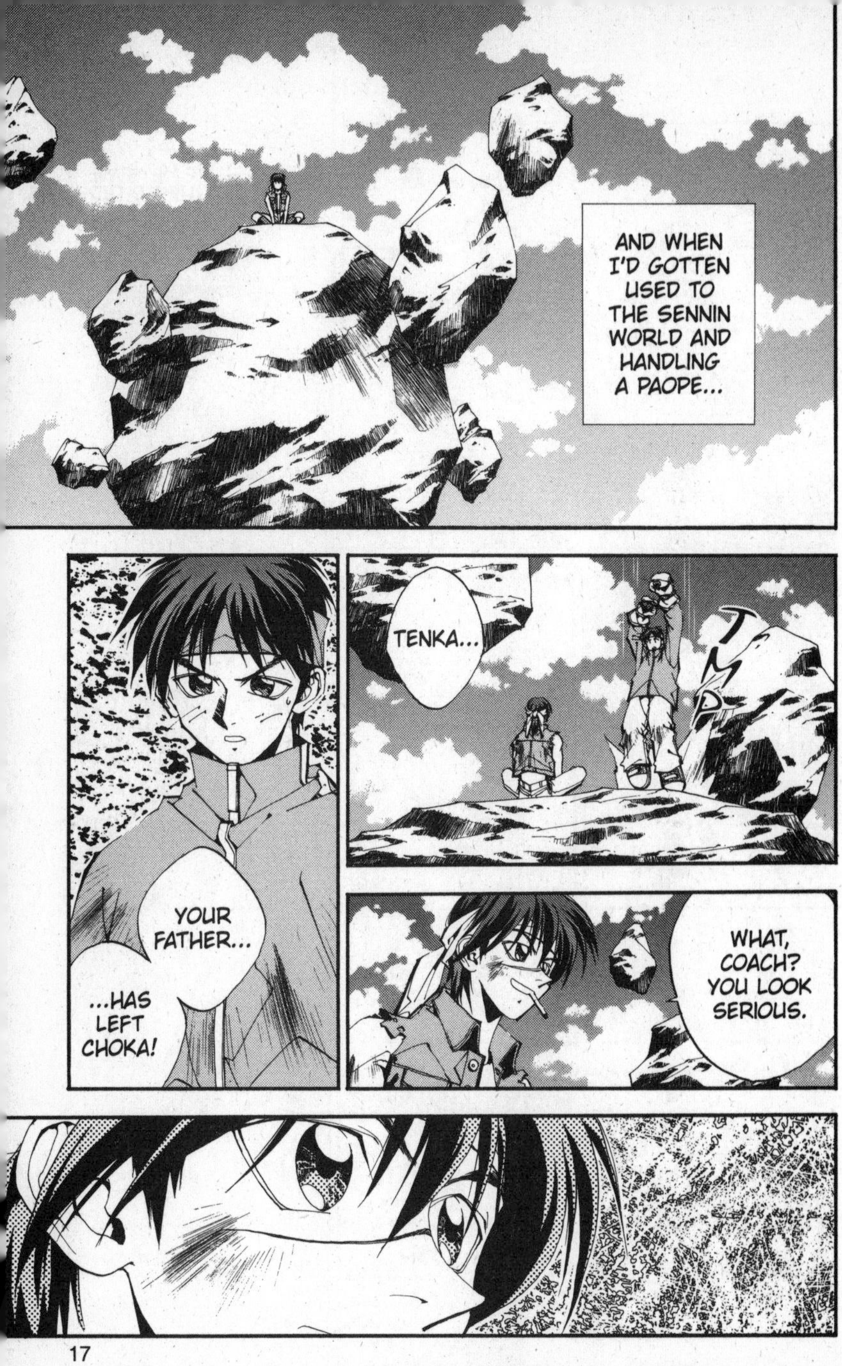
AND WHEN I'D GOTTEN USED TO THE SENNIN WORLD AND HANDLING A PAOPE...
TENKA...
TMP
WHAT, COACH? YOU LOOK SERIOUS.
YOUR FATHER...
...HAS LEFT CHOKA!

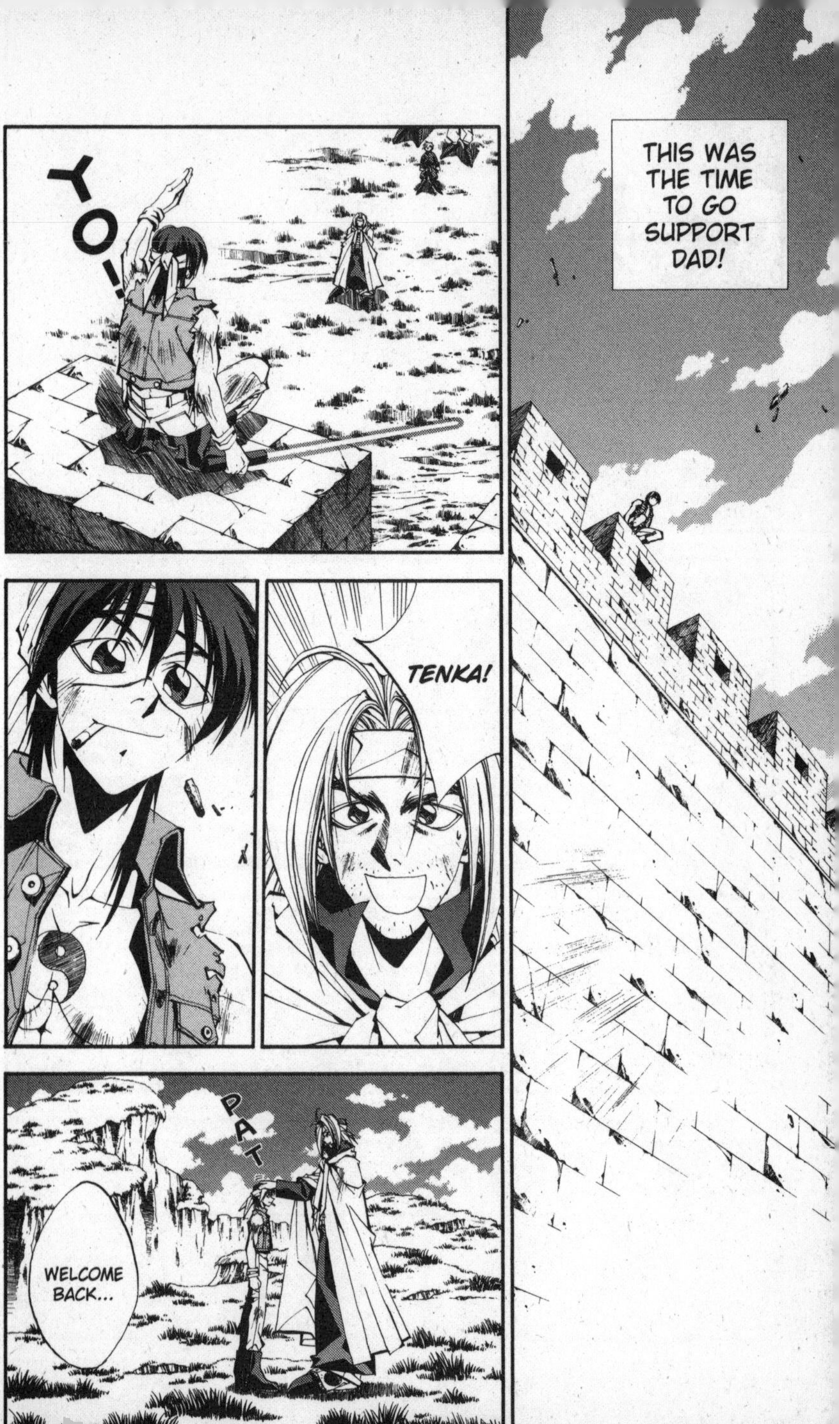
THIS WAS THE TIME TO GO SUPPORT DAD!
YO!
TENKA!
PAT
WELCOME BACK...

READ THIS WAY

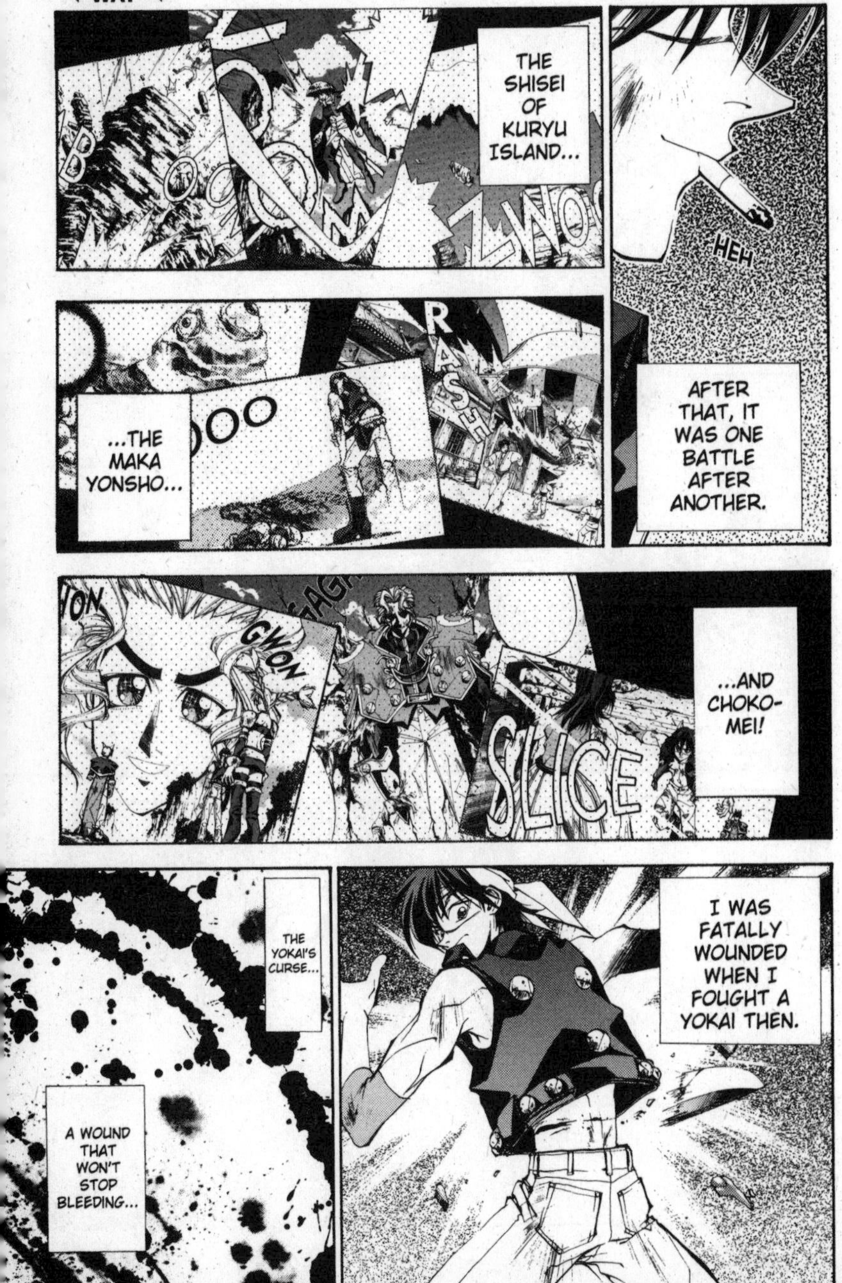
HEH
AFTER THAT, IT WAS ONE BATTLE AFTER ANOTHER.
THE SHISEI OF KURYU ISLAND...
...THE MAKA YONSHO...
...AND CHOKO-MEI!
SLICE
GWON
I WAS FATALLY WOUNDED WHEN I FOUGHT A YOKAI THEN.
THE YOKAI'S CURSE...
A WOUND THAT WON'T STOP BLEEDING...

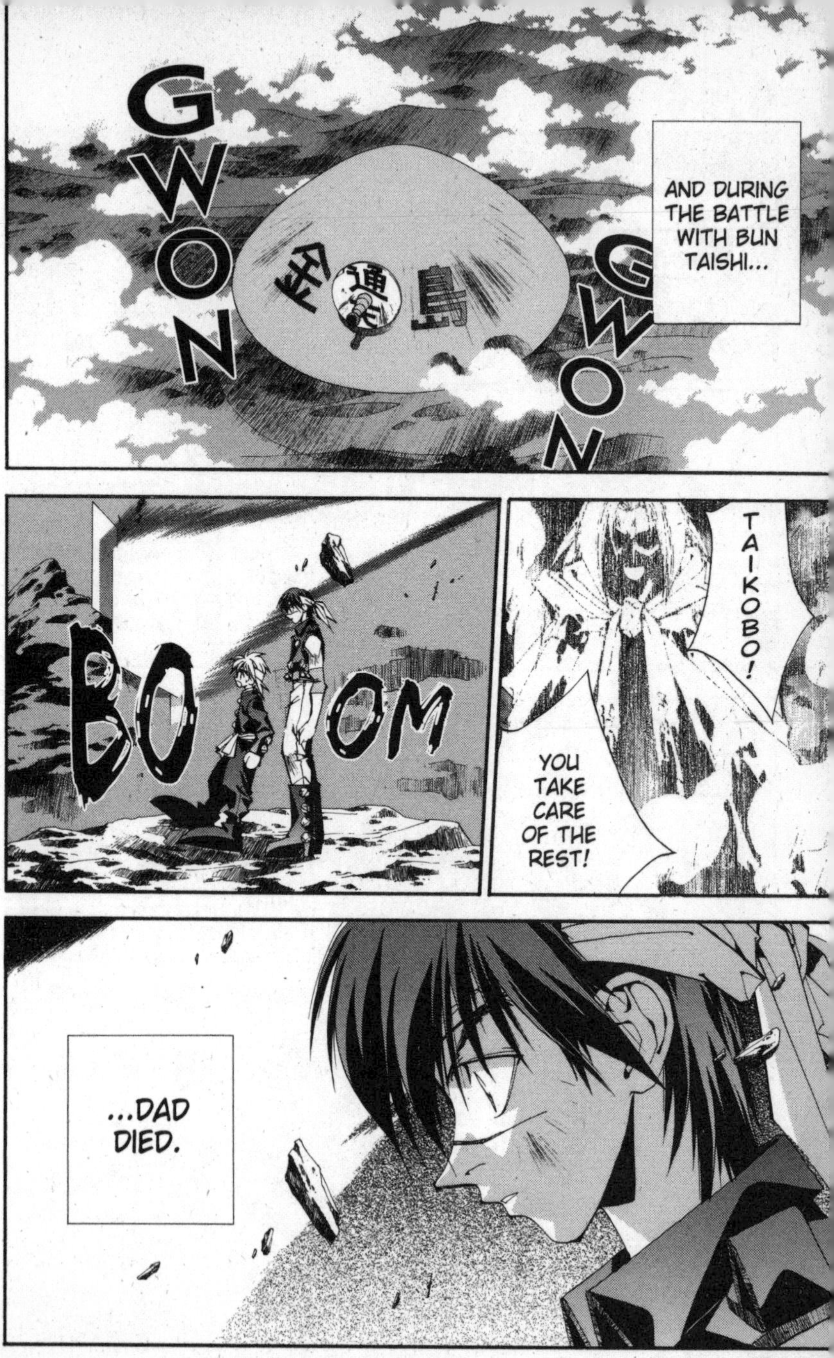
GWON
GWON
AND DURING THE BATTLE WITH BUN TAISHI...
TAIKOBO!
YOU TAKE CARE OF THE REST!
BOOM
...DAD DIED.

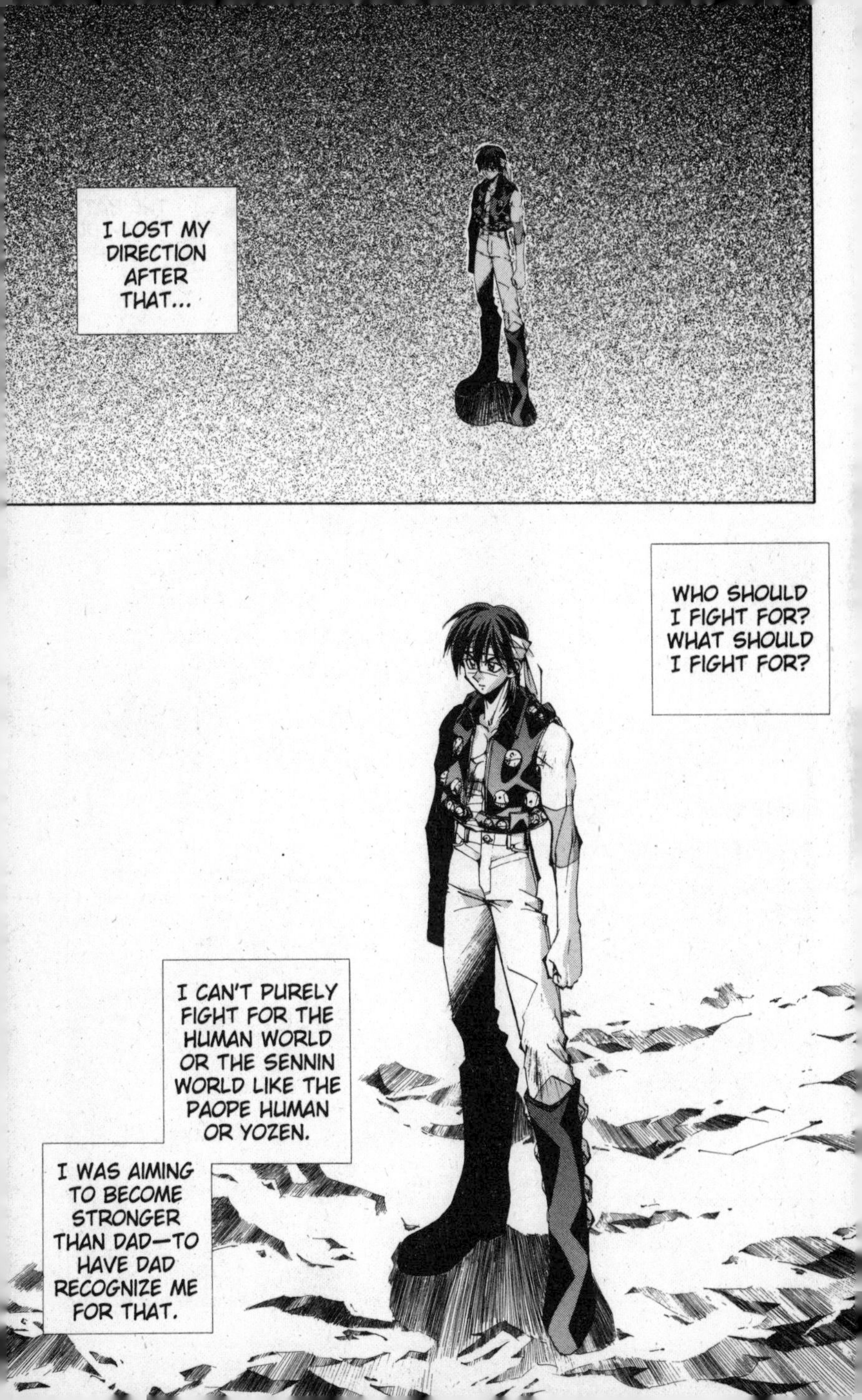
I LOST MY DIRECTION AFTER THAT...
WHO SHOULD I FIGHT FOR? WHAT SHOULD I FIGHT FOR?
I CAN'T PURELY FIGHT FOR THE HUMAN WORLD OR THE SENNIN WORLD LIKE THE PAOPE HUMAN OR YOZEN.
I WAS AIMING TO BECOME STRONGER THAN DAD—TO HAVE DAD RECOGNIZE ME FOR THAT.

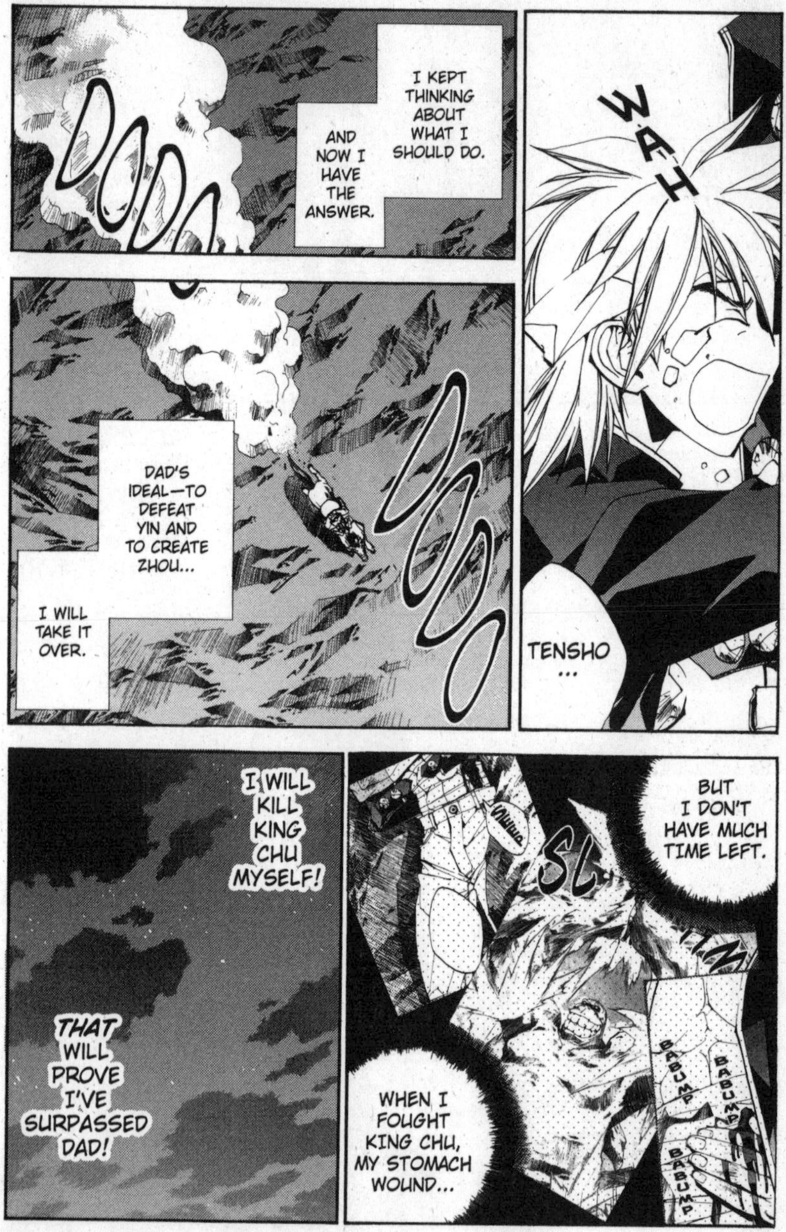
WAH
TENSHO ...
I KEPT THINKING ABOUT WHAT I SHOULD DO.
AND NOW I HAVE THE ANSWER.
DODO
DAD'S IDEAL—TO DEFEAT YIN AND TO CREATE ZHOU...
I WILL TAKE IT OVER.
BUT I DON'T HAVE MUCH TIME LEFT.
WHEN I FOUGHT KING CHU, MY STOMACH WOUND...
BABUMP BABUMP BABUMP
I WILL KILL KING CHU MYSELF!
THAT WILL PROVE I'VE SURPASSED DAD!

READ THIS WAY

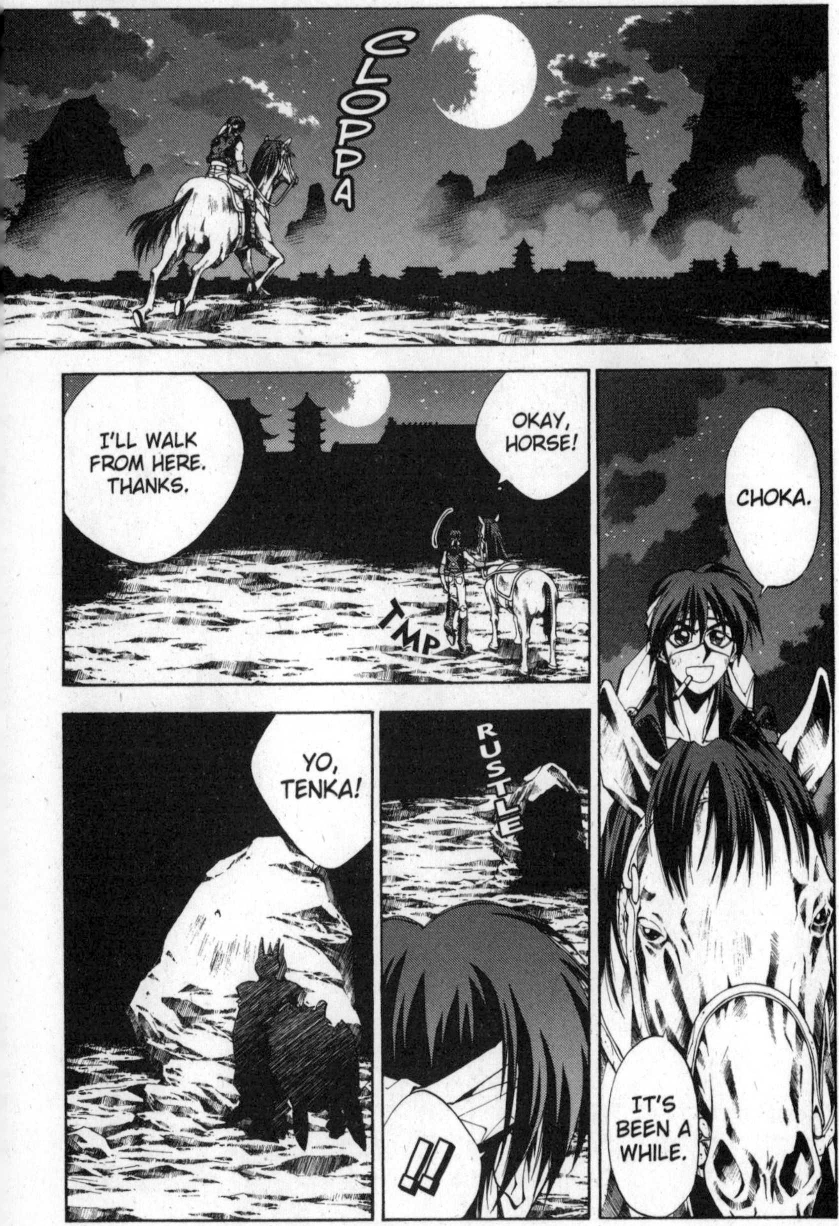

CLOPPA
OKAY, HORSE!
I'LL WALK FROM HERE. THANKS.
TMP
RUSTLE
!!
YO, TENKA!
CHOKA.
IT'S BEEN A WHILE.

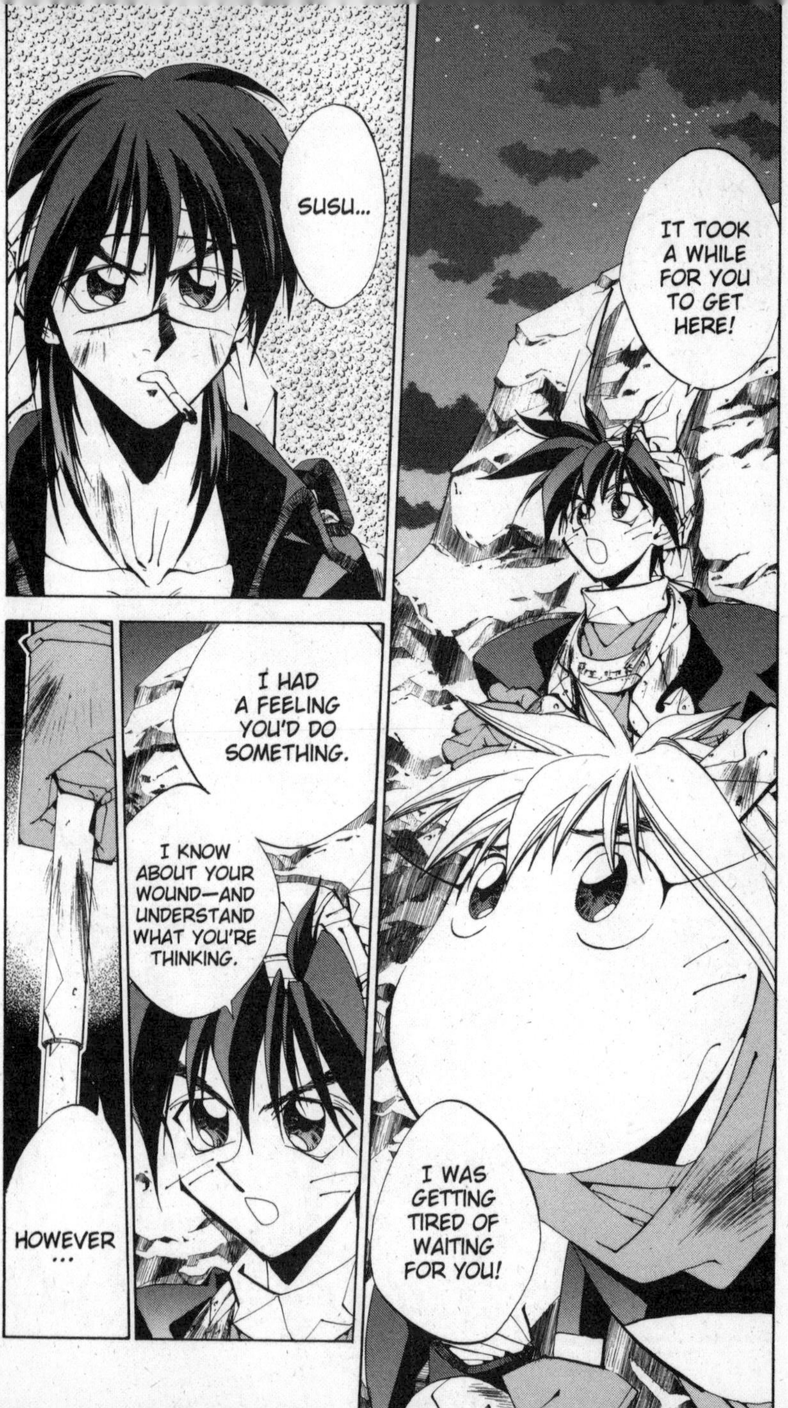
IT TOOK A WHILE FOR YOU TO GET HERE!
I WAS GETTING TIRED OF WAITING FOR YOU!
SUSU...
I HAD A FEELING YOU'D DO SOMETHING.
I KNOW ABOUT YOUR WOUND—AND UNDERSTAND WHAT YOU'RE THINKING.
HOWEVER ...

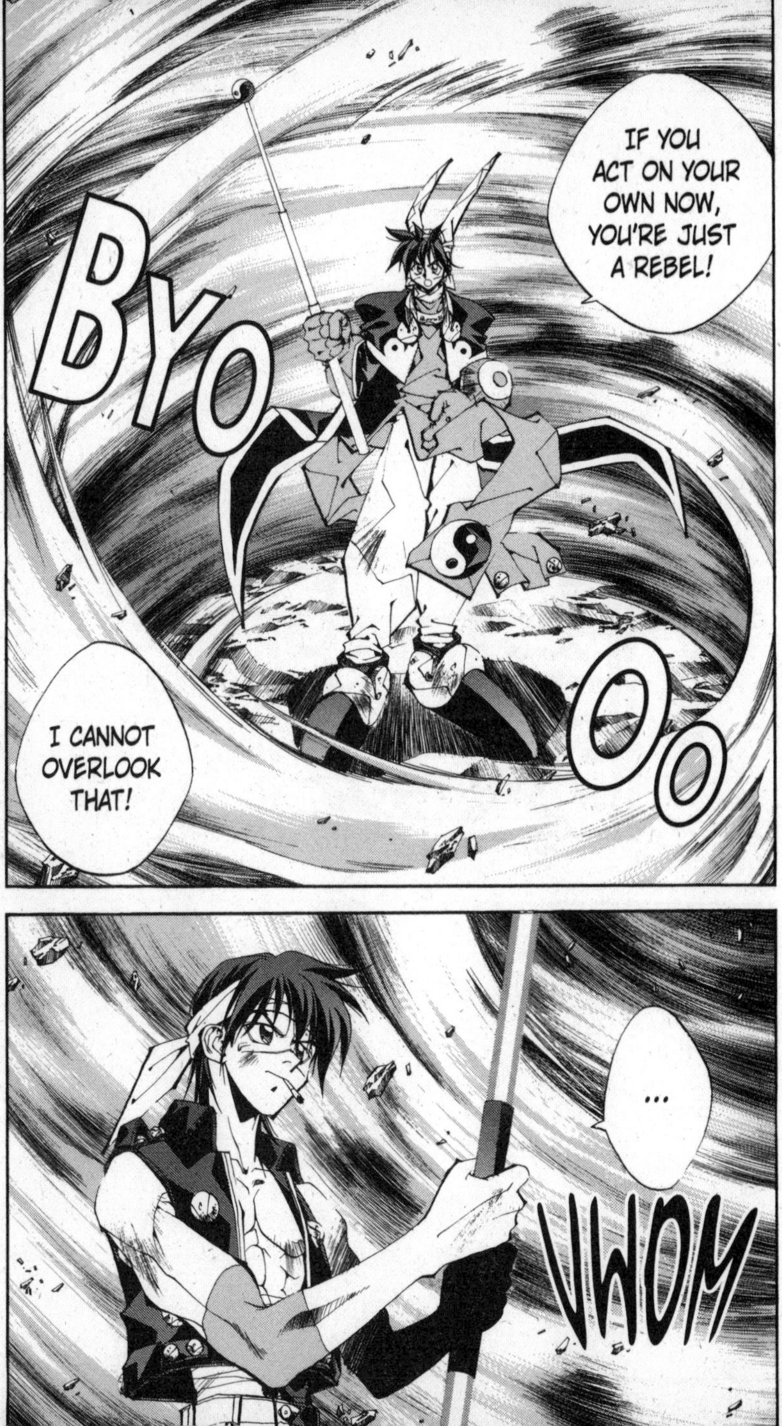
IF YOU ACT ON YOUR OWN NOW, YOU'RE JUST A REBEL!
BYOOOO
I CANNOT OVERLOOK THAT!
...
VWOM

封神演義

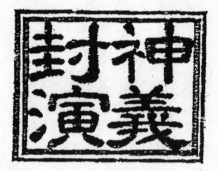

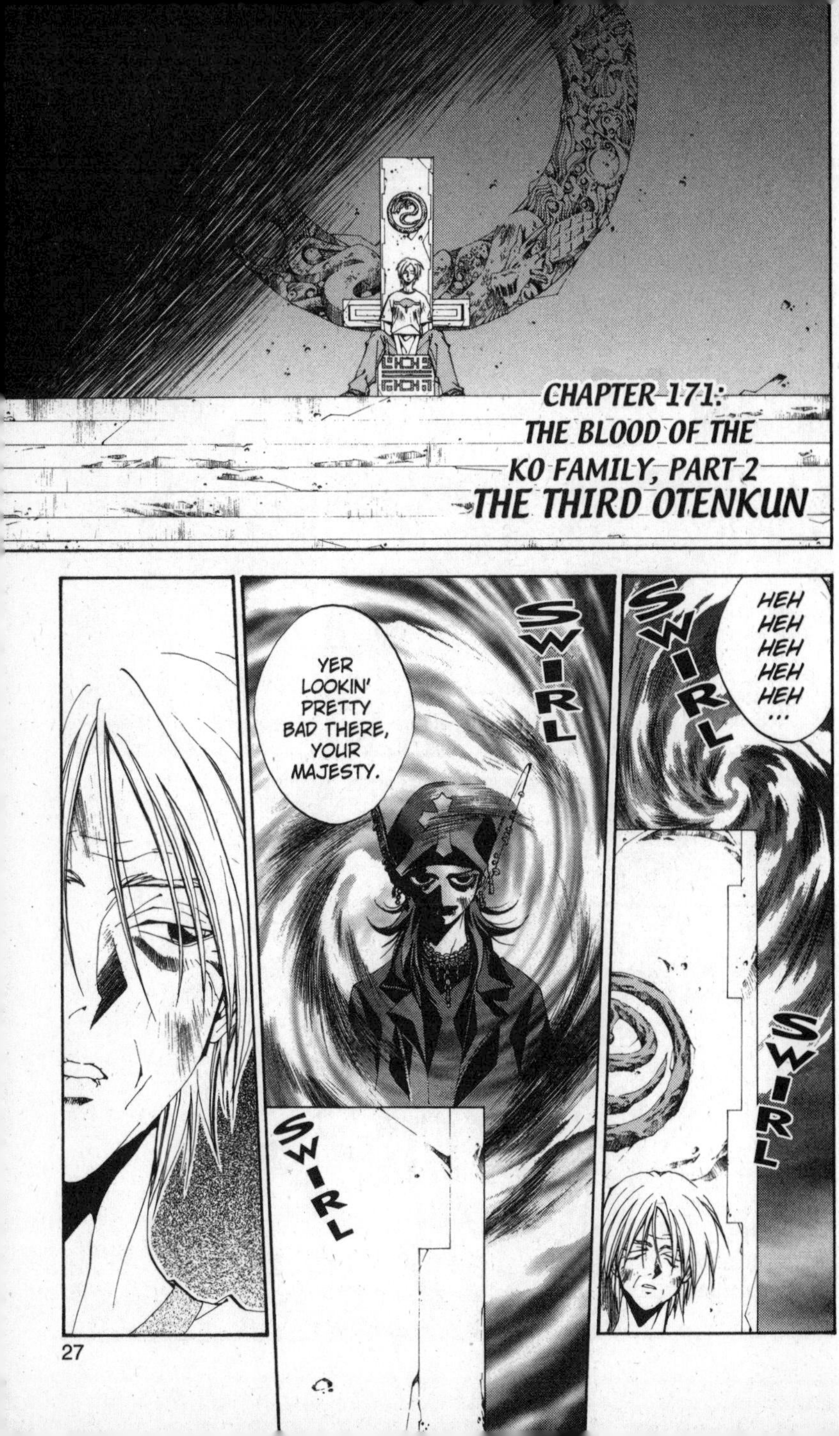
CHAPTER 171:
THE BLOOD OF THE
KO FAMILY, PART 2
THE THIRD OTENKUN
SWIRL
HEH HEH HEH HEH HEH ...
SWIRL
YER LOOKIN' PRETTY BAD THERE, YOUR MAJESTY.
SWIRL
SWIRL

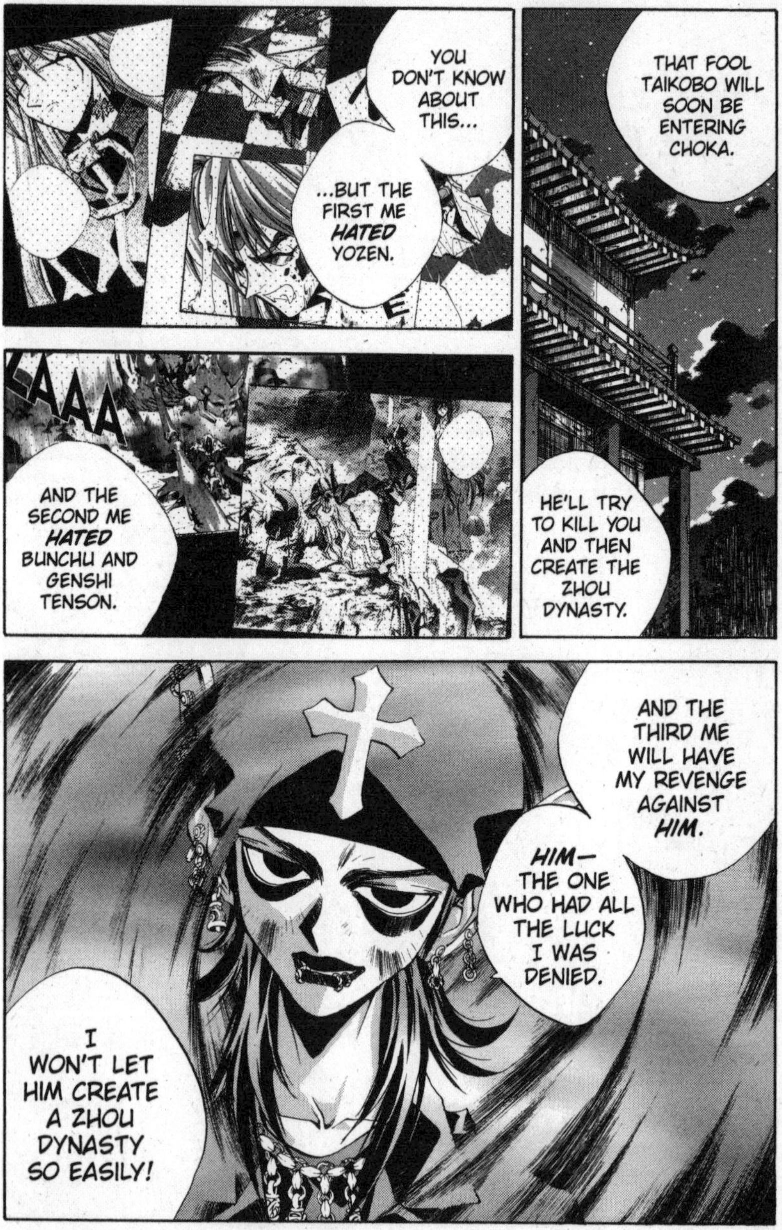
THAT FOOL TAIKOBO WILL SOON BE ENTERING CHOKA.
HE'LL TRY TO KILL YOU AND THEN CREATE THE ZHOU DYNASTY.
YOU DON'T KNOW ABOUT THIS...
...BUT THE FIRST ME *HATED* YOZEN.
AND THE SECOND ME *HATED* BUNCHU AND GENSHI TENSON.
AND THE THIRD ME WILL HAVE MY REVENGE AGAINST *HIM*.
HIM— THE ONE WHO HAD ALL THE LUCK I WAS DENIED.
I WON'T LET HIM CREATE A ZHOU DYNASTY SO EASILY!

THE BLOOD OF THE KO FAMILY, PART 2
THE THIRD OTENKUN

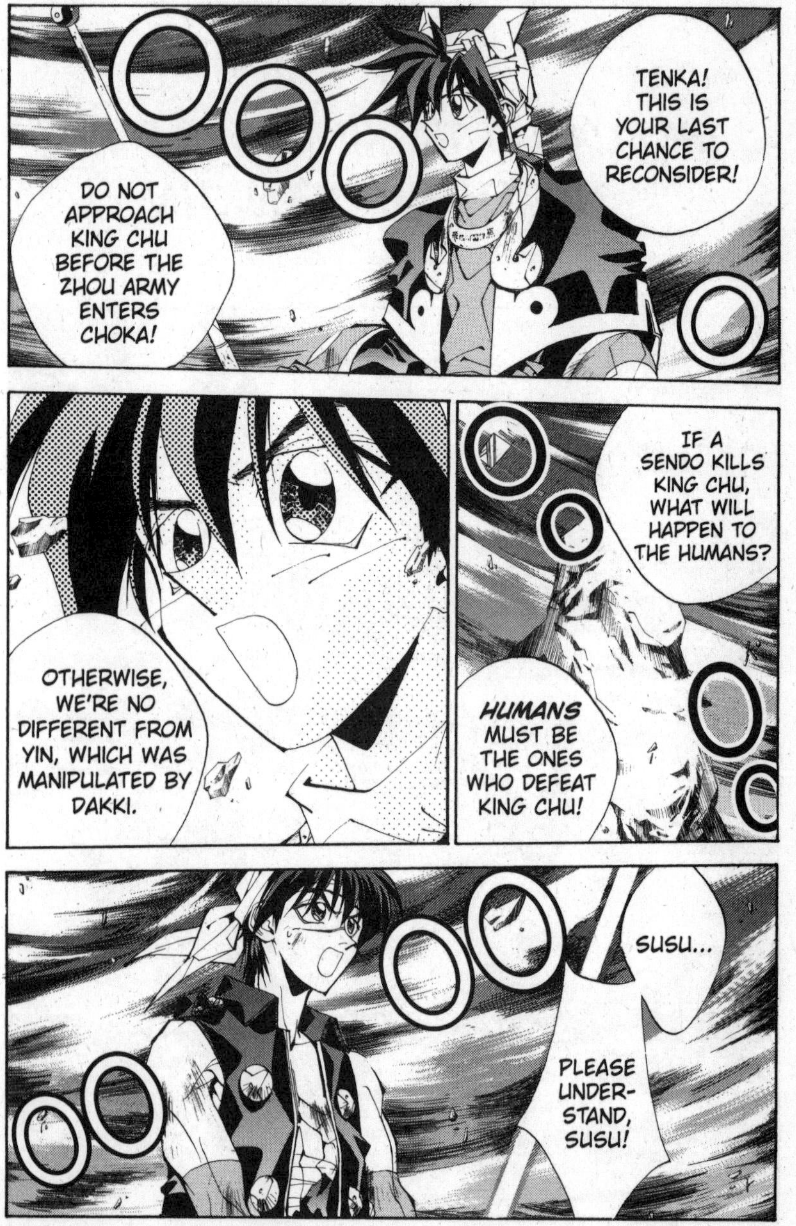
TENKA! THIS IS YOUR LAST CHANCE TO RECONSIDER!
DO NOT APPROACH KING CHU BEFORE THE ZHOU ARMY ENTERS CHOKA!
IF A SENDO KILLS KING CHU, WHAT WILL HAPPEN TO THE HUMANS?
HUMANS MUST BE THE ONES WHO DEFEAT KING CHU!
OTHERWISE, WE'RE NO DIFFERENT FROM YIN, WHICH WAS MANIPULATED BY DAKKI.
SUSU...
PLEASE UNDER-STAND, SUSU!

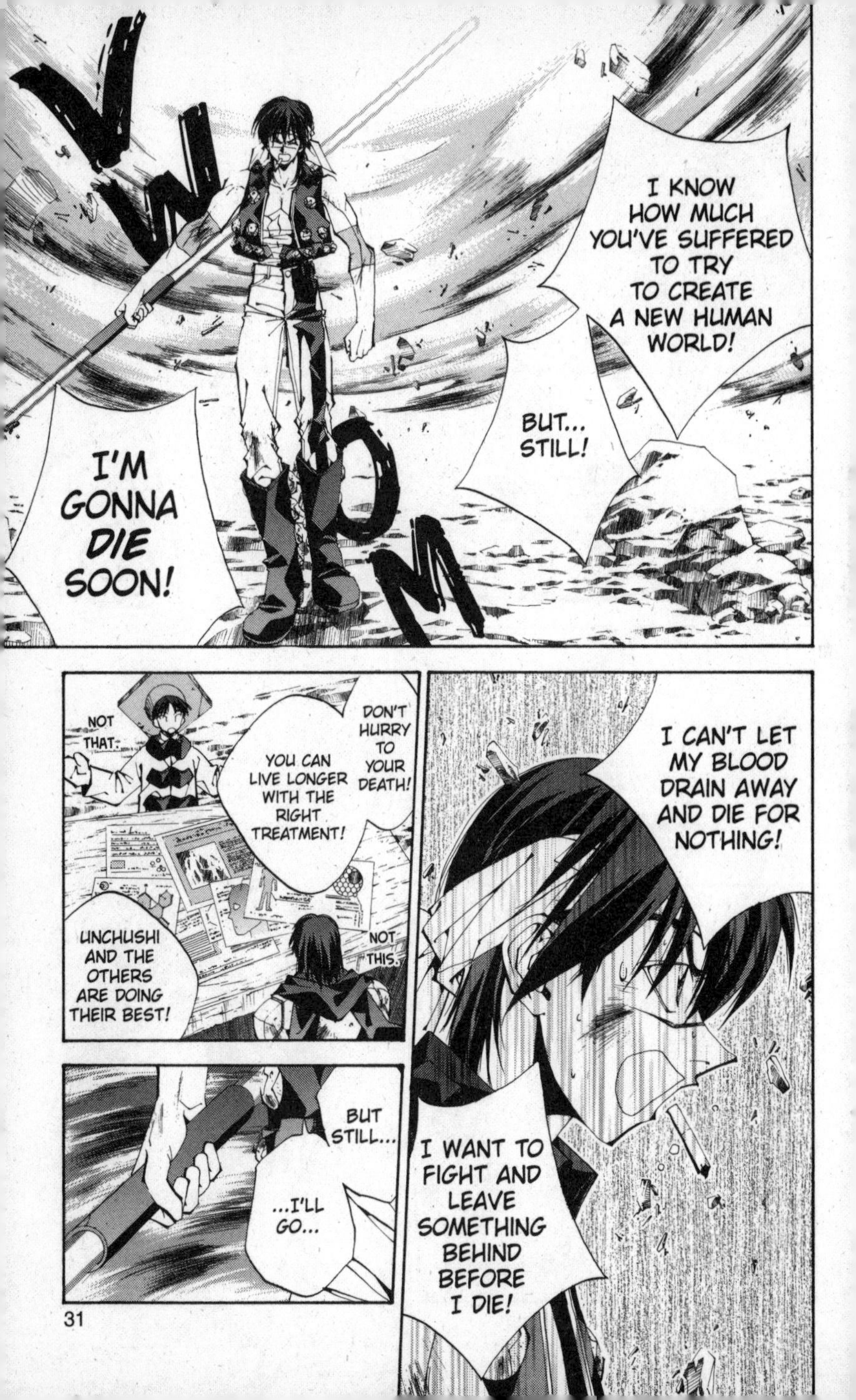
I KNOW HOW MUCH YOU'VE SUFFERED TO TRY TO CREATE A NEW HUMAN WORLD!
BUT... STILL!
I'M GONNA DIE SOON!
VWOM
I CAN'T LET MY BLOOD DRAIN AWAY AND DIE FOR NOTHING!
DON'T HURRY TO YOUR DEATH!
YOU CAN LIVE LONGER WITH THE RIGHT TREATMENT!
NOT THAT.
NOT THIS.
UNCHUSHI AND THE OTHERS ARE DOING THEIR BEST!
I WANT TO FIGHT AND LEAVE SOMETHING BEHIND BEFORE I DIE!
BUT STILL...
...I'LL GO...

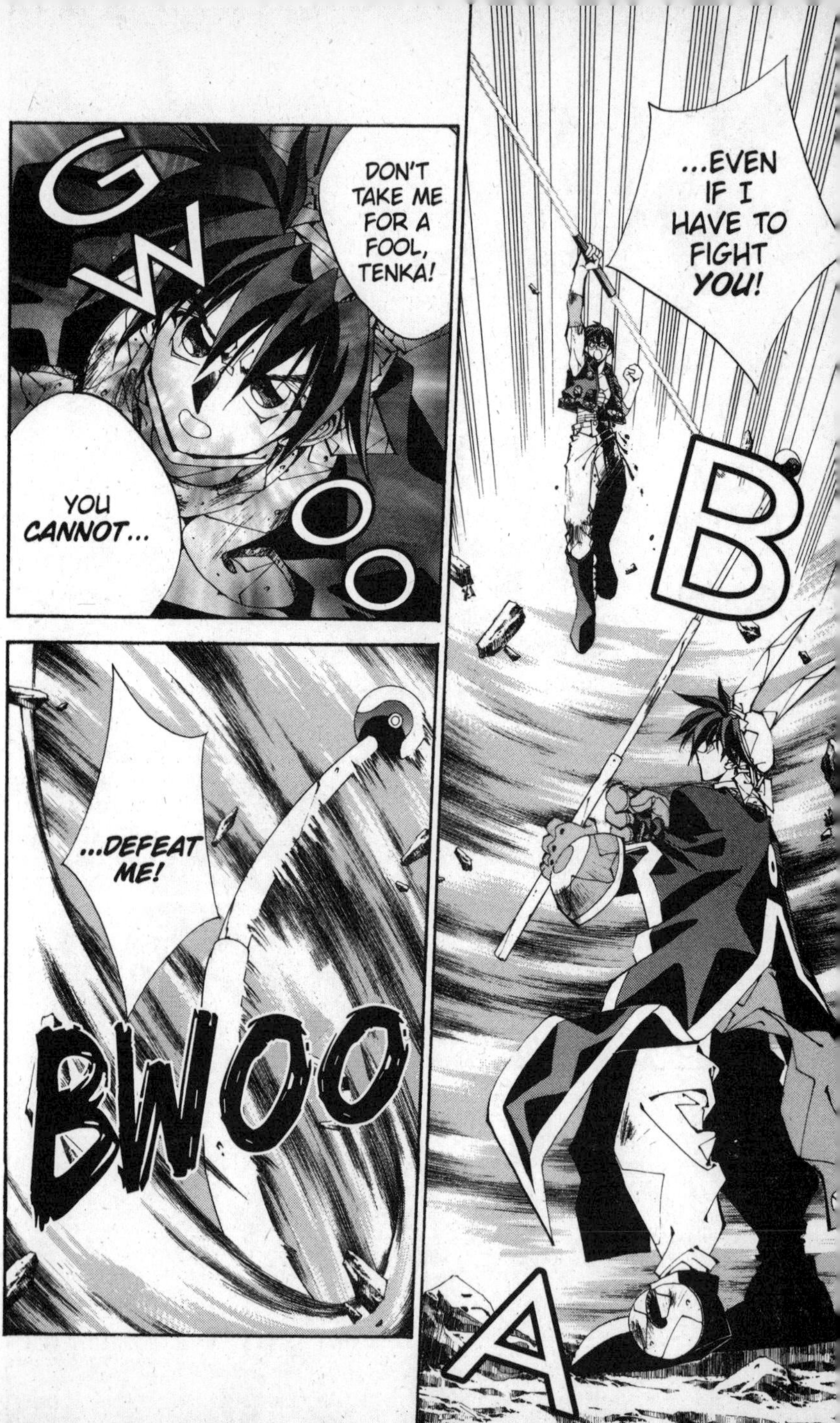
...EVEN IF I HAVE TO FIGHT YOU!
BA
DON'T TAKE ME FOR A FOOL, TENKA!
GWOO
YOU CANNOT...
...DEFEAT ME!
BWOO

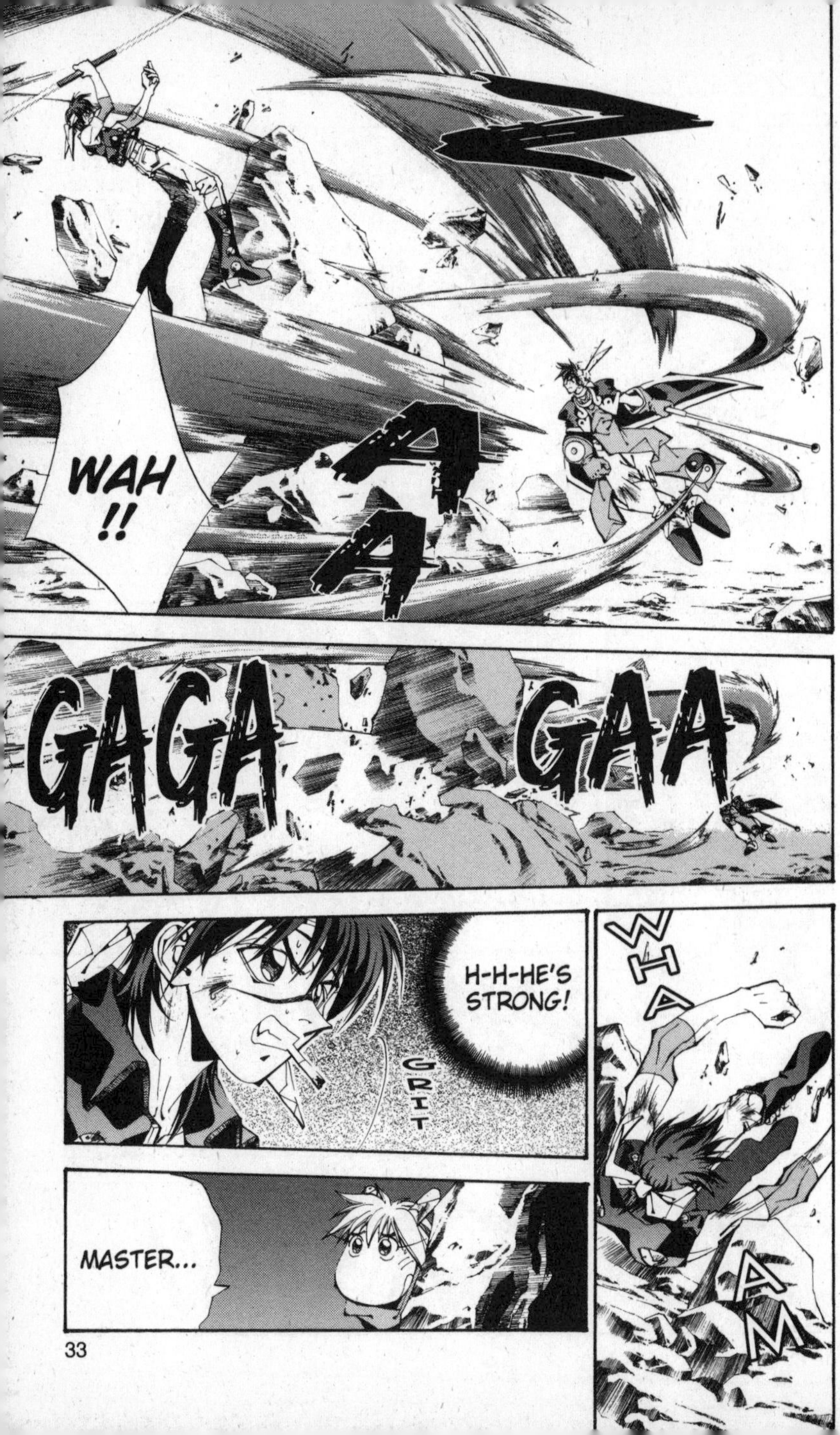
WAH!!
GAGA GAA
WHAAM
H-H-HE'S STRONG!
GRIT
MASTER...

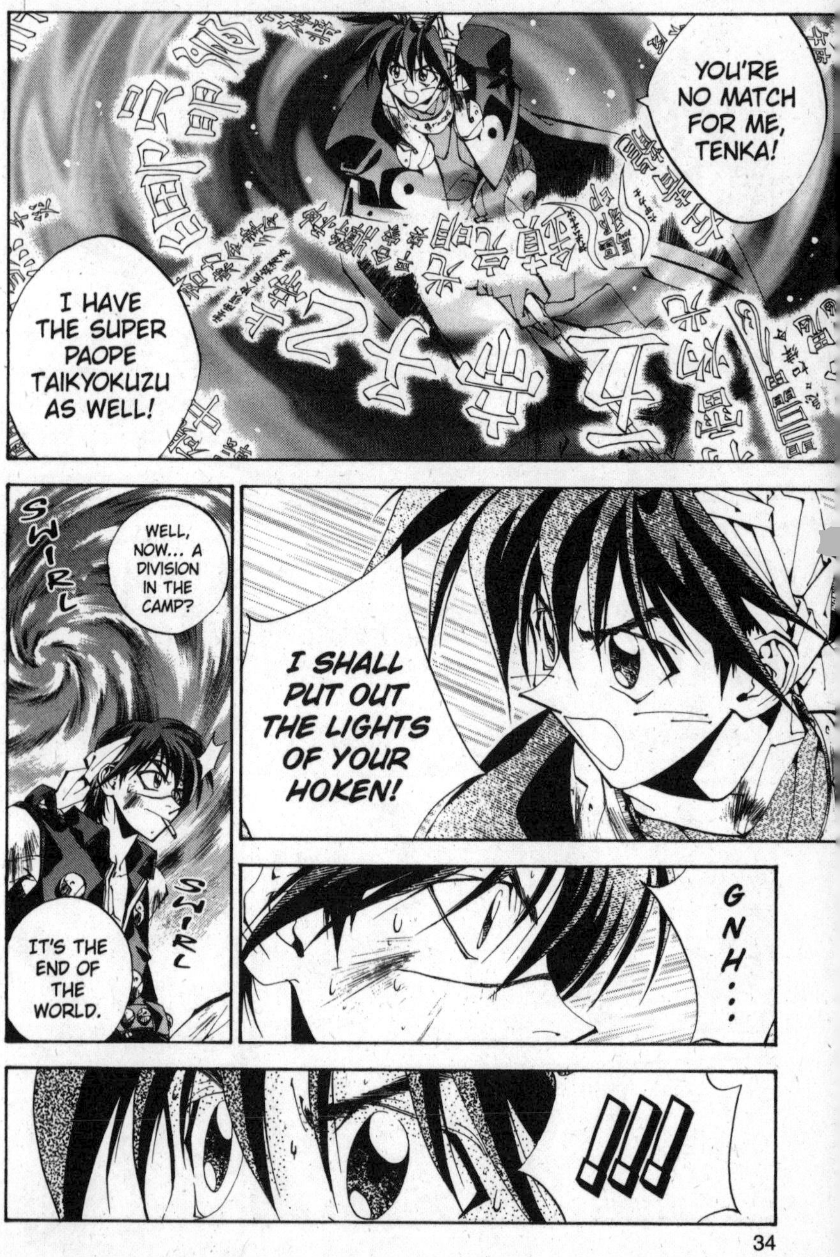
YOU'RE NO MATCH FOR ME, TENKA!
I HAVE THE SUPER PAOPE TAIKYOKUZU AS WELL!
I SHALL PUT OUT THE LIGHTS OF YOUR HOKEN!
WELL, NOW... A DIVISION IN THE CAMP?
SWIRL
SWIRL
IT'S THE END OF THE WORLD.
GNH...
!!!

READ THIS WAY

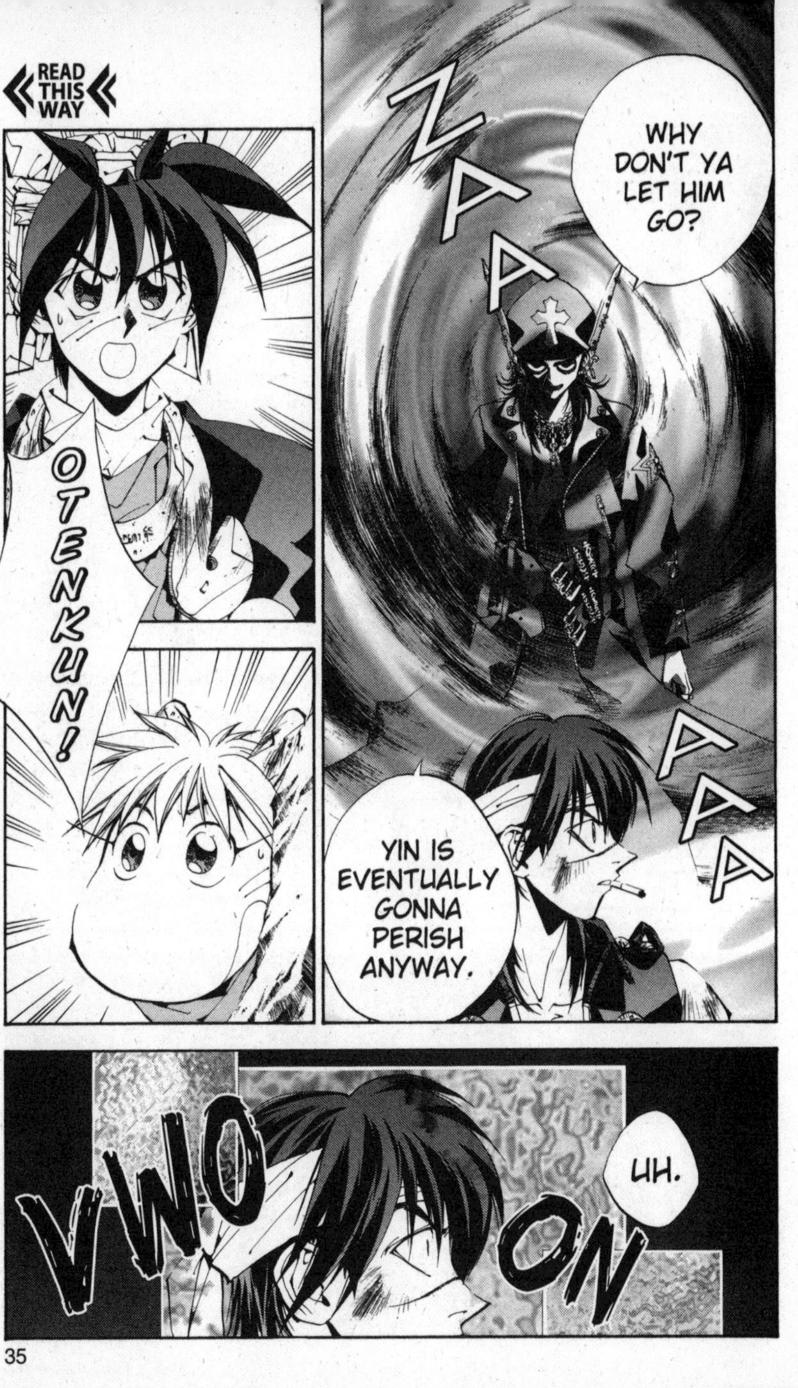
ZAAA
WHY DON'T YA LET HIM GO?
AAA
YIN IS EVENTUALLY GONNA PERISH ANYWAY.
OTENKUN!
UH.
VWOON

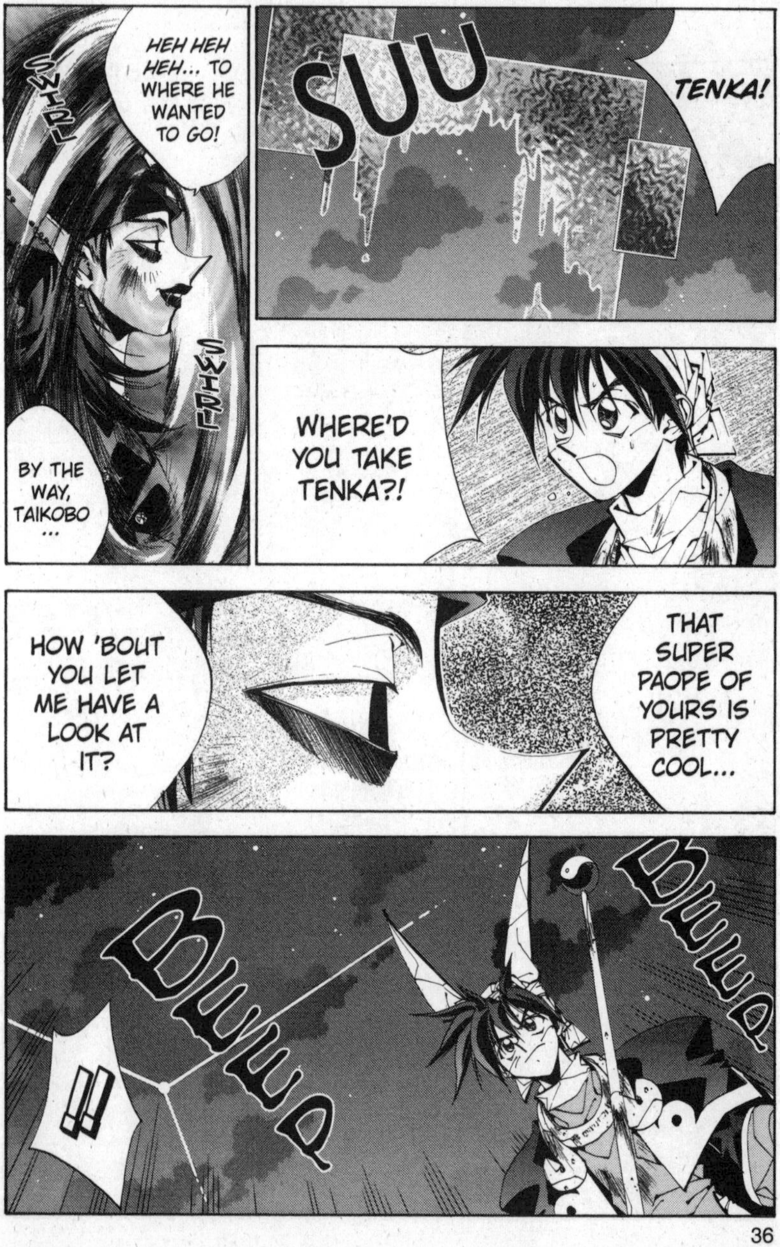
TENKA!
SUU
WHERE'D YOU TAKE TENKA?!
HEH HEH HEH... TO WHERE HE WANTED TO GO!
SWIRL
SWIRL
BY THE WAY, TAIKOBO ...
THAT SUPER PAOPE OF YOURS IS PRETTY COOL...
HOW 'BOUT YOU LET ME HAVE A LOOK AT IT?
BUWA
BUWA
!!

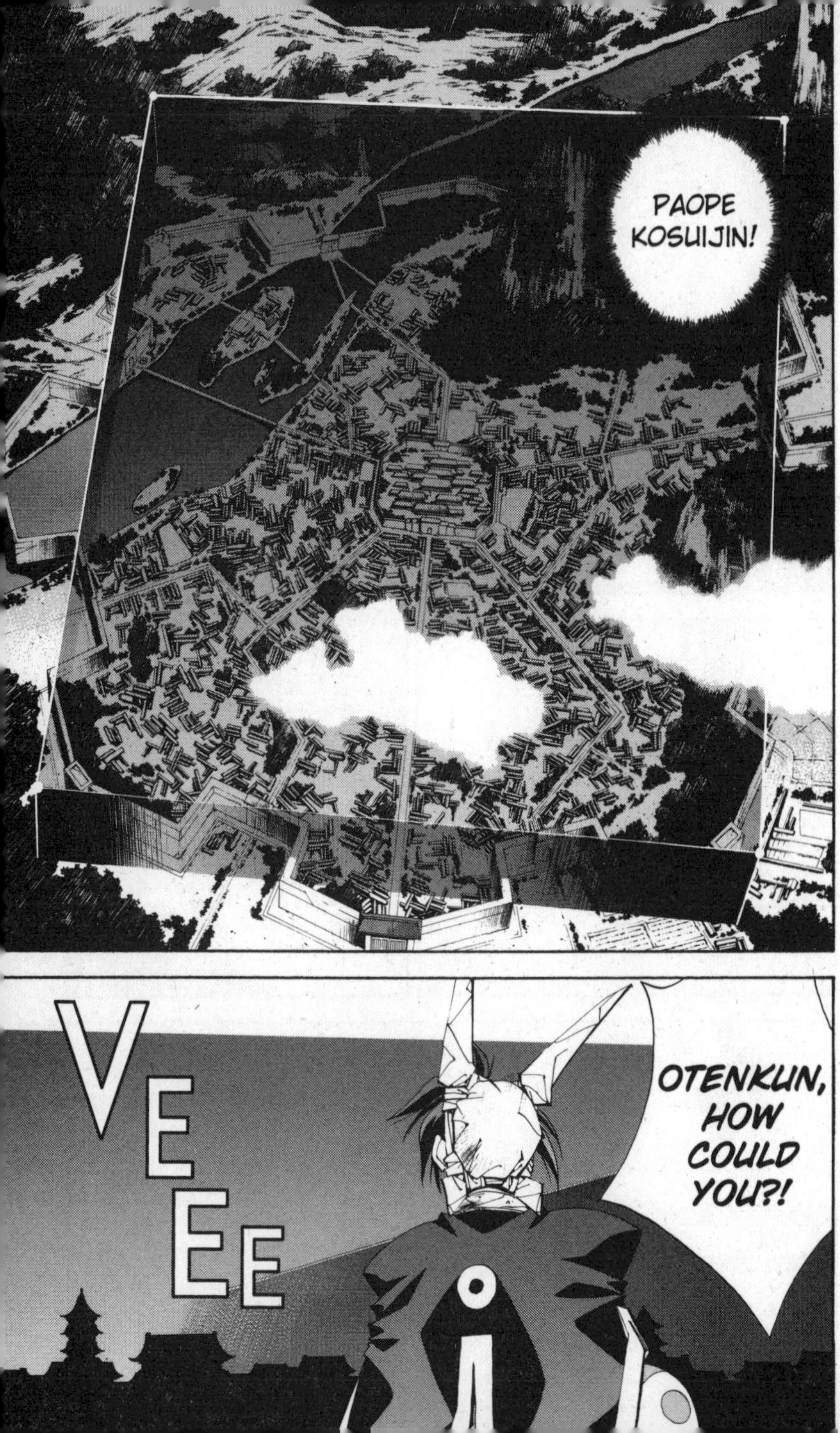
PAOPE KOSUIJIN!
OTENKUN, HOW COULD YOU?!
VEEE

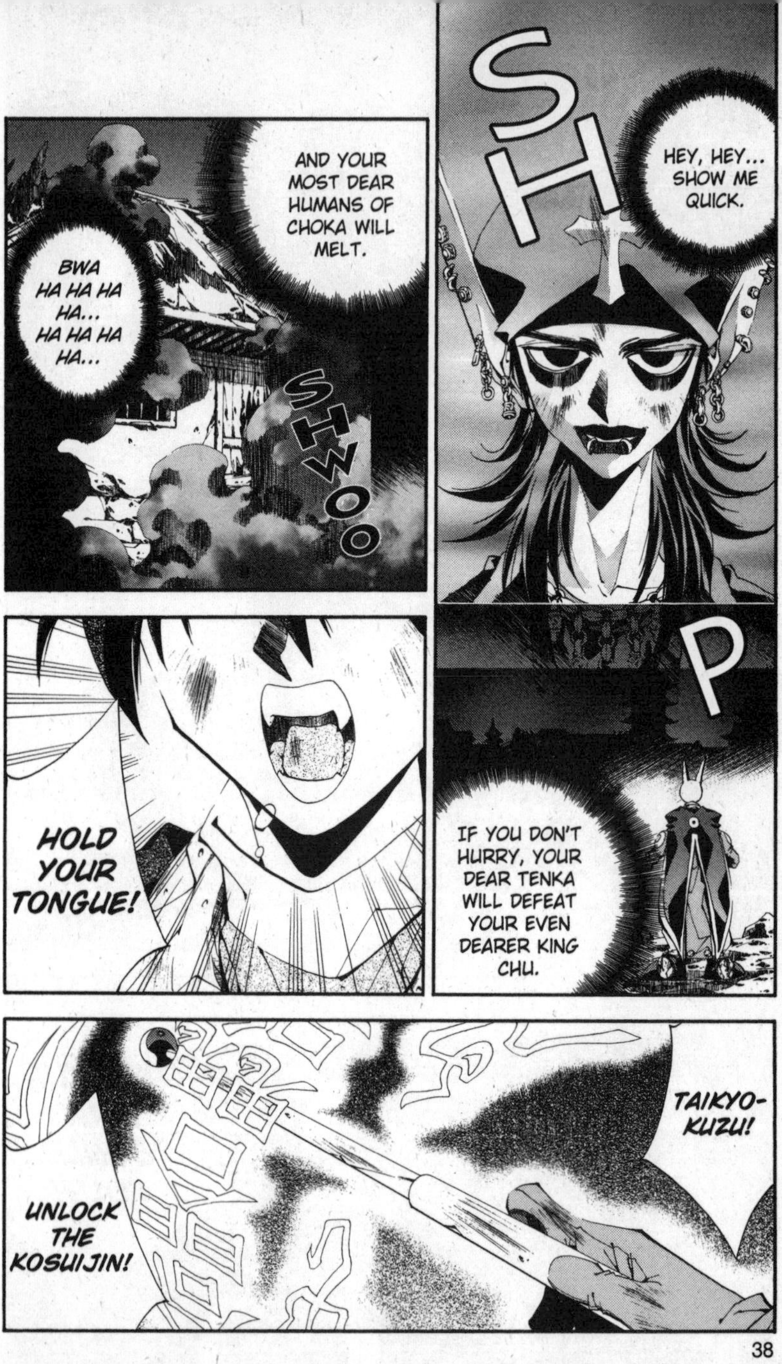
SH
HEY, HEY... SHOW ME QUICK.
AND YOUR MOST DEAR HUMANS OF CHOKA WILL MELT.
BWA HA HA HA HA... HA HA HA HA...
SHWOO
P
IF YOU DON'T HURRY, YOUR DEAR TENKA WILL DEFEAT YOUR EVEN DEARER KING CHU.
HOLD YOUR TONGUE!
TAIKYO-KUZU!
UNLOCK THE KOSUIJIN!

READ THIS WAY

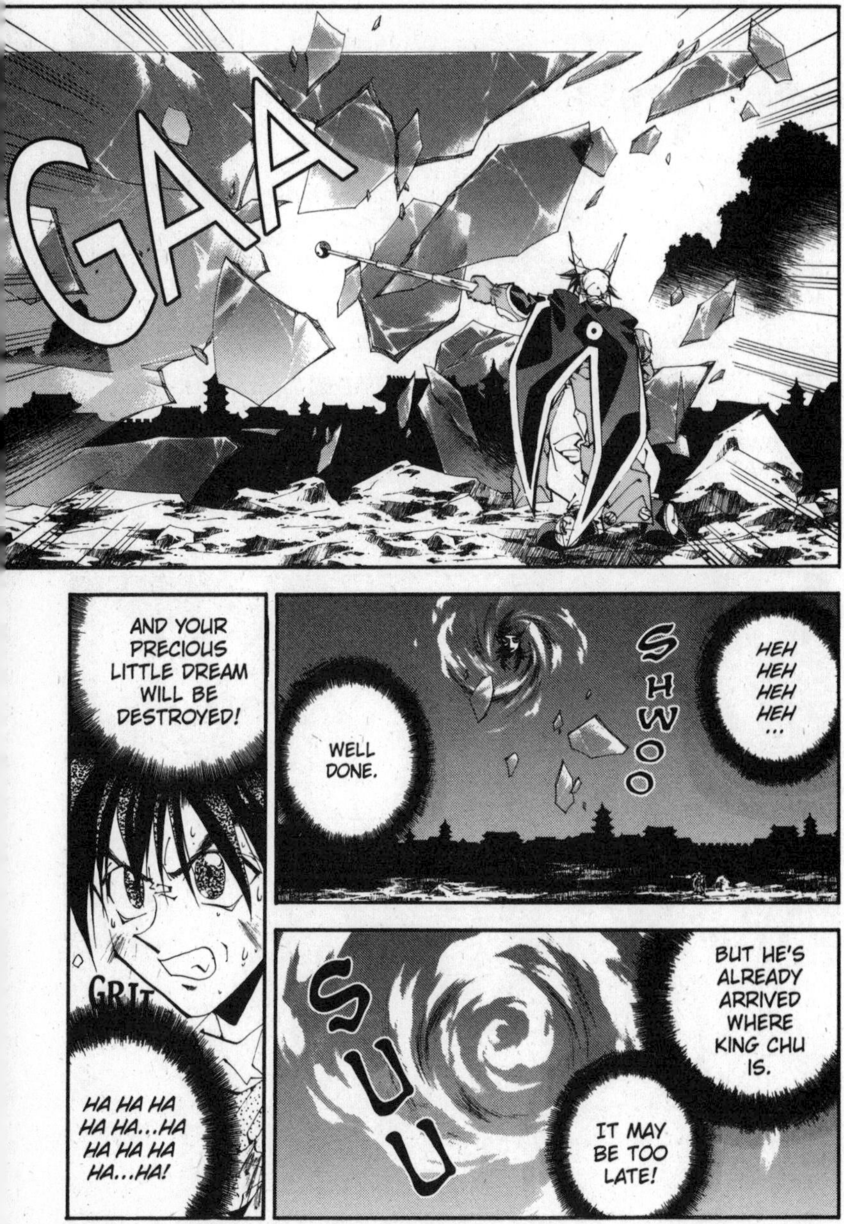
GAA
HEH HEH HEH HEH...
SHWOOO
WELL DONE.
AND YOUR PRECIOUS LITTLE DREAM WILL BE DESTROYED!
GRIT
HA HA HA HA HA...HA HA HA HA HA...HA!
BUT HE'S ALREADY ARRIVED WHERE KING CHU IS.
SUU
IT MAY BE TOO LATE!

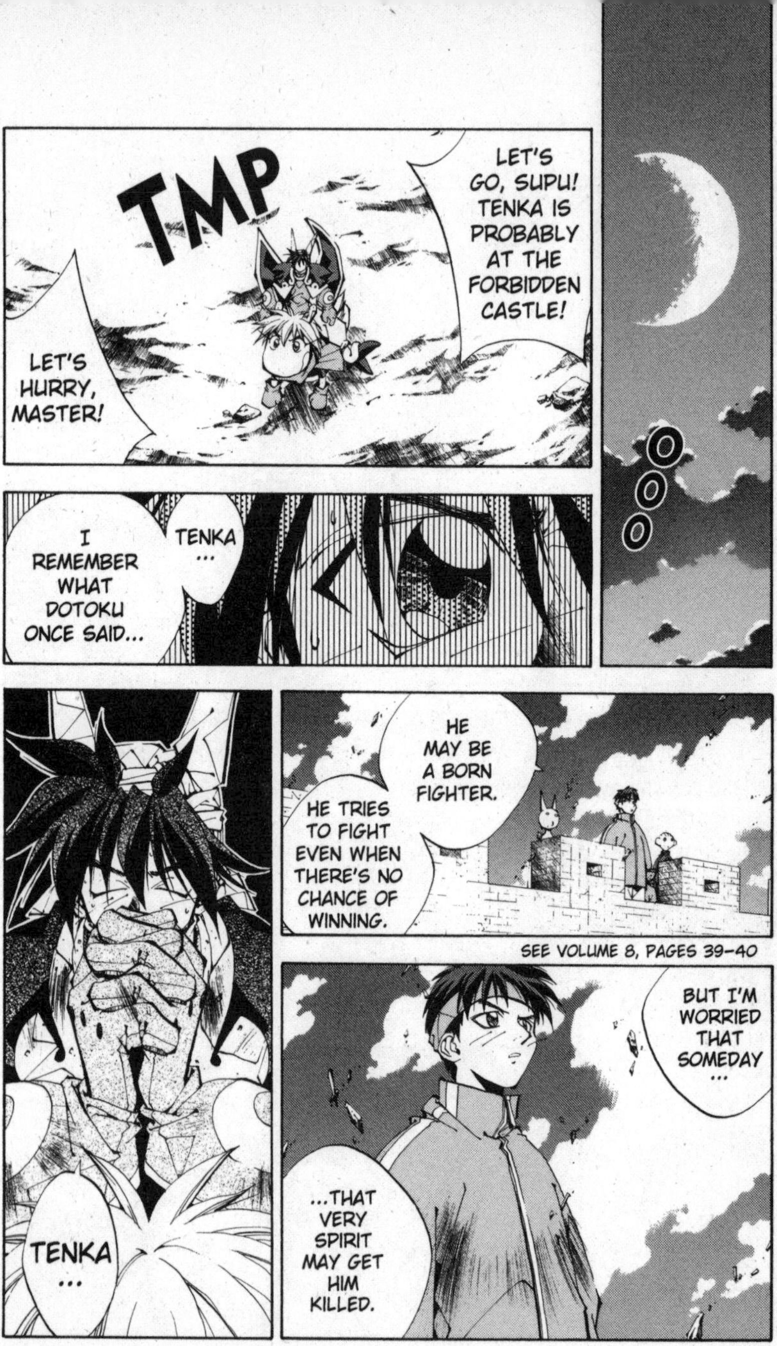
TMP
LET'S GO, SUPU! TENKA IS PROBABLY AT THE FORBIDDEN CASTLE!
LET'S HURRY, MASTER!
TENKA...
I REMEMBER WHAT DOTOKU ONCE SAID...
HE MAY BE A BORN FIGHTER.
HE TRIES TO FIGHT EVEN WHEN THERE'S NO CHANCE OF WINNING.
BUT I'M WORRIED THAT SOMEDAY...
...THAT VERY SPIRIT MAY GET HIM KILLED.
TENKA...
SEE VOLUME 8, PAGES 39-40

READ THIS WAY

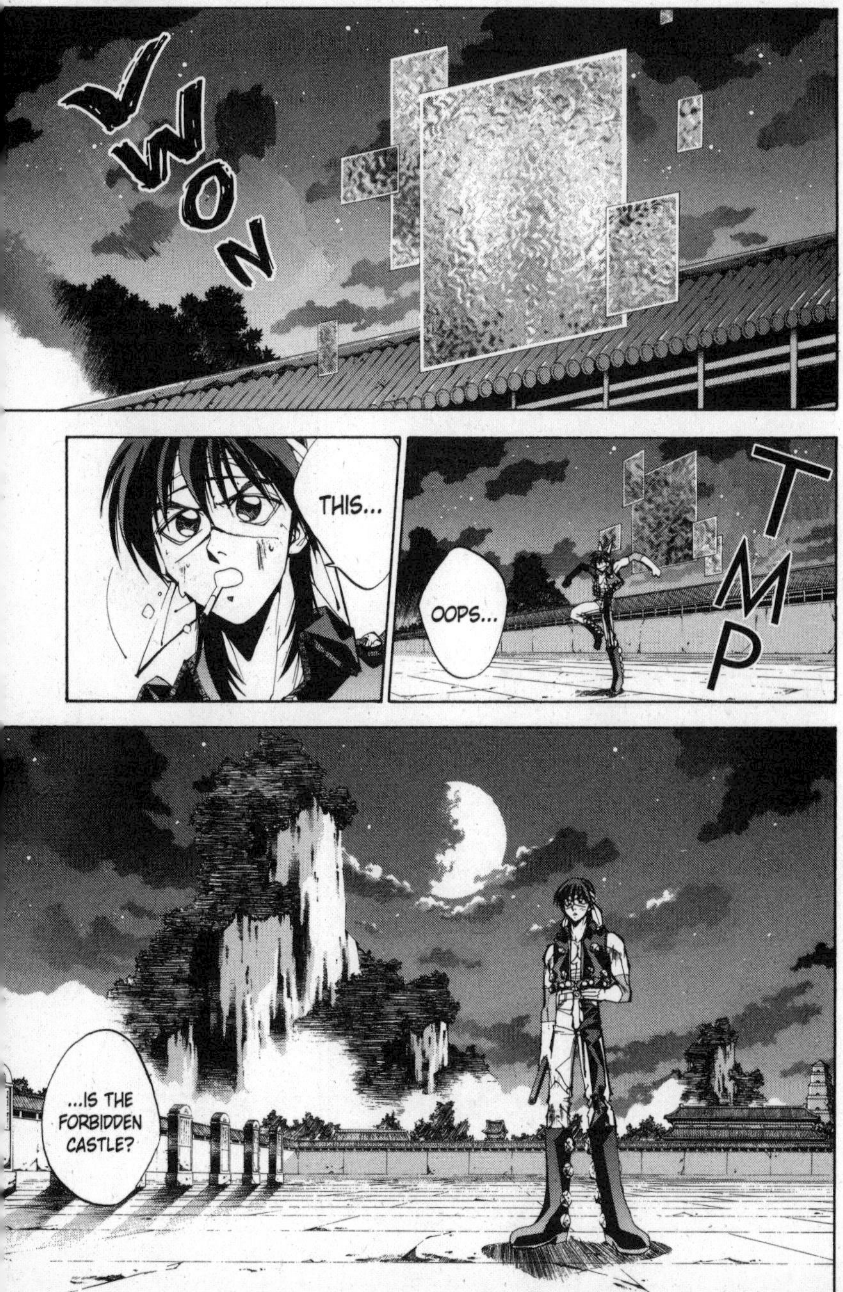
VWON
TMP
OOPS...
THIS...
...IS THE FORBIDDEN CASTLE?

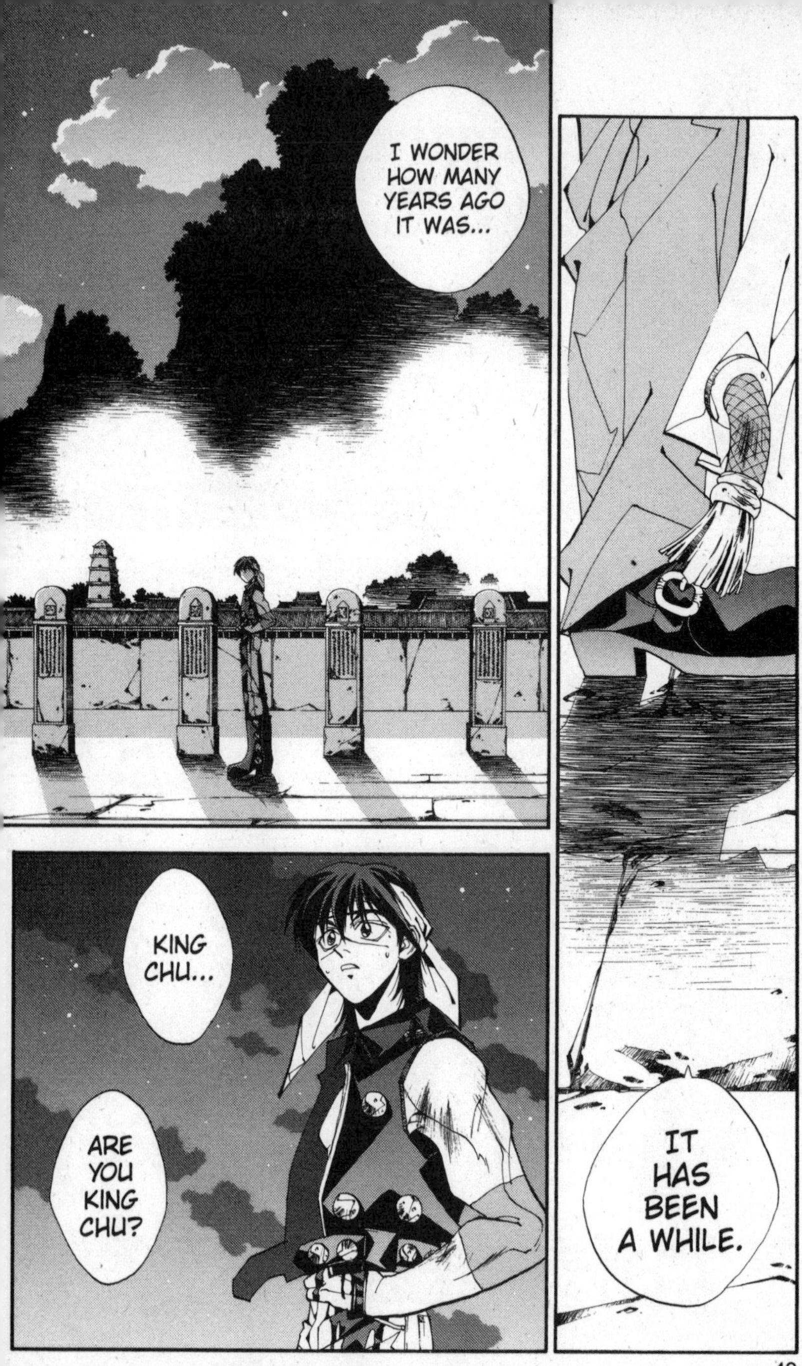
I WONDER HOW MANY YEARS AGO IT WAS...
IT HAS BEEN A WHILE.
KING CHU...
ARE YOU KING CHU?

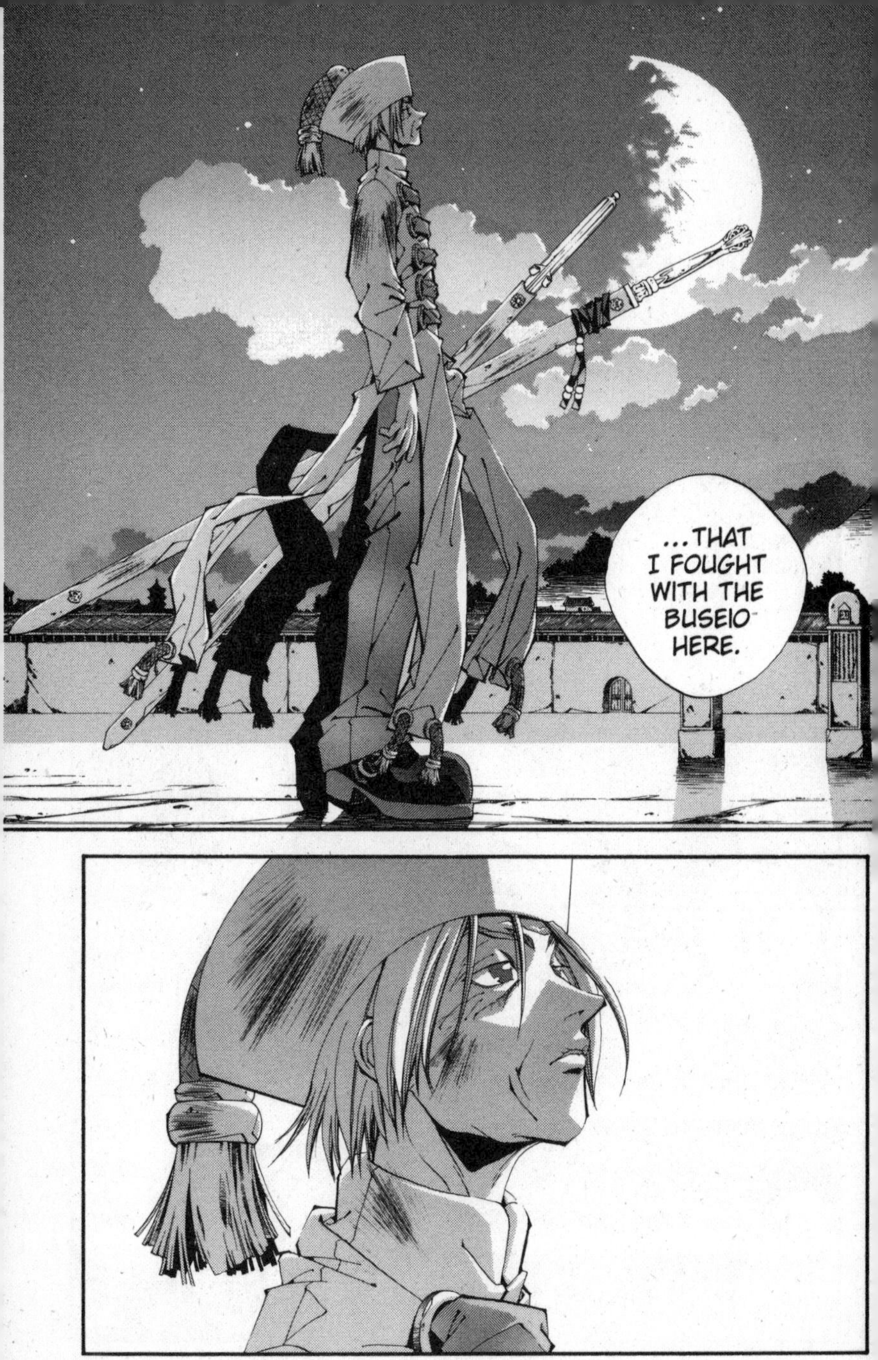
...THAT I FOUGHT WITH THE BUSEIO HERE.

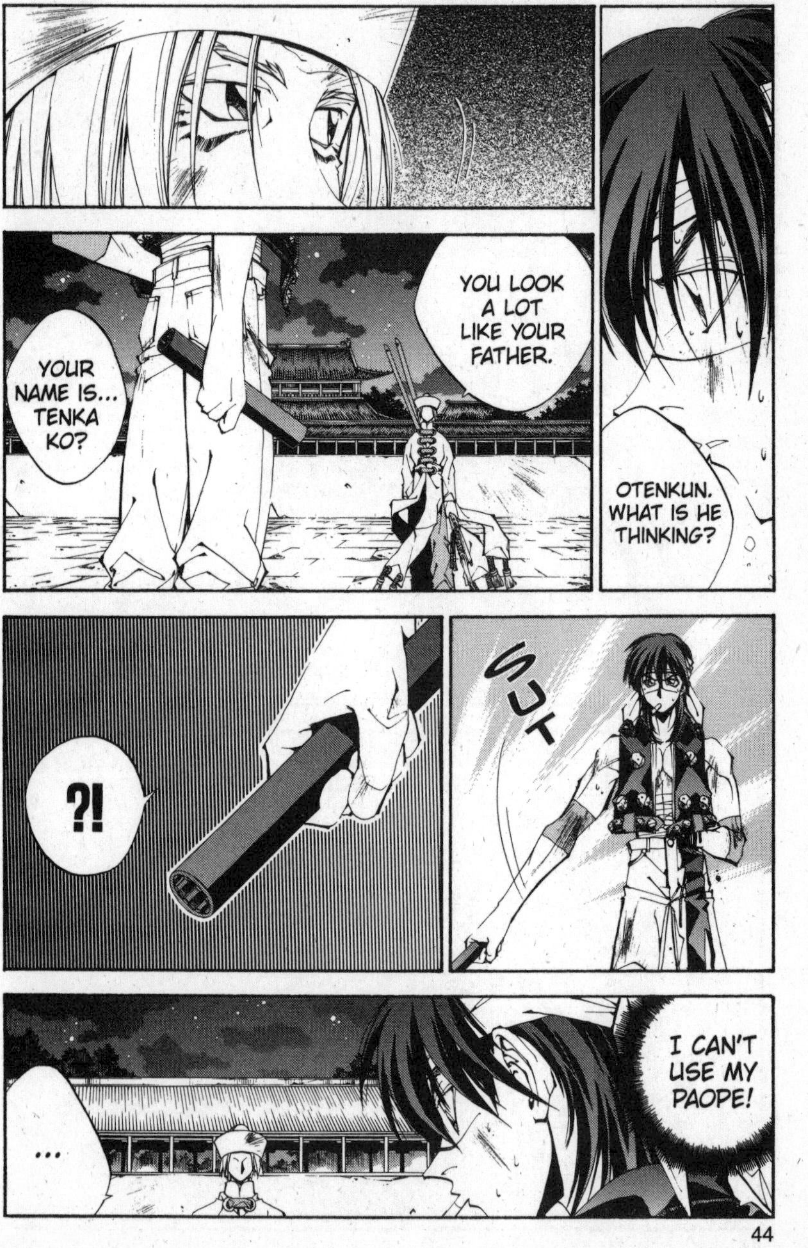
OTENKUN. WHAT IS HE THINKING?
YOU LOOK A LOT LIKE YOUR FATHER.
YOUR NAME IS... TENKA KO?
SUT
?!
I CAN'T USE MY PAOPE!
...

READ THIS WAY

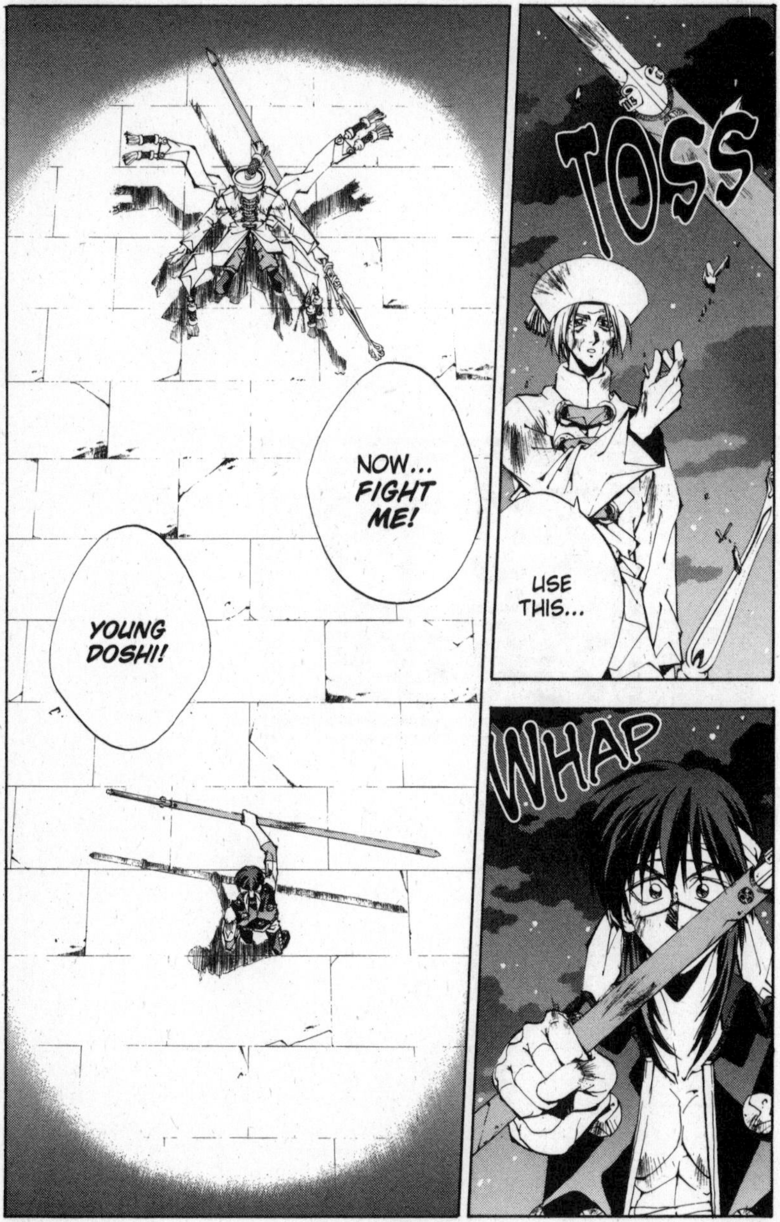
TOSS
USE THIS...
WHAP
NOW... FIGHT ME!
YOUNG DOSHI!

封神演義

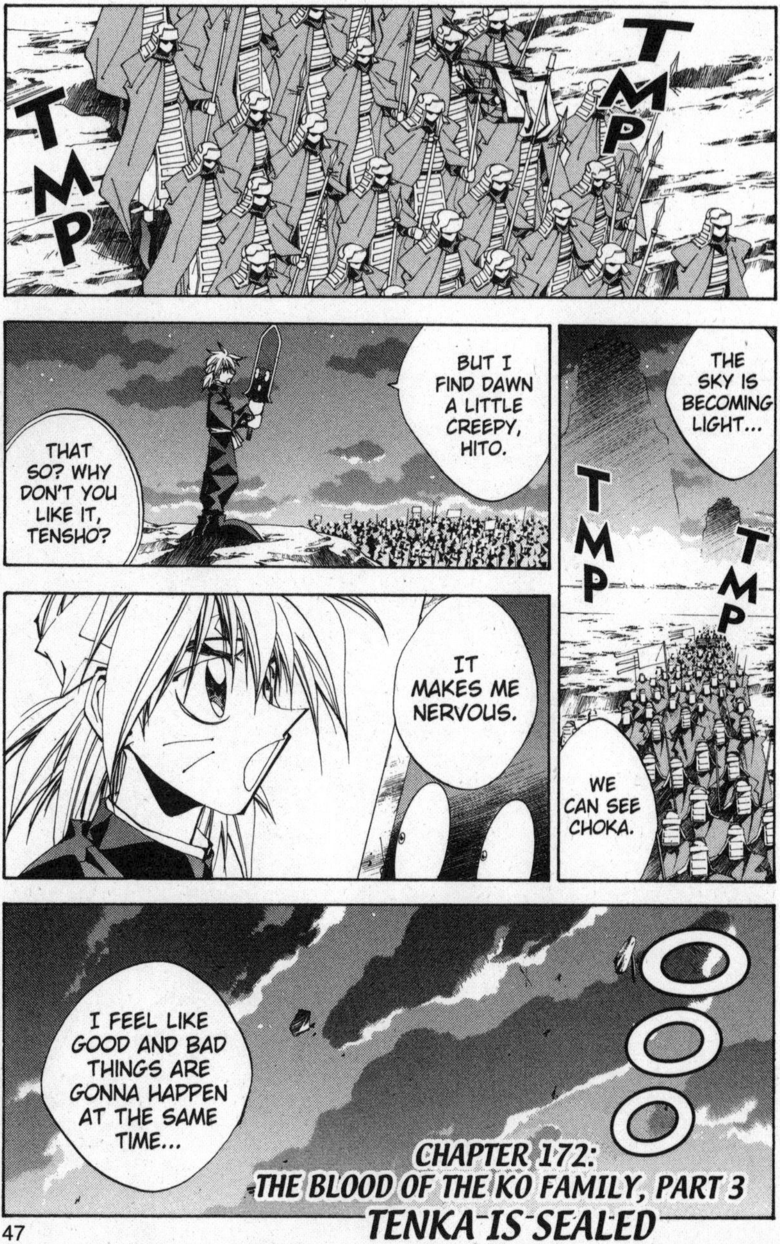
TMP
TMP
THE SKY IS BECOMING LIGHT...
TMP
TMP
WE CAN SEE CHOKA.
BUT I FIND DAWN A LITTLE CREEPY, HITO.
THAT SO? WHY DON'T YOU LIKE IT, TENSHO?
IT MAKES ME NERVOUS.
OOO
I FEEL LIKE GOOD AND BAD THINGS ARE GONNA HAPPEN AT THE SAME TIME...
CHAPTER 172:
THE BLOOD OF THE KO FAMILY, PART 3
TENKA IS SEALED

THE BLOOD OF THE KO FAMILY, PART 3
TENKA IS SEALED

READ THIS WAY

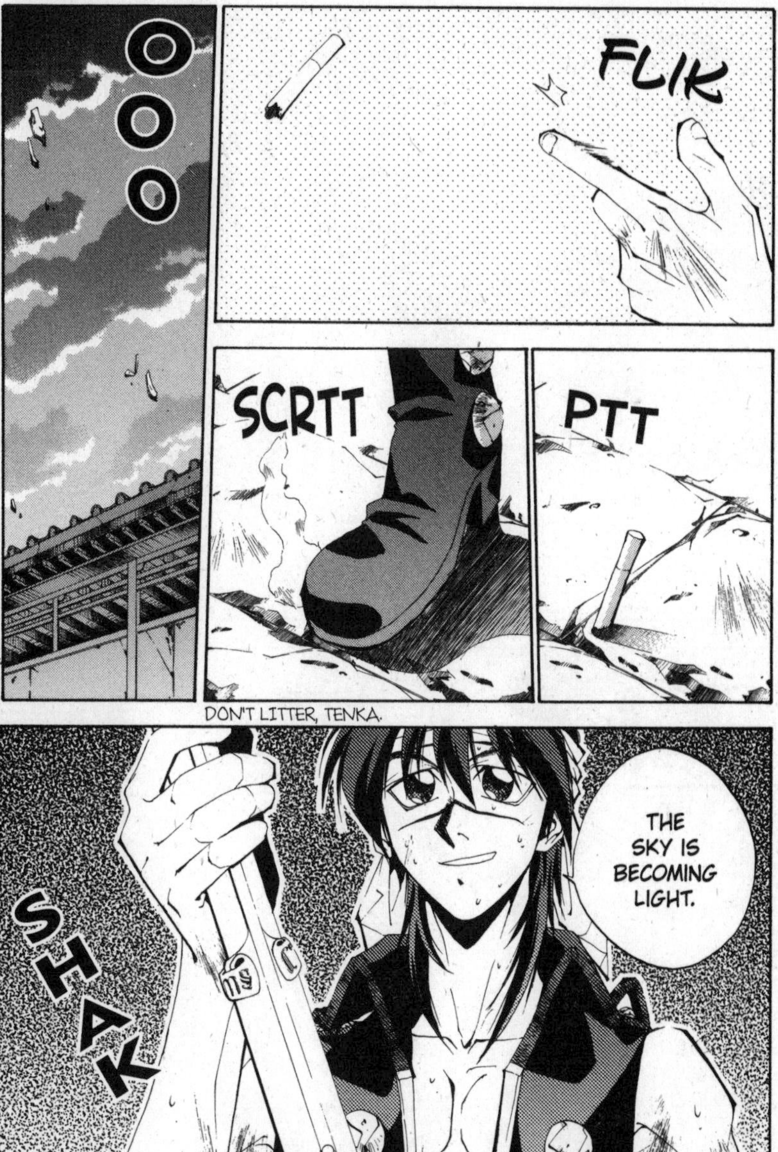

FLIK
PTT
SCRTT
OOO
DON'T LITTER, TENKA.
THE SKY IS BECOMING LIGHT.
SHAK

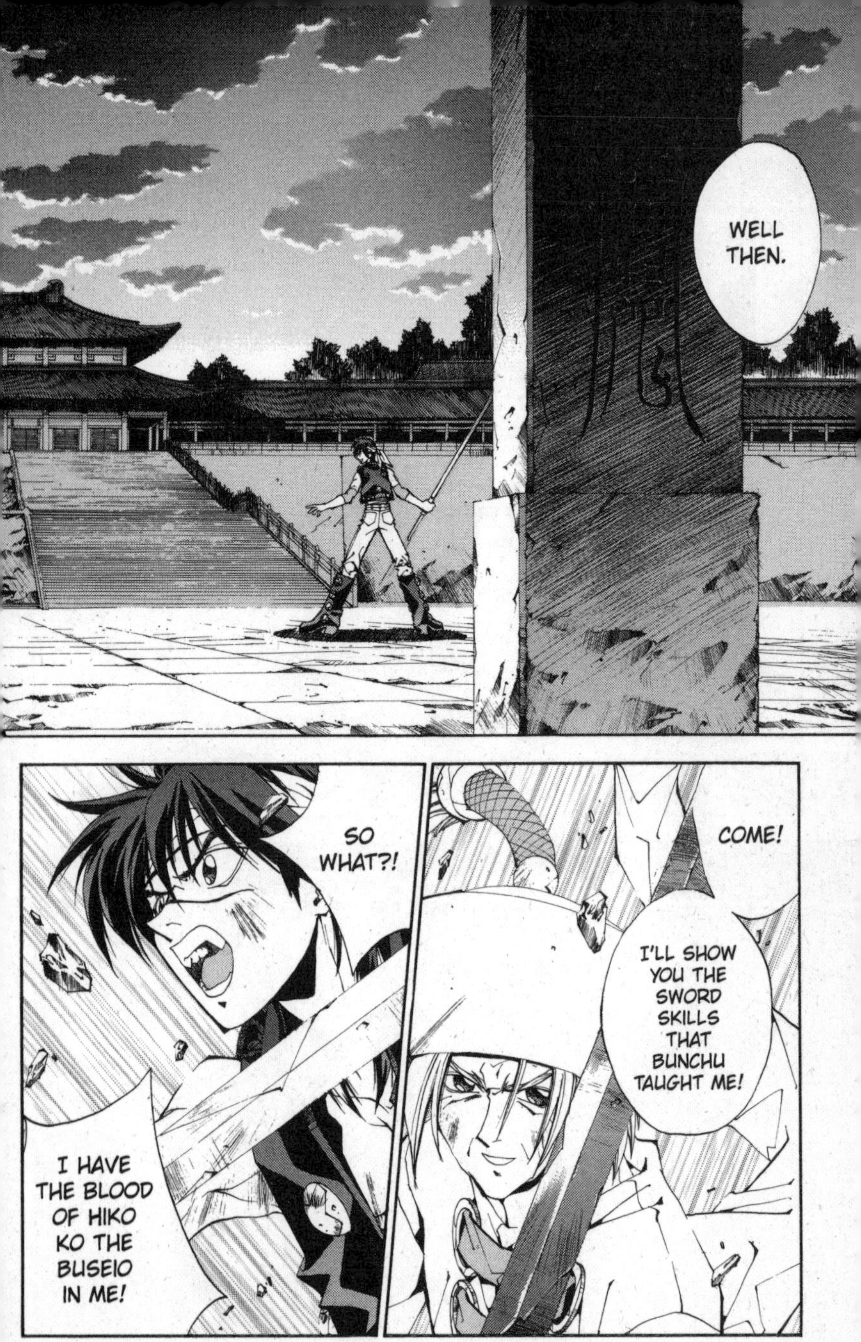
WELL THEN.
COME!
I'LL SHOW YOU THE SWORD SKILLS THAT BUNCHU TAUGHT ME!
SO WHAT?!
I HAVE THE BLOOD OF HIKO KO THE BUSEIO IN ME!

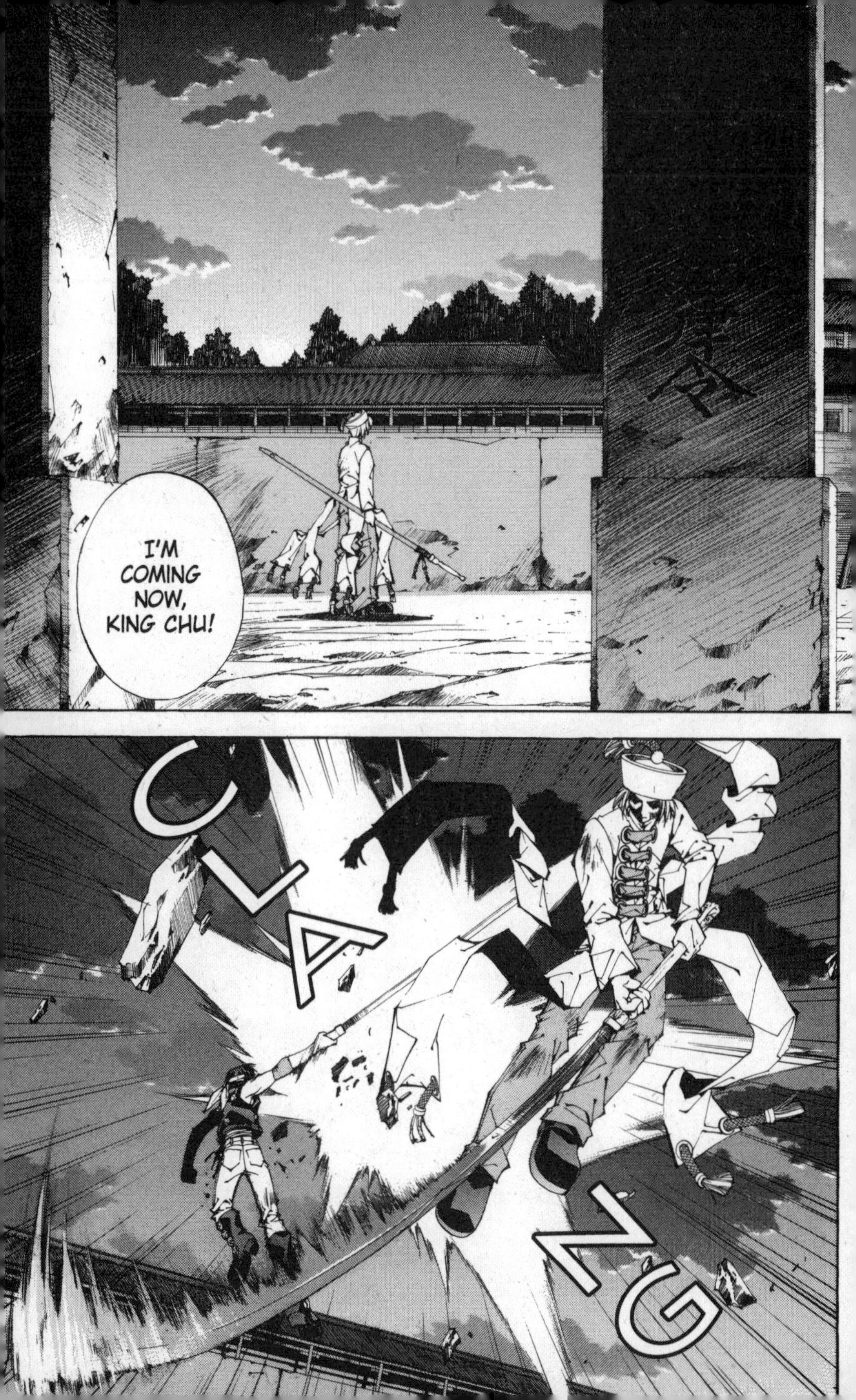
I'M COMING NOW, KING CHU!
CLANG

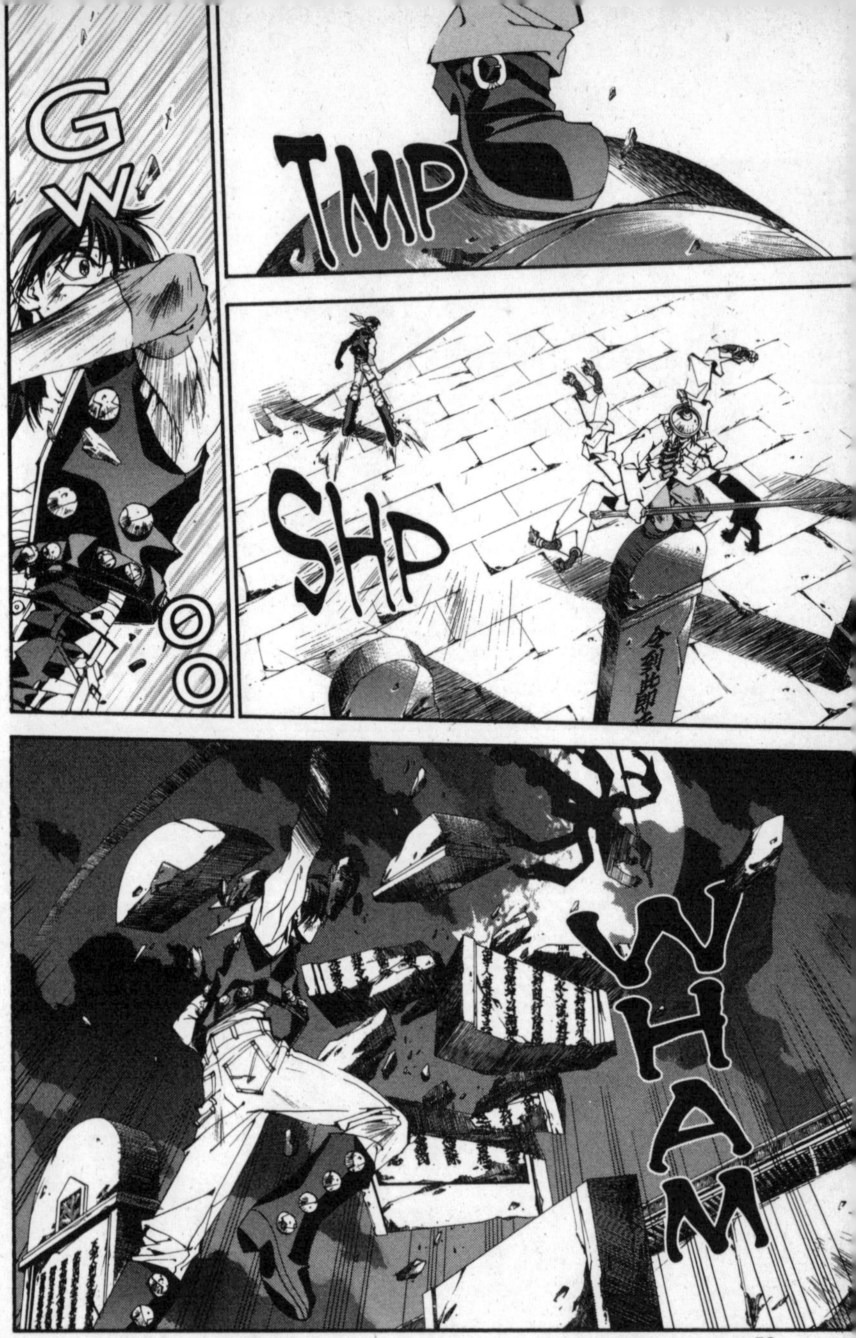
TMP
SHP
GWOO
WHAM

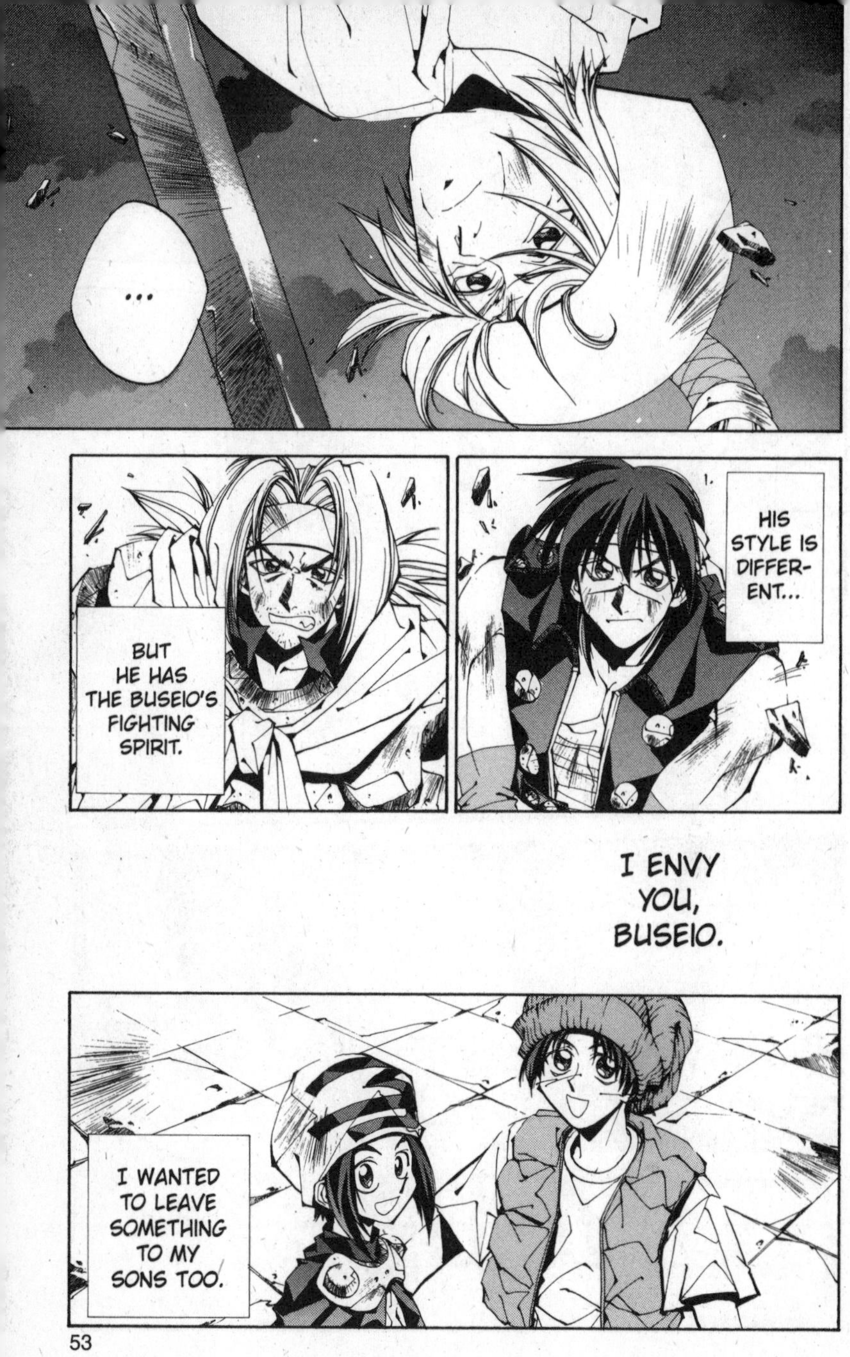
...
HIS STYLE IS DIFFERENT...
BUT HE HAS THE BUSEIO'S FIGHTING SPIRIT.
I ENVY YOU, BUSEIO.
I WANTED TO LEAVE SOMETHING TO MY SONS TOO.

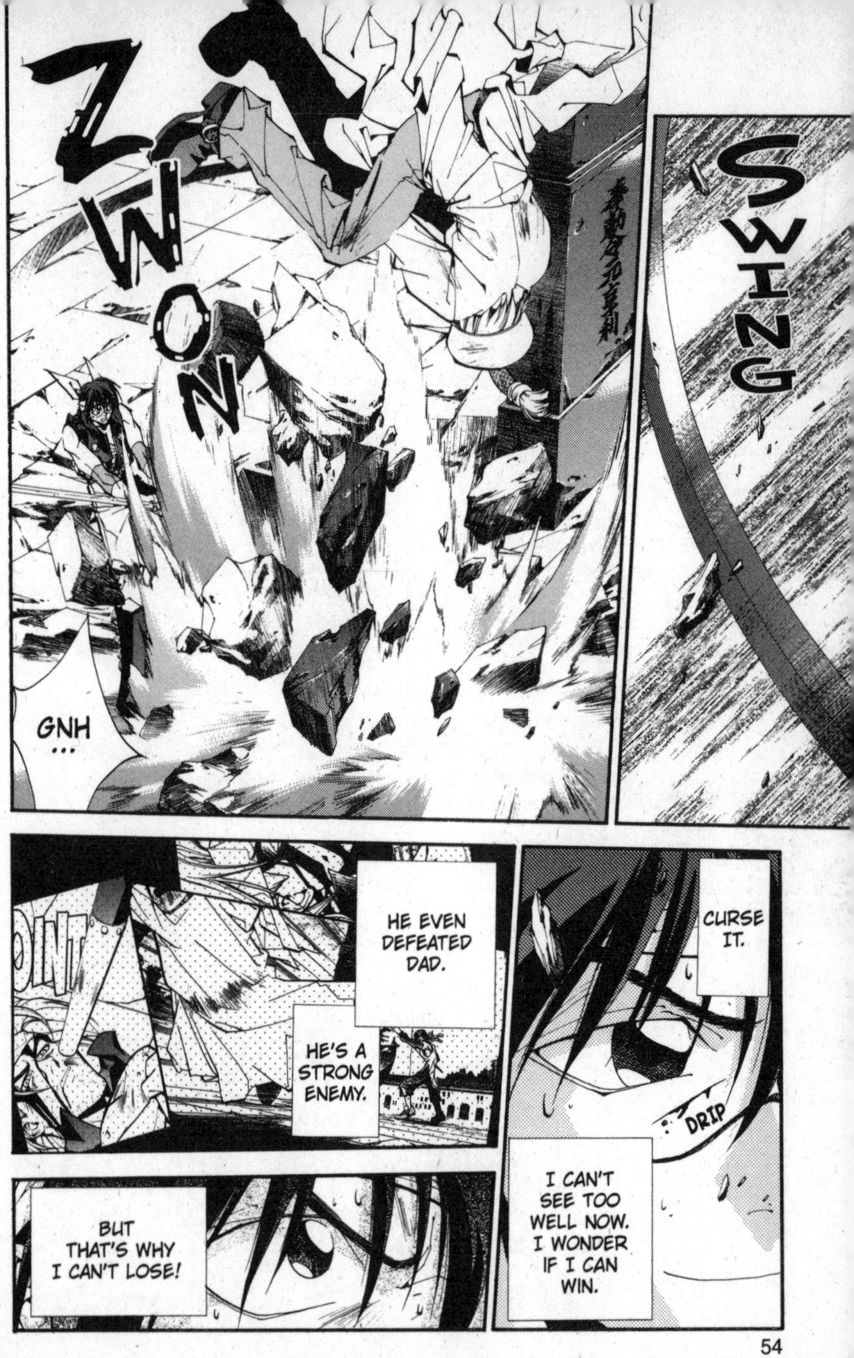
SWING
ZWON
GNH...
CURSE IT.
DRIP
HE EVEN DEFEATED DAD.
HE'S A STRONG ENEMY.
I CAN'T SEE TOO WELL NOW. I WONDER IF I CAN WIN.
BUT THAT'S WHY I CAN'T LOSE!

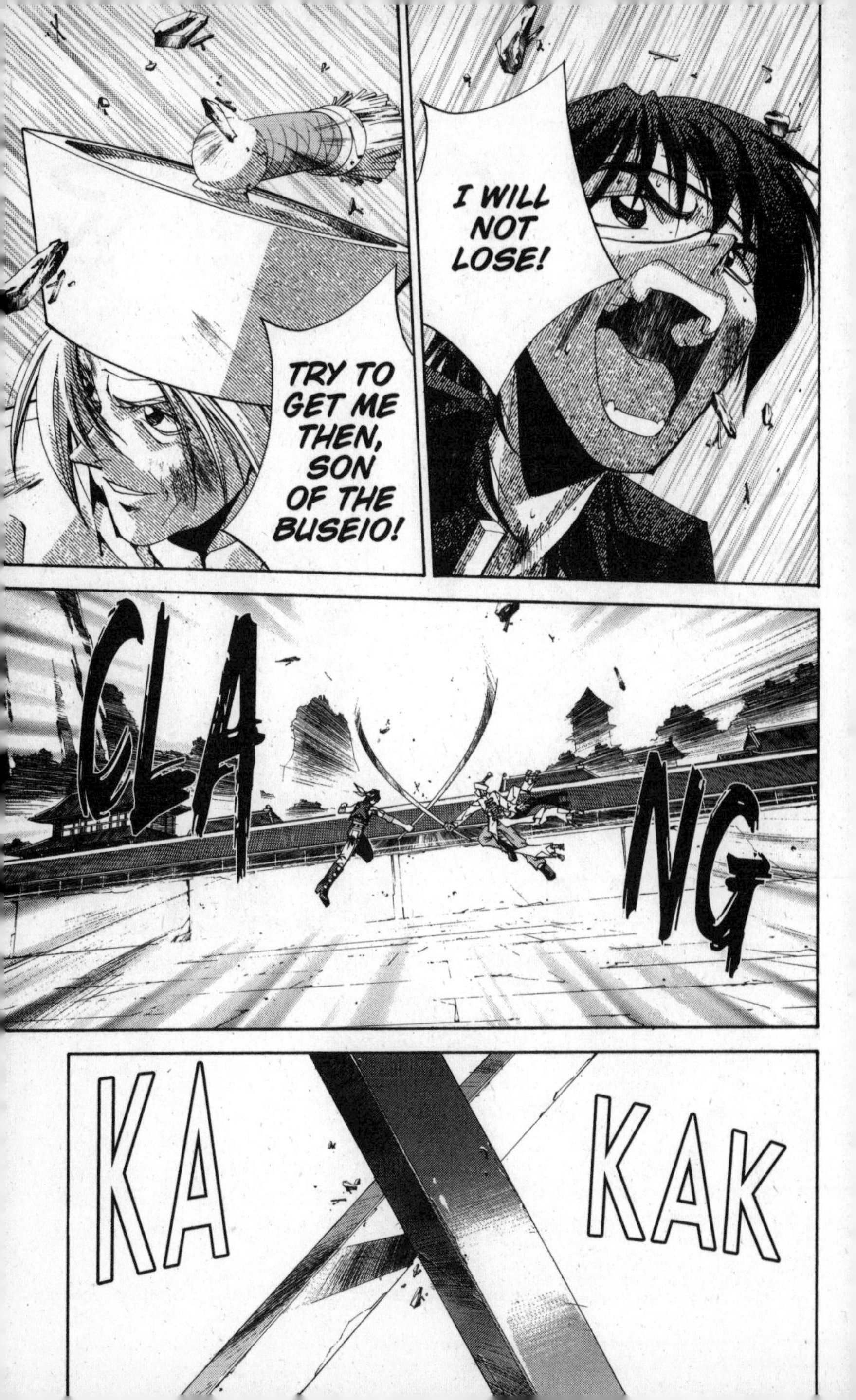
I WILL NOT LOSE!
TRY TO GET ME THEN, SON OF THE BUSEIO!
CLANG
KA
KAK

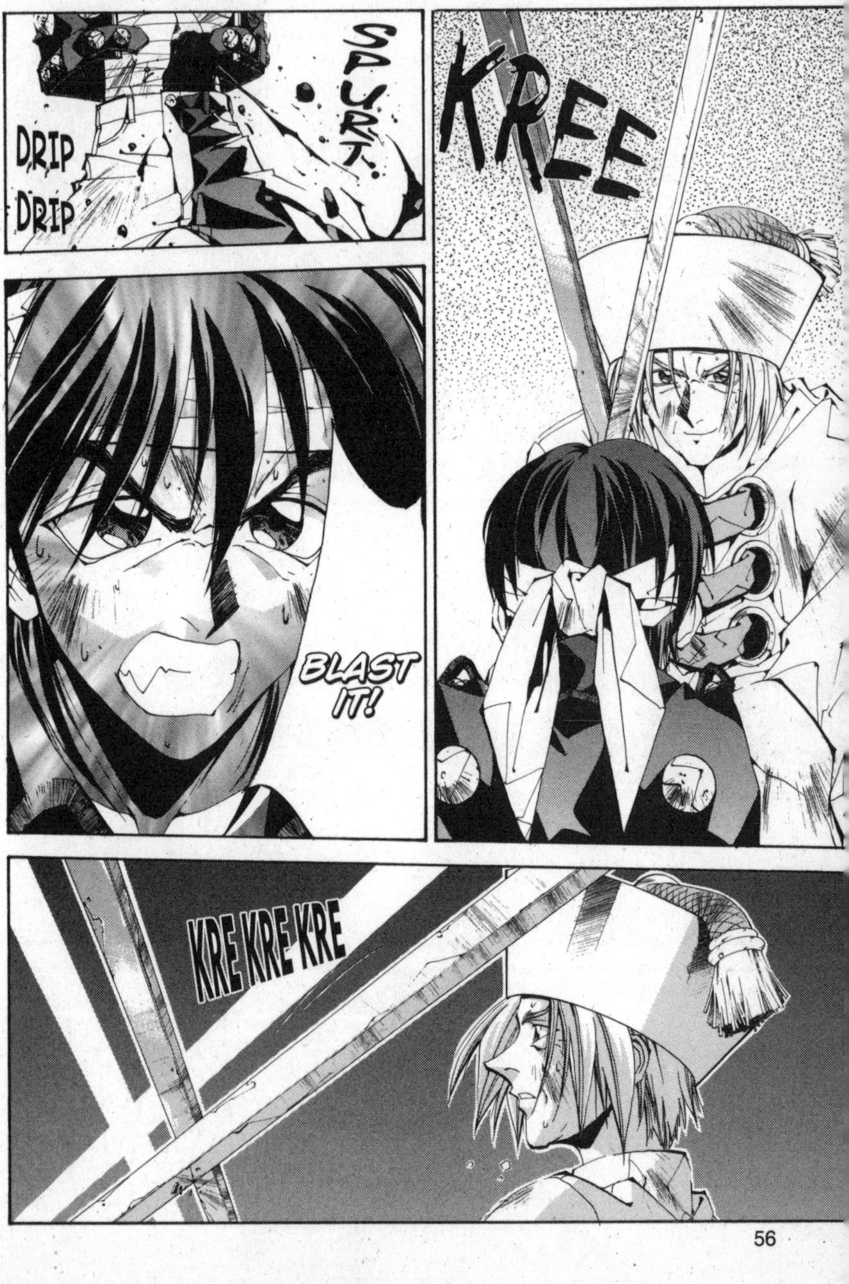
SPURT
DRIP
DRIP
KREE
BLAST IT!
KRE KRE KRE

READ THIS WAY

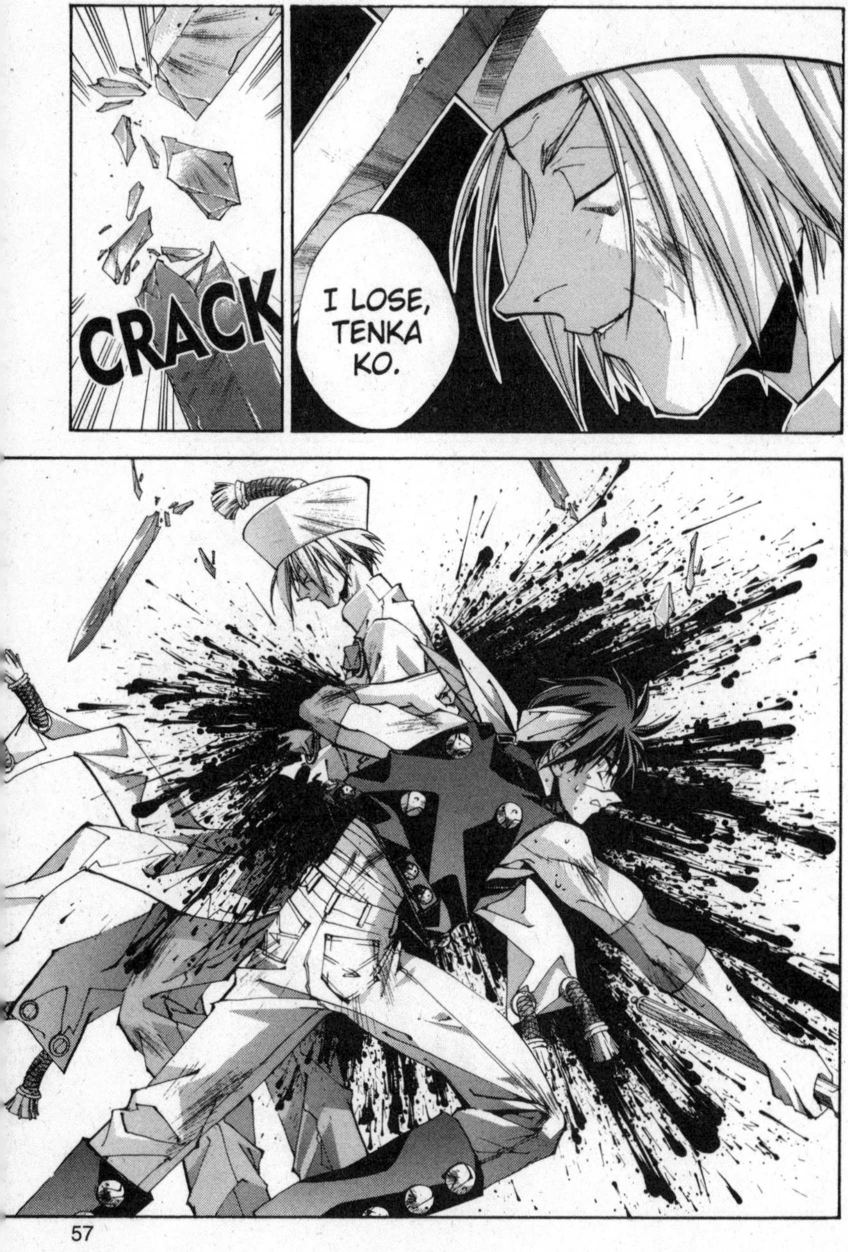
CRACK
I LOSE, TENKA KO.

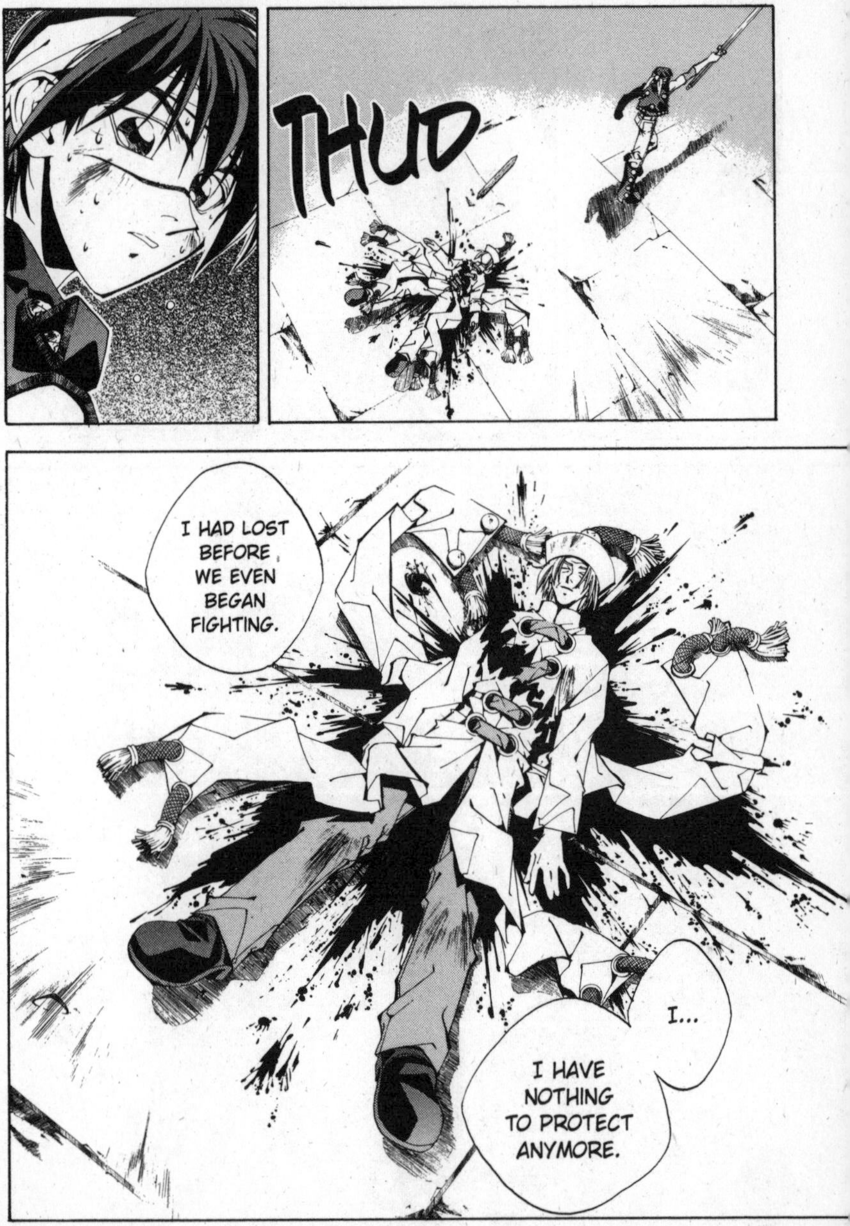
THUD
I HAD LOST BEFORE WE EVEN BEGAN FIGHTING.
I...
I HAVE NOTHING TO PROTECT ANYMORE.

READ THIS WAY

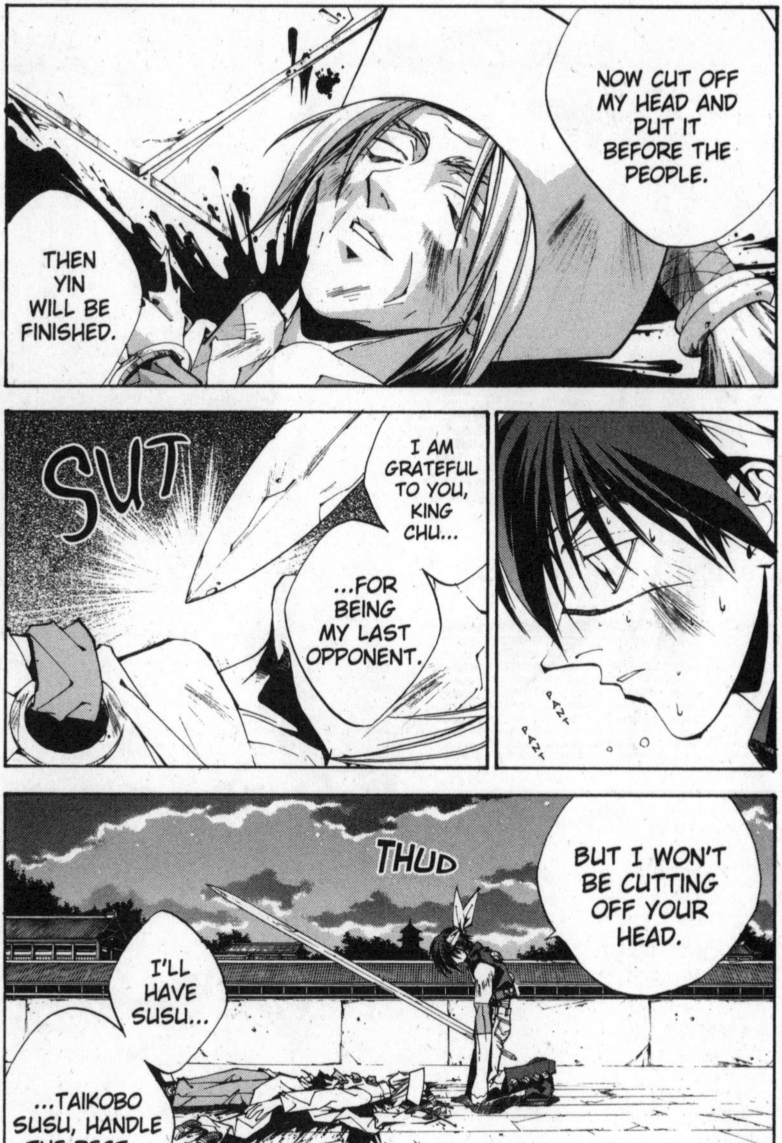
NOW CUT OFF MY HEAD AND PUT IT BEFORE THE PEOPLE.
THEN YIN WILL BE FINISHED.
PANT PANT
SUT
I AM GRATEFUL TO YOU, KING CHU...
...FOR BEING MY LAST OPPONENT.
THUD
BUT I WON'T BE CUTTING OFF YOUR HEAD.
I'LL HAVE SUSU...
...TAIKOBO SUSU, HANDLE THE REST...

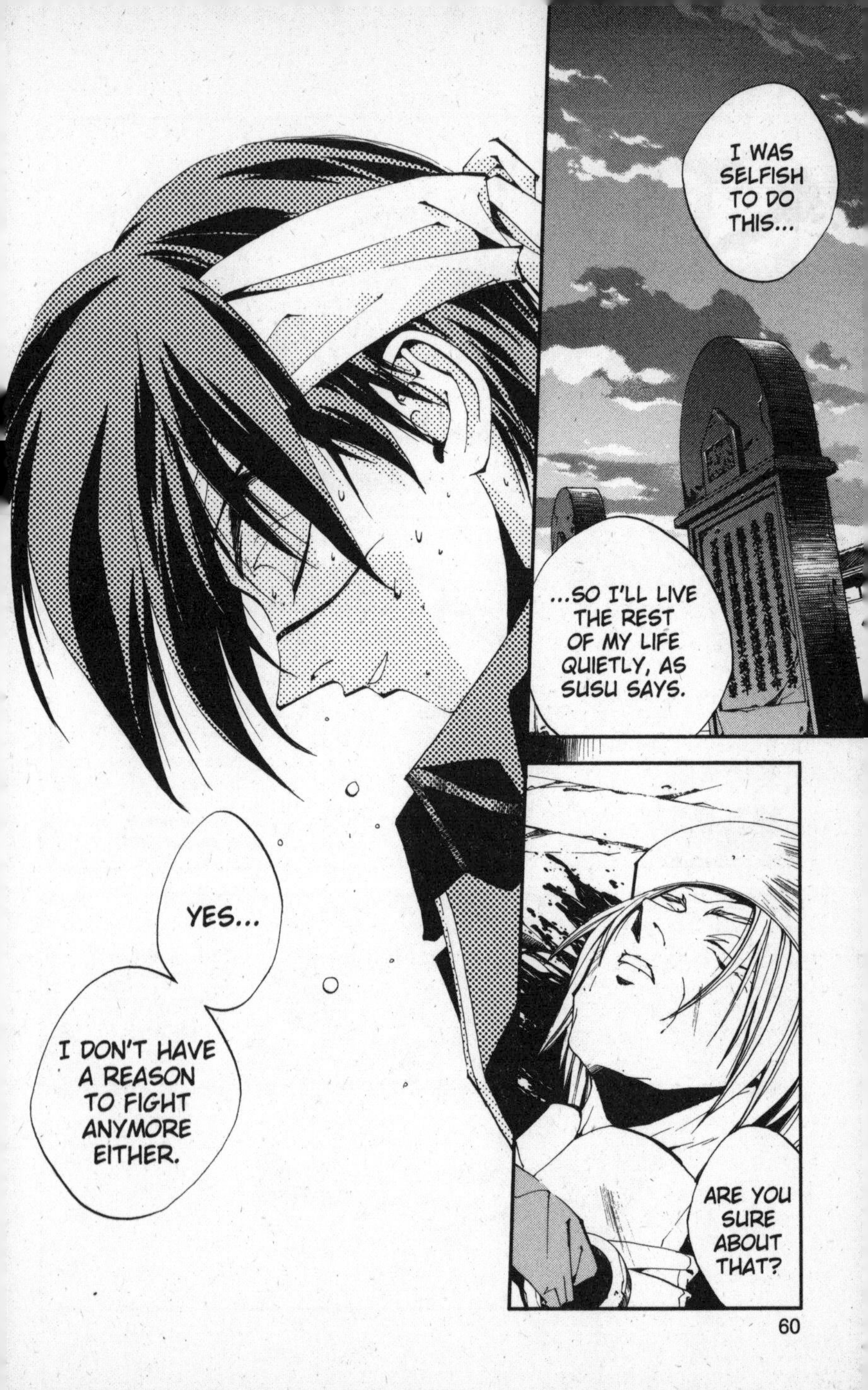
I WAS SELFISH TO DO THIS...
...SO I'LL LIVE THE REST OF MY LIFE QUIETLY, AS SUSU SAYS.
ARE YOU SURE ABOUT THAT?
YES...
I DON'T HAVE A REASON TO FIGHT ANYMORE EITHER.

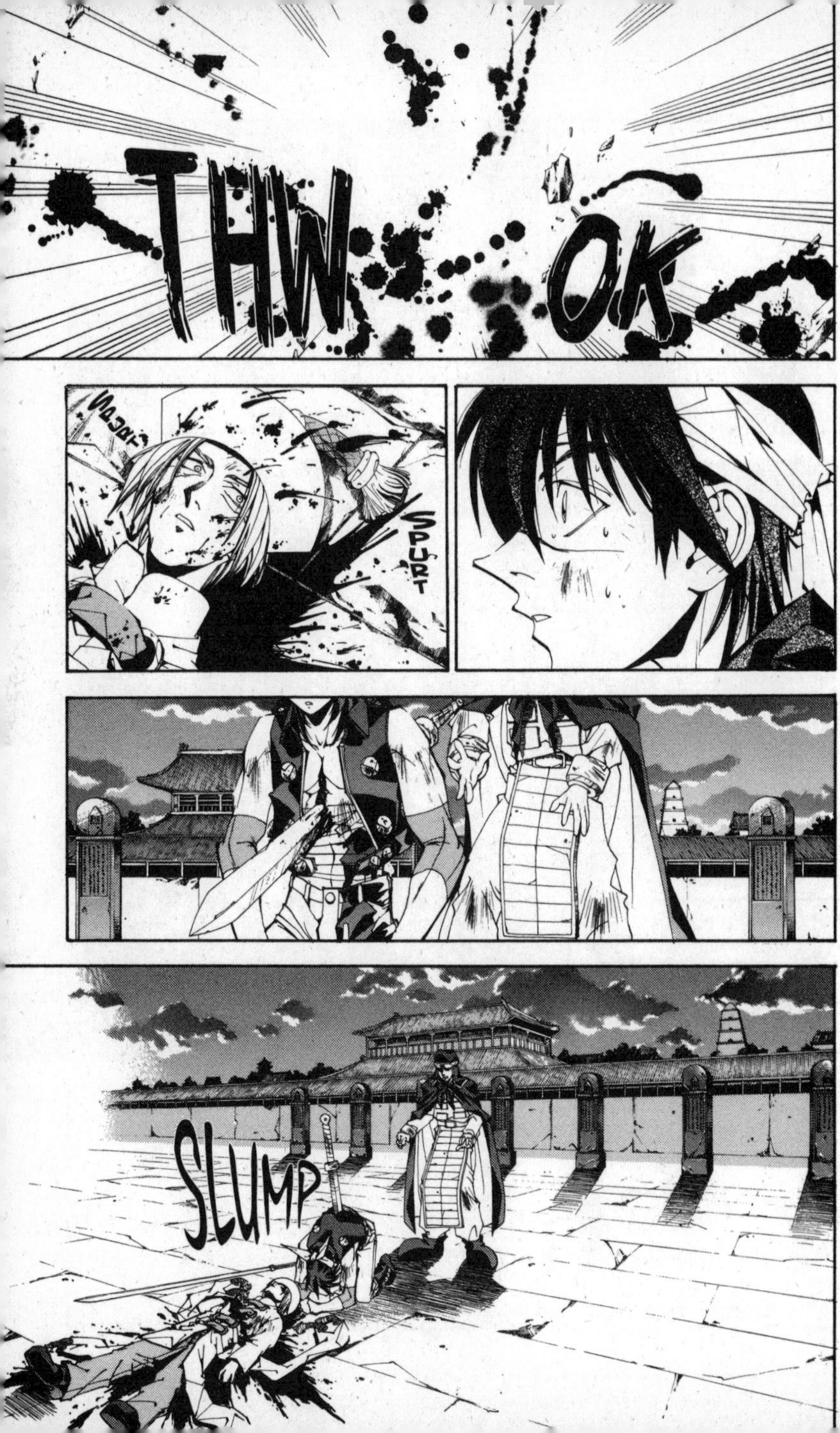
THWOK
SPURT
SLUMP

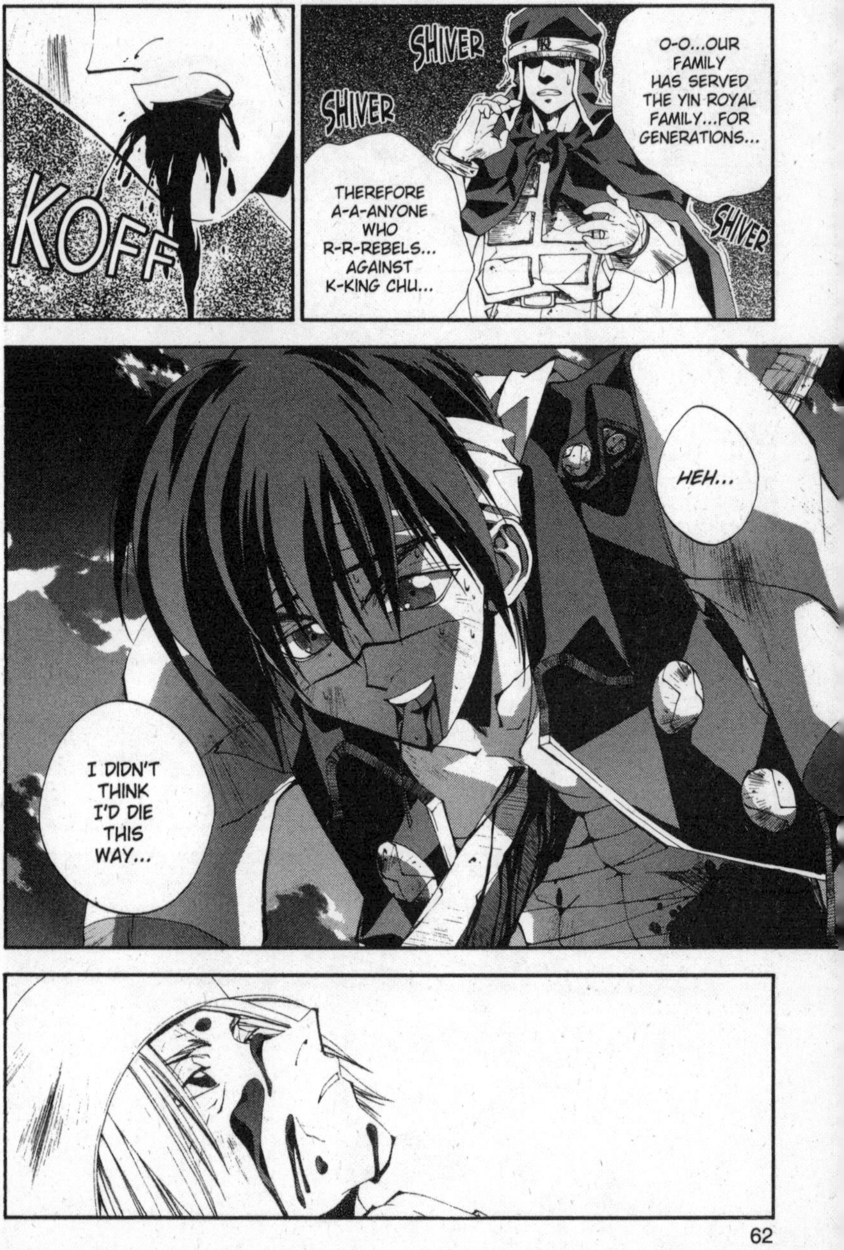
SHIVER
SHIVER
O-O...OUR FAMILY HAS SERVED THE YIN ROYAL FAMILY...FOR GENERATIONS...
SHIVER
THEREFORE A-A-ANYONE WHO R-R-REBELS... AGAINST K-KING CHU...
KOFF
HEH...
I DIDN'T THINK I'D DIE THIS WAY...

READ THIS WAY

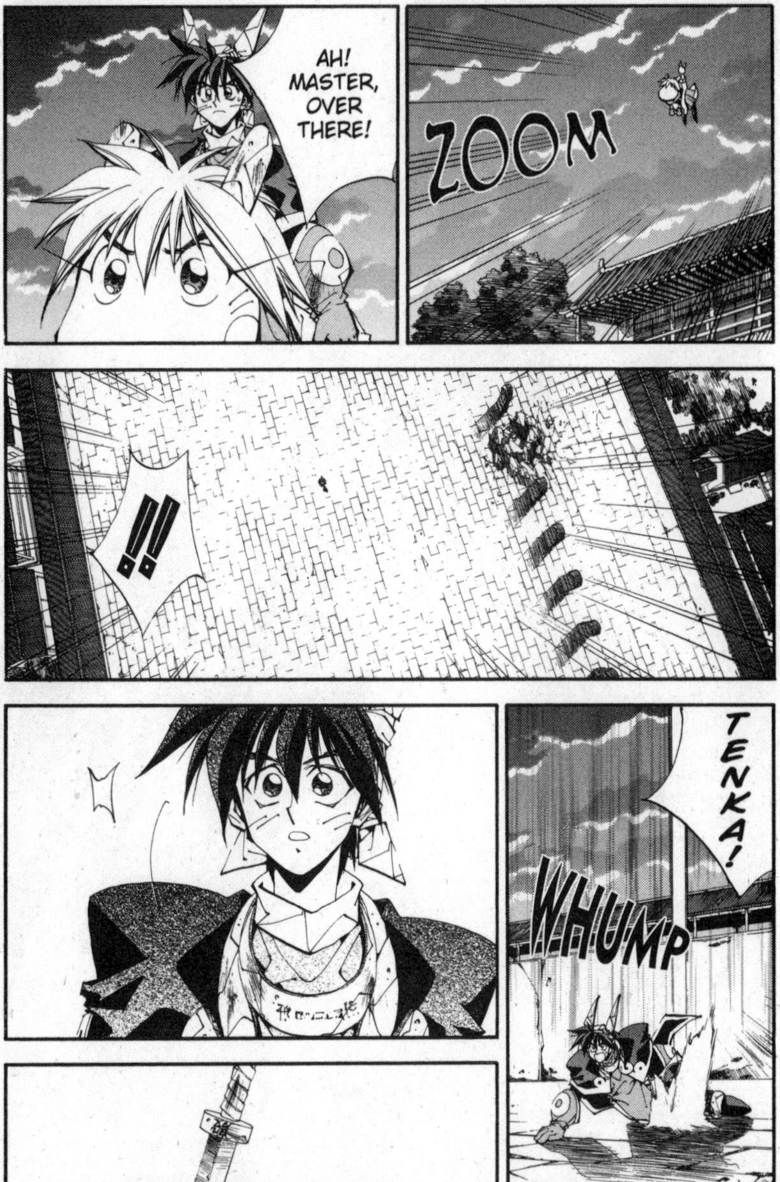
ZOOM
AH! MASTER, OVER THERE!
!!
TENKA!
WHUMP

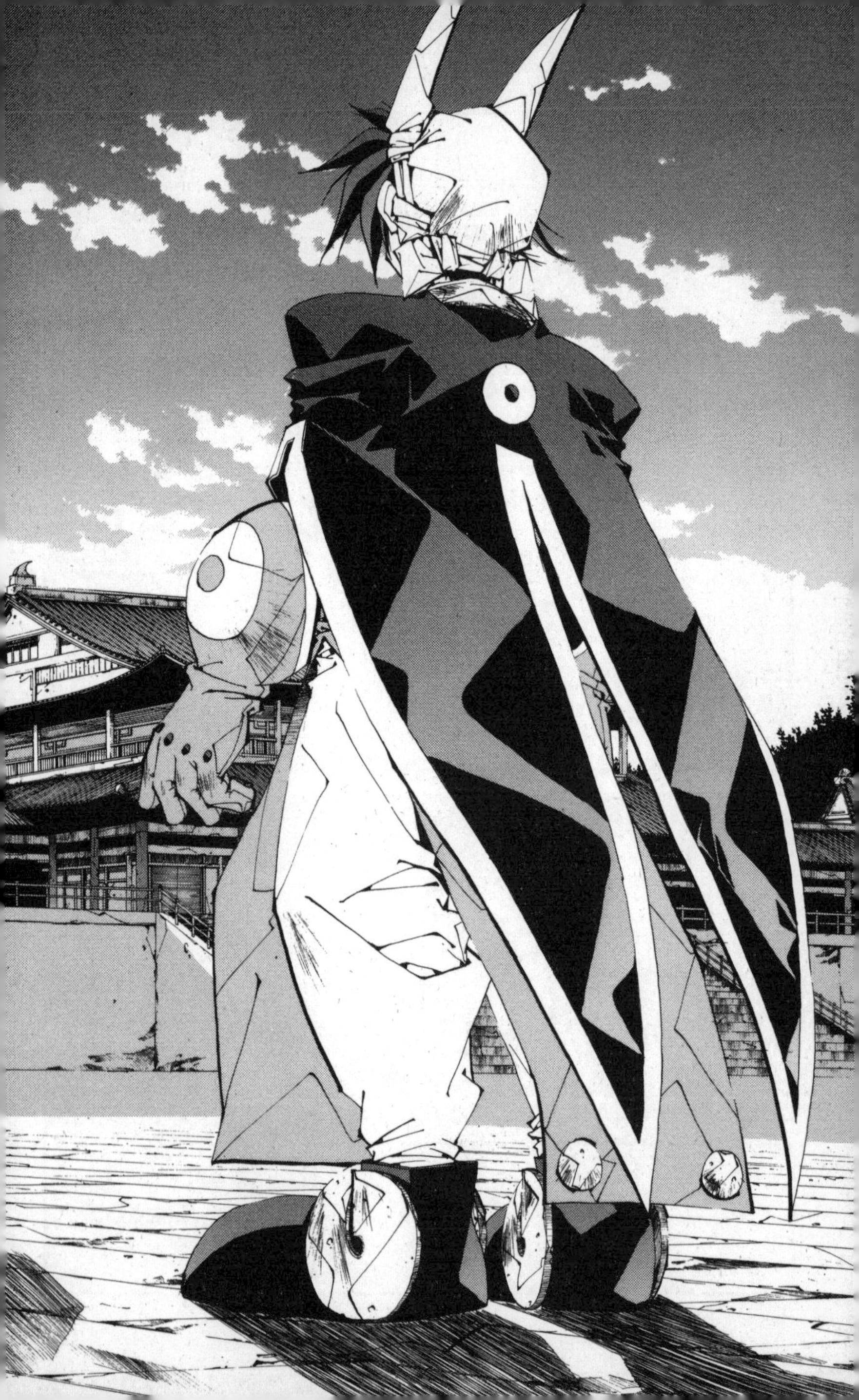

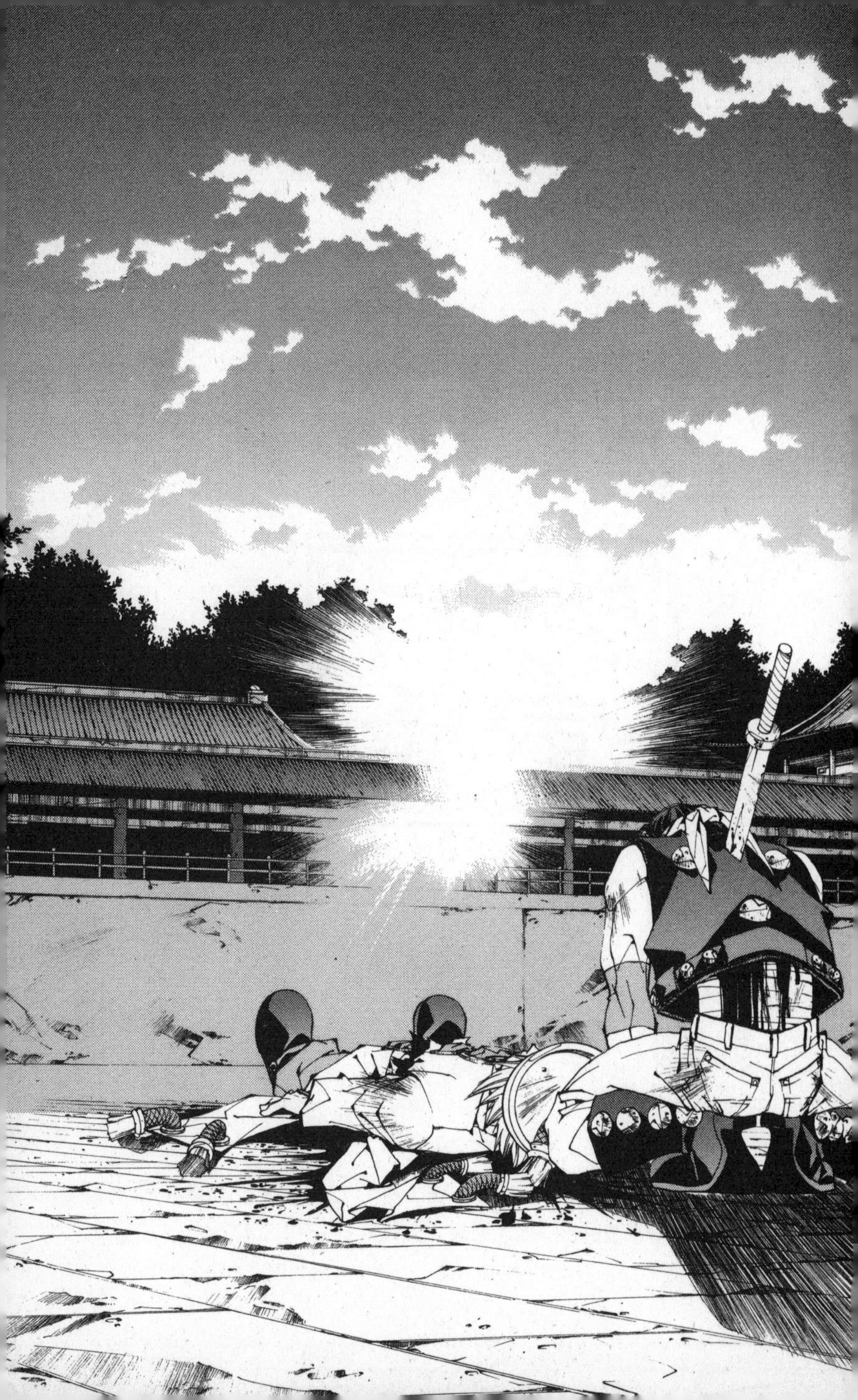

封神演義

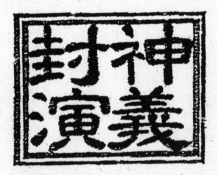

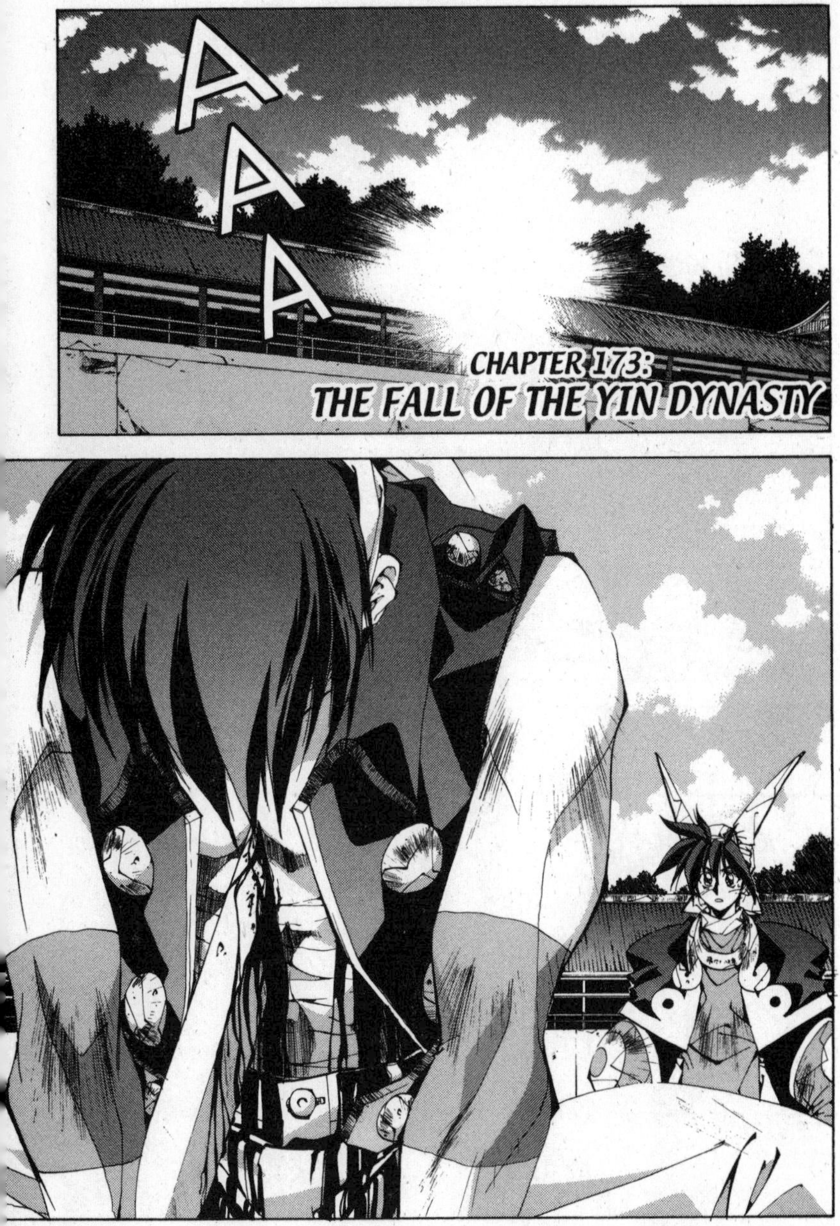
AAA
CHAPTER 173:
THE FALL OF THE YIN DYNASTY

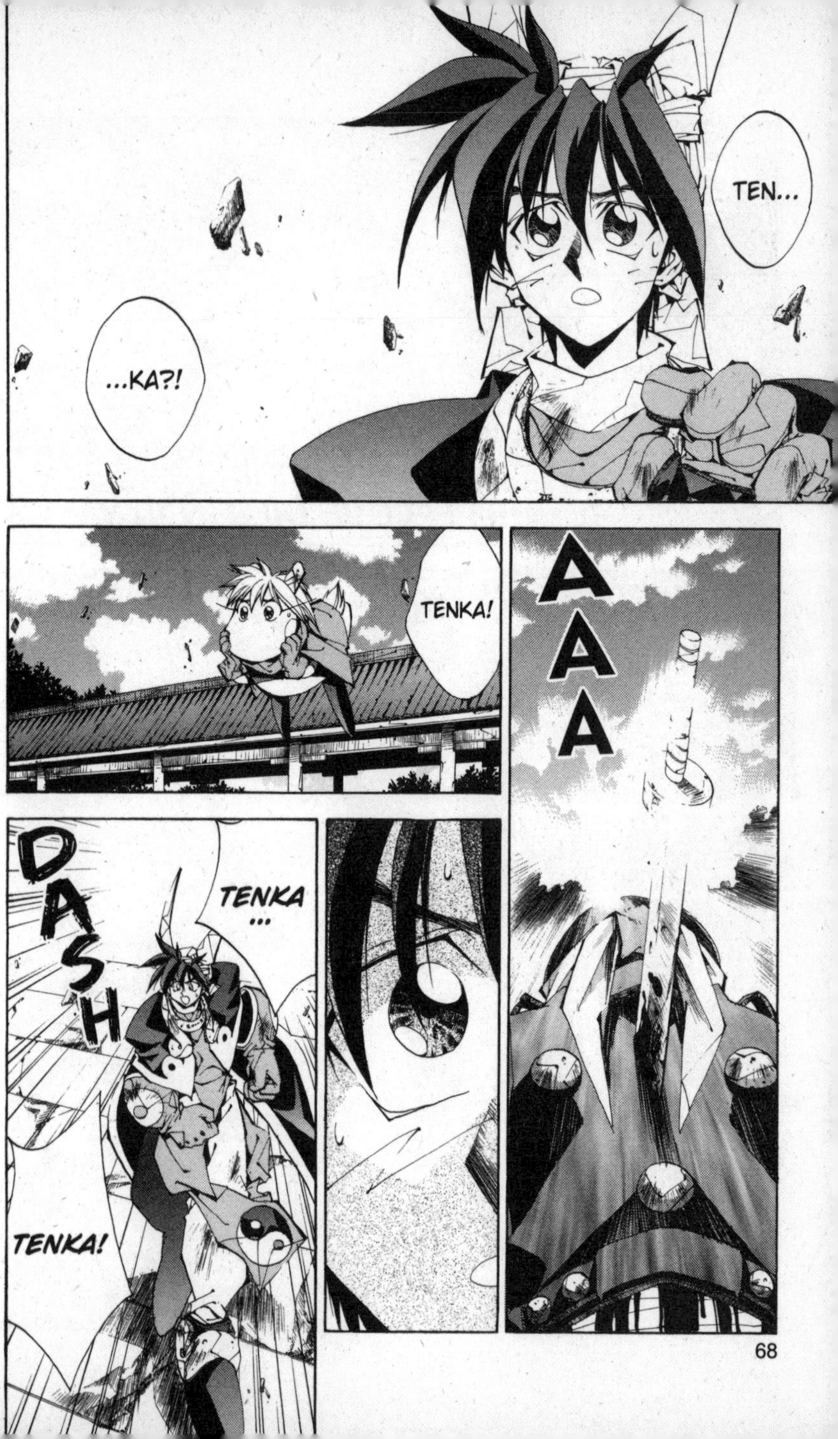
TEN...
...KA?!
AAA
TENKA!
DASH
TENKA ...
TENKA!

READ THIS WAY

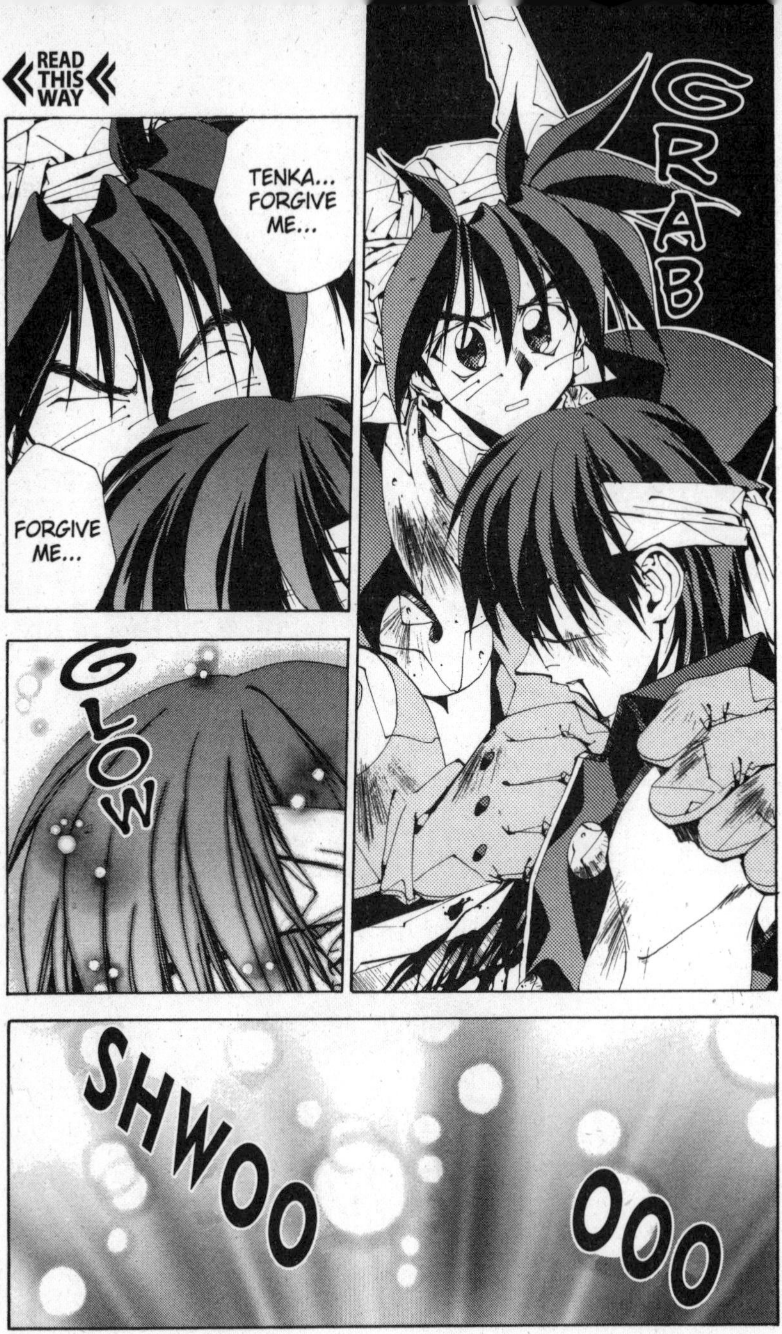
GRAB
TENKA... FORGIVE ME...
FORGIVE ME...
GLOW
SHWOO OOO

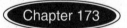
Chapter 173

THE FALL OF THE YIN DYNASTY

READ THIS WAY

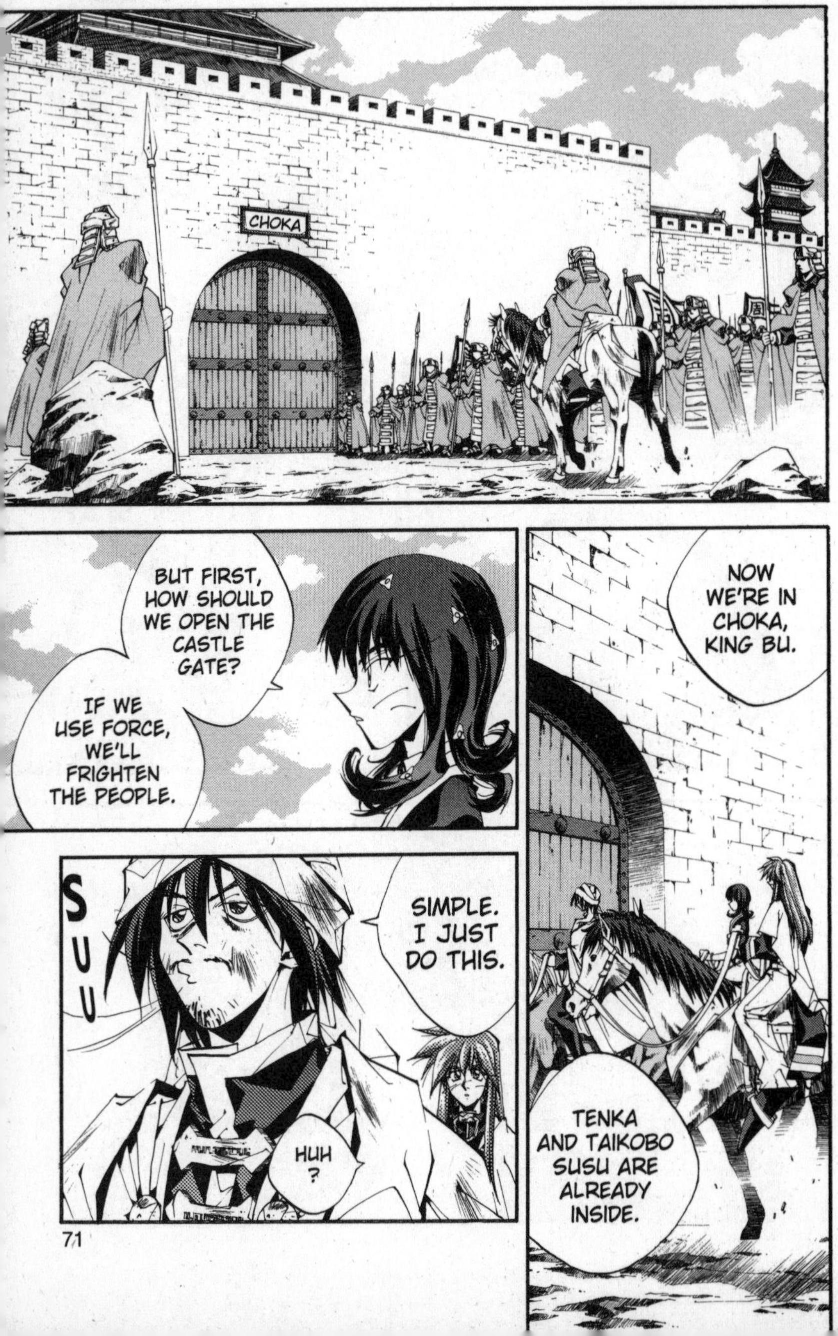

CHOKA
NOW WE'RE IN CHOKA, KING BU.
TENKA AND TAIKOBO SUSU ARE ALREADY INSIDE.
BUT FIRST, HOW SHOULD WE OPEN THE CASTLE GATE?
IF WE USE FORCE, WE'LL FRIGHTEN THE PEOPLE.
SUU
SIMPLE. I JUST DO THIS.
HUH?

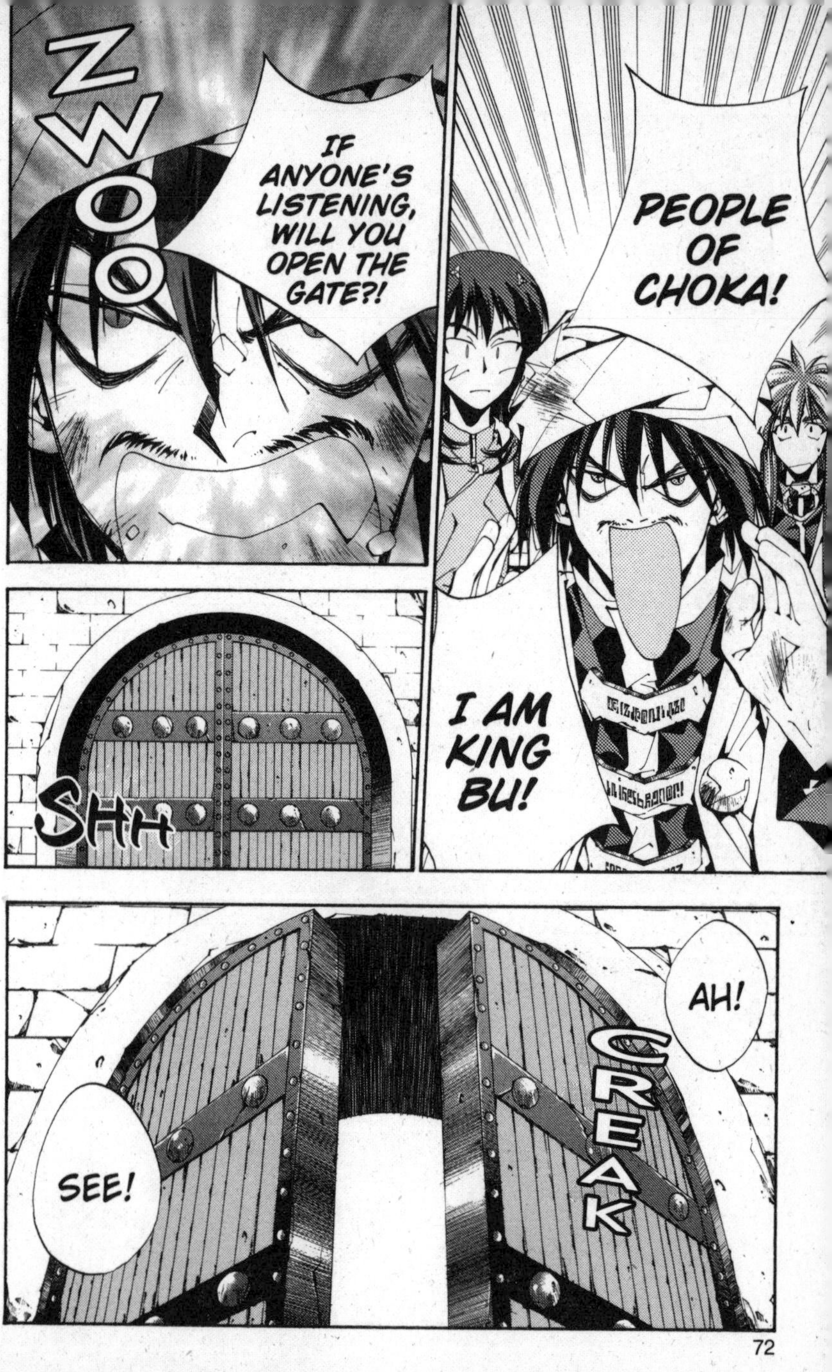
PEOPLE OF CHOKA!
ZWOOO
IF ANYONE'S LISTENING, WILL YOU OPEN THE GATE?!
I AM KING BU!
SHH
AH!
CREAK
SEE!

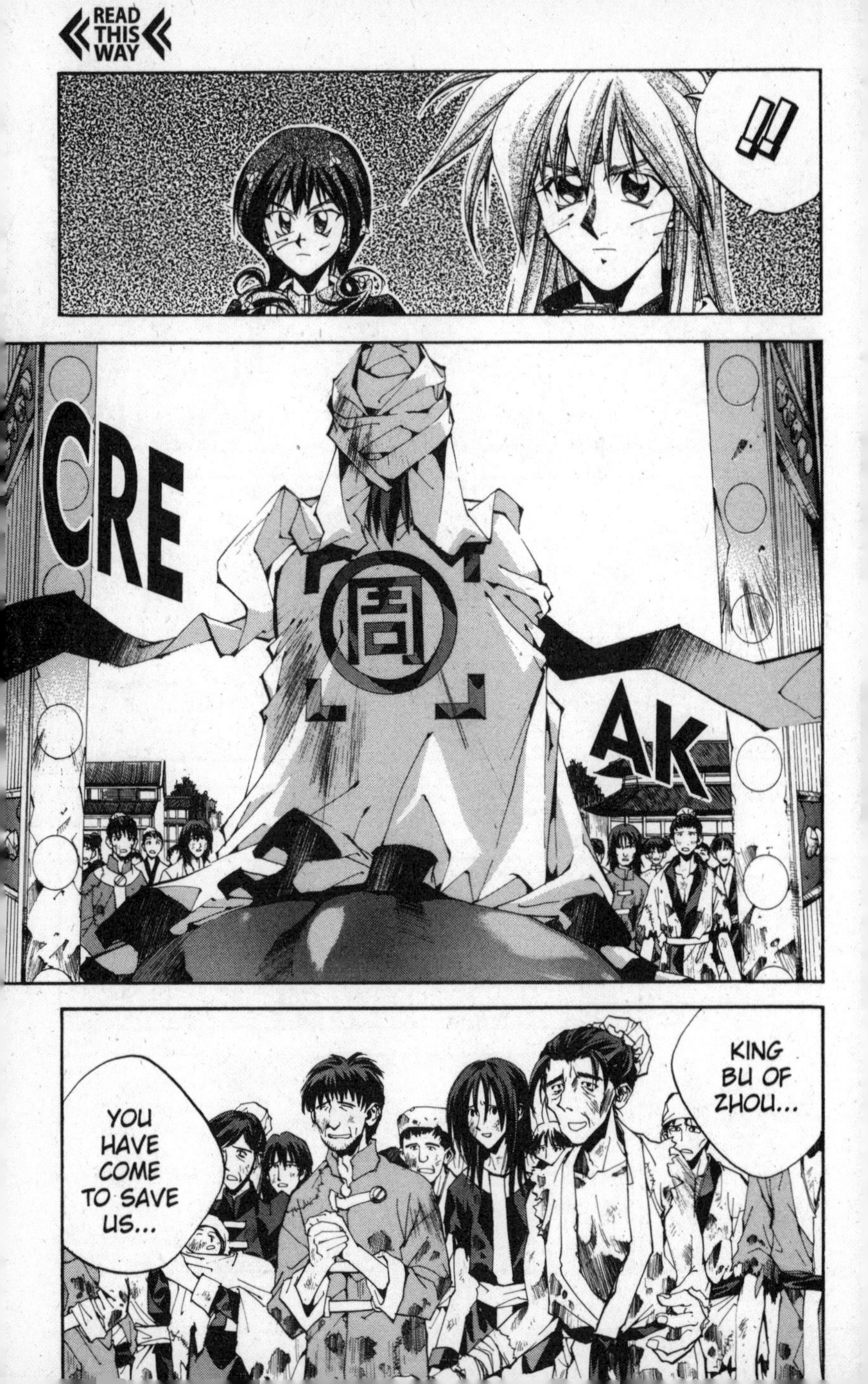
READ THIS WAY
!!
CRE
AK
KING BU OF ZHOU...
YOU HAVE COME TO SAVE US...

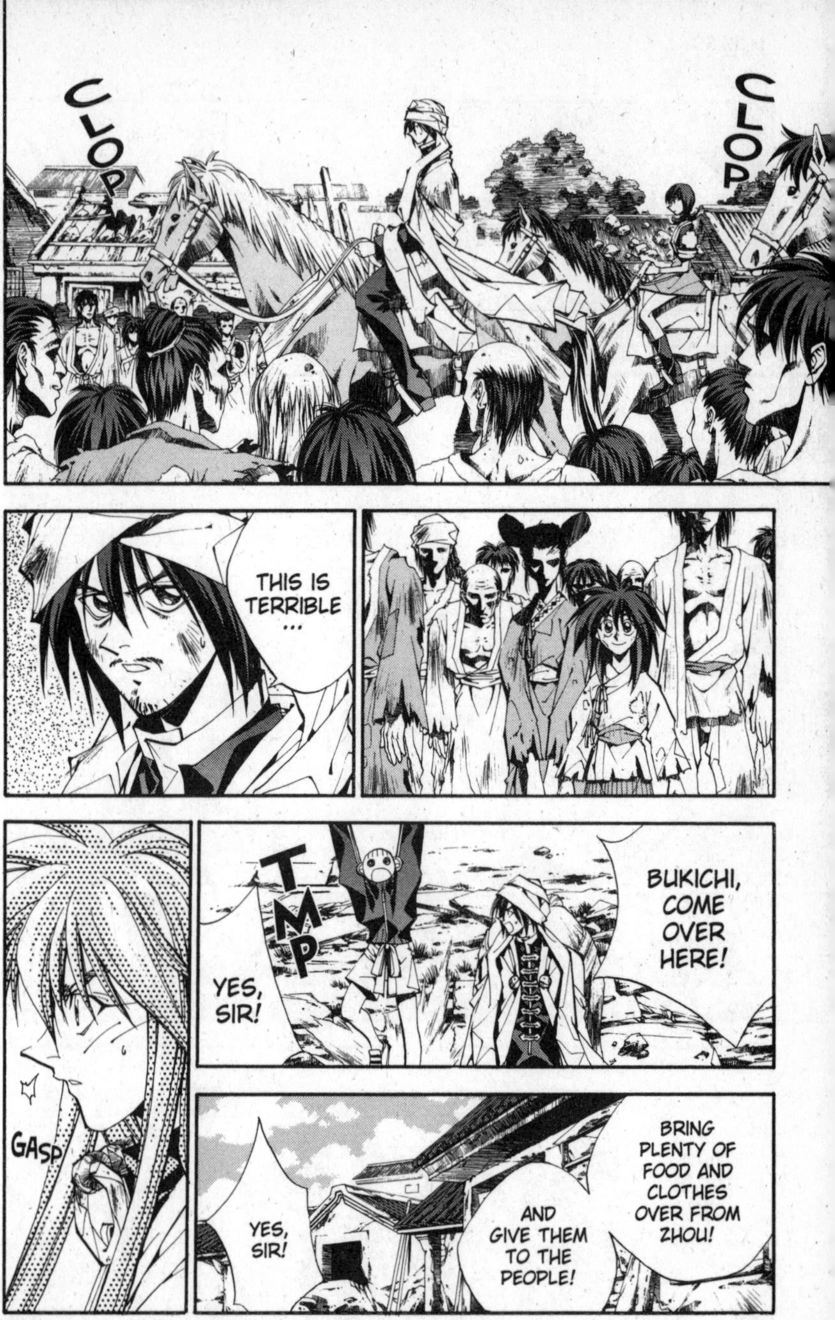
CLOP
CLOP
THIS IS TERRIBLE ...
BUKICHI, COME OVER HERE!
TMP
YES, SIR!
GASP
BRING PLENTY OF FOOD AND CLOTHES OVER FROM ZHOU!
AND GIVE THEM TO THE PEOPLE!
YES, SIR!

READ THIS WAY

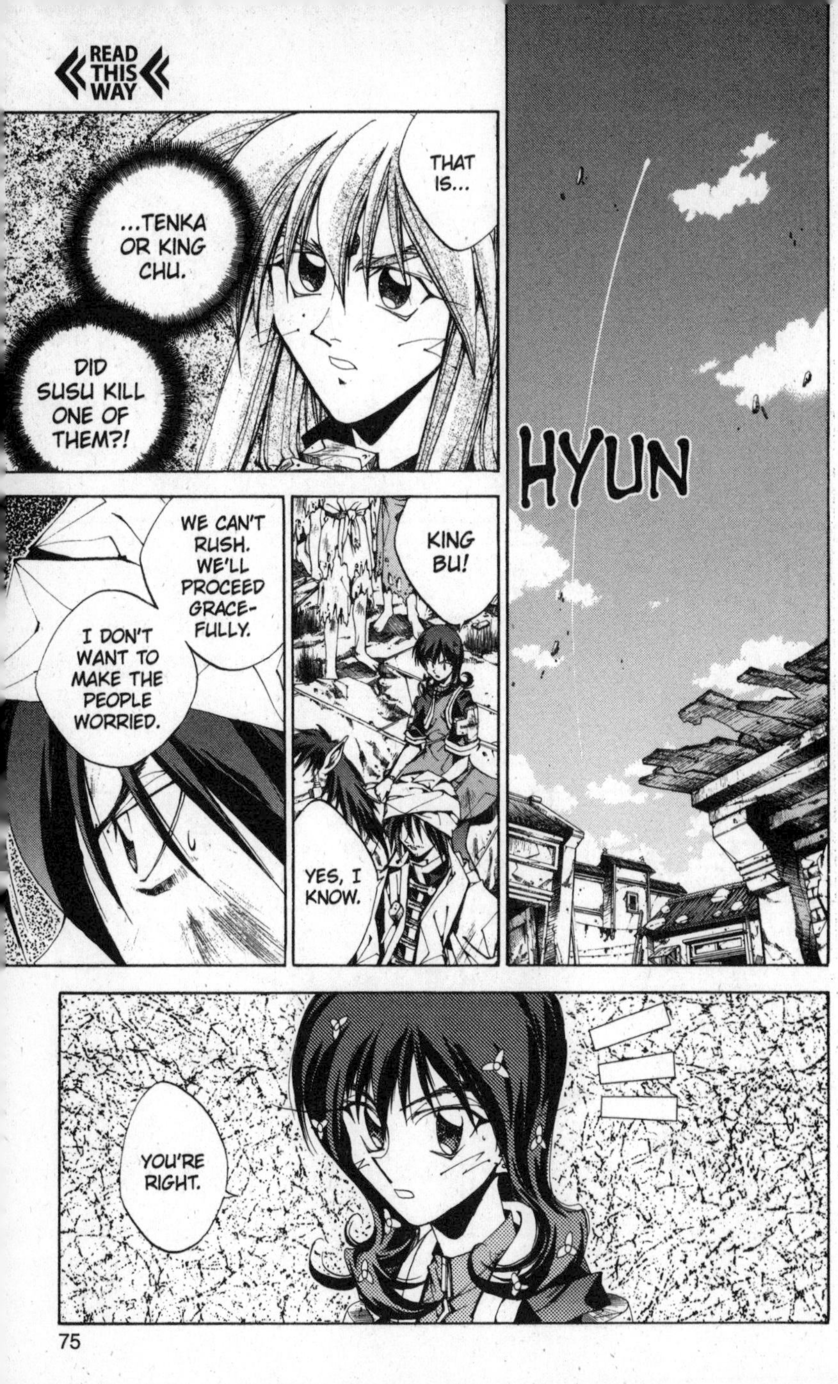
HYUN
THAT IS...
...TENKA OR KING CHU.
DID SUSU KILL ONE OF THEM?!
KING BU!
YES, I KNOW.
WE CAN'T RUSH. WE'LL PROCEED GRACE-FULLY.
I DON'T WANT TO MAKE THE PEOPLE WORRIED.
YOU'RE RIGHT.

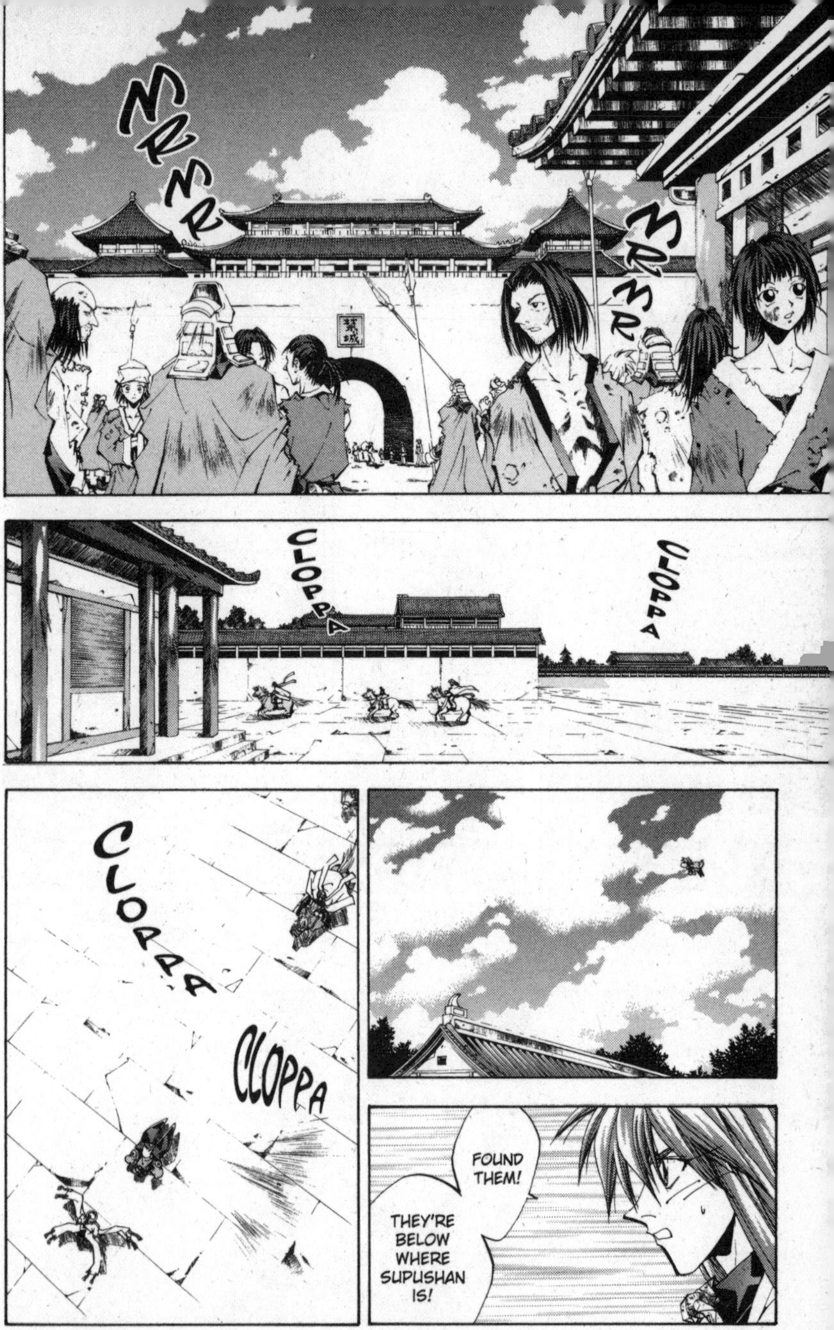
MRMR
MRMR
CLOPPA
CLOPPA
CLOPPA
CLOPPA
FOUND THEM!
THEY'RE BELOW WHERE SUPUSHAN IS!

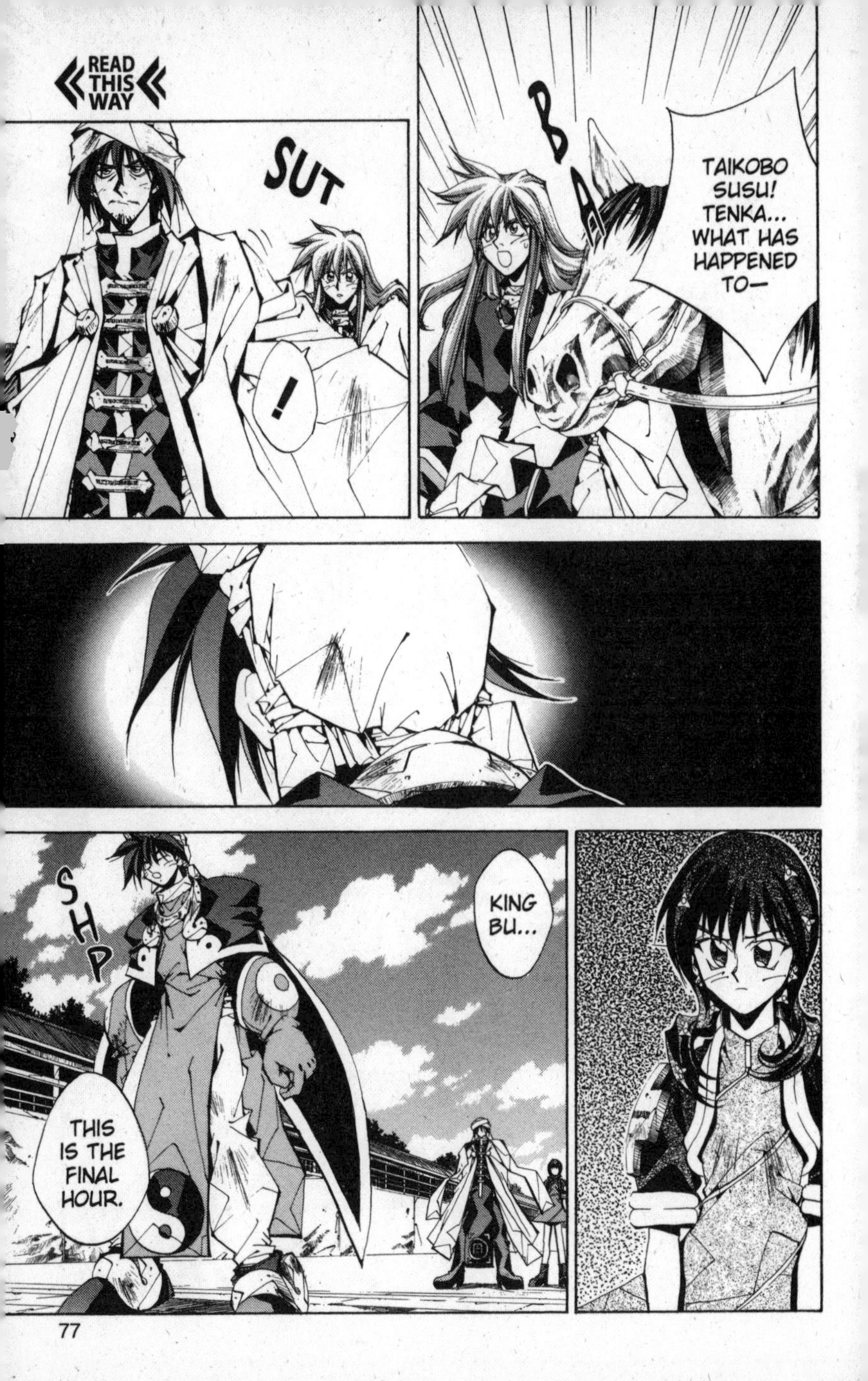
READ THIS WAY
TAIKOBO SUSU! TENKA... WHAT HAS HAPPENED TO—
BA
SUT
!
KING BU...
SHP
THIS IS THE FINAL HOUR.

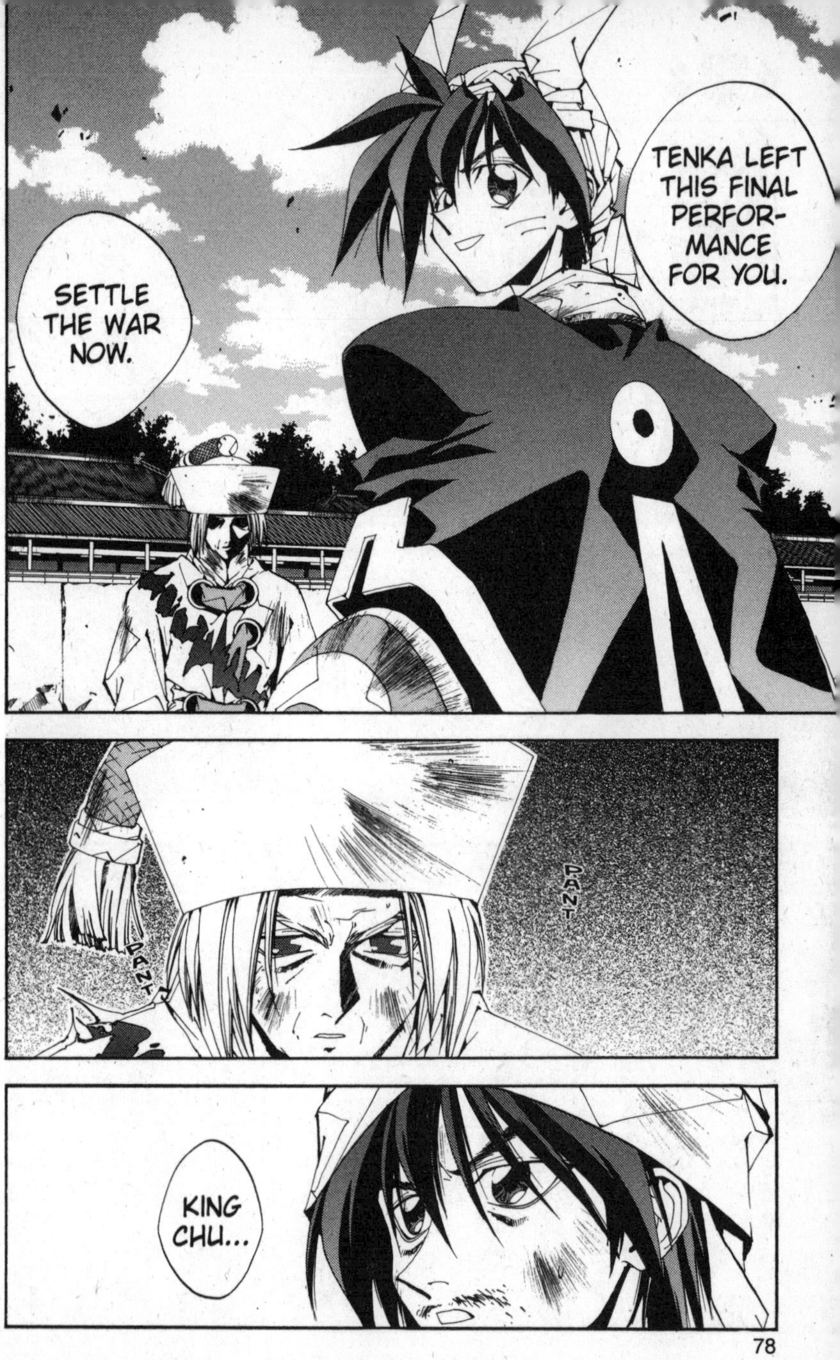
TENKA LEFT THIS FINAL PERFOR-MANCE FOR YOU.
SETTLE THE WAR NOW.
PANT
PANT
KING CHU...

READ THIS WAY

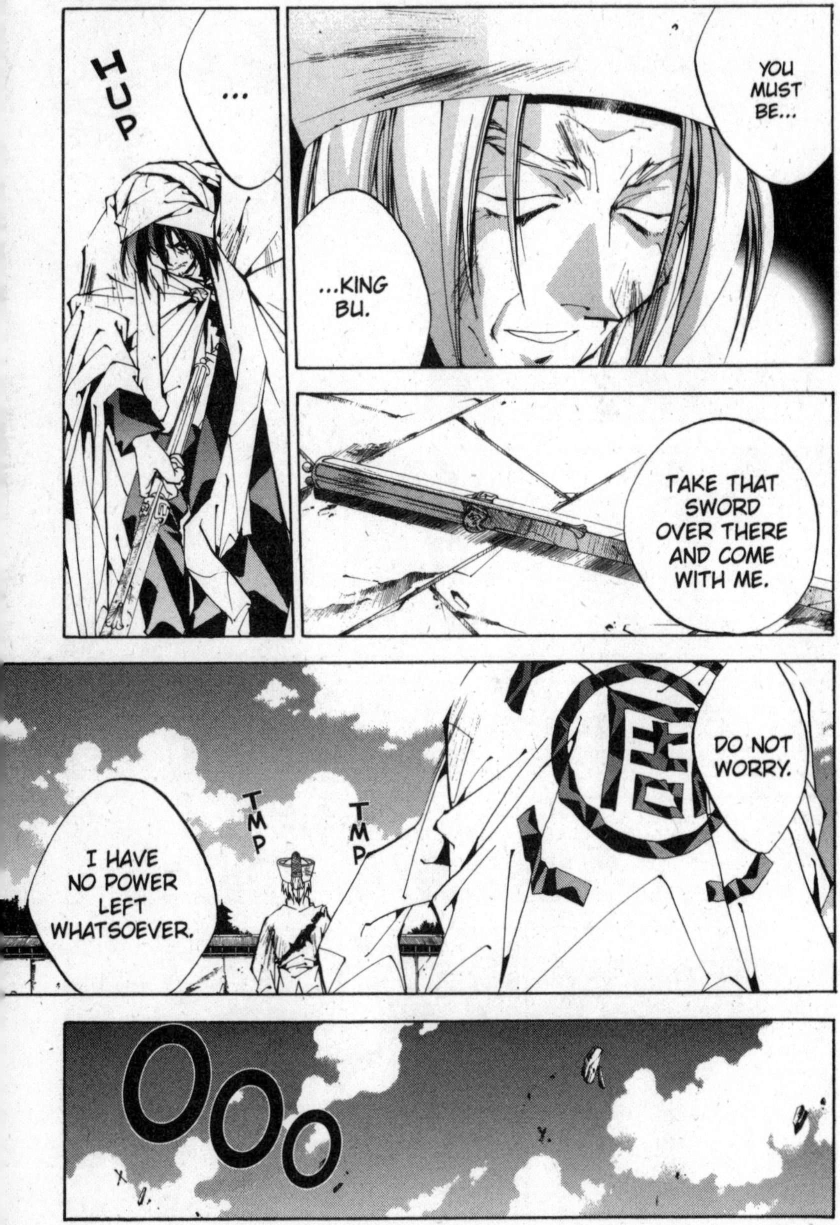
YOU MUST BE...
...KING BU.
TAKE THAT SWORD OVER THERE AND COME WITH ME.
HUP
...
DO NOT WORRY.
TMP
TMP
I HAVE NO POWER LEFT WHATSOEVER.
OOO

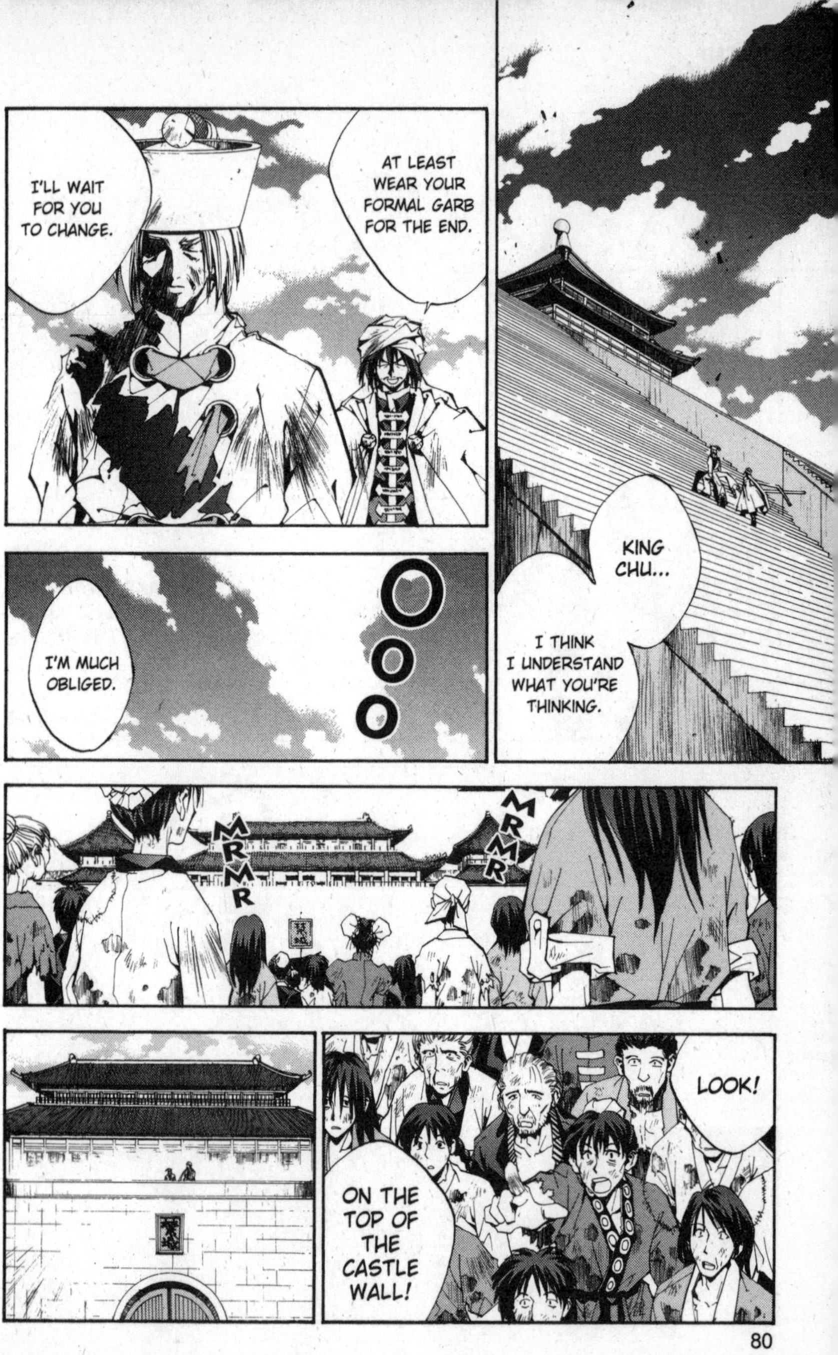
KING CHU...
I THINK I UNDERSTAND WHAT YOU'RE THINKING.
AT LEAST WEAR YOUR FORMAL GARB FOR THE END.
I'LL WAIT FOR YOU TO CHANGE.
OOO
I'M MUCH OBLIGED.
MRMR
MRMR
LOOK!
ON THE TOP OF THE CASTLE WALL!

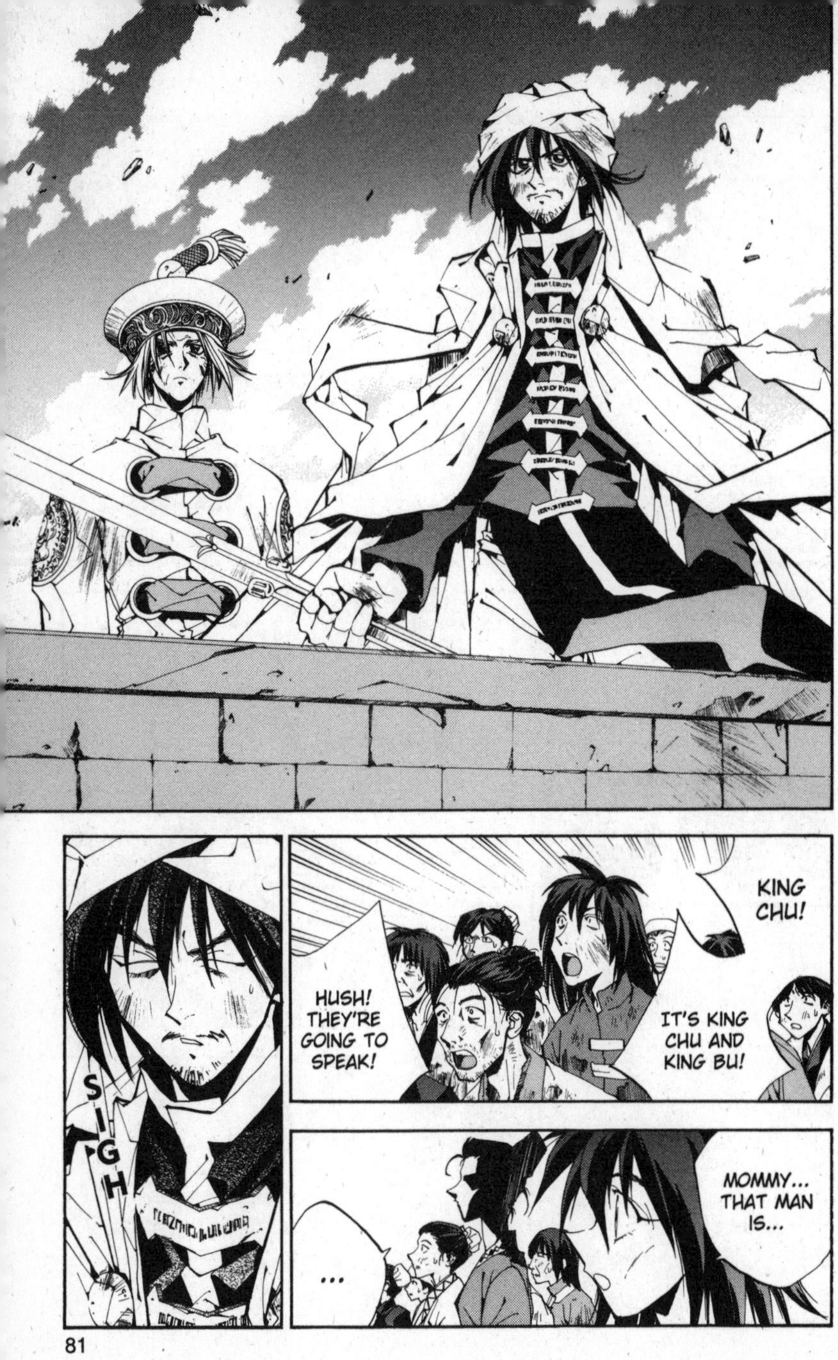
KING CHU!
IT'S KING CHU AND KING BU!
HUSH! THEY'RE GOING TO SPEAK!
MOMMY... THAT MAN IS...
...
SIGH

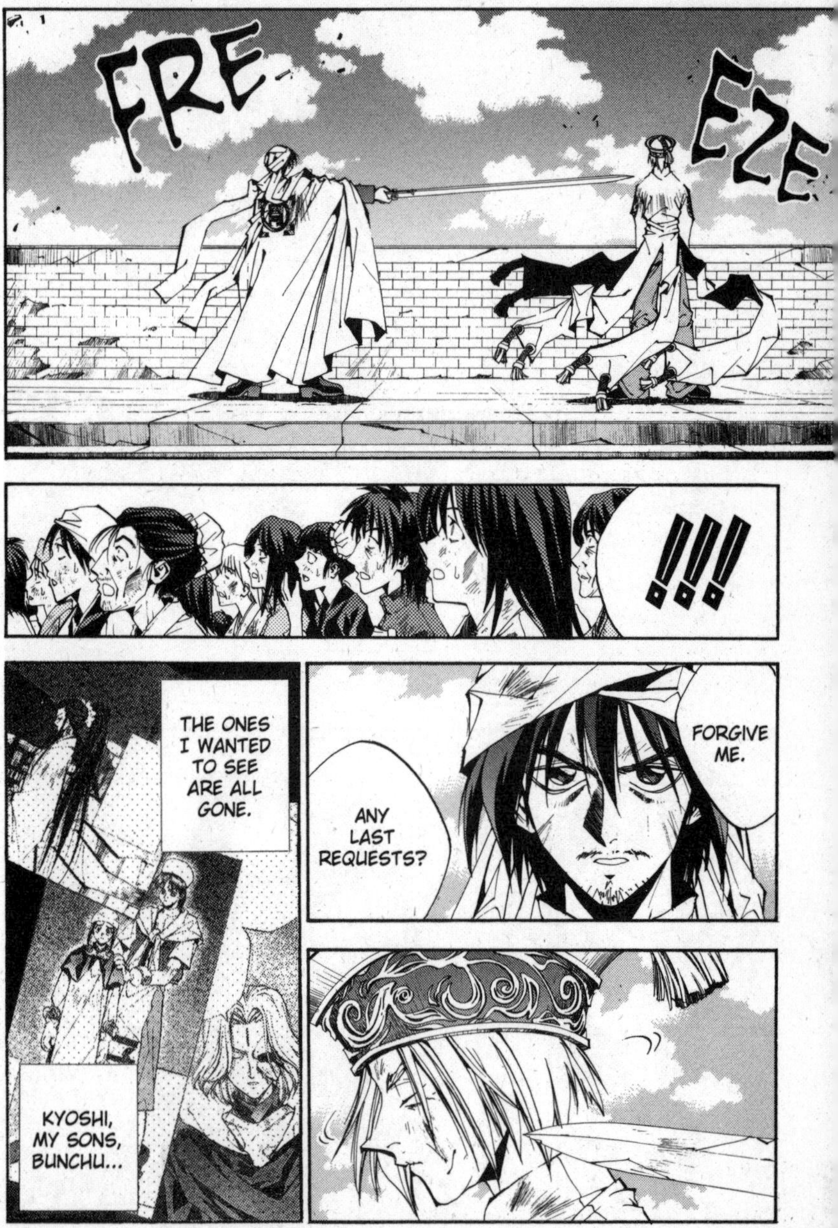
FRE
EZE
!!!
FORGIVE ME.
ANY LAST REQUESTS?
THE ONES I WANTED TO SEE ARE ALL GONE.
KYOSHI, MY SONS, BUNCHU...

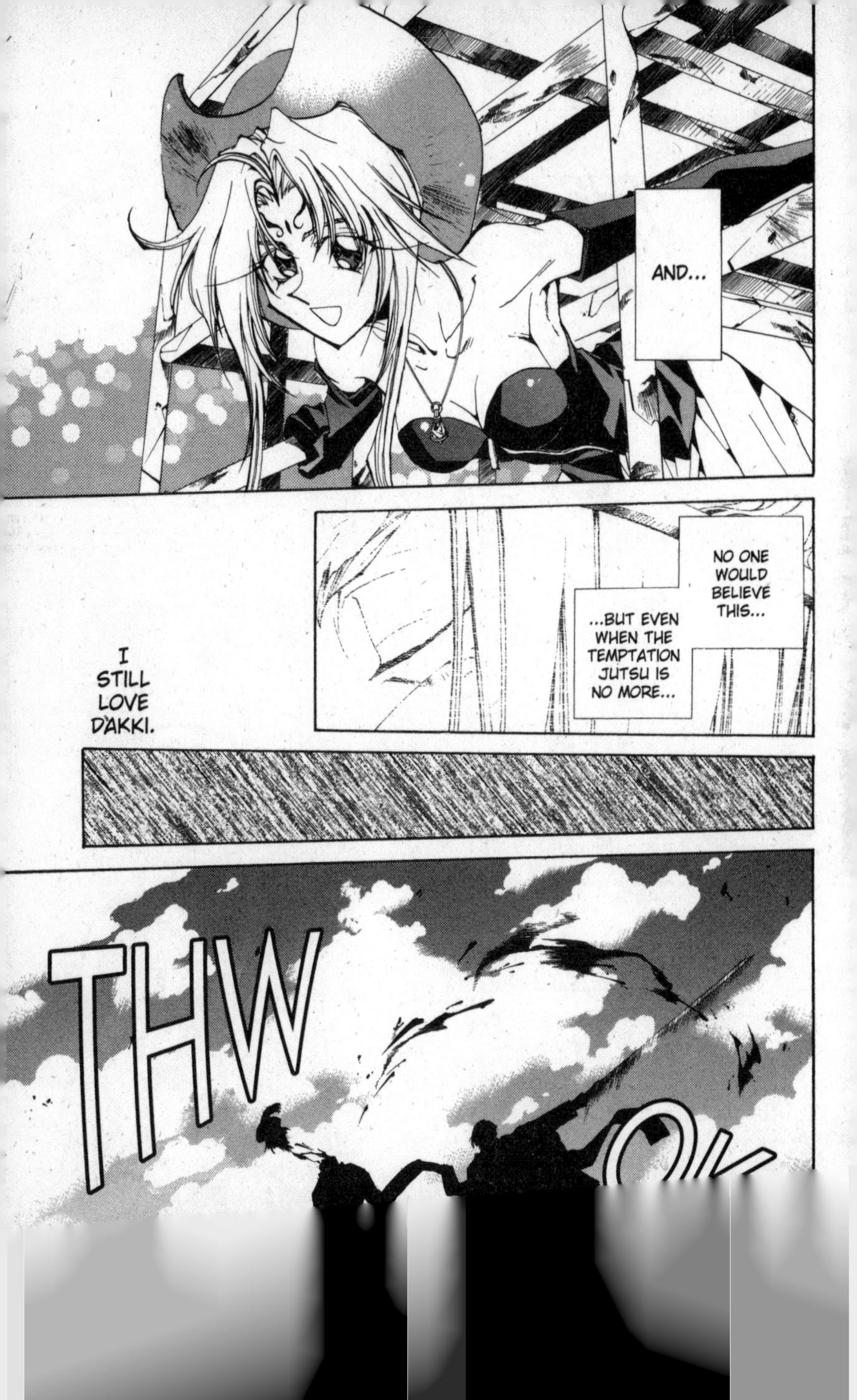
AND...
NO ONE WOULD BELIEVE THIS...
...BUT EVEN WHEN THE TEMPTATION JUTSU IS NO MORE...
I STILL LOVE DAKKI.
THW
OK

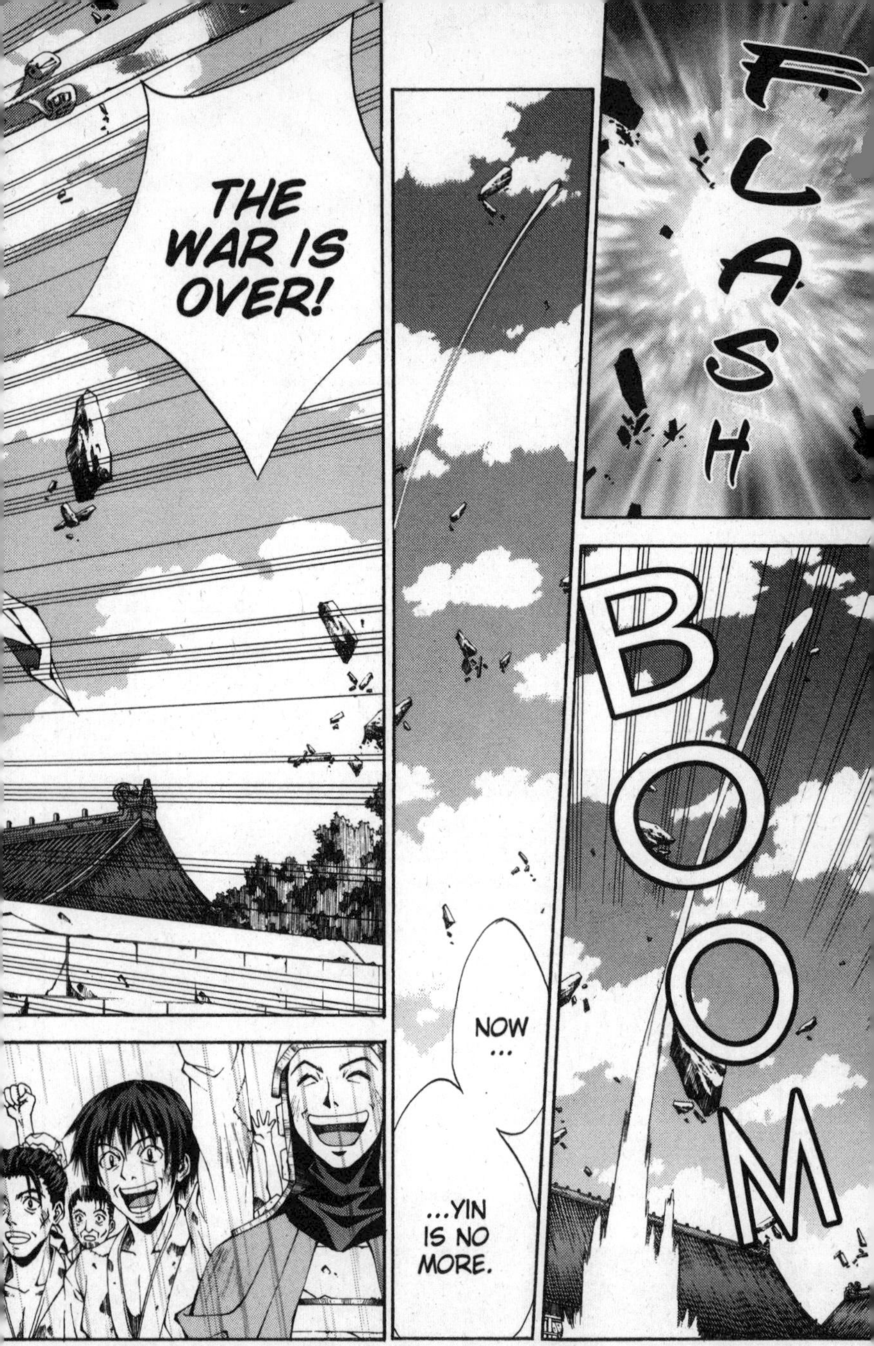
FLASH
BOOM
NOW...
...YIN IS NO MORE.
THE WAR IS OVER!

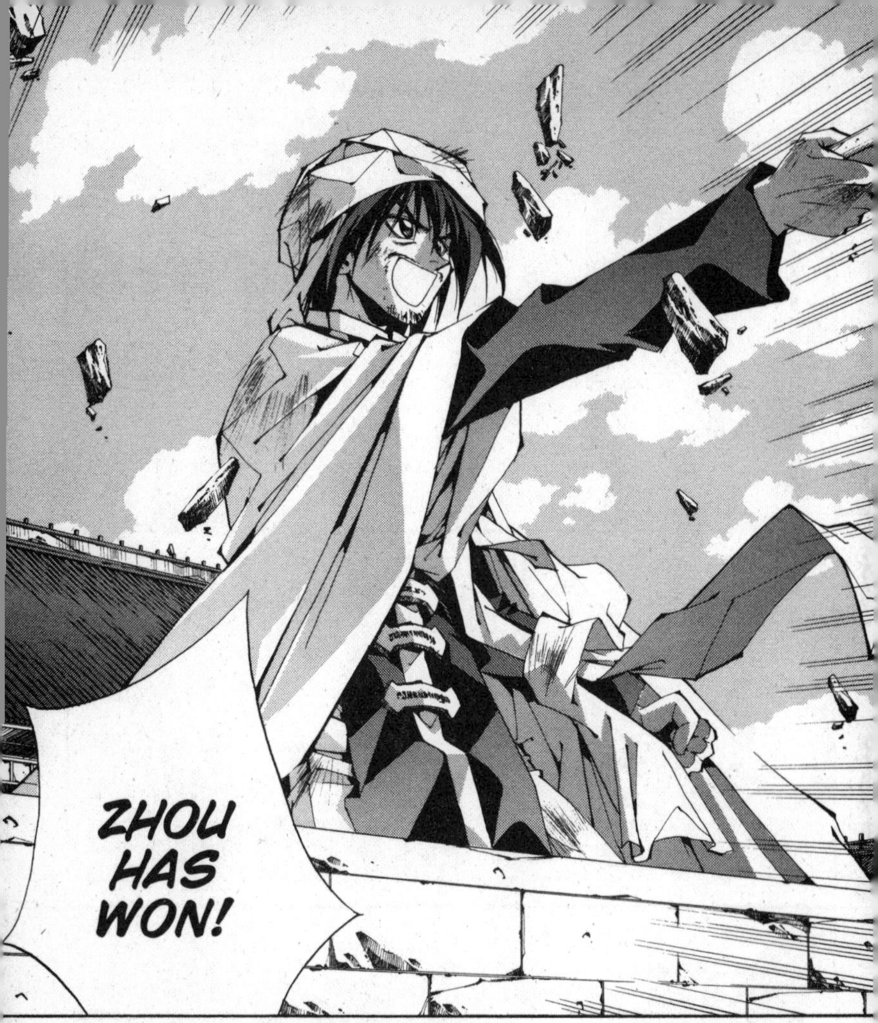
ZHOU HAS WON!

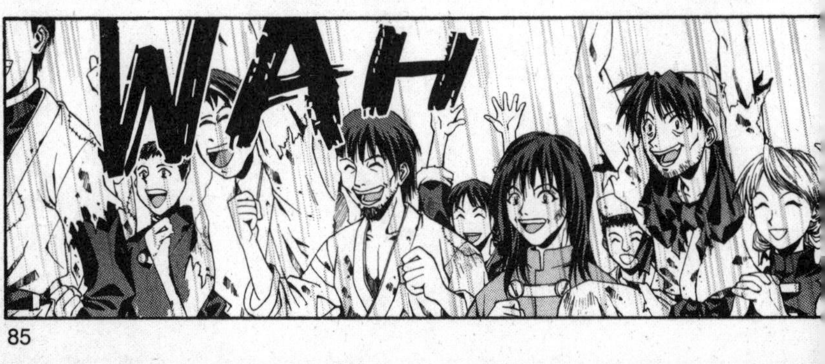
WAH

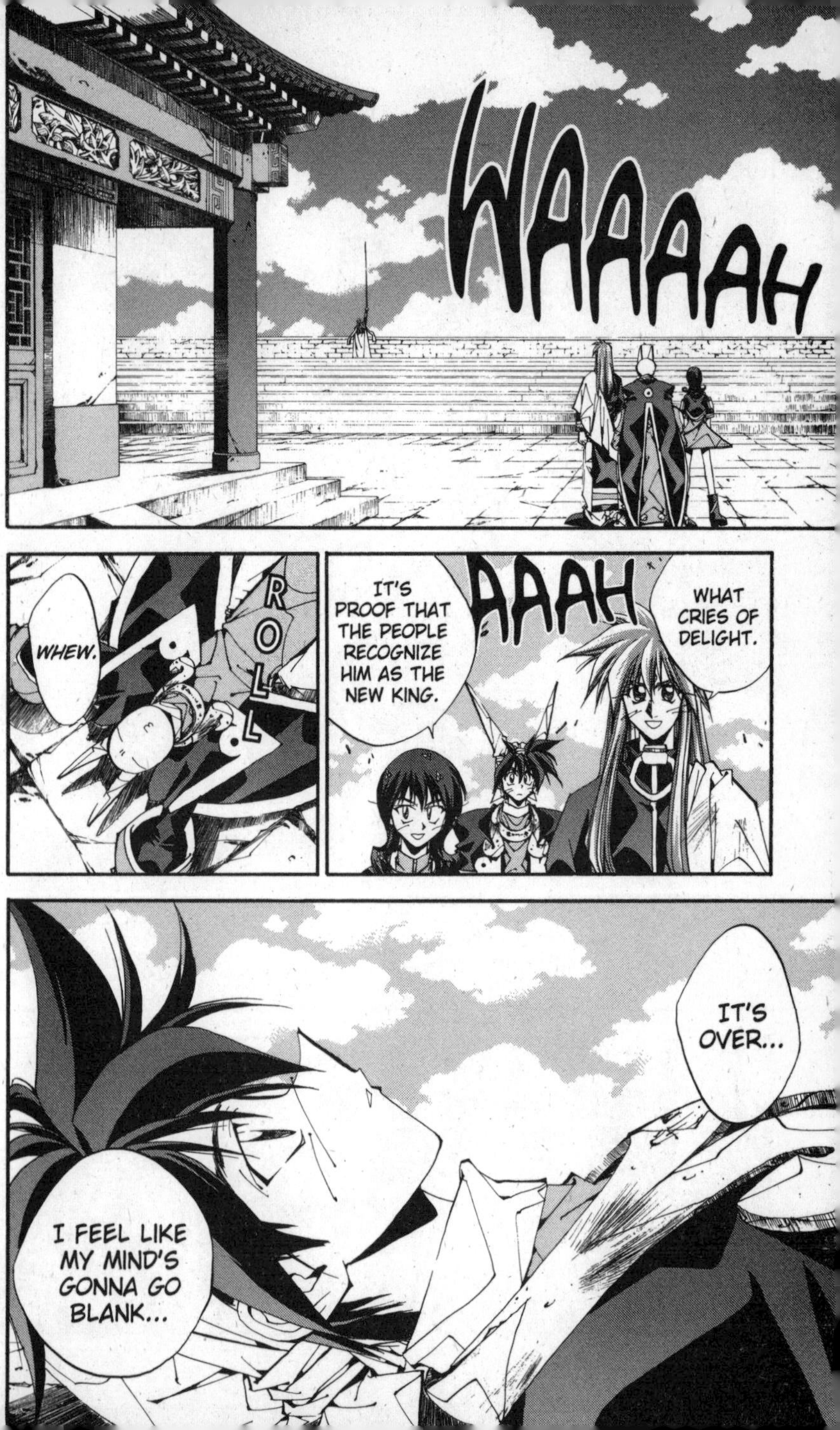
WAAAAAH
AAAH
WHAT CRIES OF DELIGHT.
IT'S PROOF THAT THE PEOPLE RECOGNIZE HIM AS THE NEW KING.
ROLL
WHEW.
IT'S OVER...
I FEEL LIKE MY MIND'S GONNA GO BLANK...

HEH HEH HEH HEH ...

SWIRL

SWIRL

WSSH

THUS YIN PERISHED AFTER 30 GENERATIONS AND 700 YEARS.

AND SO, ON A SPRING DAY IN THE SECOND HALF OF THE 11TH CENTURY B.C., THE ZHOU ERA BEGAN.

封神演義

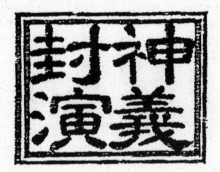

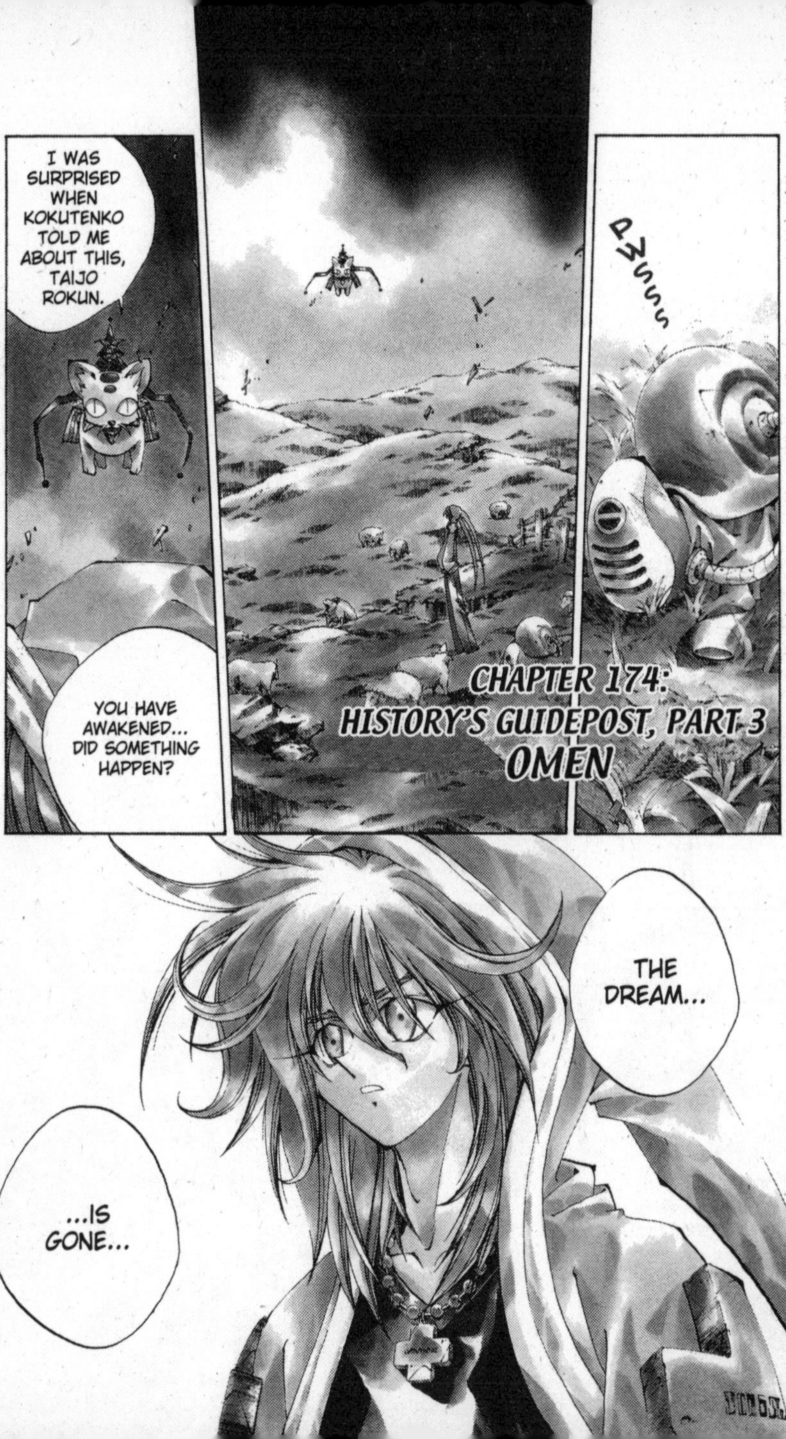
PWSSSS
CHAPTER 174:
HISTORY'S GUIDEPOST, PART 3
OMEN
I WAS SURPRISED WHEN KOKUTENKO TOLD ME ABOUT THIS, TAIJO ROKUN.
YOU HAVE AWAKENED... DID SOMETHING HAPPEN?
THE DREAM...
...IS GONE...

Chapter 174

HISTORY'S GUIDEPOST, PART 3
OMEN

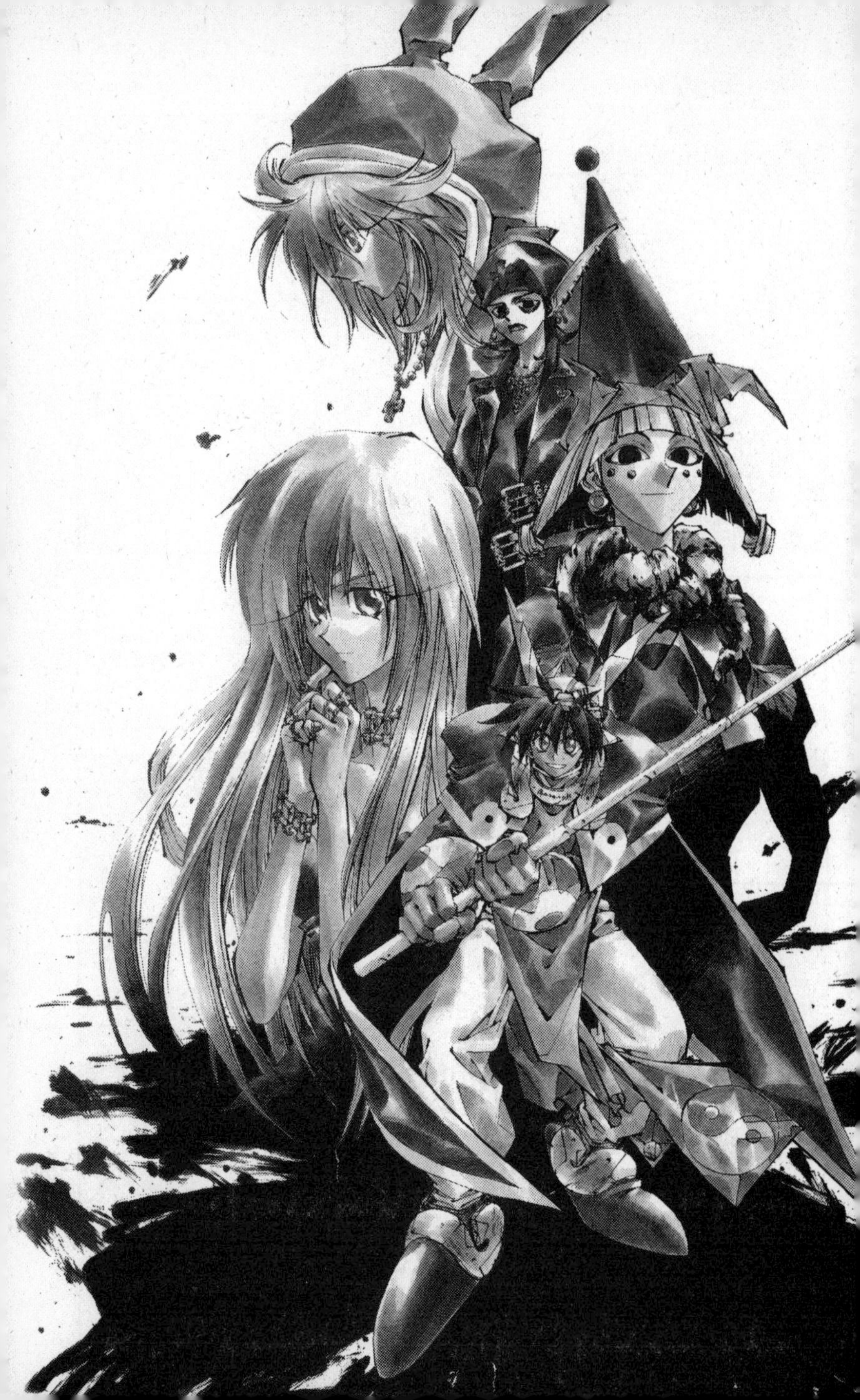

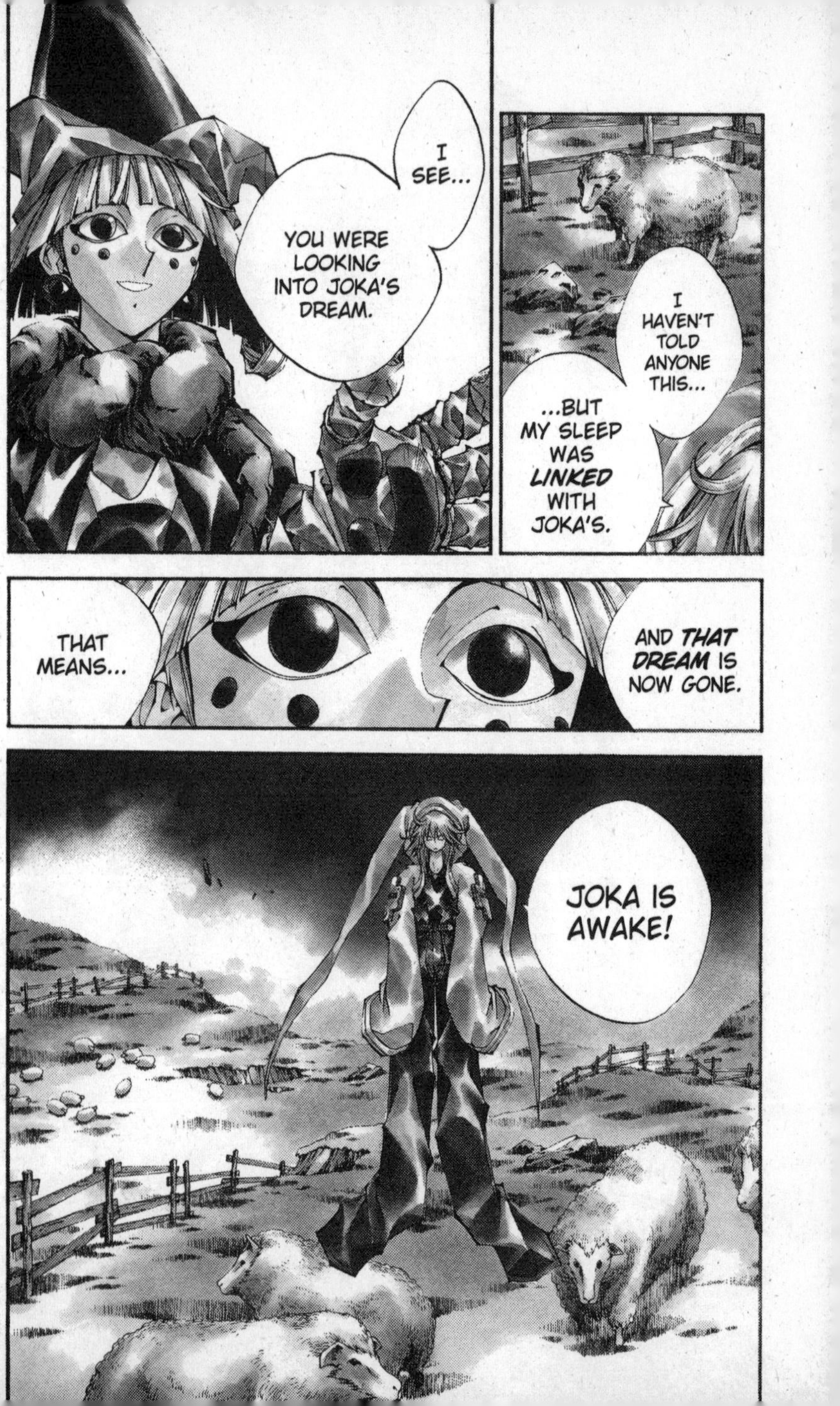
I HAVEN'T TOLD ANYONE THIS...
...BUT MY SLEEP WAS *LINKED* WITH JOKA'S.
I SEE...
YOU WERE LOOKING INTO JOKA'S DREAM.
AND *THAT DREAM* IS NOW GONE.
THAT MEANS...
JOKA IS AWAKE!

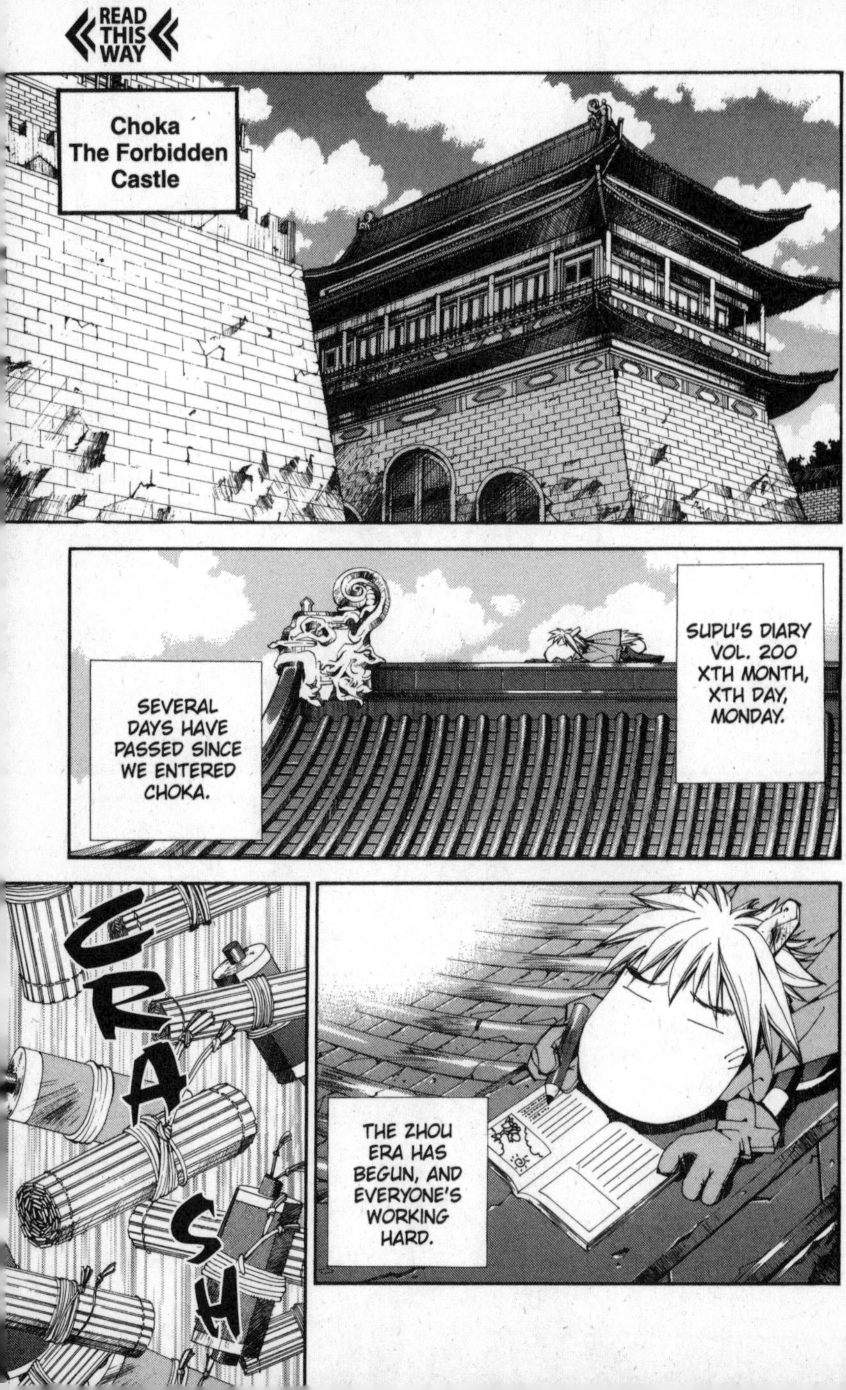
READ THIS WAY
Choka The Forbidden Castle
SUPU'S DIARY VOL. 200 XTH MONTH, XTH DAY, MONDAY.
SEVERAL DAYS HAVE PASSED SINCE WE ENTERED CHOKA.
THE ZHOU ERA HAS BEGUN, AND EVERYONE'S WORKING HARD.
CRASH

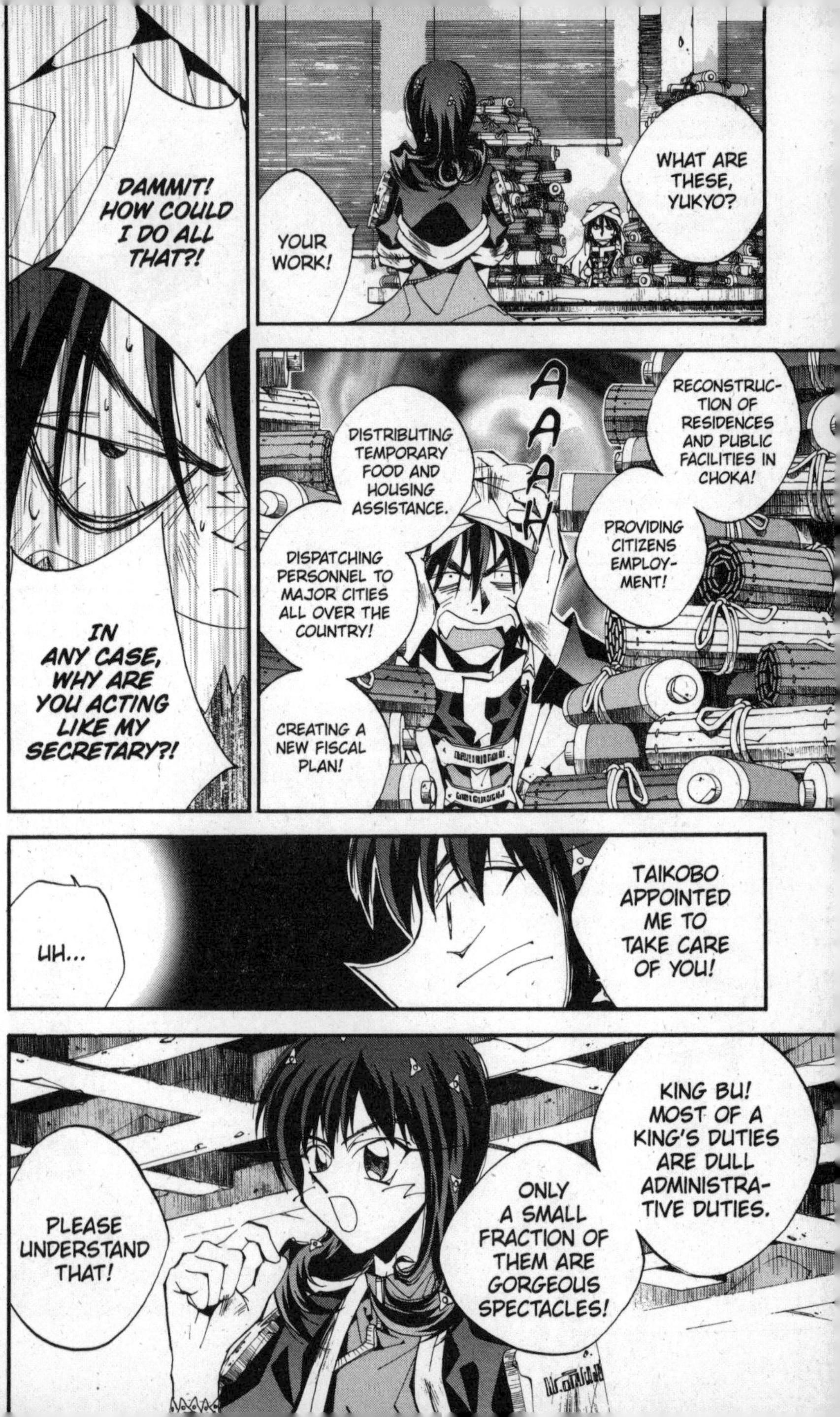
WHAT ARE THESE, YUKYO?
YOUR WORK!
RECONSTRUCTION OF RESIDENCES AND PUBLIC FACILITIES IN CHOKA!
PROVIDING CITIZENS EMPLOYMENT!
AAAH
DISTRIBUTING TEMPORARY FOOD AND HOUSING ASSISTANCE.
DISPATCHING PERSONNEL TO MAJOR CITIES ALL OVER THE COUNTRY!
CREATING A NEW FISCAL PLAN!
DAMMIT! HOW COULD I DO ALL THAT?!
IN ANY CASE, WHY ARE YOU ACTING LIKE MY SECRETARY?!
TAIKOBO APPOINTED ME TO TAKE CARE OF YOU!
UH...
KING BU! MOST OF A KING'S DUTIES ARE DULL ADMINISTRATIVE DUTIES.
ONLY A SMALL FRACTION OF THEM ARE GORGEOUS SPECTACLES!
PLEASE UNDERSTAND THAT!

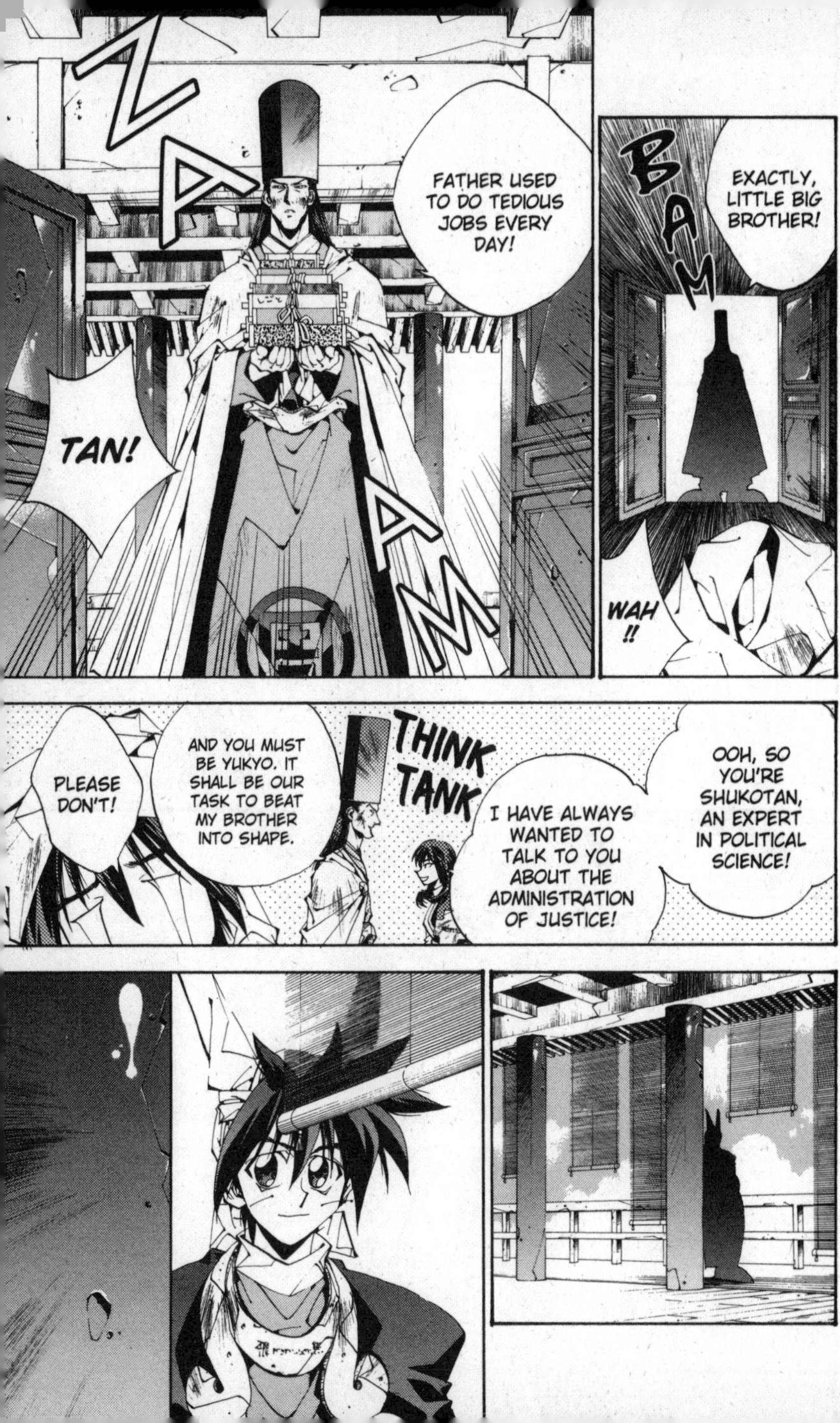
BAM
EXACTLY, LITTLE BIG BROTHER!
WAH!!
ZAAM
FATHER USED TO DO TEDIOUS JOBS EVERY DAY!
TAN!
OOH, SO YOU'RE SHUKOTAN, AN EXPERT IN POLITICAL SCIENCE!
I HAVE ALWAYS WANTED TO TALK TO YOU ABOUT THE ADMINISTRATION OF JUSTICE!
THINK TANK
AND YOU MUST BE YUKYO. IT SHALL BE OUR TASK TO BEAT MY BROTHER INTO SHAPE.
PLEASE DON'T!
!

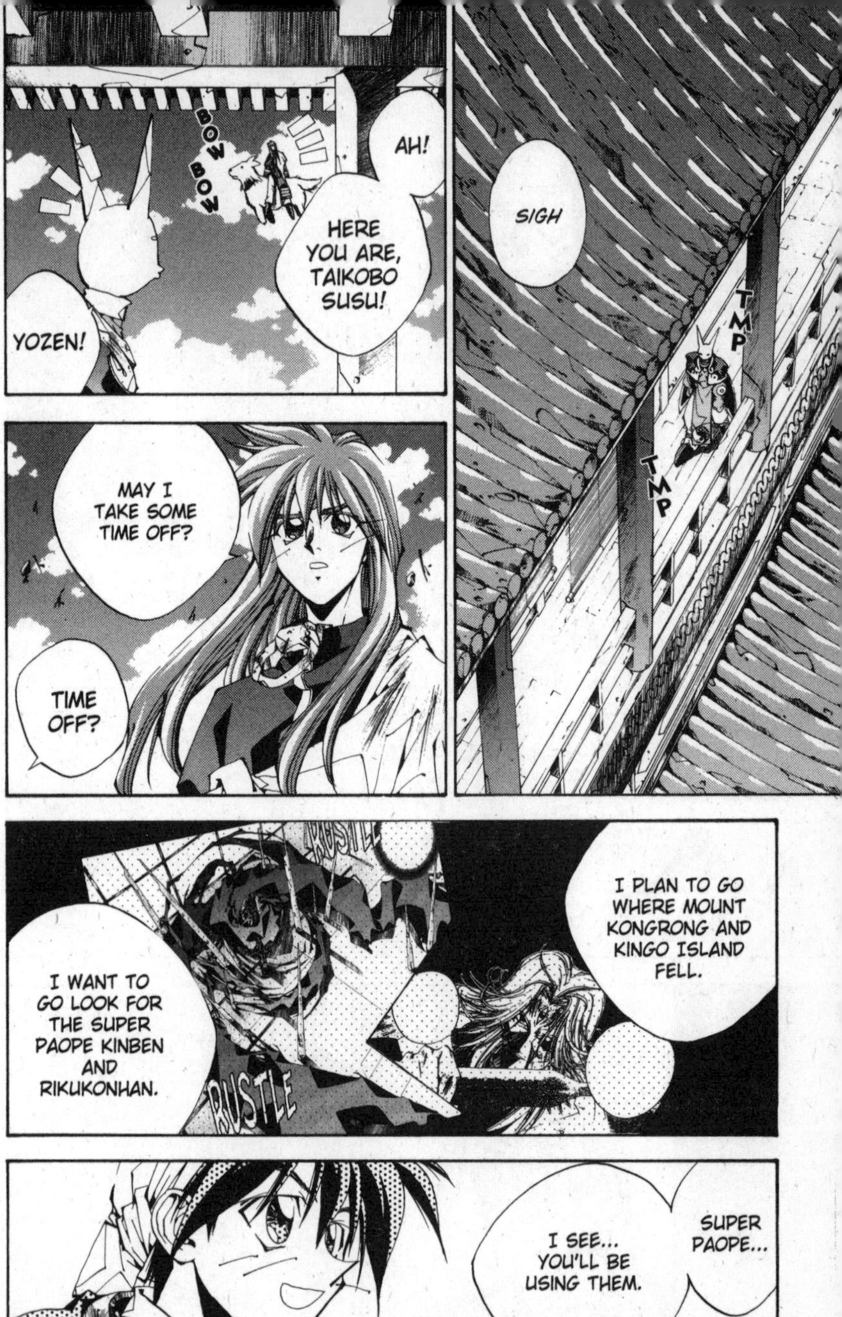
SIGH
TMP
TMP
AH!
HERE YOU ARE, TAIKOBO SUSU!
BOW BOW
YOZEN!
MAY I TAKE SOME TIME OFF?
TIME OFF?
I PLAN TO GO WHERE MOUNT KONGRONG AND KINGO ISLAND FELL.
I WANT TO GO LOOK FOR THE SUPER PAOPE KINBEN AND RIKUKONHAN.
RUSTLE
RUSTLE
SUPER PAOPE...
I SEE... YOU'LL BE USING THEM.

READ THIS WAY

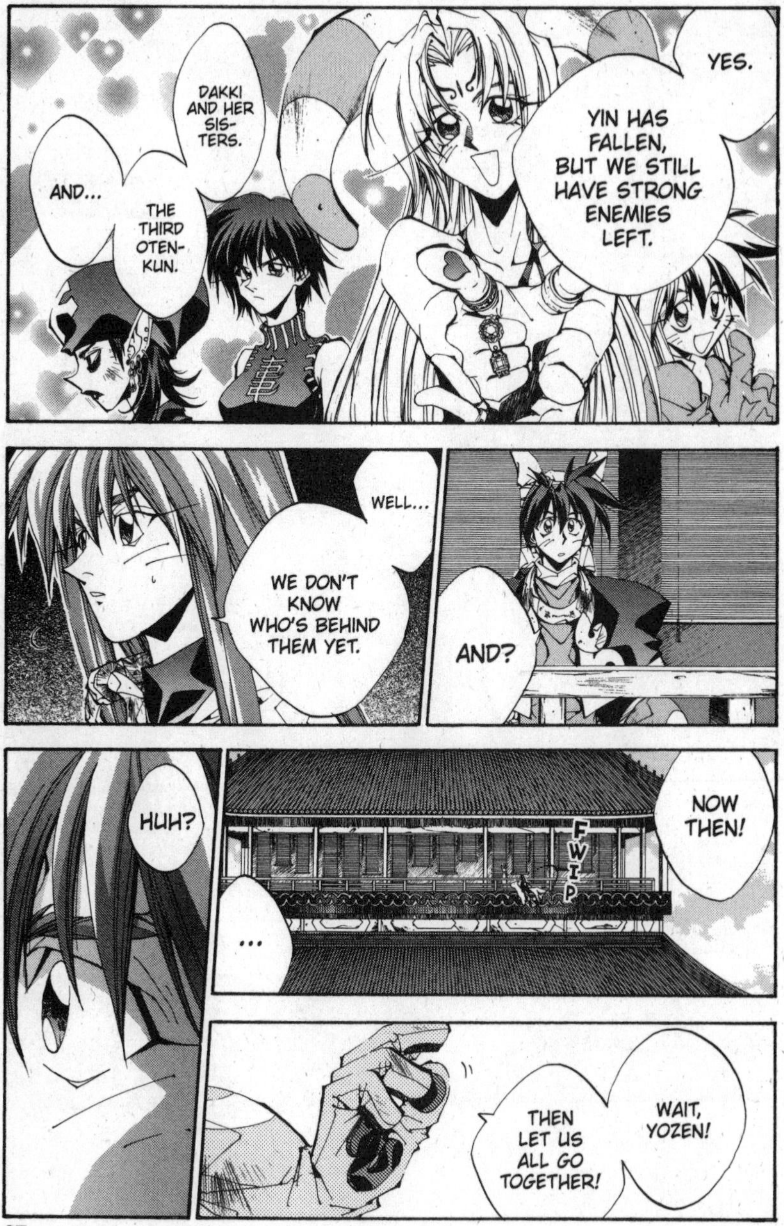

YES.
YIN HAS FALLEN, BUT WE STILL HAVE STRONG ENEMIES LEFT.
DAKKI AND HER SIS-TERS.
AND...
THE THIRD OTEN-KUN.
AND?
WELL...
WE DON'T KNOW WHO'S BEHIND THEM YET.
NOW THEN!
FWIP
...
HUH?
WAIT, YOZEN!
THEN LET US ALL GO TOGETHER!

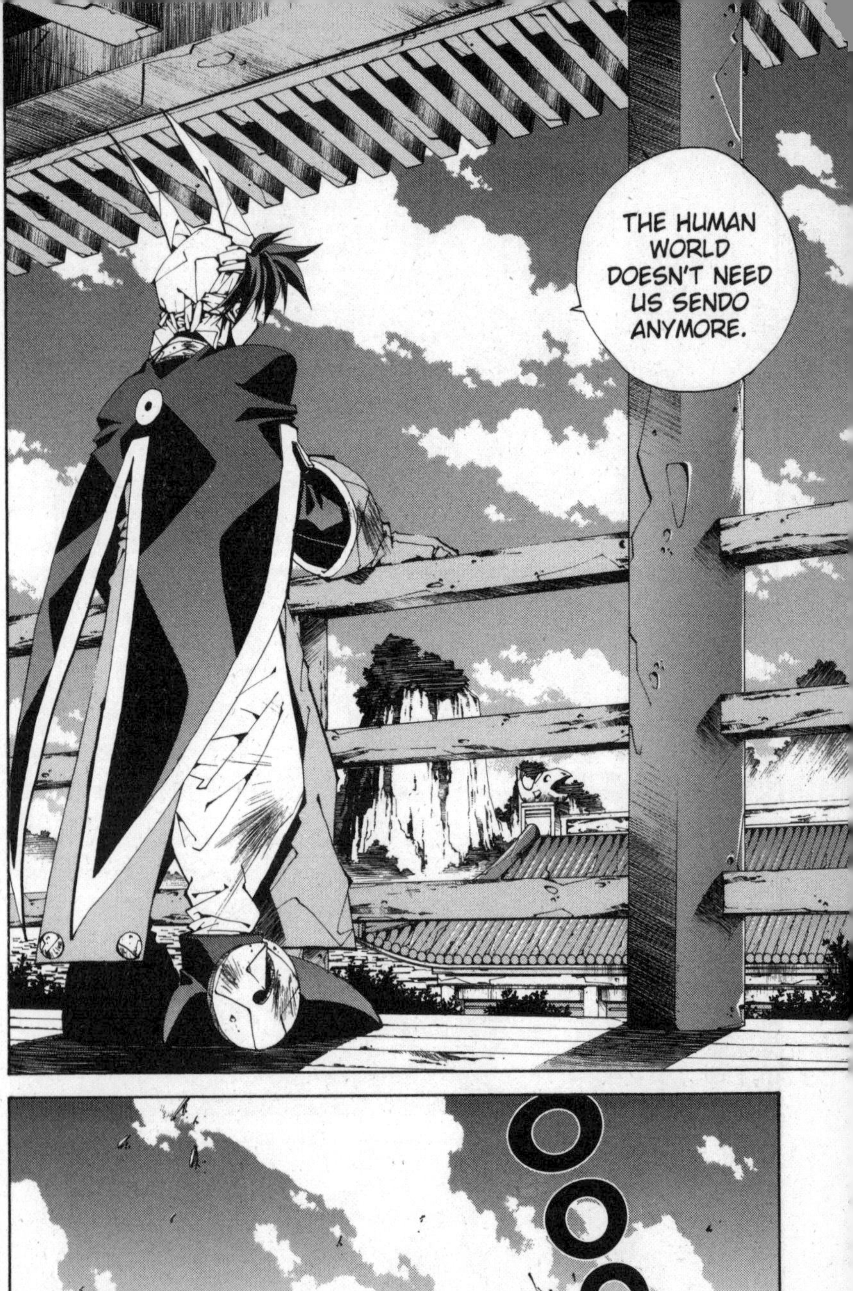
THE HUMAN WORLD DOESN'T NEED US SENDO ANYMORE.

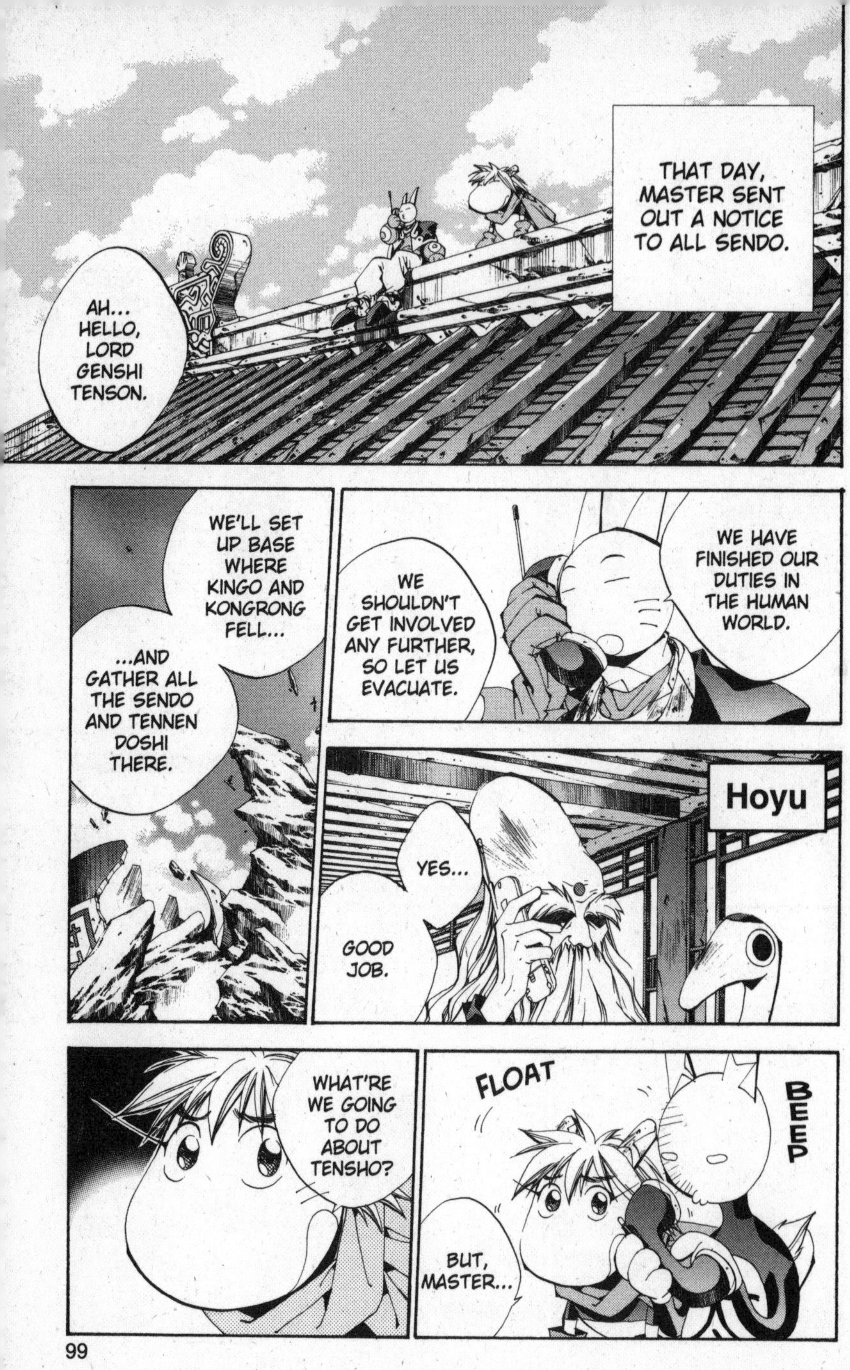
THAT DAY, MASTER SENT OUT A NOTICE TO ALL SENDO.
AH... HELLO, LORD GENSHI TENSON.
WE HAVE FINISHED OUR DUTIES IN THE HUMAN WORLD.
WE SHOULDN'T GET INVOLVED ANY FURTHER, SO LET US EVACUATE.
Hoyu
YES...
GOOD JOB.
WE'LL SET UP BASE WHERE KINGO AND KONGRONG FELL...
...AND GATHER ALL THE SENDO AND TENNEN DOSHI THERE.
FLOAT
BEEP
BUT, MASTER...
WHAT'RE WE GOING TO DO ABOUT TENSHO?

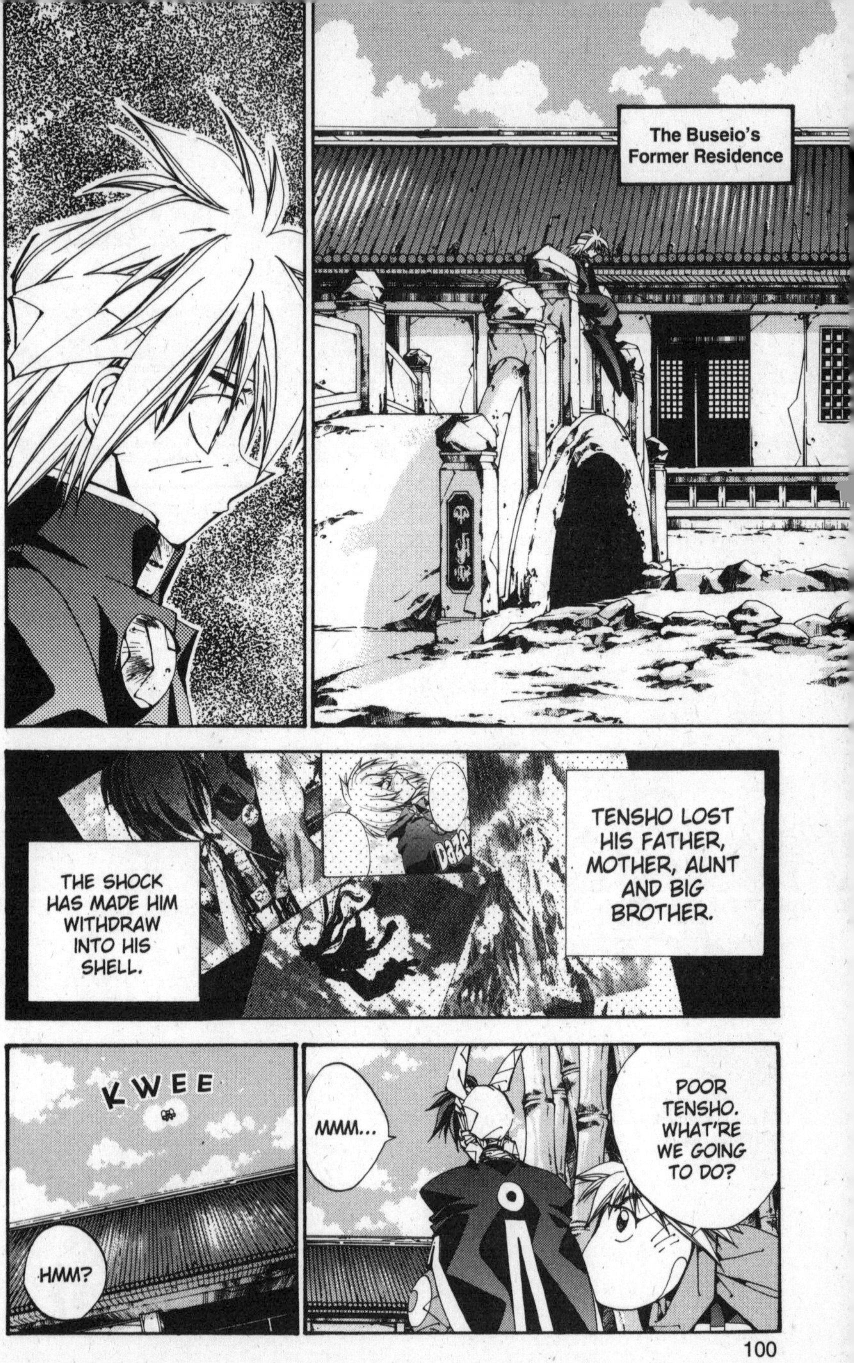
The Buseio's Former Residence
TENSHO LOST HIS FATHER, MOTHER, AUNT AND BIG BROTHER.
Daze
THE SHOCK HAS MADE HIM WITHDRAW INTO HIS SHELL.
POOR TENSHO. WHAT'RE WE GOING TO DO?
MMM...
KWEE
HMM?

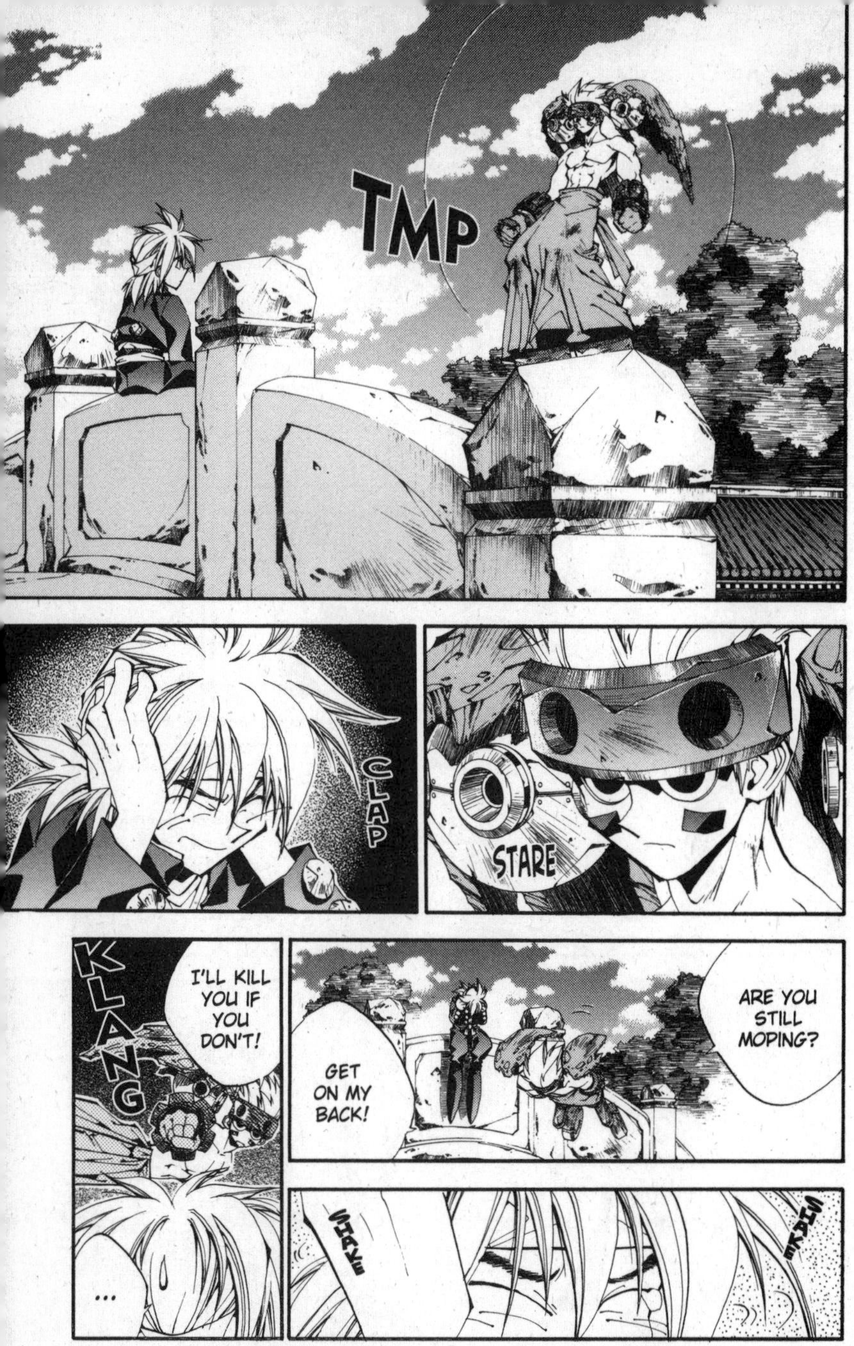
TMP
STARE
CLAP
ARE YOU STILL MOPING?
GET ON MY BACK!
SHAKE
SHAKE
KLANG
I'LL KILL YOU IF YOU DON'T!
...

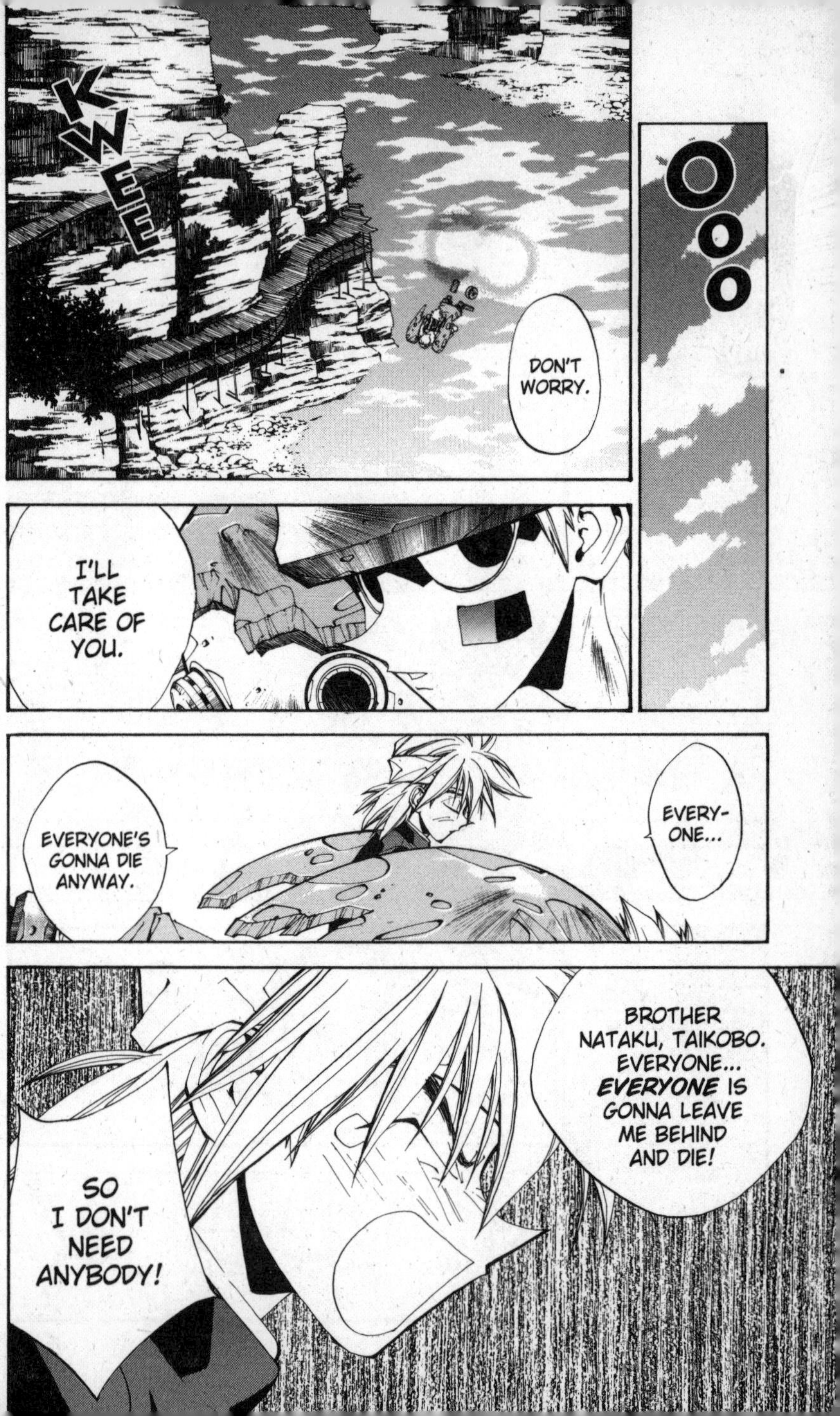
OOO
KWEEE
DON'T WORRY.
I'LL TAKE CARE OF YOU.
EVERY-ONE...
EVERYONE'S GONNA DIE ANYWAY.
BROTHER NATAKU, TAIKOBO. EVERYONE... EVERYONE IS GONNA LEAVE ME BEHIND AND DIE!
SO I DON'T NEED ANYBODY!

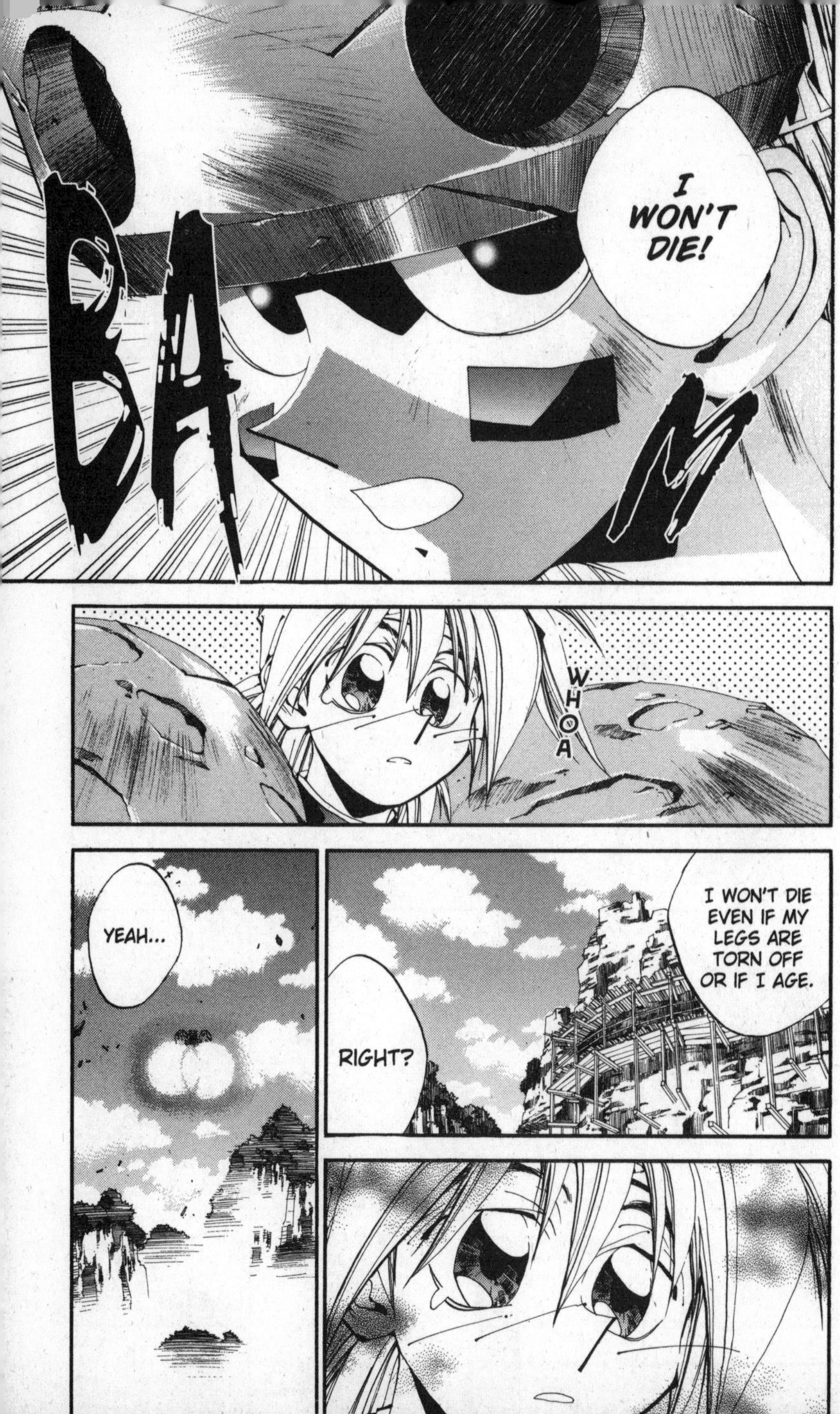
I WON'T DIE!
BAM
WHOA
I WON'T DIE EVEN IF MY LEGS ARE TORN OFF OR IF I AGE.
RIGHT?
YEAH...

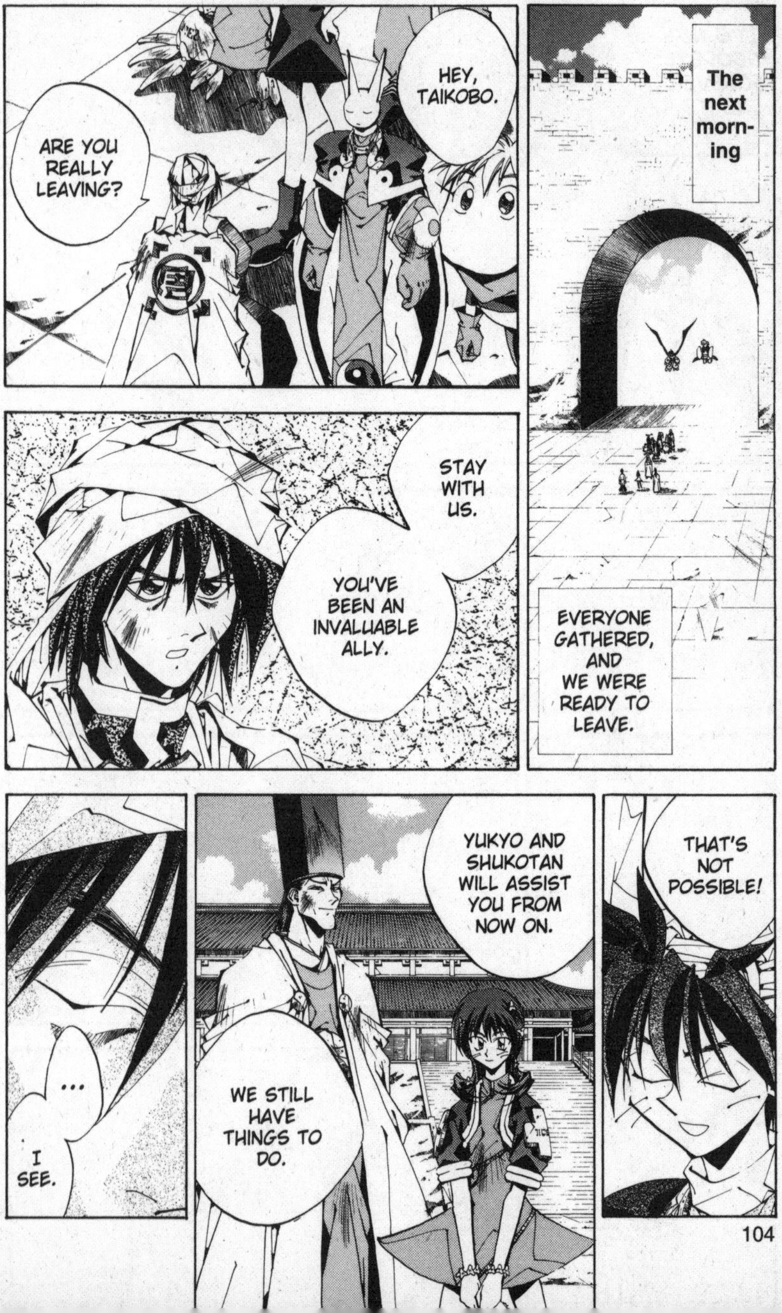
The next morning
EVERYONE GATHERED, AND WE WERE READY TO LEAVE.
HEY, TAIKOBO.
ARE YOU REALLY LEAVING?
STAY WITH US.
YOU'VE BEEN AN INVALUABLE ALLY.
THAT'S NOT POSSIBLE!
YUKYO AND SHUKOTAN WILL ASSIST YOU FROM NOW ON.
WE STILL HAVE THINGS TO DO.
...
I SEE.

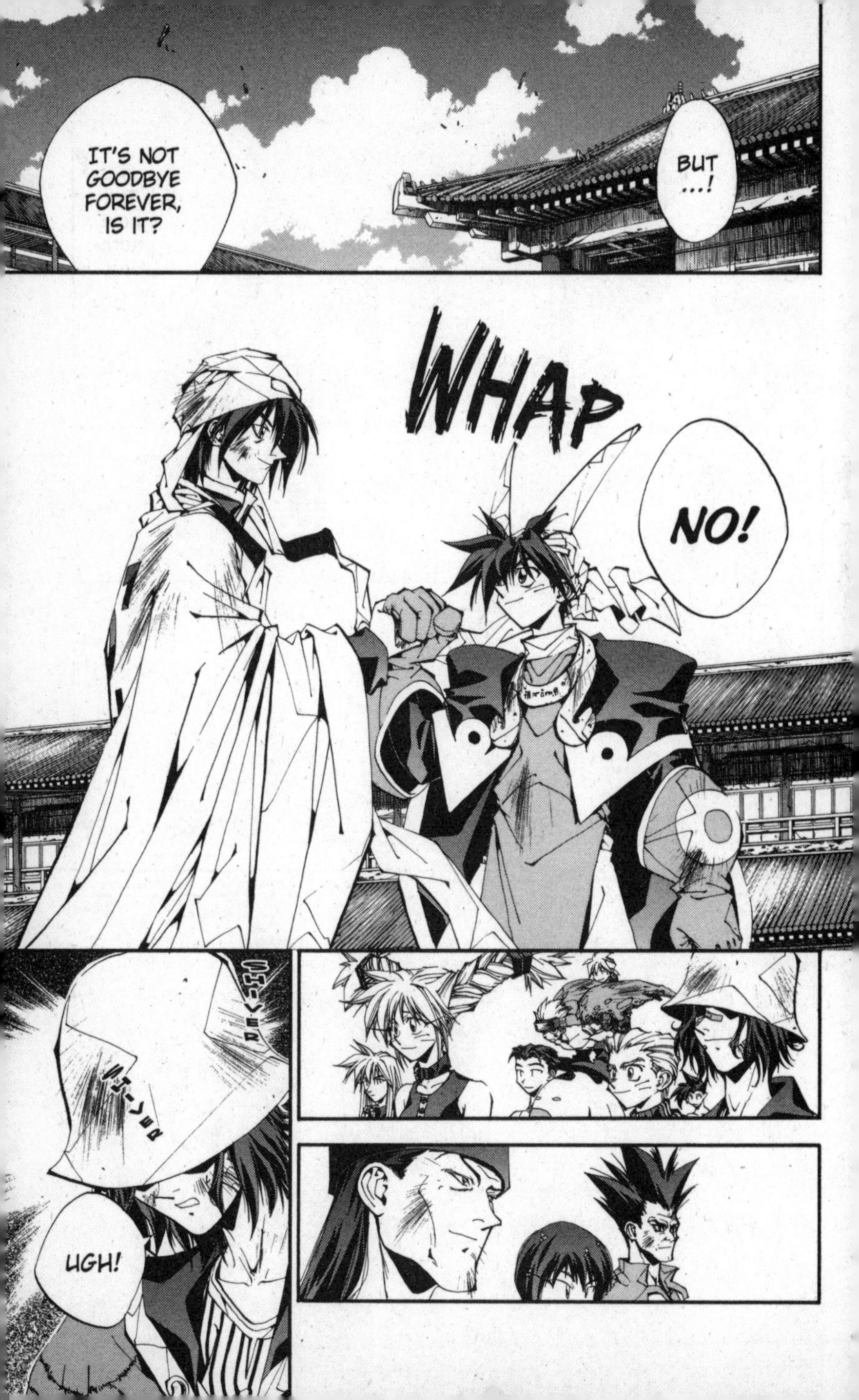
BUT ...!
IT'S NOT GOODBYE FOREVER, IS IT?
WHAP
NO!
SHIVER
UGH!

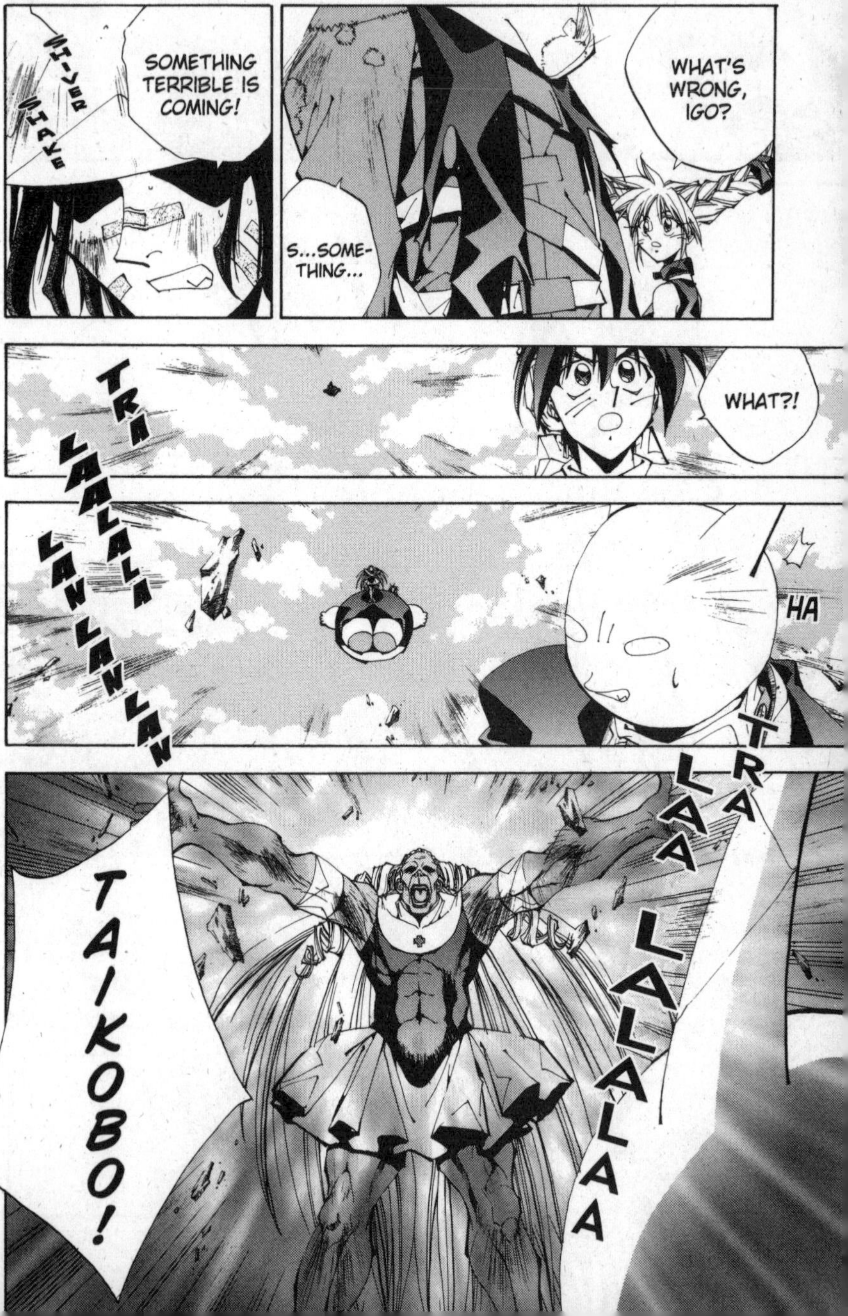
WHAT'S WRONG, IGO?
S...SOME-THING...
SOMETHING TERRIBLE IS COMING!
SHIVER SHAKE
WHAT?!
TRA LALALA LAAA
LAN LAN LAN LAN
HA
TRA LAA LALALALAA
TAIKOBO!

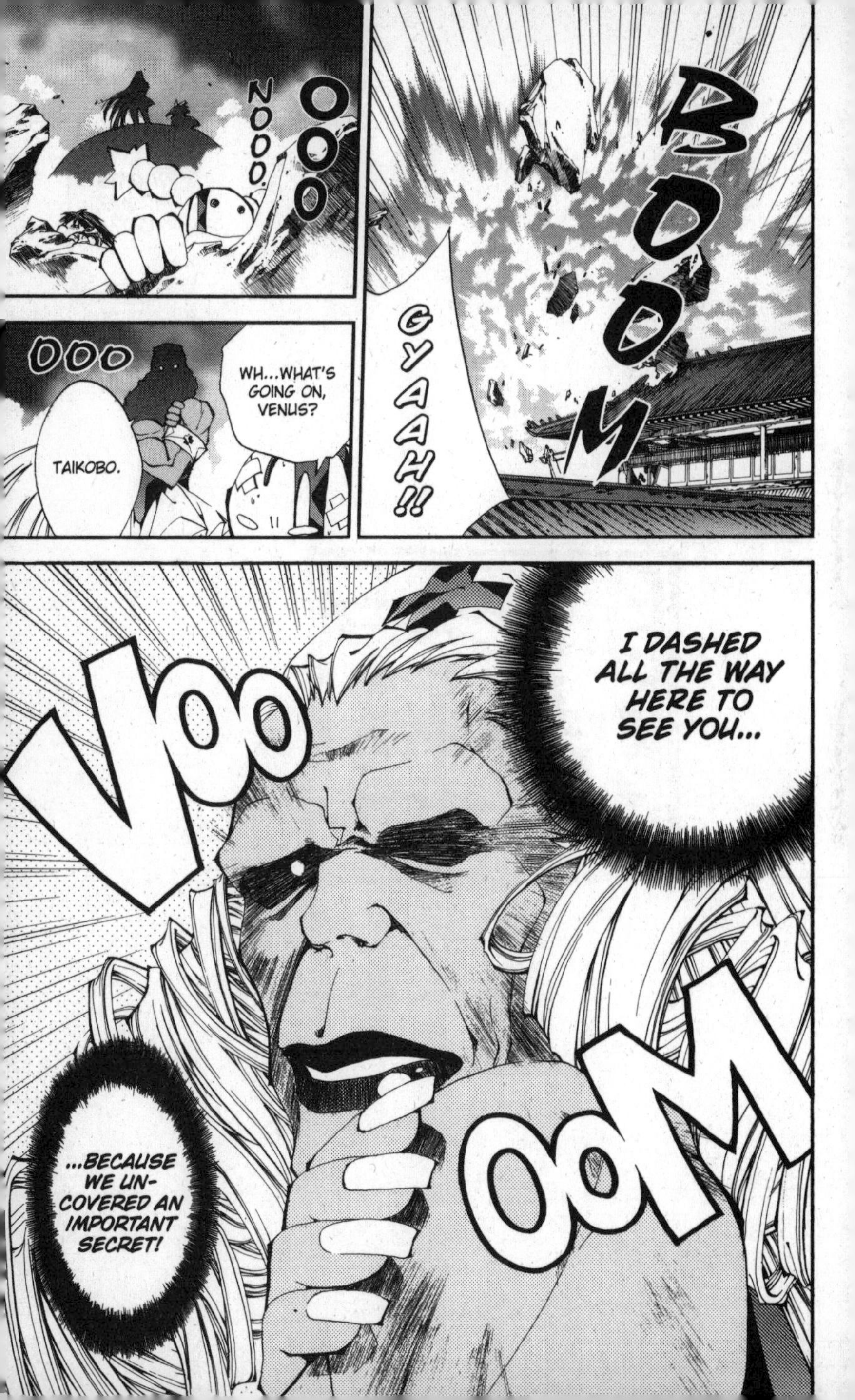
BOOOM
GYAAAH!!
OOOO
NOOOO.
WH...WHAT'S GOING ON, VENUS?
OOO
TAIKOBO.
I DASHED ALL THE WAY HERE TO SEE YOU...
VOOOOM
...BECAUSE WE UN-COVERED AN IMPORTANT SECRET!

封神演義

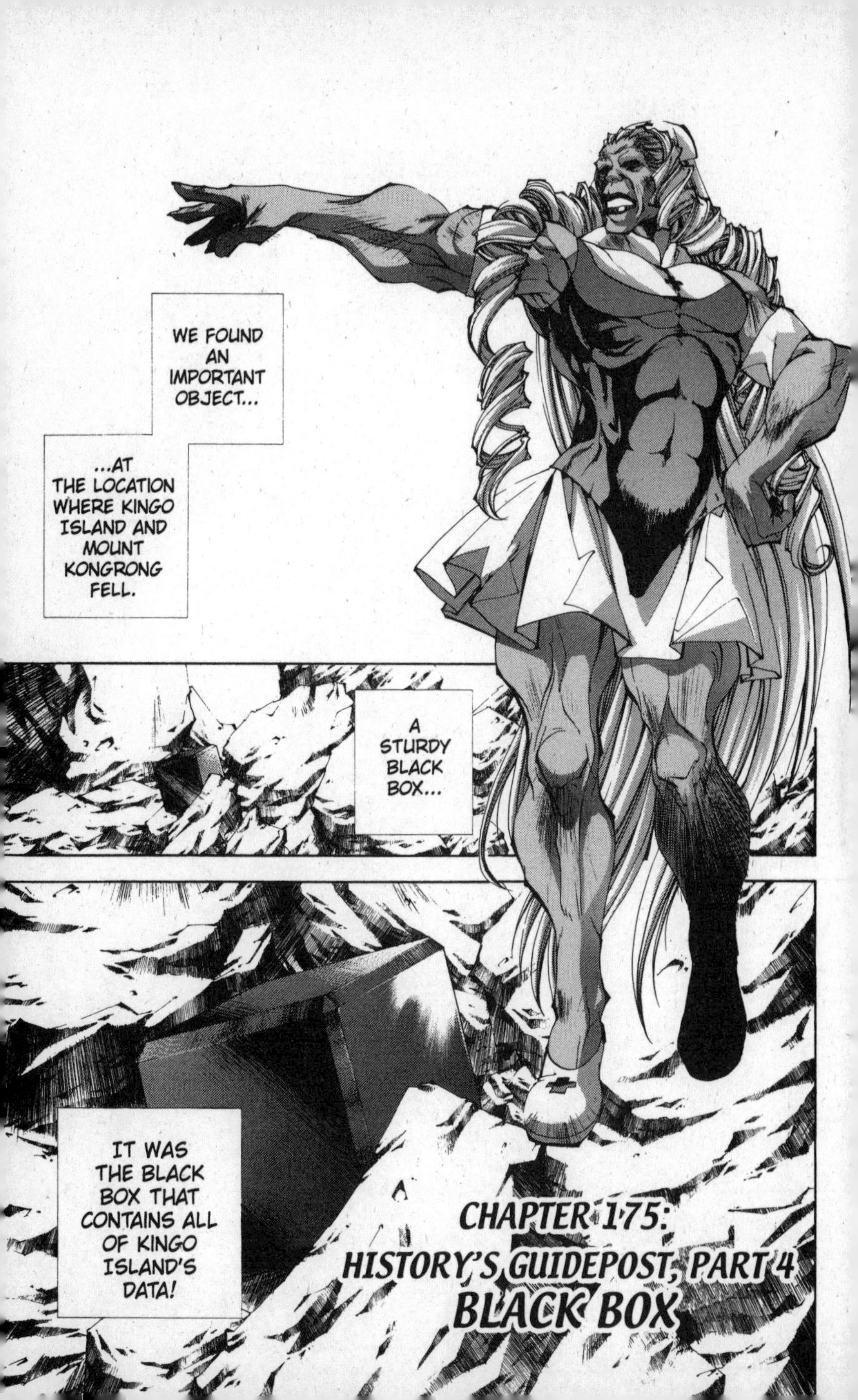
WE FOUND AN IMPORTANT OBJECT...
...AT THE LOCATION WHERE KINGO ISLAND AND MOUNT KONGRONG FELL.
A STURDY BLACK BOX...
IT WAS THE BLACK BOX THAT CONTAINS ALL OF KINGO ISLAND'S DATA!
CHAPTER 175:
HISTORY'S GUIDEPOST, PART 4
BLACK BOX

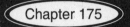
HISTORY'S GUIDEPOST, PART 4
BLACK BOX

BLACK BOX

USUALLY A PIECE OF EQUIPMENT ON AN AIRPLANE
THAT RECORDS FLIGHT DATA.
IN THE EVENT OF AN AIRPLANE CRASH, THE BLACK BOX IS
USED TO INVESTIGATE THE CAUSE OF THE ACCIDENT.

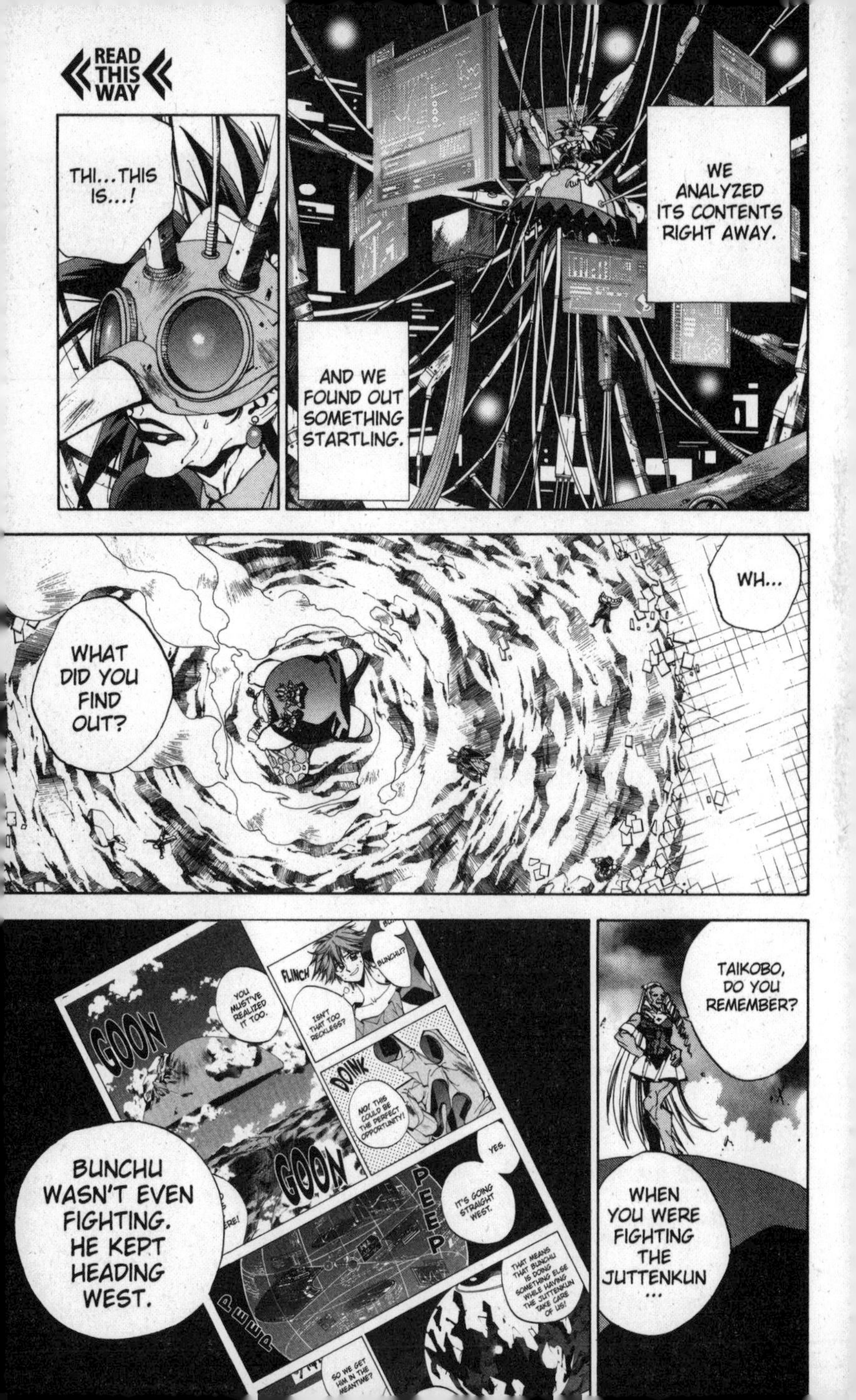
READ THIS WAY
WE ANALYZED ITS CONTENTS RIGHT AWAY.
AND WE FOUND OUT SOMETHING STARTLING.
THI...THIS IS...!
WH...
WHAT DID YOU FIND OUT?
TAIKOBO, DO YOU REMEMBER?
WHEN YOU WERE FIGHTING THE JUTTENKUN...
BUNCHU?
FLINCH
ISN'T THAT TOO RECKLESS?
YOU MUST'VE REALIZED IT TOO.
GOON
DOINK
NO! THIS COULD BE THE PERFECT OPPORTUNITY!
GOON
YES.
IT'S GOING STRAIGHT WEST.
PEEP
PEEP
THAT MEANS THAT BUNCHU IS DOING SOMETHING ELSE WHILE HAVING THE JUTTENKUN TAKE CARE OF US!
SO WE GET HIM IN THE MEANTIME?
BUNCHU WASN'T EVEN FIGHTING. HE KEPT HEADING WEST.

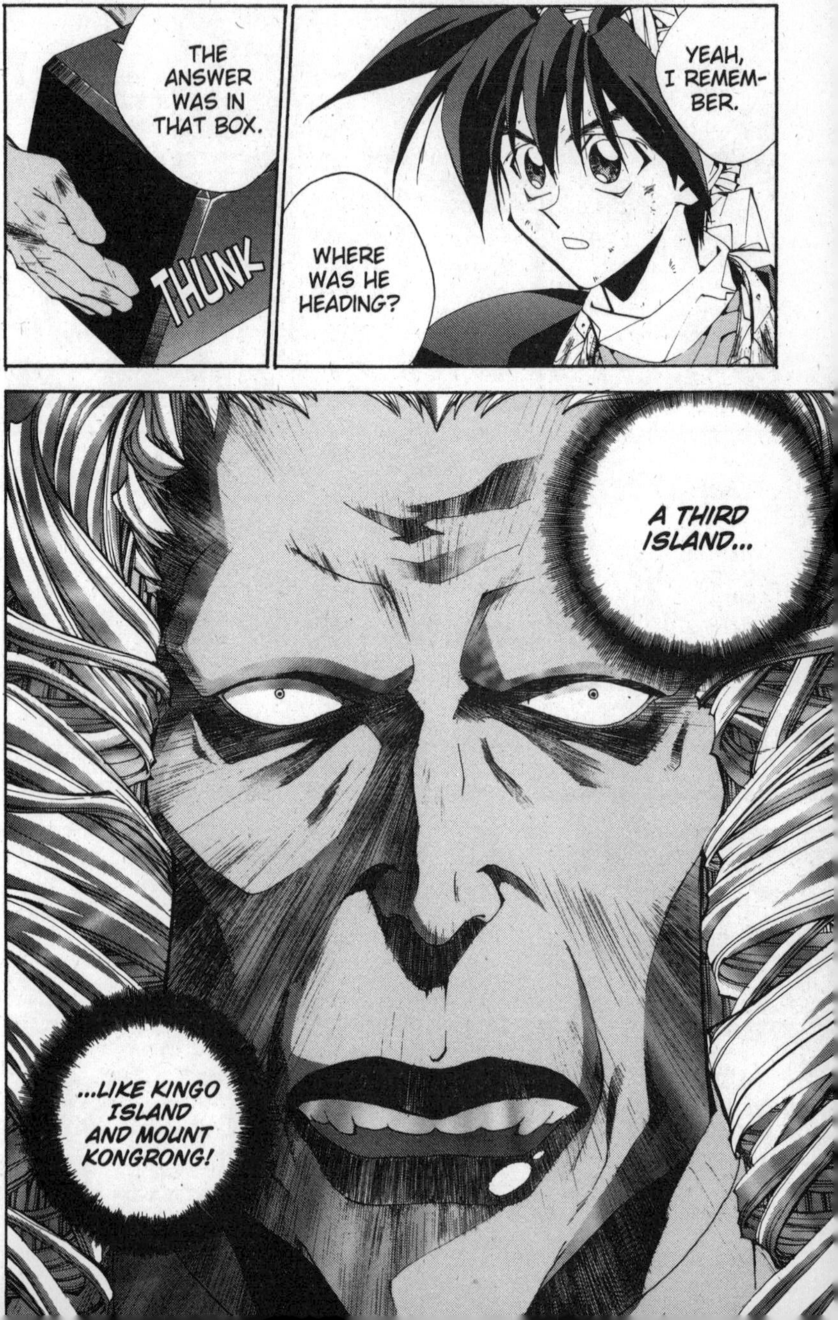
YEAH, I REMEM-BER.
WHERE WAS HE HEADING?
THE ANSWER WAS IN THAT BOX.
THUNK
A THIRD ISLAND...
...LIKE KINGO ISLAND AND MOUNT KONGRONG!

READ THIS WAY

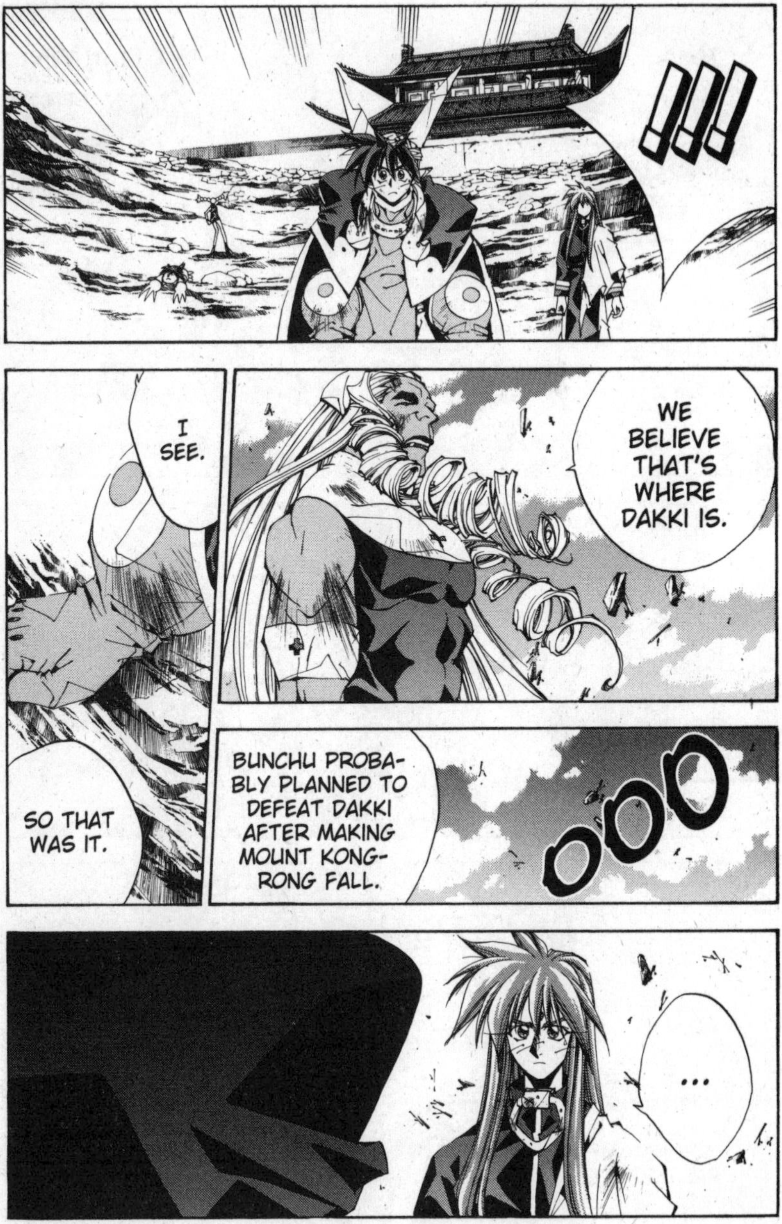
!!!
WE BELIEVE THAT'S WHERE DAKKI IS.
I SEE.
BUNCHU PROBA-BLY PLANNED TO DEFEAT DAKKI AFTER MAKING MOUNT KONG-RONG FALL.
SO THAT WAS IT.
...

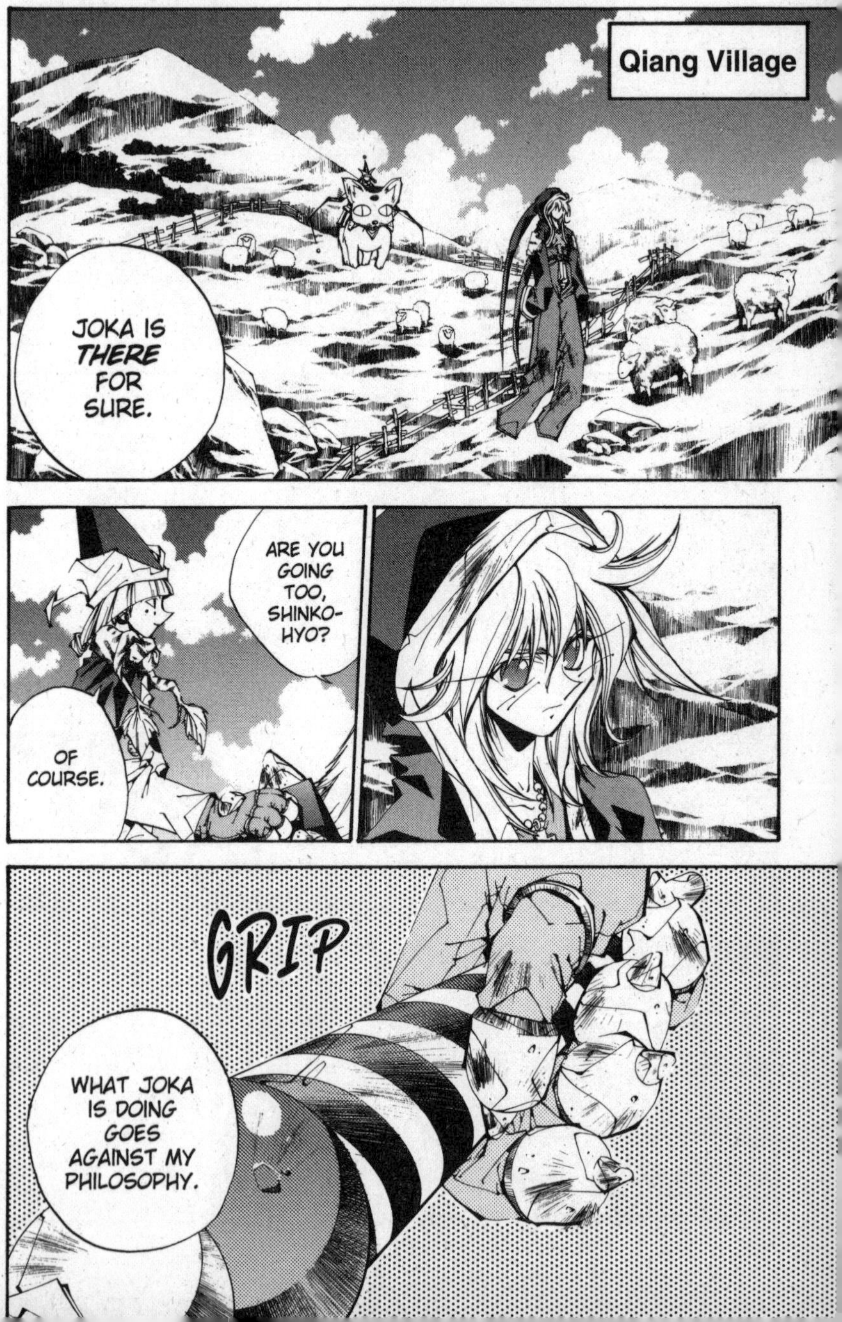
Qiang Village
JOKA IS *THERE* FOR SURE.
ARE YOU GOING TOO, SHINKO-HYO?
OF COURSE.
GRIP
WHAT JOKA IS DOING GOES AGAINST MY PHILOSOPHY.

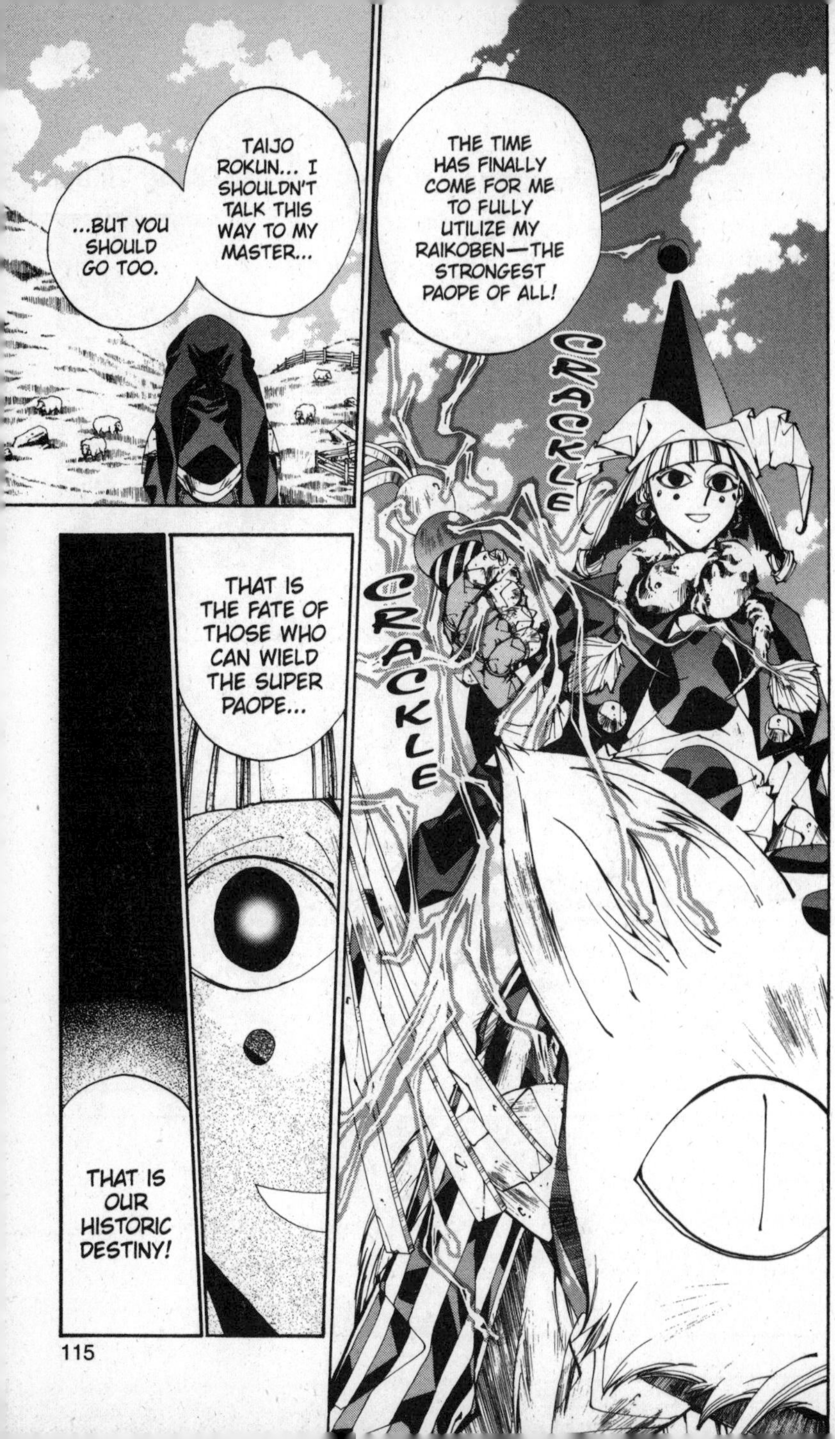
THE TIME HAS FINALLY COME FOR ME TO FULLY UTILIZE MY RAIKOBEN—THE STRONGEST PAOPE OF ALL!
CRACKLE
CRACKLE
TAIJO ROKUN... I SHOULDN'T TALK THIS WAY TO MY MASTER...
...BUT YOU SHOULD GO TOO.
THAT IS THE FATE OF THOSE WHO CAN WIELD THE SUPER PAOPE...
THAT IS OUR HISTORIC DESTINY!

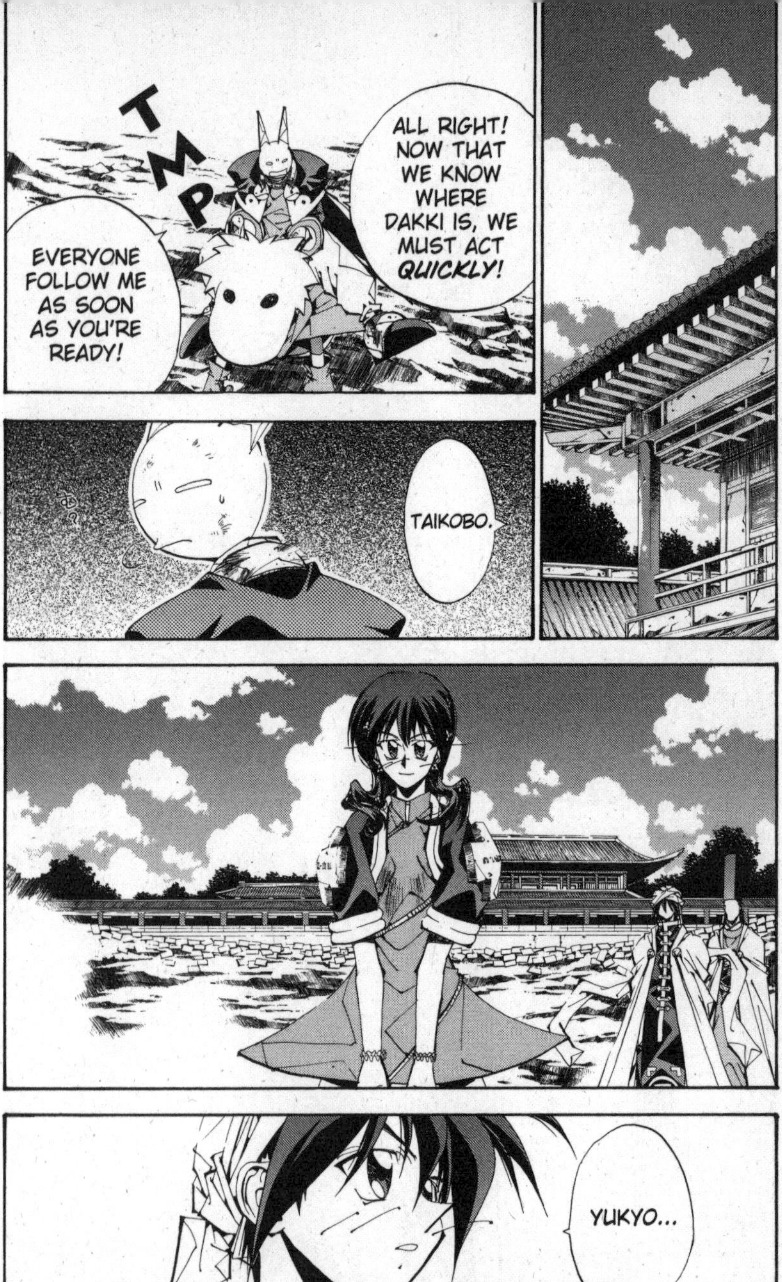
TMP
ALL RIGHT! NOW THAT WE KNOW WHERE DAKKI IS, WE MUST ACT QUICKLY!
EVERYONE FOLLOW ME AS SOON AS YOU'RE READY!
TAIKOBO.
YUKYO...

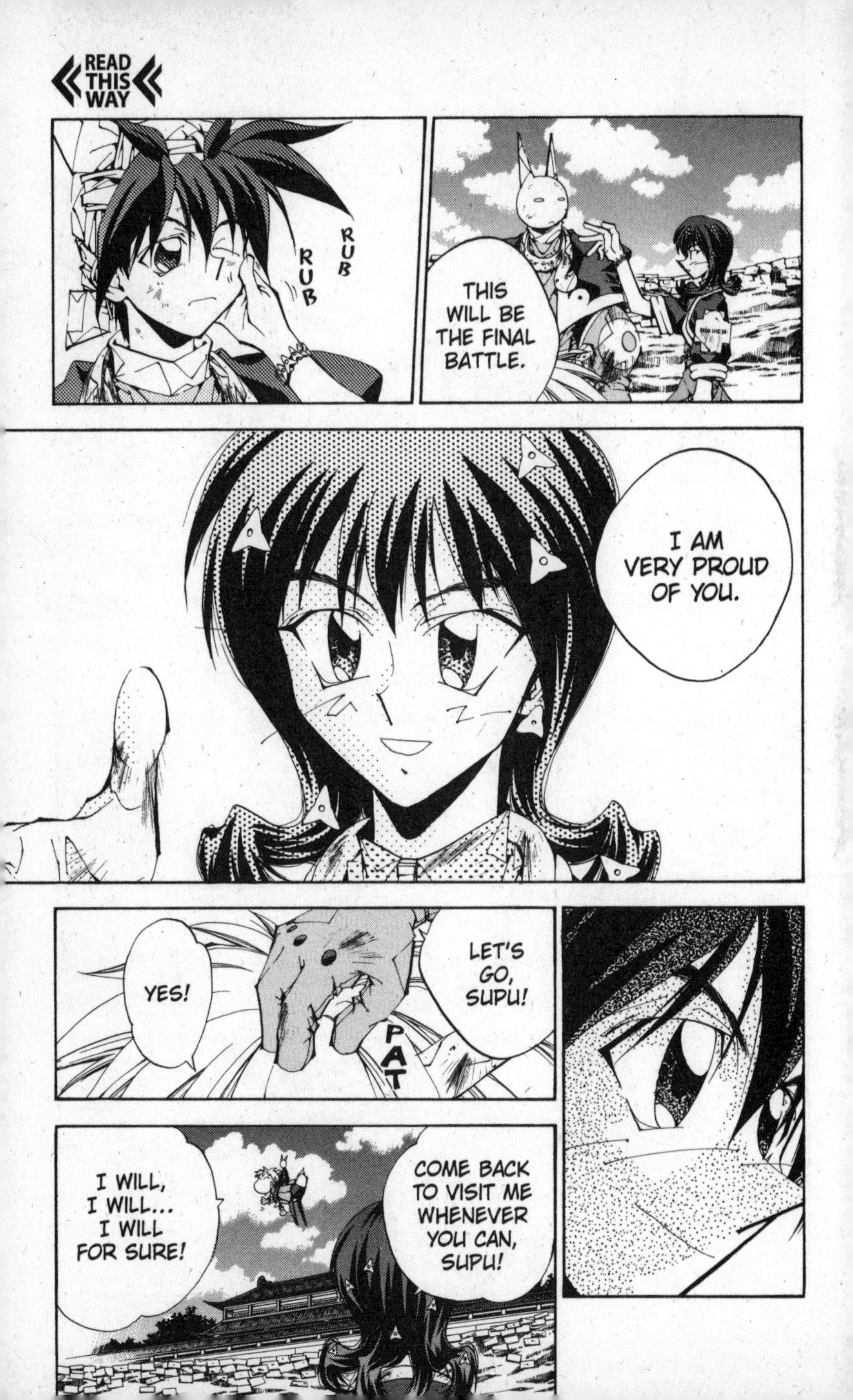
READ THIS WAY
THIS WILL BE THE FINAL BATTLE.
RUB RUB
I AM VERY PROUD OF YOU.
LET'S GO, SUPU!
PAT
YES!
COME BACK TO VISIT ME WHENEVER YOU CAN, SUPU!
I WILL, I WILL... I WILL FOR SURE!

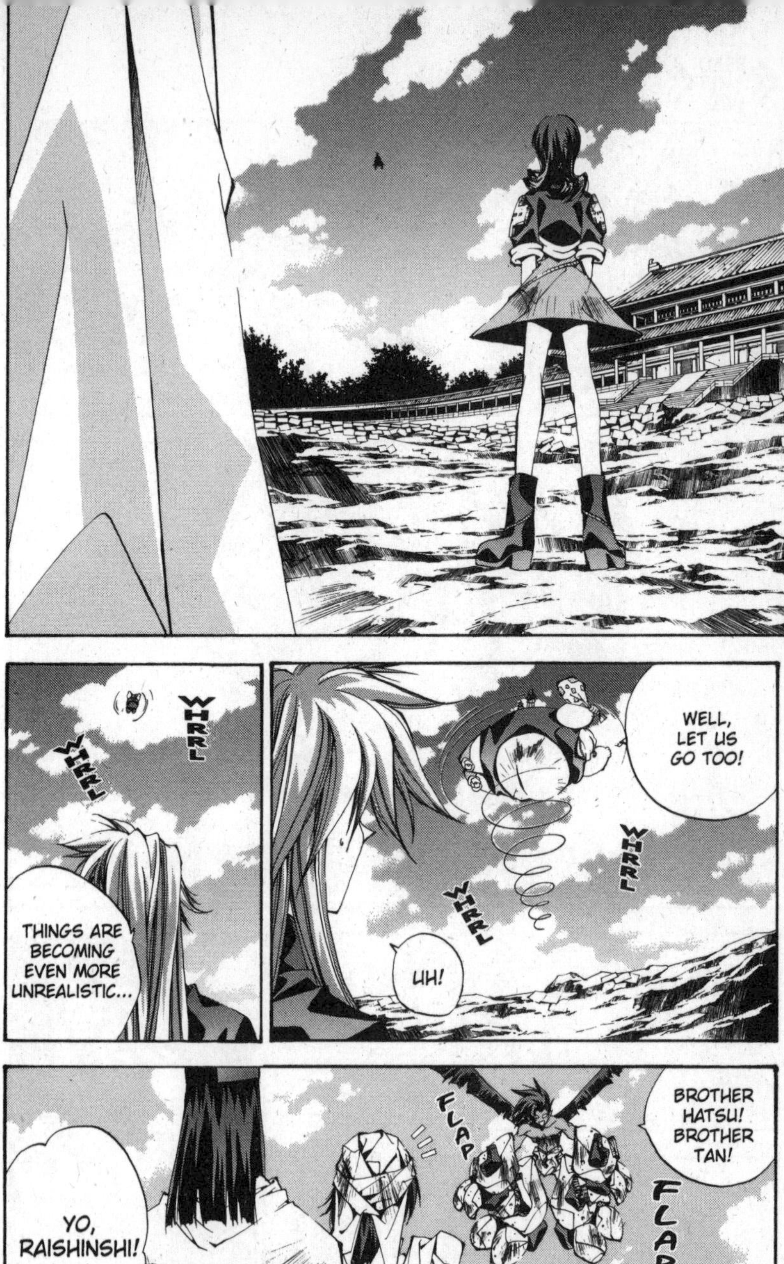

WELL, LET US GO TOO!
WHRRL
WHRRL
UH!
WHRRL
WHRRL
THINGS ARE BECOMING EVEN MORE UNREALISTIC...
BROTHER HATSU! BROTHER TAN!
FLAP
FLAP
YO, RAISHINSHI!

READ THIS WAY

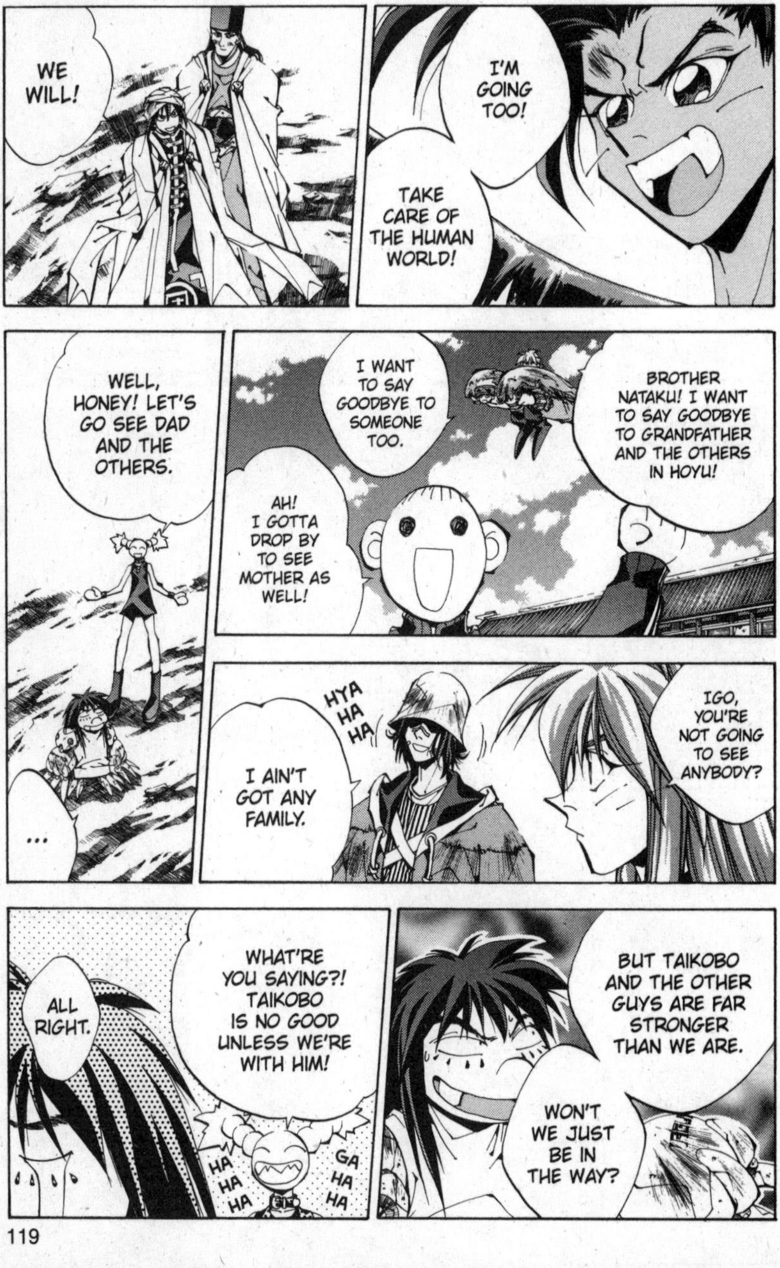
I'M GOING TOO!
TAKE CARE OF THE HUMAN WORLD!
WE WILL!
BROTHER NATAKU! I WANT TO SAY GOODBYE TO GRANDFATHER AND THE OTHERS IN HOYU!
I WANT TO SAY GOODBYE TO SOMEONE TOO.
AH! I GOTTA DROP BY TO SEE MOTHER AS WELL!
IGO, YOU'RE NOT GOING TO SEE ANYBODY?
HYA HA HA HA
I AIN'T GOT ANY FAMILY.
WELL, HONEY! LET'S GO SEE DAD AND THE OTHERS.
...
BUT TAIKOBO AND THE OTHER GUYS ARE FAR STRONGER THAN WE ARE.
WON'T WE JUST BE IN THE WAY?
WHAT'RE YOU SAYING?! TAIKOBO IS NO GOOD UNLESS WE'RE WITH HIM!
GA HA HA
HA HA HA
ALL RIGHT.

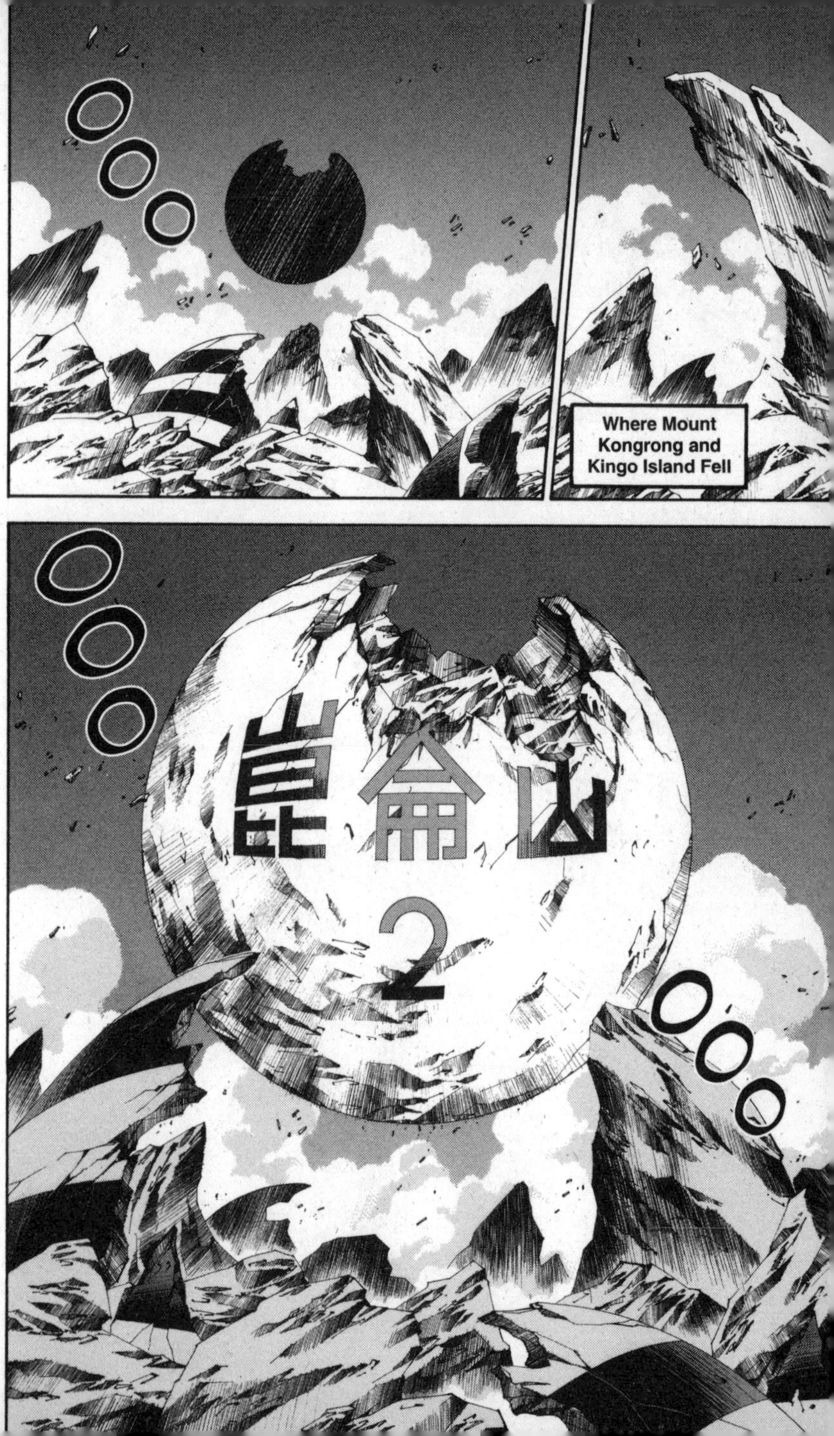
Where Mount Kongrong and Kingo Island Fell
OOO
OOO
崑崙山 2
OOO

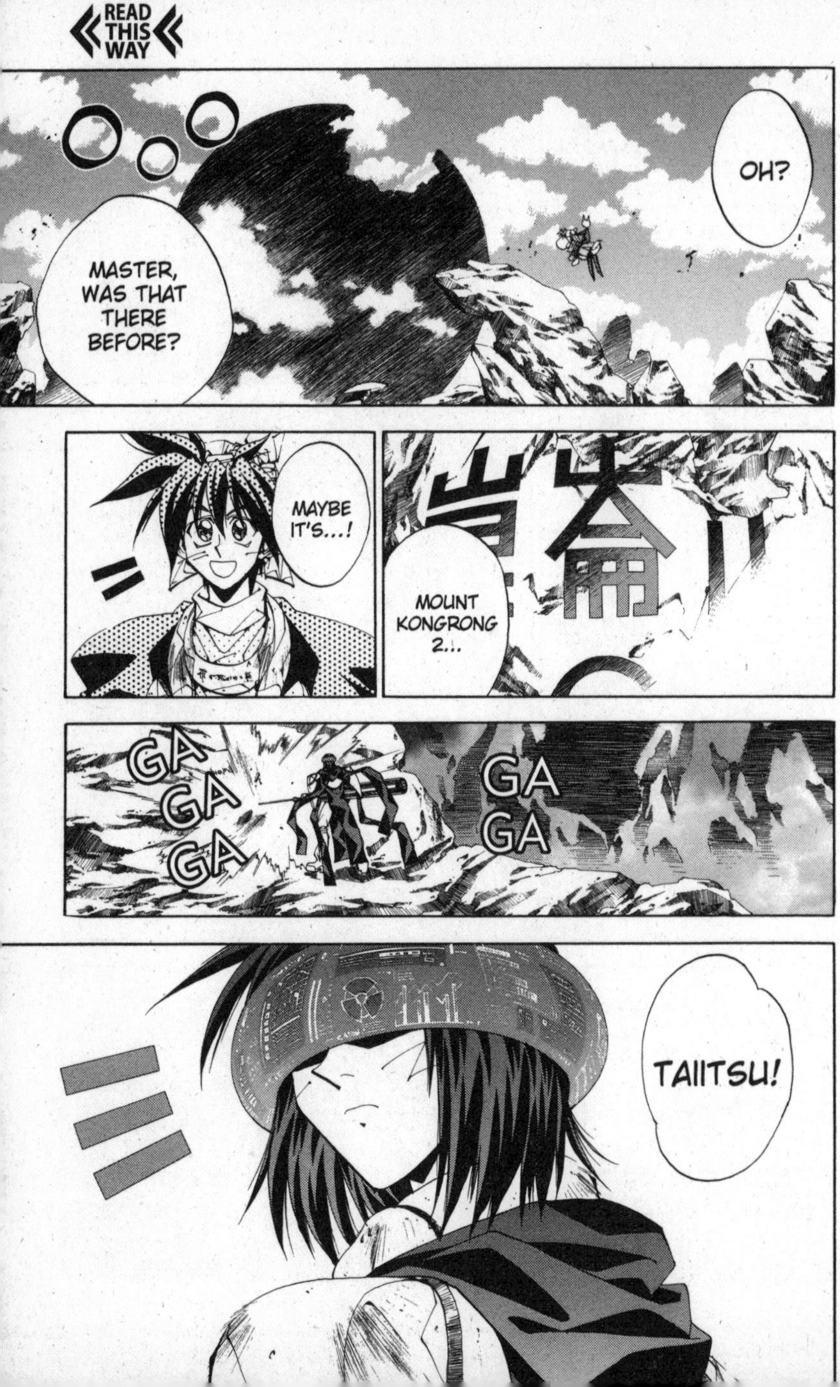
READ THIS WAY
OH?
MASTER, WAS THAT THERE BEFORE?
MOUNT KONGRONG 2...
MAYBE IT'S...!
GA GA
GA GA GA
TAIITSU!

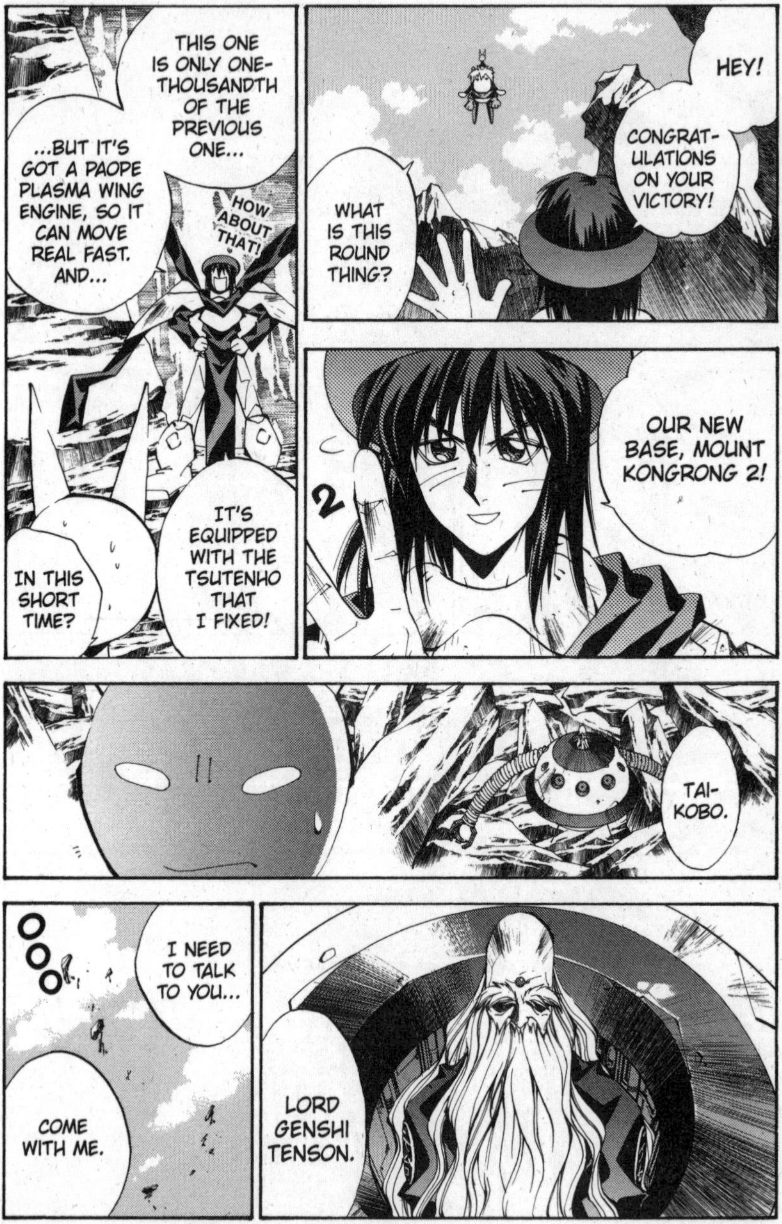
HEY!
CONGRAT-ULATIONS ON YOUR VICTORY!
WHAT IS THIS ROUND THING?
OUR NEW BASE, MOUNT KONGRONG 2!
2
THIS ONE IS ONLY ONE-THOUSANDTH OF THE PREVIOUS ONE...
...BUT IT'S GOT A PAOPE PLASMA WING ENGINE, SO IT CAN MOVE REAL FAST. AND...
HOW ABOUT THAT!
IT'S EQUIPPED WITH THE TSUTENHO THAT I FIXED!
IN THIS SHORT TIME?
TAI-KOBO.
LORD GENSHI TENSON.
I NEED TO TALK TO YOU...
COME WITH ME.
OOO

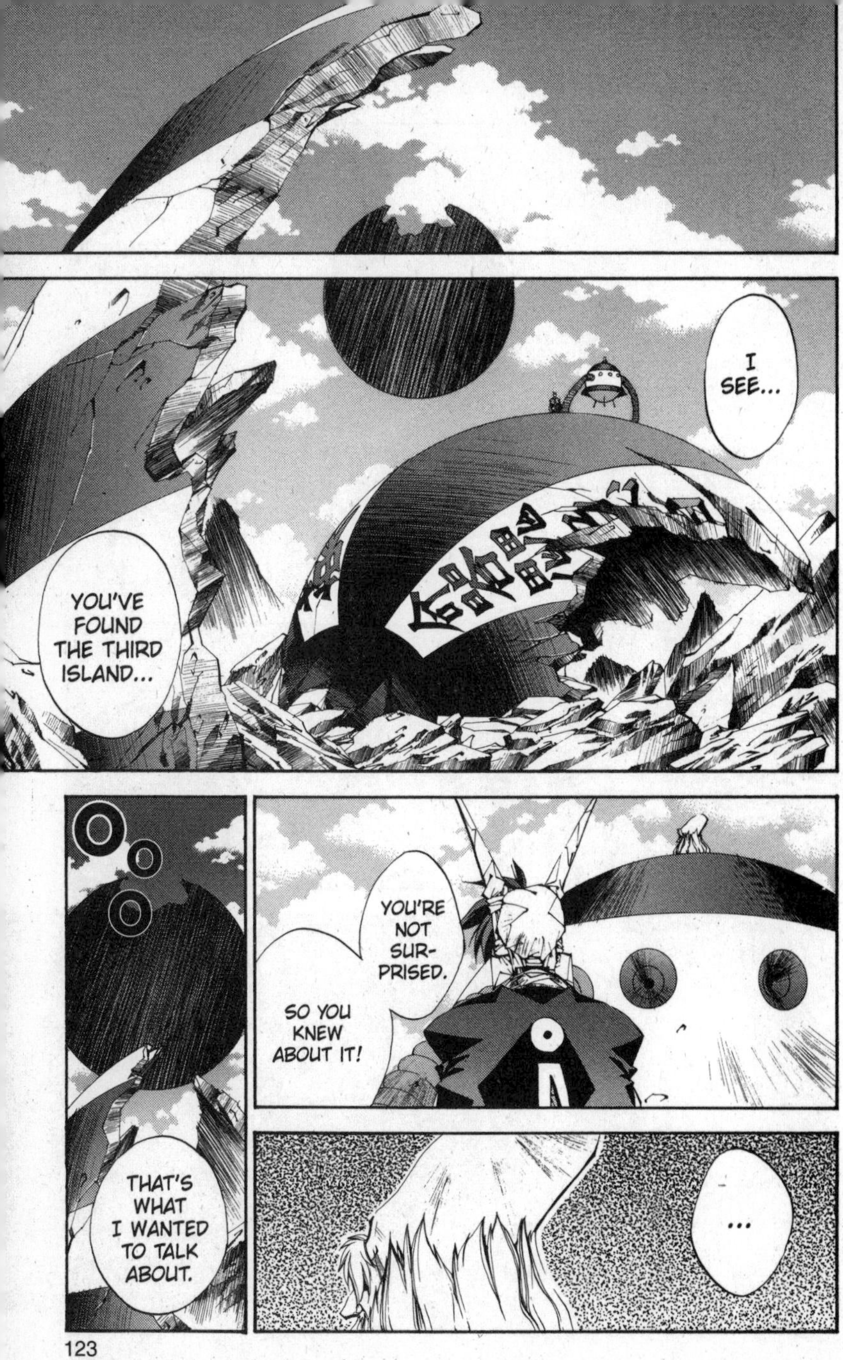
I SEE...
YOU'VE FOUND THE THIRD ISLAND...
YOU'RE NOT SUR-PRISED.
SO YOU KNEW ABOUT IT!
...
THAT'S WHAT I WANTED TO TALK ABOUT.

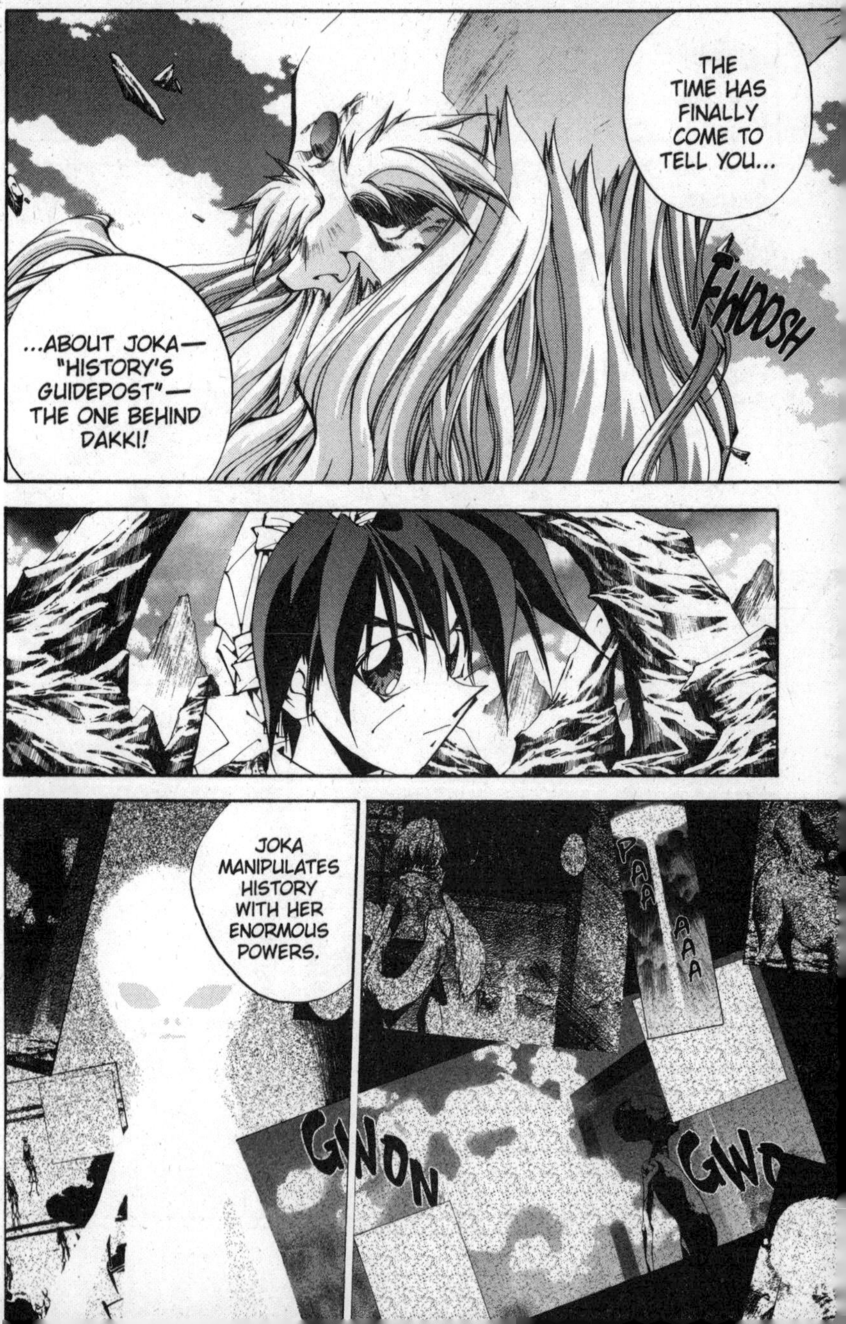
THE TIME HAS FINALLY COME TO TELL YOU...
FWOOSH
...ABOUT JOKA—"HISTORY'S GUIDEPOST"—THE ONE BEHIND DAKKI!
JOKA MANIPULATES HISTORY WITH HER ENORMOUS POWERS.
GWO
GNON

READ THIS WAY

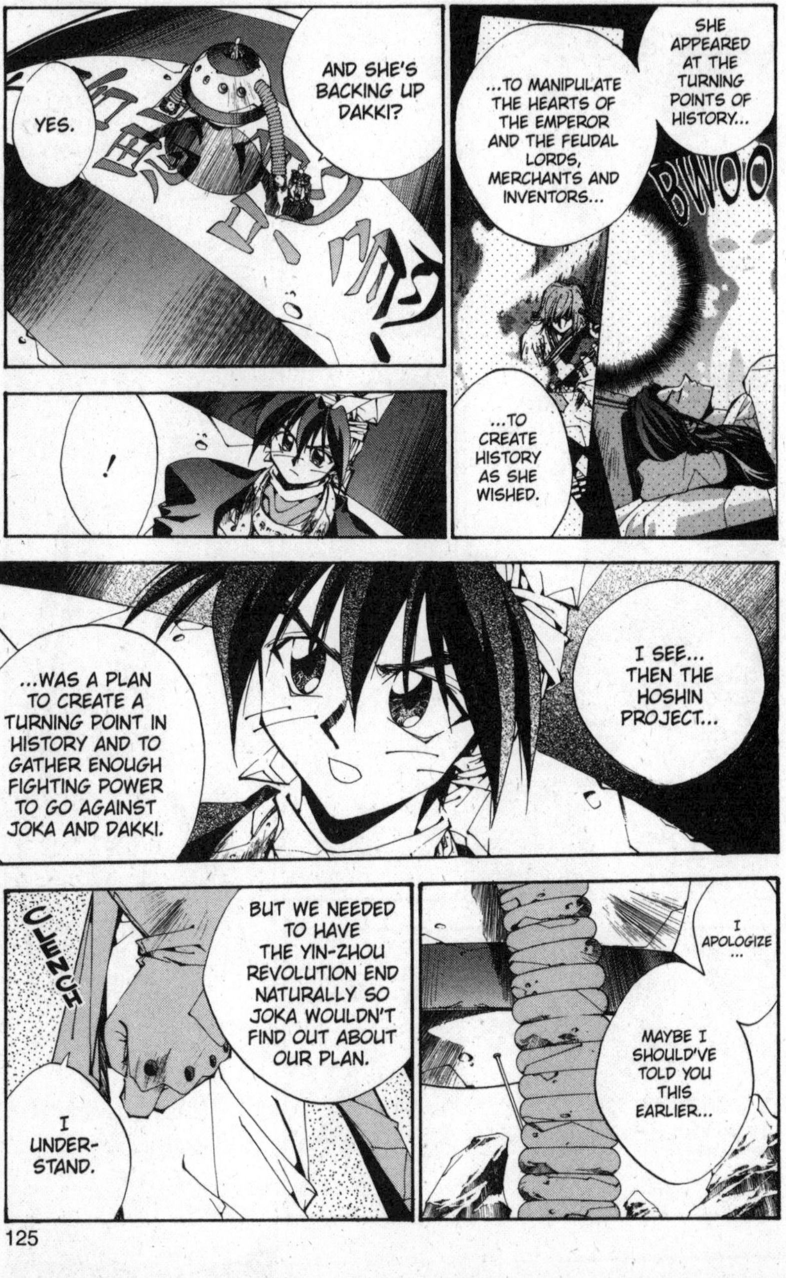
SHE APPEARED AT THE TURNING POINTS OF HISTORY...
...TO MANIPULATE THE HEARTS OF THE EMPEROR AND THE FEUDAL LORDS, MERCHANTS AND INVENTORS...
BWOO
...TO CREATE HISTORY AS SHE WISHED.
AND SHE'S BACKING UP DAKKI?
YES.
!
I SEE... THEN THE HOSHIN PROJECT...
...WAS A PLAN TO CREATE A TURNING POINT IN HISTORY AND TO GATHER ENOUGH FIGHTING POWER TO GO AGAINST JOKA AND DAKKI.
I APOLOGIZE...
MAYBE I SHOULD'VE TOLD YOU THIS EARLIER...
BUT WE NEEDED TO HAVE THE YIN-ZHOU REVOLUTION END NATURALLY SO JOKA WOULDN'T FIND OUT ABOUT OUR PLAN.
CLENCH
I UNDER-STAND.

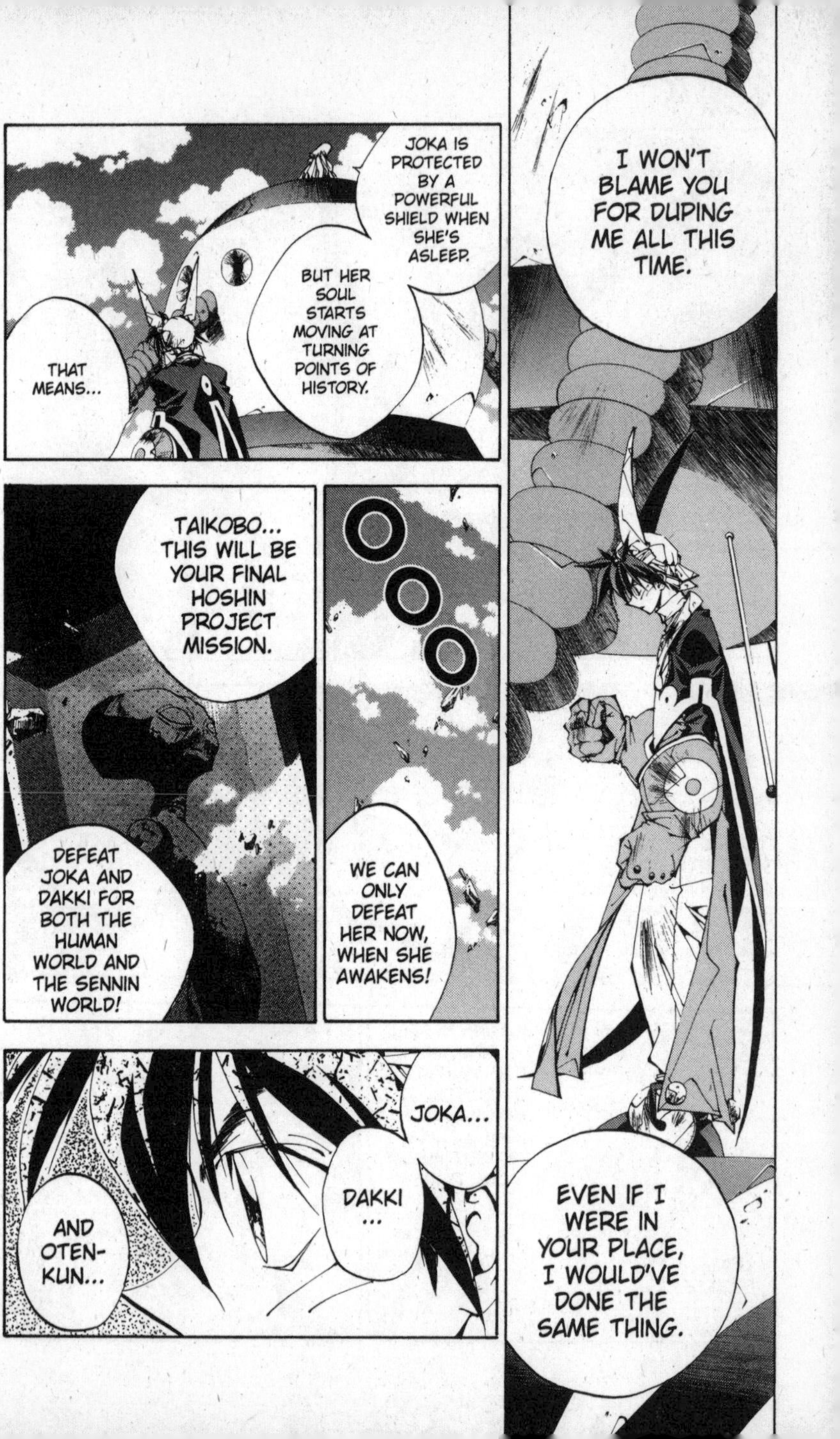
JOKA IS PROTECTED BY A POWERFUL SHIELD WHEN SHE'S ASLEEP.
BUT HER SOUL STARTS MOVING AT TURNING POINTS OF HISTORY.
THAT MEANS...
WE CAN ONLY DEFEAT HER NOW, WHEN SHE AWAKENS!
TAIKOBO... THIS WILL BE YOUR FINAL HOSHIN PROJECT MISSION.
DEFEAT JOKA AND DAKKI FOR BOTH THE HUMAN WORLD AND THE SENNIN WORLD!
JOKA...
DAKKI...
AND OTEN-KUN...
I WON'T BLAME YOU FOR DUPING ME ALL THIS TIME.
EVEN IF I WERE IN YOUR PLACE, I WOULD'VE DONE THE SAME THING.

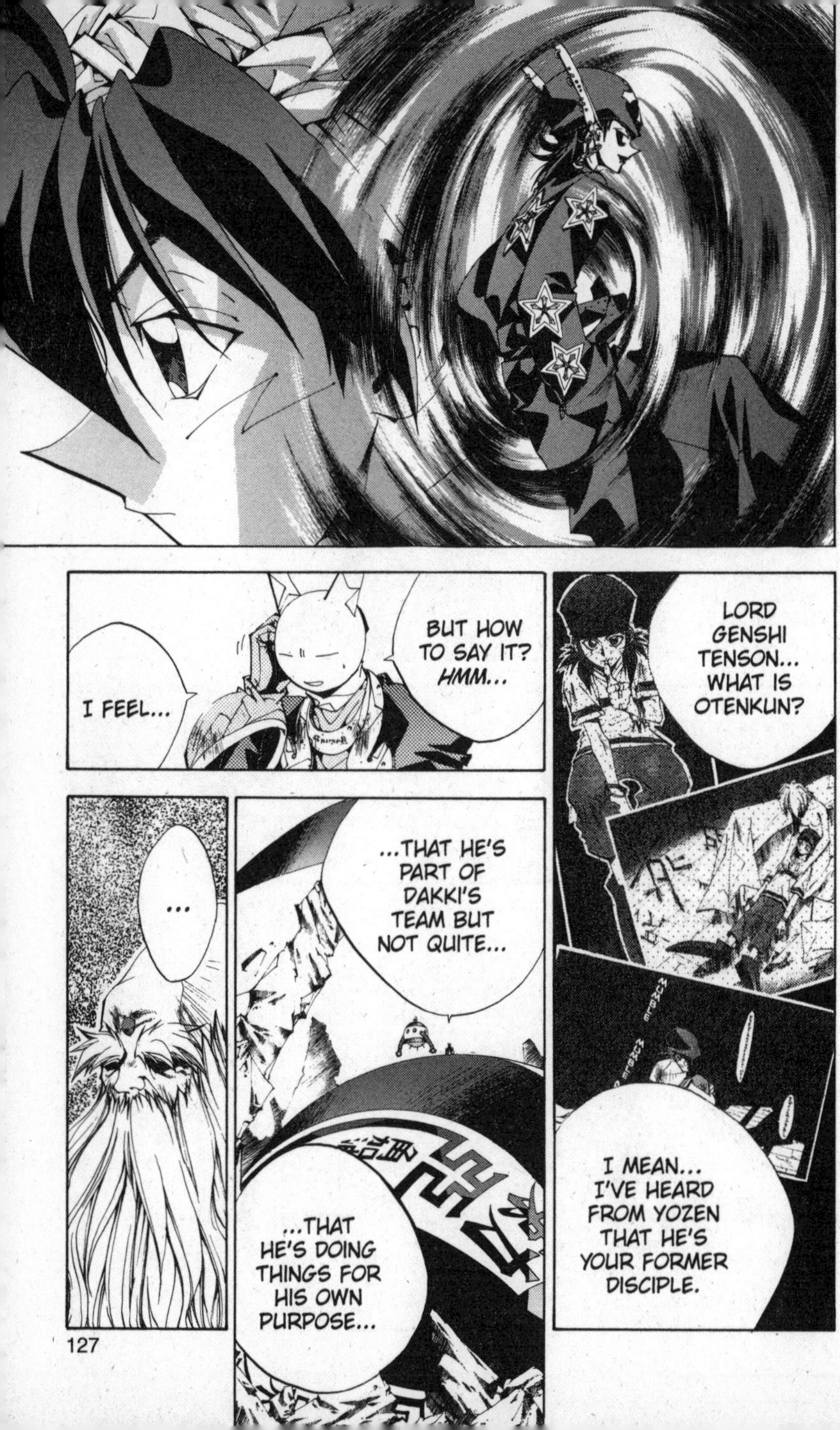
LORD GENSHI TENSON... WHAT IS OTENKUN?
MUMBLE
MUMBLE
I MEAN... I'VE HEARD FROM YOZEN THAT HE'S YOUR FORMER DISCIPLE.
BUT HOW TO SAY IT? HMM...
I FEEL...
...THAT HE'S PART OF DAKKI'S TEAM BUT NOT QUITE...
...THAT HE'S DOING THINGS FOR HIS OWN PURPOSE...
...

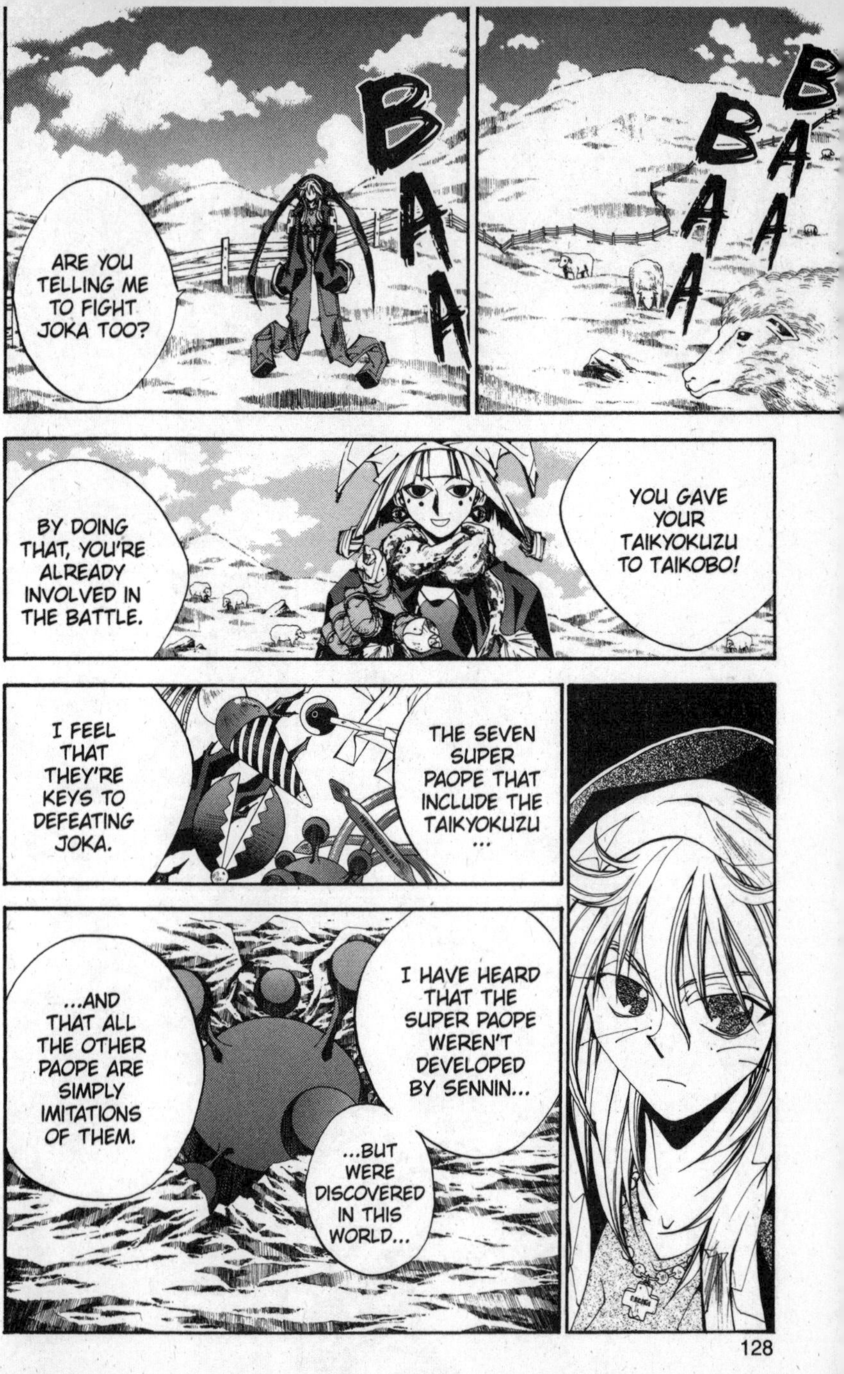
BAA
BAAA
BAA
ARE YOU TELLING ME TO FIGHT JOKA TOO?
YOU GAVE YOUR TAIKYOKUZU TO TAIKOBO!
BY DOING THAT, YOU'RE ALREADY INVOLVED IN THE BATTLE.
THE SEVEN SUPER PAOPE THAT INCLUDE THE TAIKYOKUZU ...
I FEEL THAT THEY'RE KEYS TO DEFEATING JOKA.
I HAVE HEARD THAT THE SUPER PAOPE WEREN'T DEVELOPED BY SENNIN...
...BUT WERE DISCOVERED IN THIS WORLD...
...AND THAT ALL THE OTHER PAOPE ARE SIMPLY IMITATIONS OF THEM.

READ THIS WAY

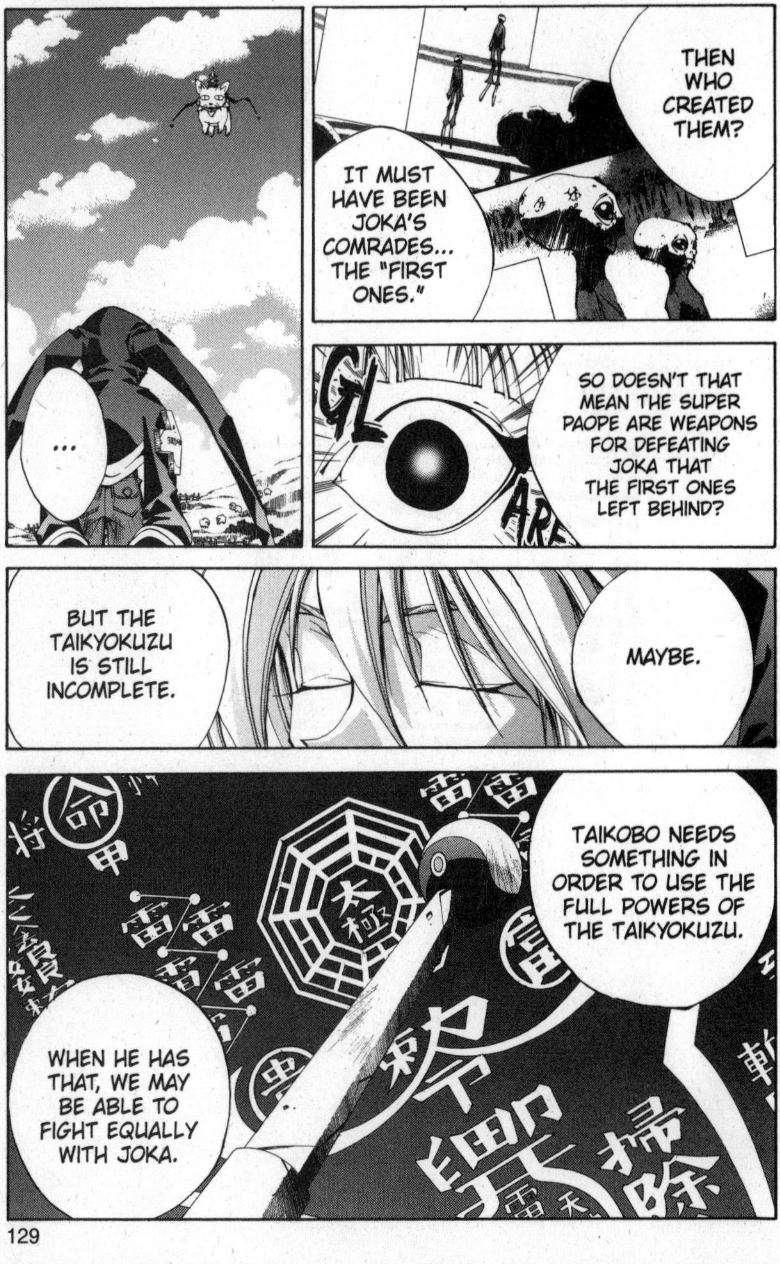
THEN WHO CREATED THEM?
IT MUST HAVE BEEN JOKA'S COMRADES... THE "FIRST ONES."
SO DOESN'T THAT MEAN THE SUPER PAOPE ARE WEAPONS FOR DEFEATING JOKA THAT THE FIRST ONES LEFT BEHIND?
...
MAYBE.
BUT THE TAIKYOKUZU IS STILL INCOMPLETE.
TAIKOBO NEEDS SOMETHING IN ORDER TO USE THE FULL POWERS OF THE TAIKYOKUZU.
WHEN HE HAS THAT, WE MAY BE ABLE TO FIGHT EQUALLY WITH JOKA.

封神演義

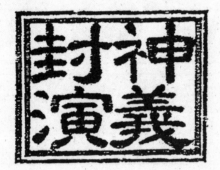

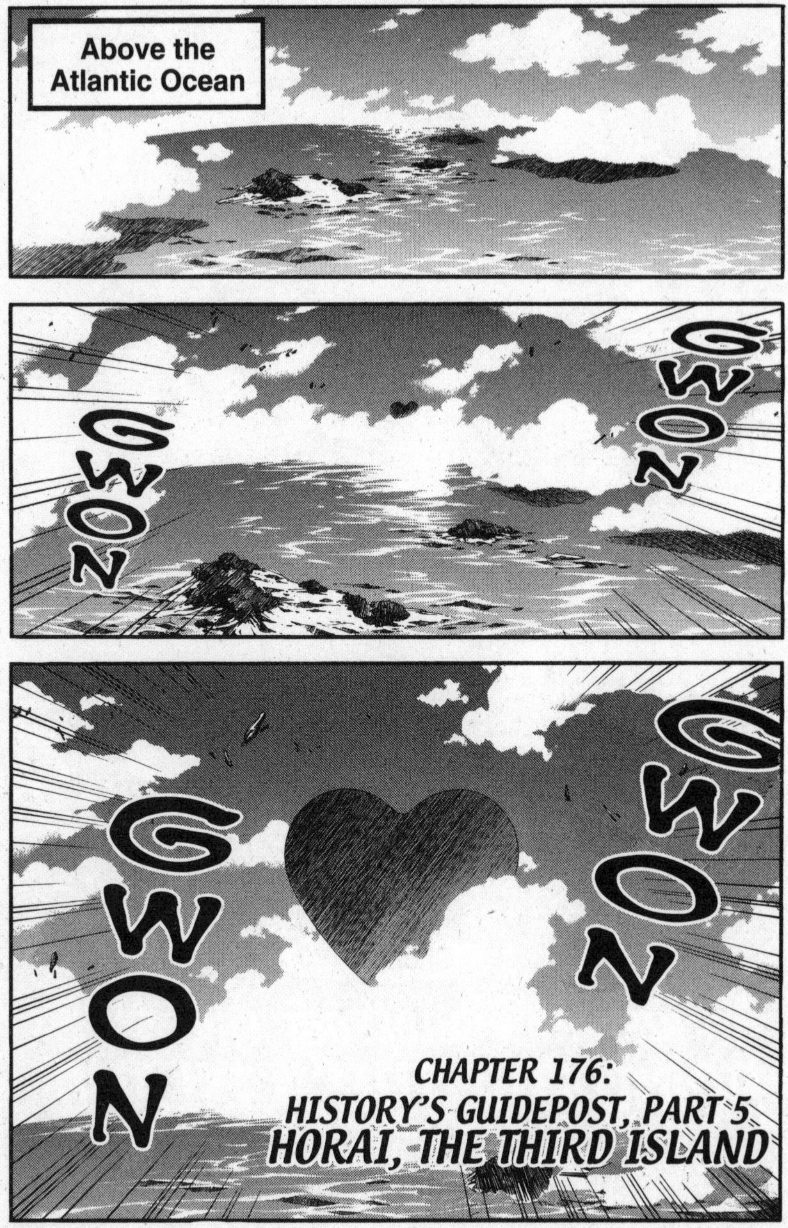
Above the Atlantic Ocean
GWON
GWON
GWON
GWON
CHAPTER 176:
HISTORY'S GUIDEPOST, PART 5
HORAI, THE THIRD ISLAND

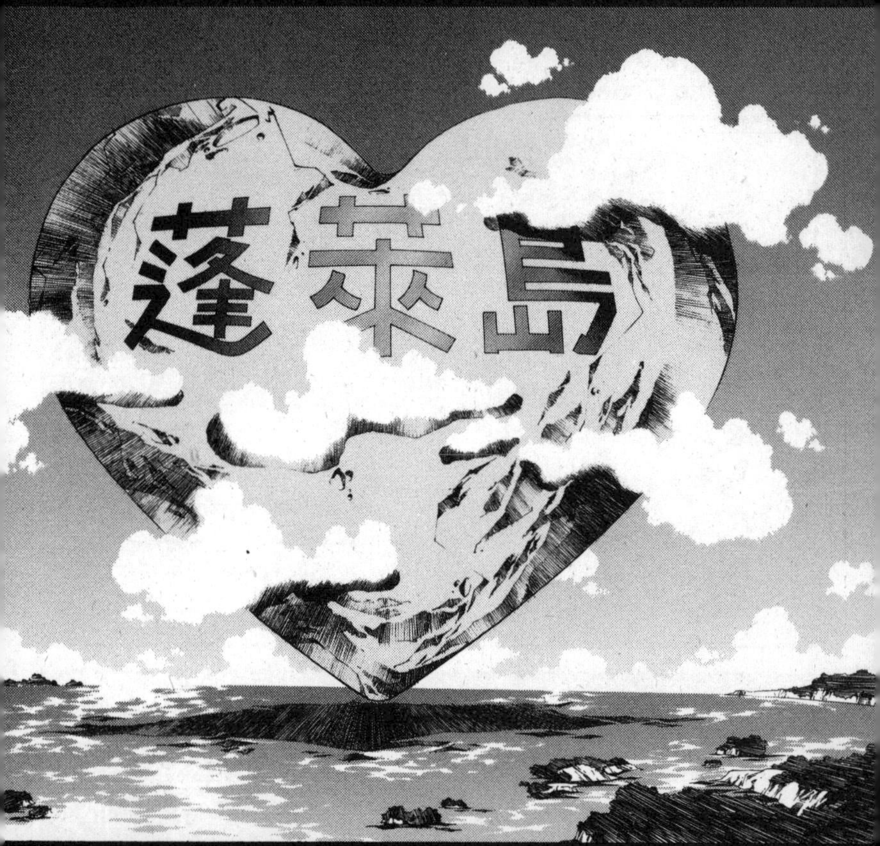
蓬莱島

Chapter 176

HISTORY'S GUIDEPOST, PART 5

HORAI, THE THIRD ISLAND

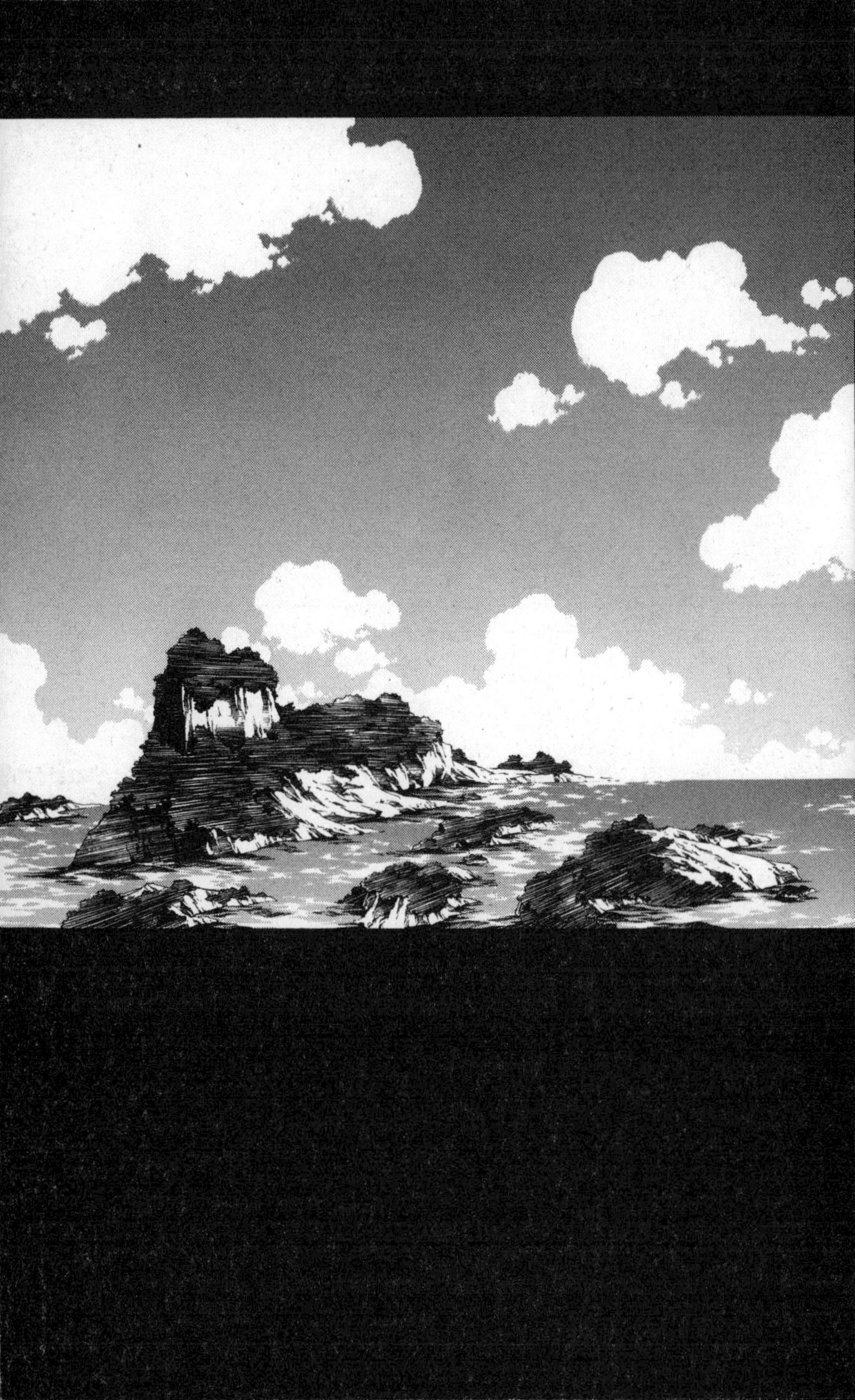

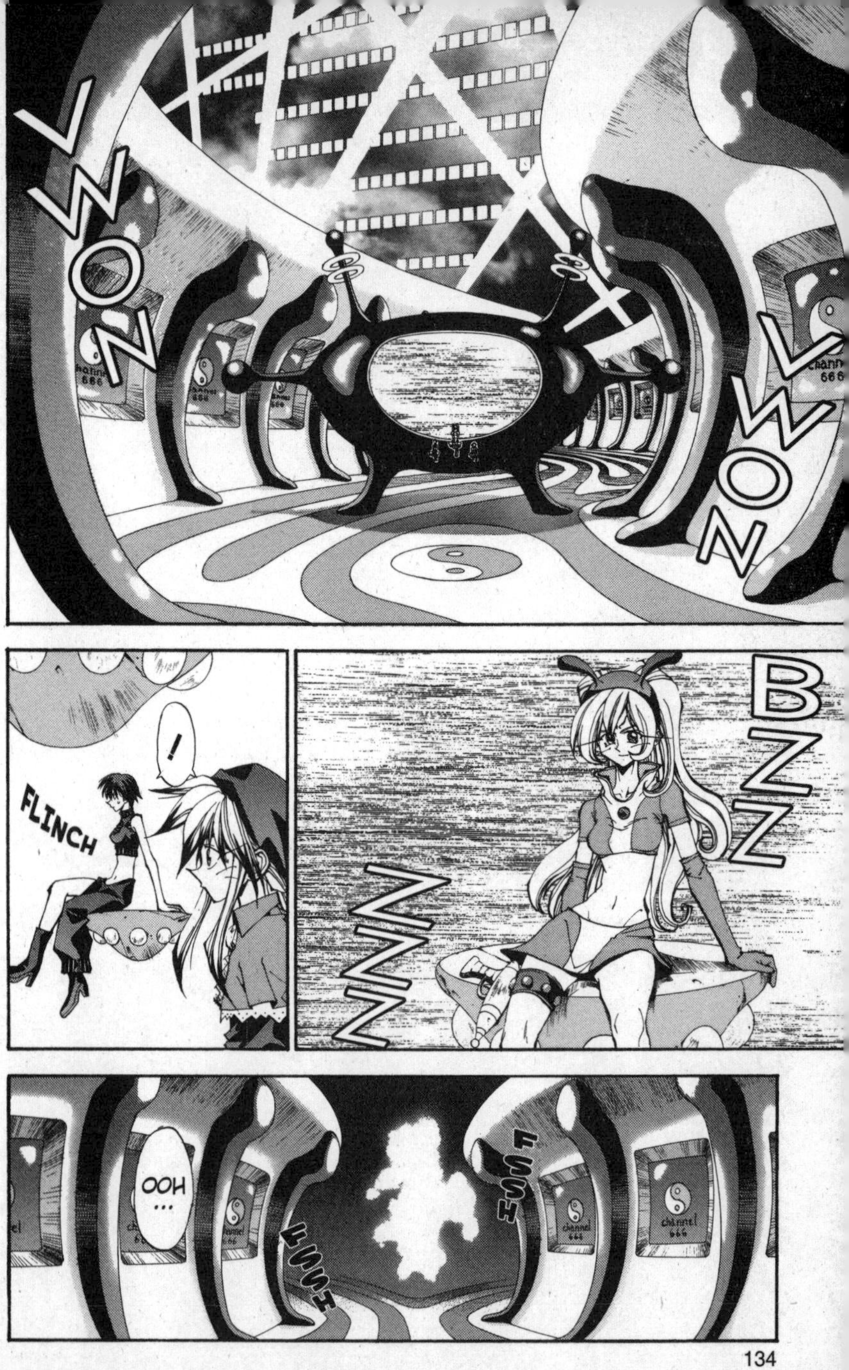
VWOWN
VWOWN
channel 666
channel 666
BZZZ
ZZZZ
!
FLINCH
FSSH
OOH ...
FSSH
channel 666
channel 666

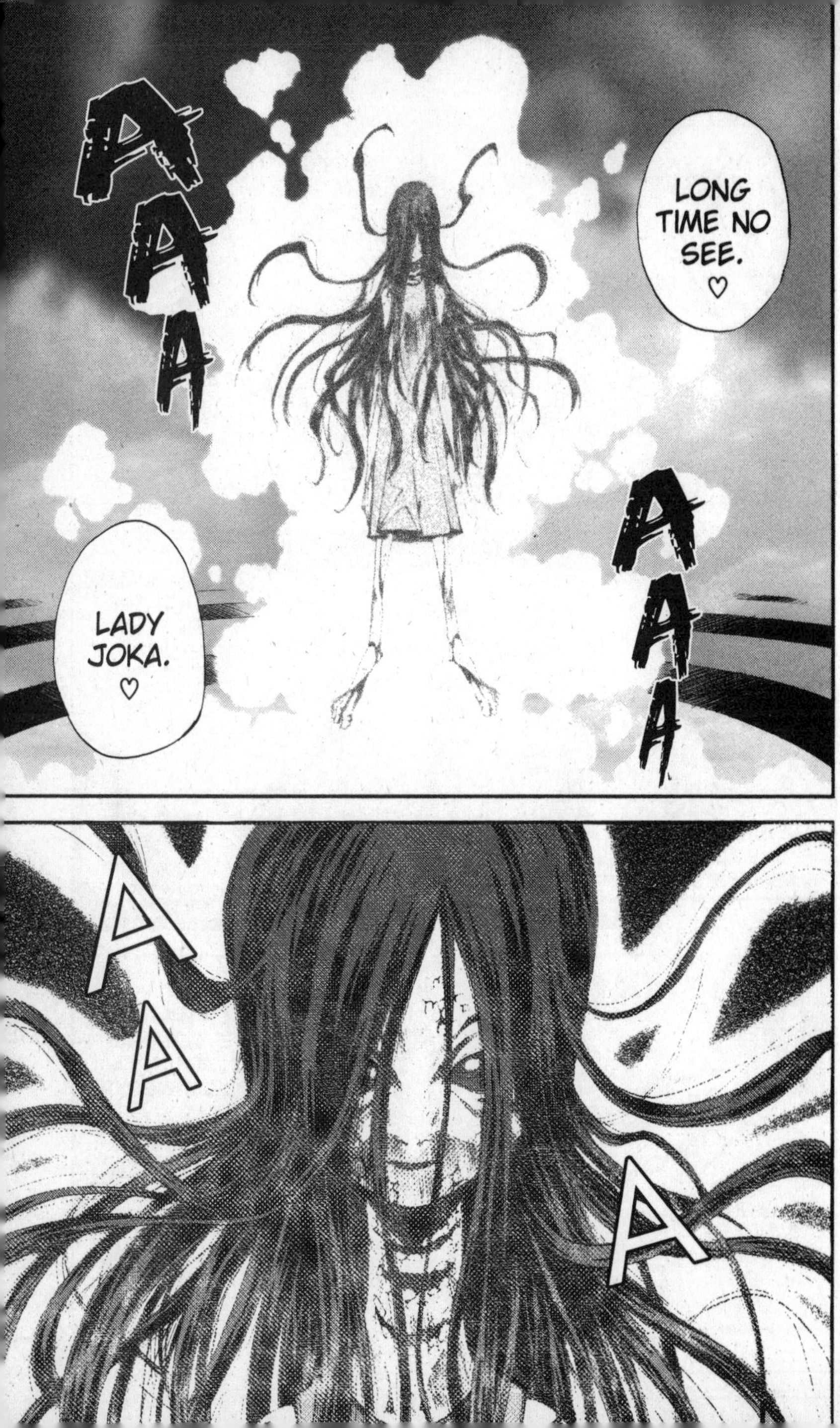

AAA
LONG TIME NO SEE. ♡
AAA
LADY JOKA. ♡
AAA

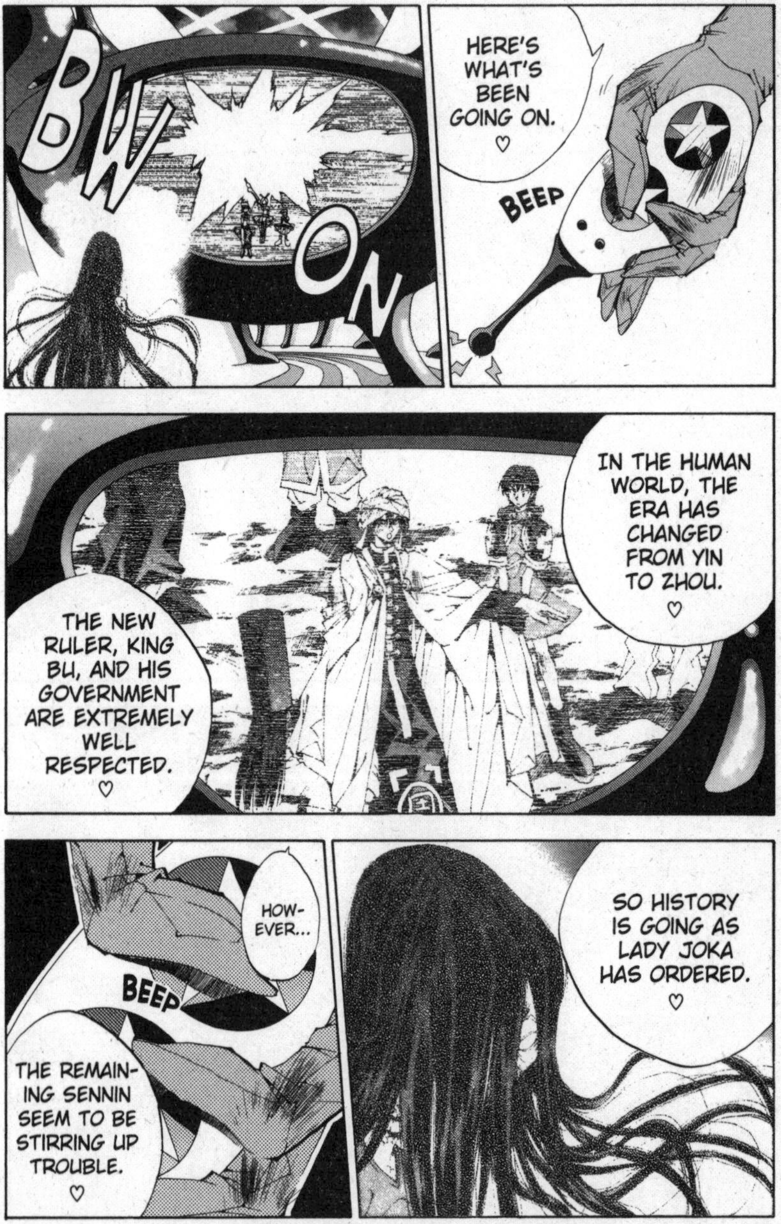
HERE'S WHAT'S BEEN GOING ON. ♡
BEEP
BWOON
IN THE HUMAN WORLD, THE ERA HAS CHANGED FROM YIN TO ZHOU. ♡
THE NEW RULER, KING BU, AND HIS GOVERNMENT ARE EXTREMELY WELL RESPECTED. ♡
SO HISTORY IS GOING AS LADY JOKA HAS ORDERED. ♡
HOW-EVER...
BEEP
THE REMAIN-ING SENNIN SEEM TO BE STIRRING UP TROUBLE. ♡

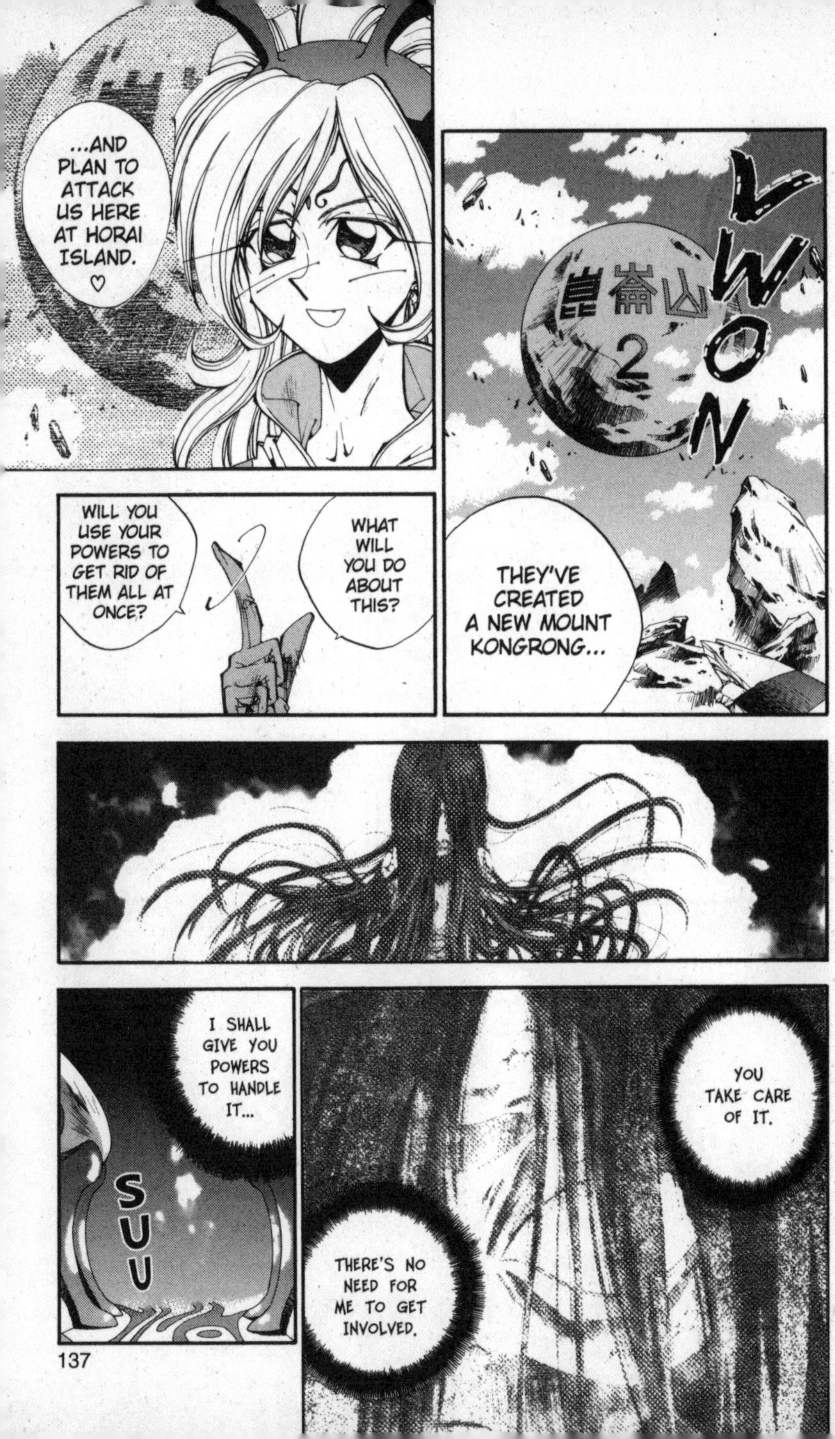
VWON
崑崙山
2
THEY'VE CREATED A NEW MOUNT KONGRONG...
...AND PLAN TO ATTACK US HERE AT HORAI ISLAND. ♡
WHAT WILL YOU DO ABOUT THIS?
WILL YOU USE YOUR POWERS TO GET RID OF THEM ALL AT ONCE?
YOU TAKE CARE OF IT.
THERE'S NO NEED FOR ME TO GET INVOLVED.
I SHALL GIVE YOU POWERS TO HANDLE IT...
SUU

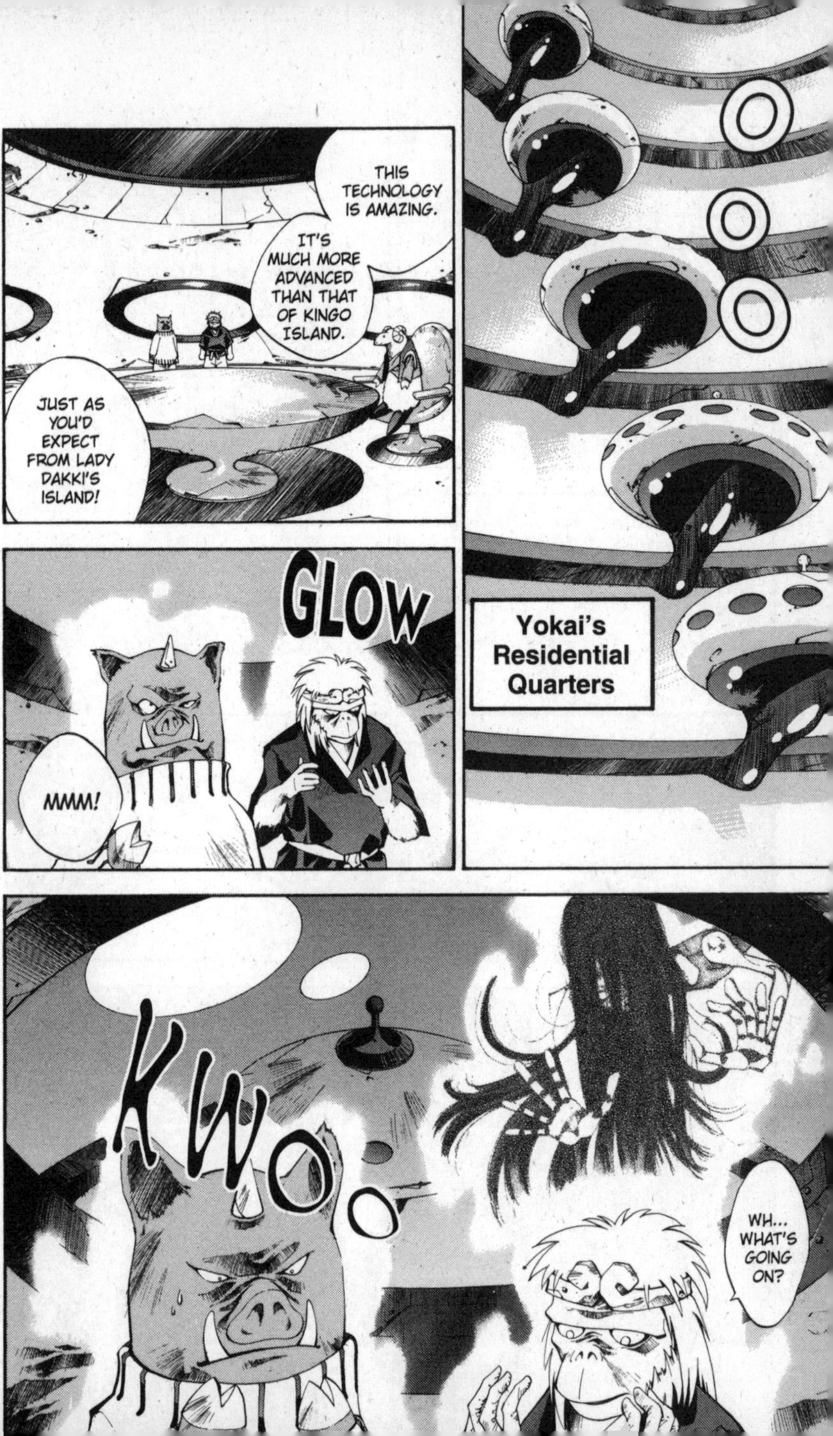
Yokai's Residential Quarters
THIS TECHNOLOGY IS AMAZING.
IT'S MUCH MORE ADVANCED THAN THAT OF KINGO ISLAND.
JUST AS YOU'D EXPECT FROM LADY DAKKI'S ISLAND!
GLOW
MMM!
KWOO
WH... WHAT'S GOING ON?

READ THIS WAY

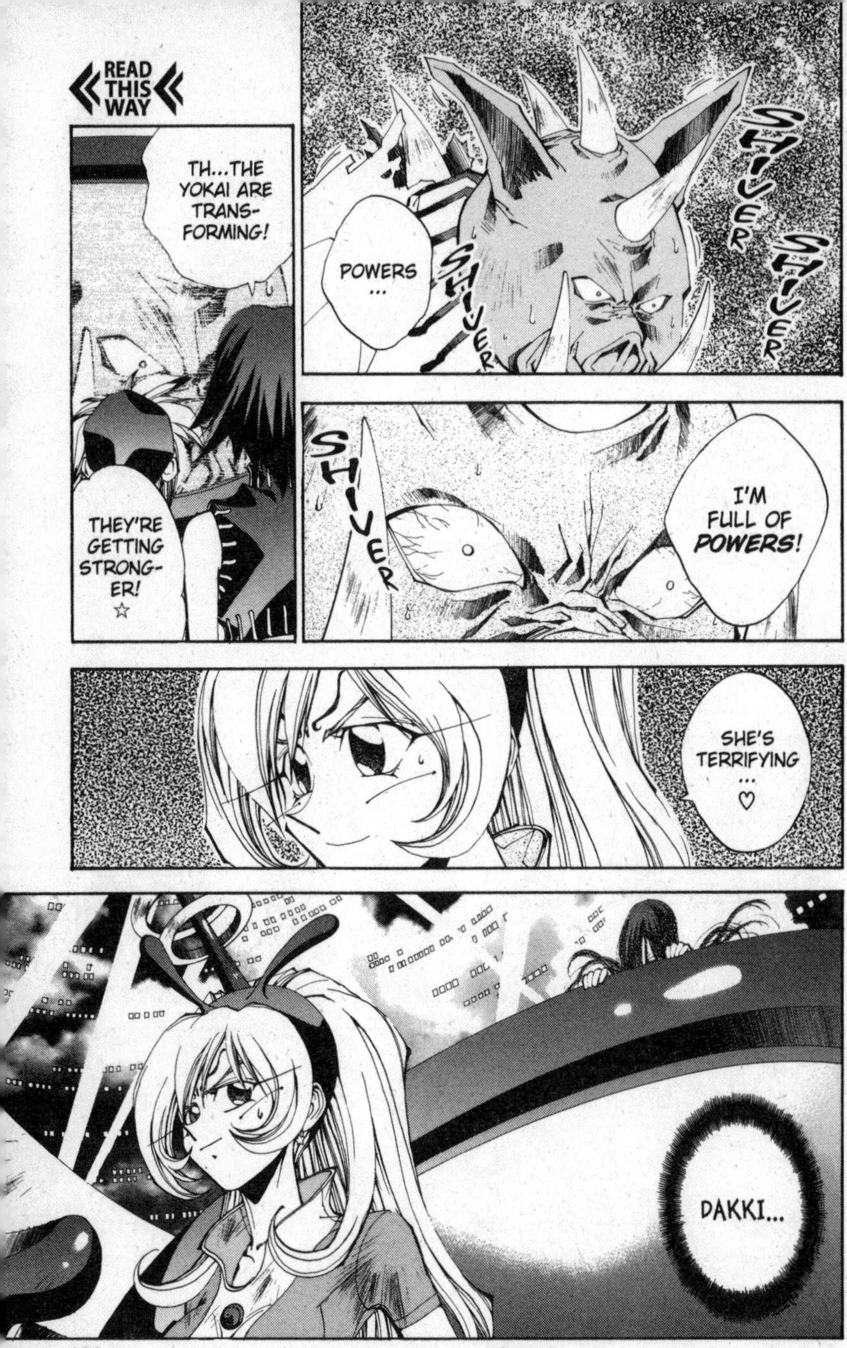

SHIVER SHIVER
POWERS...
SHIVER
TH...THE YOKAI ARE TRANSFORMING!
THEY'RE GETTING STRONGER! ☆
SHIVER
I'M FULL OF POWERS!
SHE'S TERRIFYING... ♡
DAKKI...

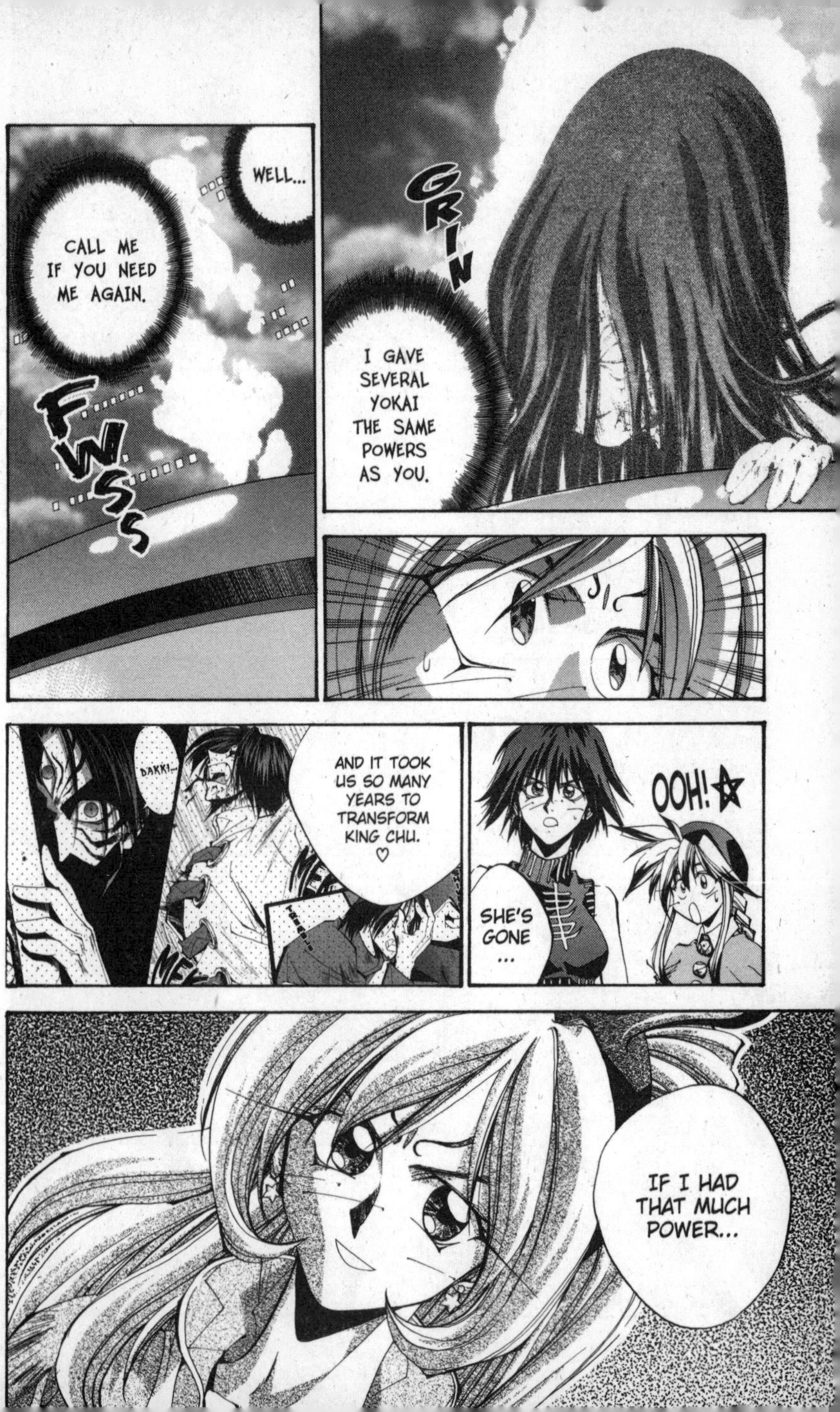
GRIN
I GAVE SEVERAL YOKAI THE SAME POWERS AS YOU.
WELL...
CALL ME IF YOU NEED ME AGAIN.
FWSSS
OOH!☆
SHE'S GONE ...
AND IT TOOK US SO MANY YEARS TO TRANSFORM KING CHU. ♡
DAKKI...
IF I HAD THAT MUCH POWER...

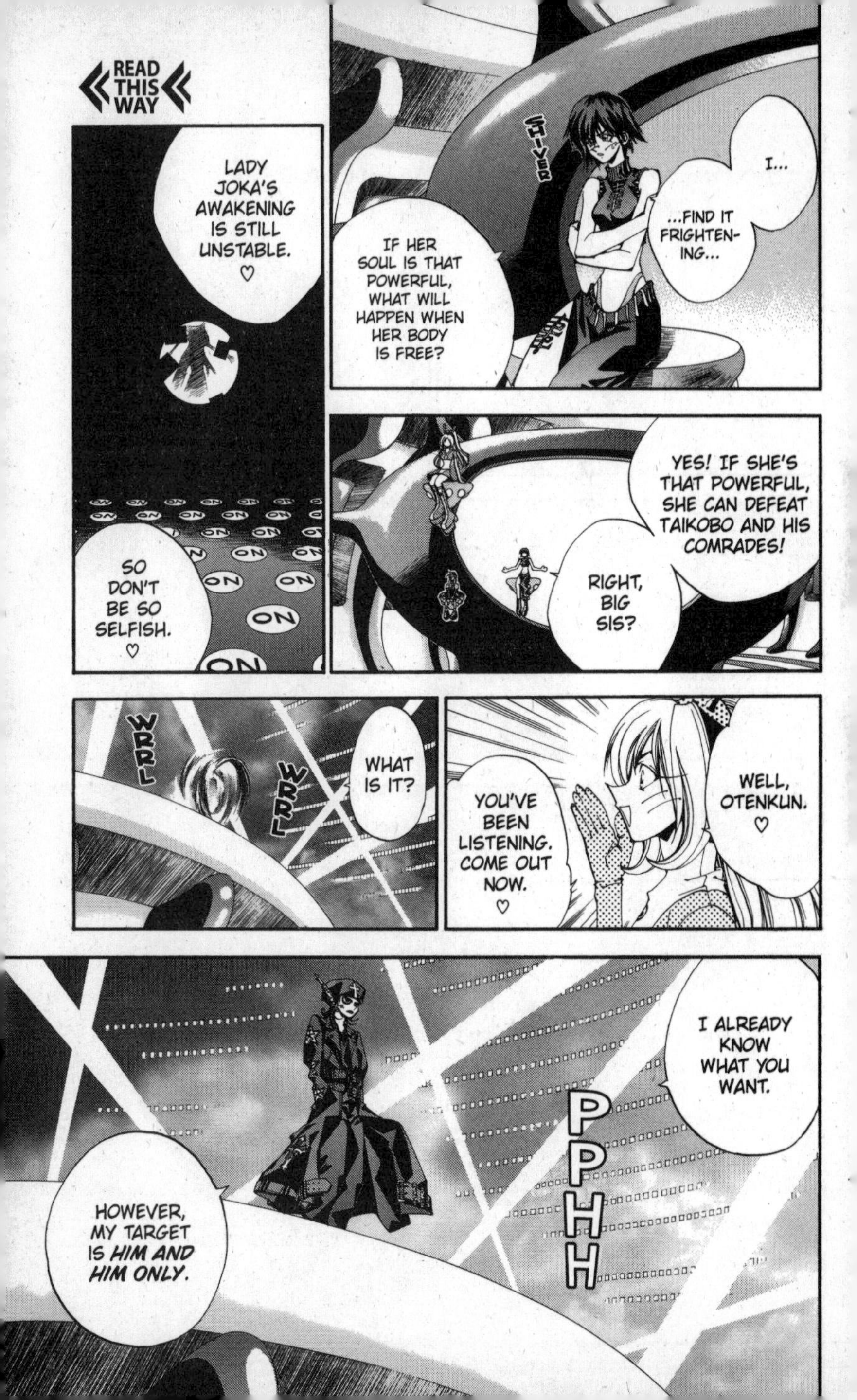
READ THIS WAY
SHIVER
I...
...FIND IT FRIGHTENING...
IF HER SOUL IS THAT POWERFUL, WHAT WILL HAPPEN WHEN HER BODY IS FREE?
YES! IF SHE'S THAT POWERFUL, SHE CAN DEFEAT TAIKOBO AND HIS COMRADES!
RIGHT, BIG SIS?
LADY JOKA'S AWAKENING IS STILL UNSTABLE. ♡
SO DON'T BE SO SELFISH. ♡
ON
WELL, OTENKUN. ♡
YOU'VE BEEN LISTENING. COME OUT NOW. ♡
WHAT IS IT?
WRRL
WRRL
I ALREADY KNOW WHAT YOU WANT.
PPHH
HOWEVER, MY TARGET IS *HIM AND HIM ONLY*.

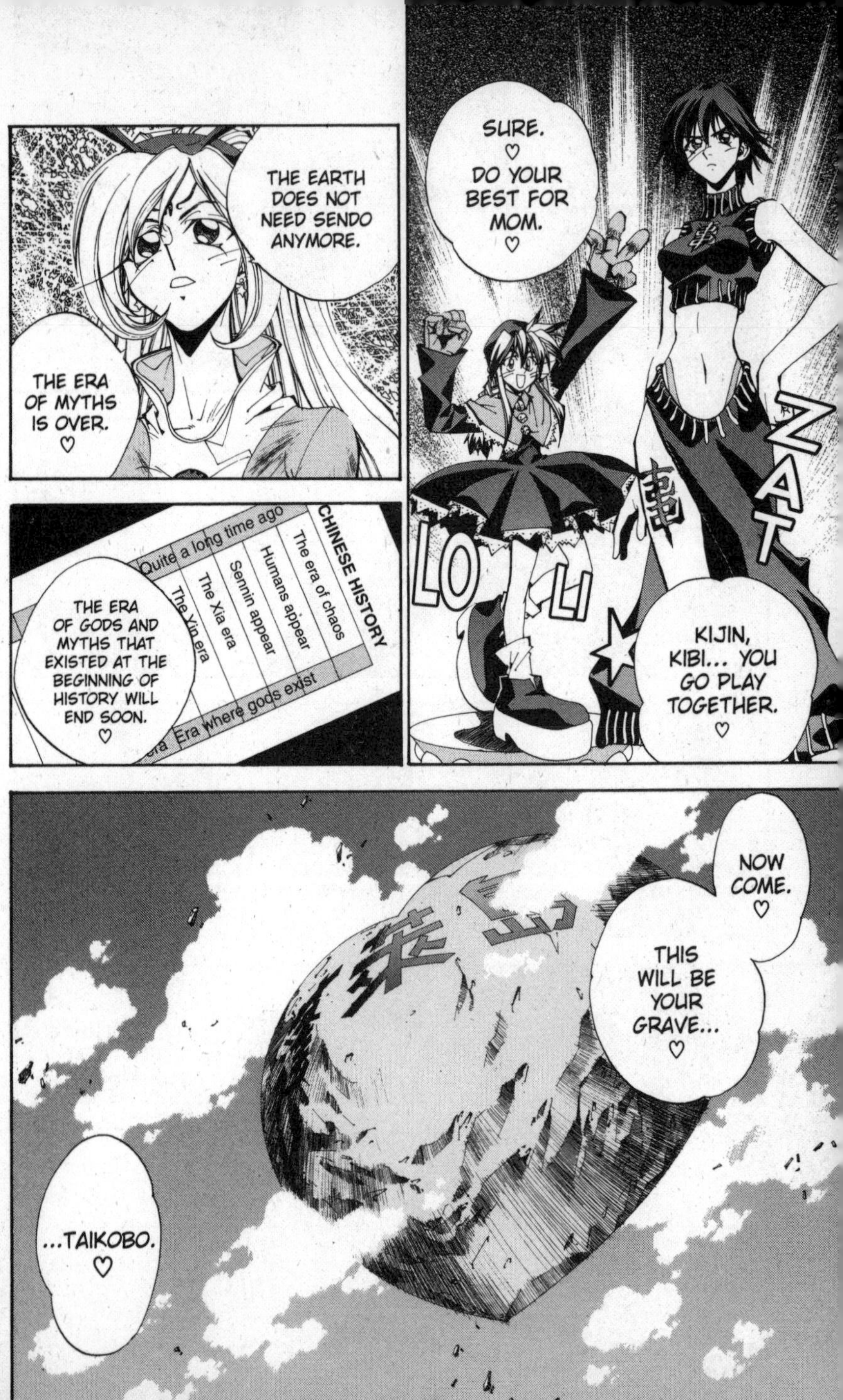
SURE. ♡ DO YOUR BEST FOR MOM. ♡
ZAT
LO
LI
KIJIN, KIBI... YOU GO PLAY TOGETHER. ♡
THE EARTH DOES NOT NEED SENDO ANYMORE.
THE ERA OF MYTHS IS OVER. ♡
CHINESE HISTORY
Quite a long time ago
The era of chaos
Humans appear
Sennin appear
The Xia era
The Yin era
Era where gods exist
era
THE ERA OF GODS AND MYTHS THAT EXISTED AT THE BEGINNING OF HISTORY WILL END SOON. ♡
NOW COME. ♡
THIS WILL BE YOUR GRAVE... ♡
...TAIKOBO. ♡

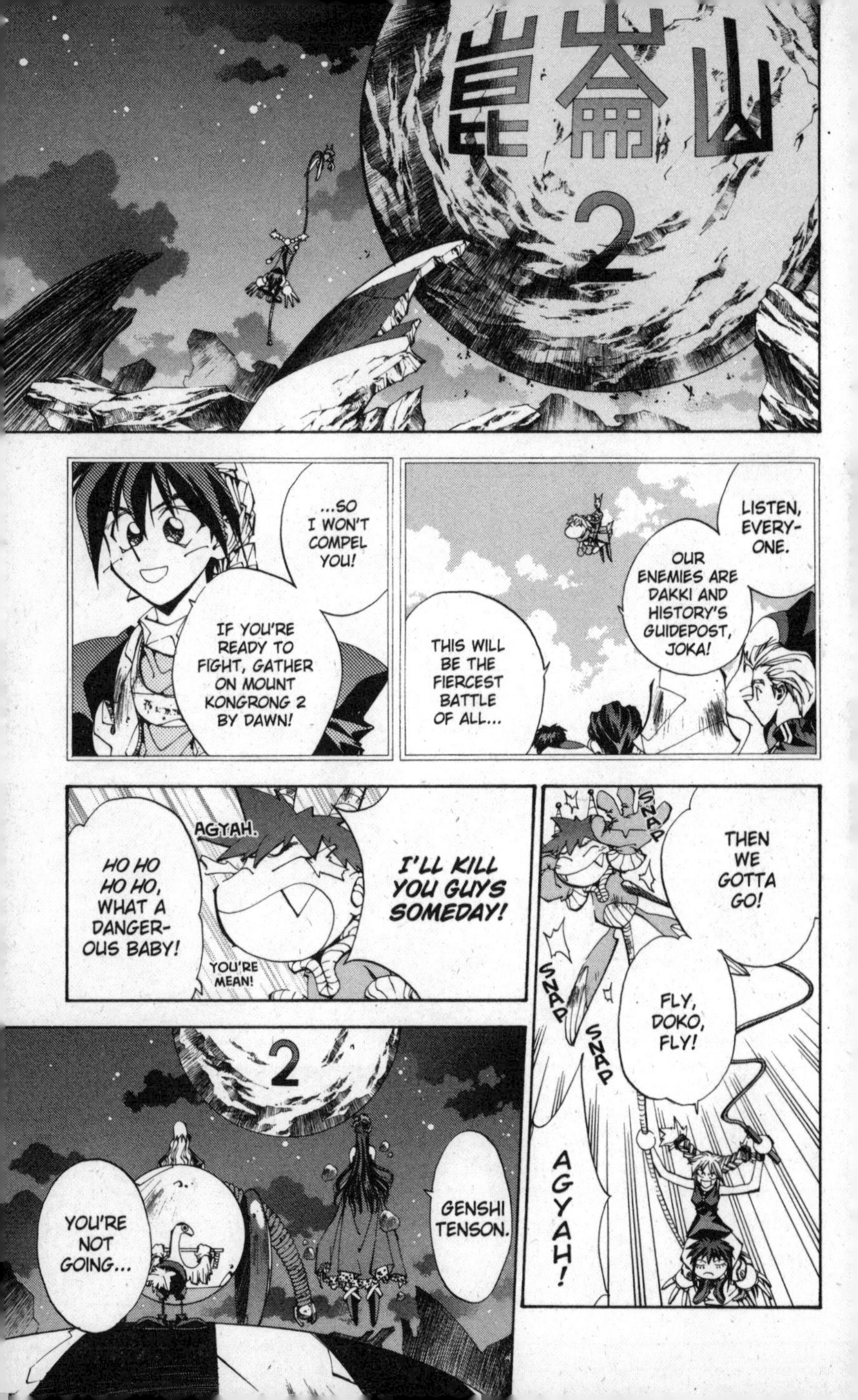
崑崙山
2
LISTEN, EVERY-ONE.
OUR ENEMIES ARE DAKKI AND HISTORY'S GUIDEPOST, JOKA!
THIS WILL BE THE FIERCEST BATTLE OF ALL...
...SO I WON'T COMPEL YOU!
IF YOU'RE READY TO FIGHT, GATHER ON MOUNT KONGRONG 2 BY DAWN!
SNAP
THEN WE GOTTA GO!
FLY, DOKO, FLY!
SNAP
SNAP
AGYAH!
I'LL KILL YOU GUYS SOMEDAY!
AGYAH.
HO HO HO HO, WHAT A DANGER-OUS BABY!
YOU'RE MEAN!
2
GENSHI TENSON.
YOU'RE NOT GOING...

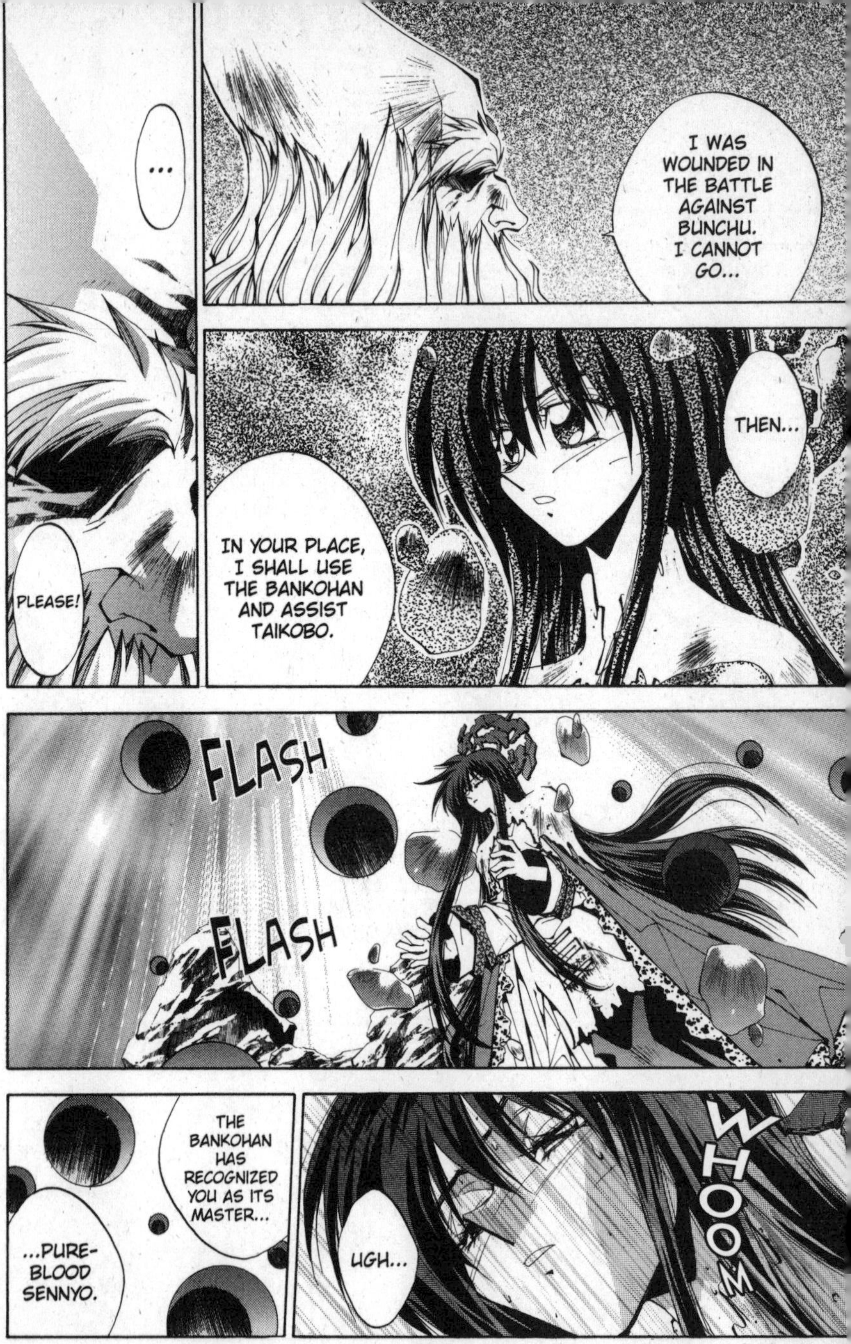
I WAS WOUNDED IN THE BATTLE AGAINST BUNCHU. I CANNOT GO...
...
THEN...
IN YOUR PLACE, I SHALL USE THE BANKOHAN AND ASSIST TAIKOBO.
PLEASE!
FLASH
FLASH
WHOOM
UGH...
THE BANKOHAN HAS RECOGNIZED YOU AS ITS MASTER...
...PURE-BLOOD SENNYO.

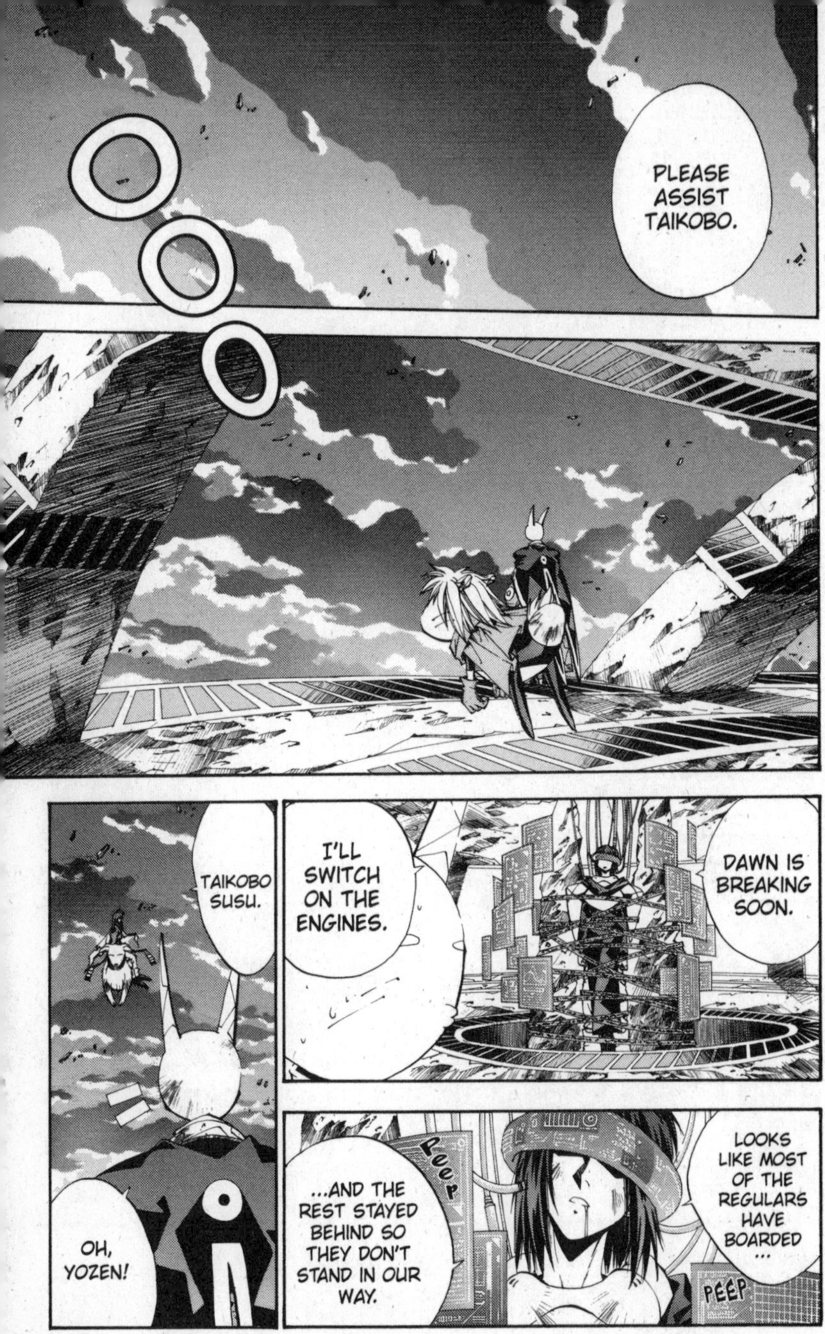
PLEASE ASSIST TAIKOBO.
DAWN IS BREAKING SOON.
I'LL SWITCH ON THE ENGINES.
LOOKS LIKE MOST OF THE REGULARS HAVE BOARDED ...
PEEP
...AND THE REST STAYED BEHIND SO THEY DON'T STAND IN OUR WAY.
Peep
TAIKOBO SUSU.
OH, YOZEN!

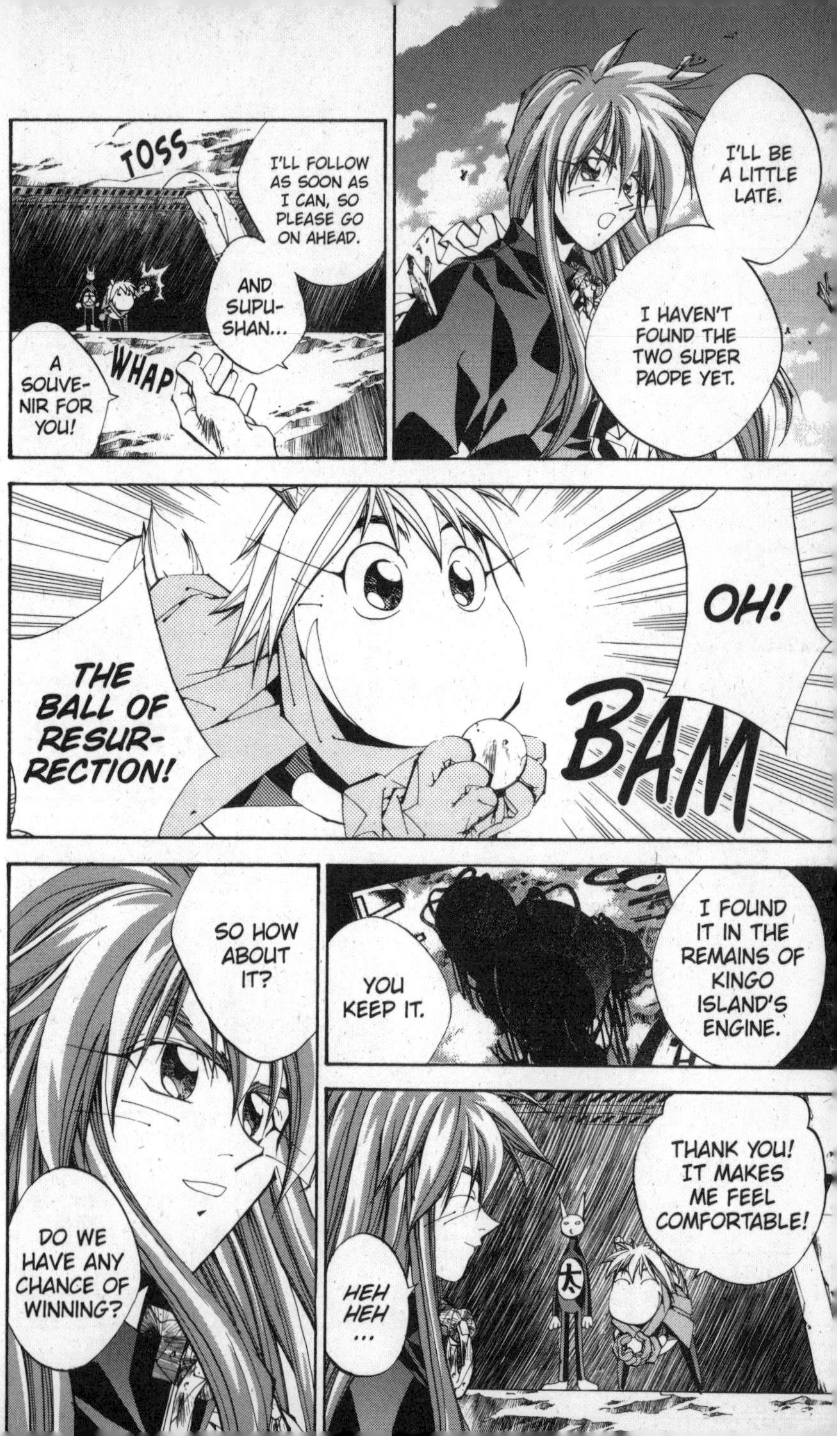
I'LL BE A LITTLE LATE.
I HAVEN'T FOUND THE TWO SUPER PAOPE YET.
I'LL FOLLOW AS SOON AS I CAN, SO PLEASE GO ON AHEAD.
TOSS
AND SUPU-SHAN...
A SOUVENIR FOR YOU!
WHAP
OH!
BAM
THE BALL OF RESURRECTION!
I FOUND IT IN THE REMAINS OF KINGO ISLAND'S ENGINE.
YOU KEEP IT.
THANK YOU! IT MAKES ME FEEL COMFORTABLE!
HEH HEH ...
SO HOW ABOUT IT?
DO WE HAVE ANY CHANCE OF WINNING?

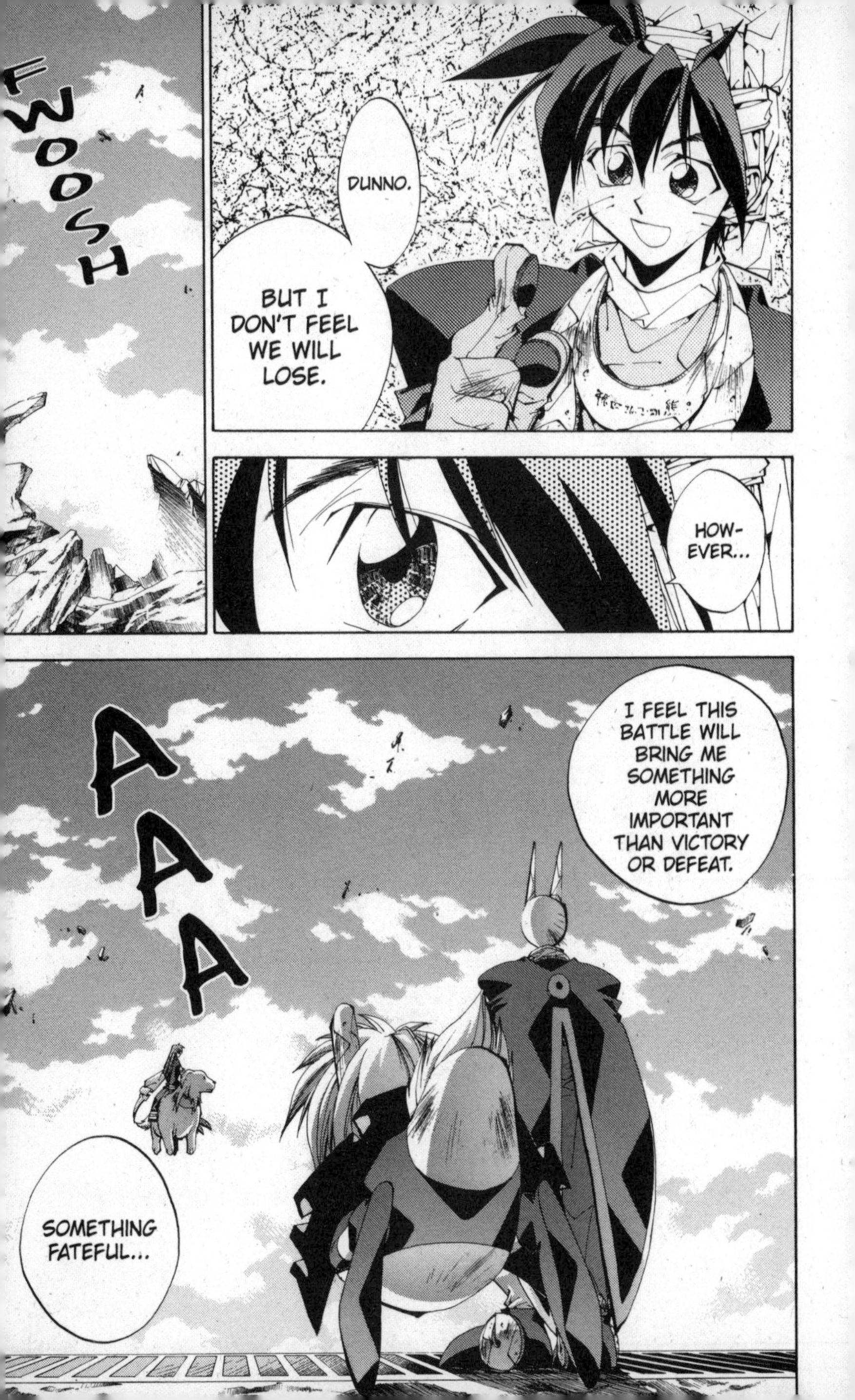
DUNNO.
BUT I DON'T FEEL WE WILL LOSE.
FWOOSH
HOW-EVER...
I FEEL THIS BATTLE WILL BRING ME SOMETHING MORE IMPORTANT THAN VICTORY OR DEFEAT.
AAA
SOMETHING FATEFUL...

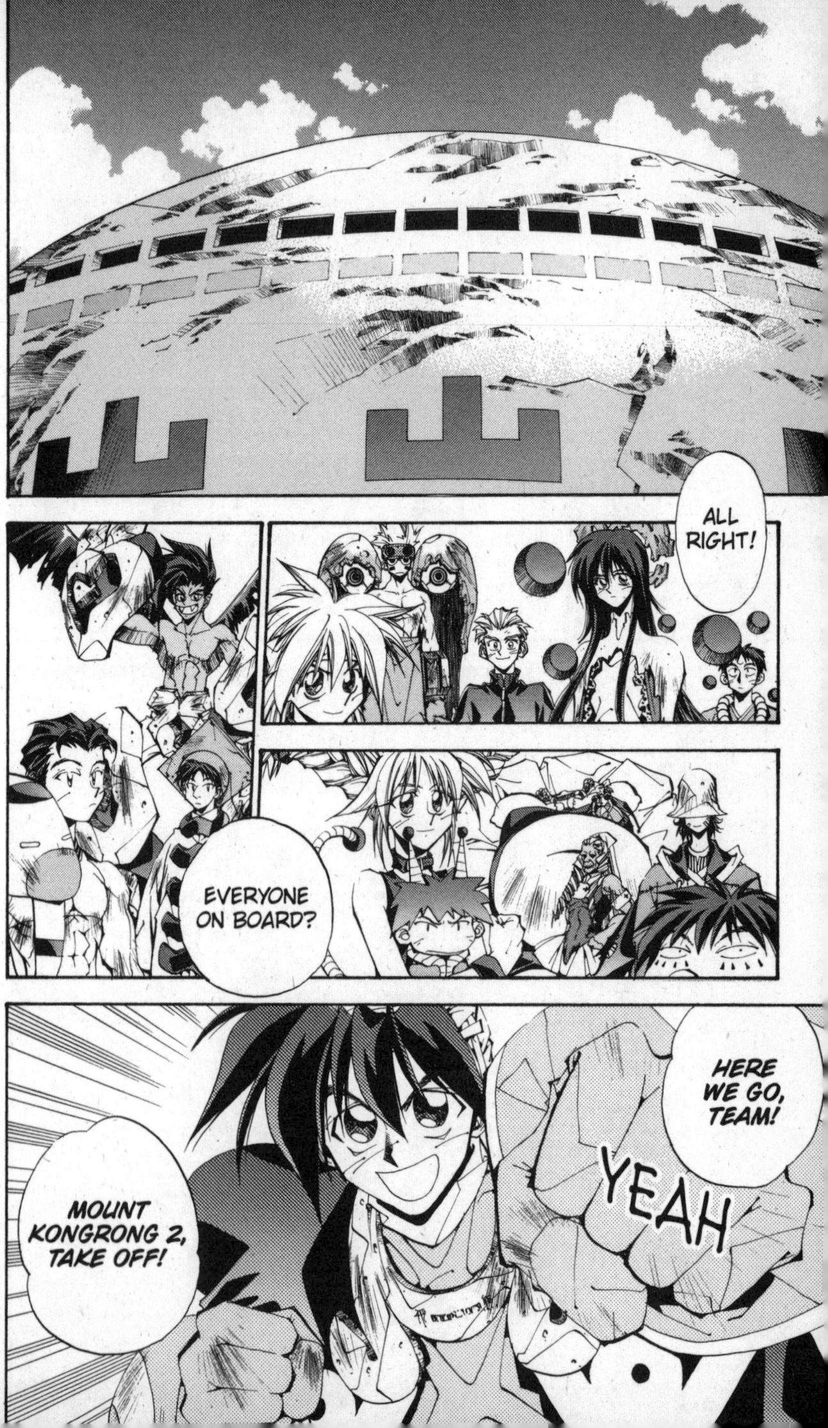
ALL RIGHT!
EVERYONE ON BOARD?
HERE WE GO, TEAM!
YEAH
MOUNT KONGRONG 2, TAKE OFF!

READ THIS WAY

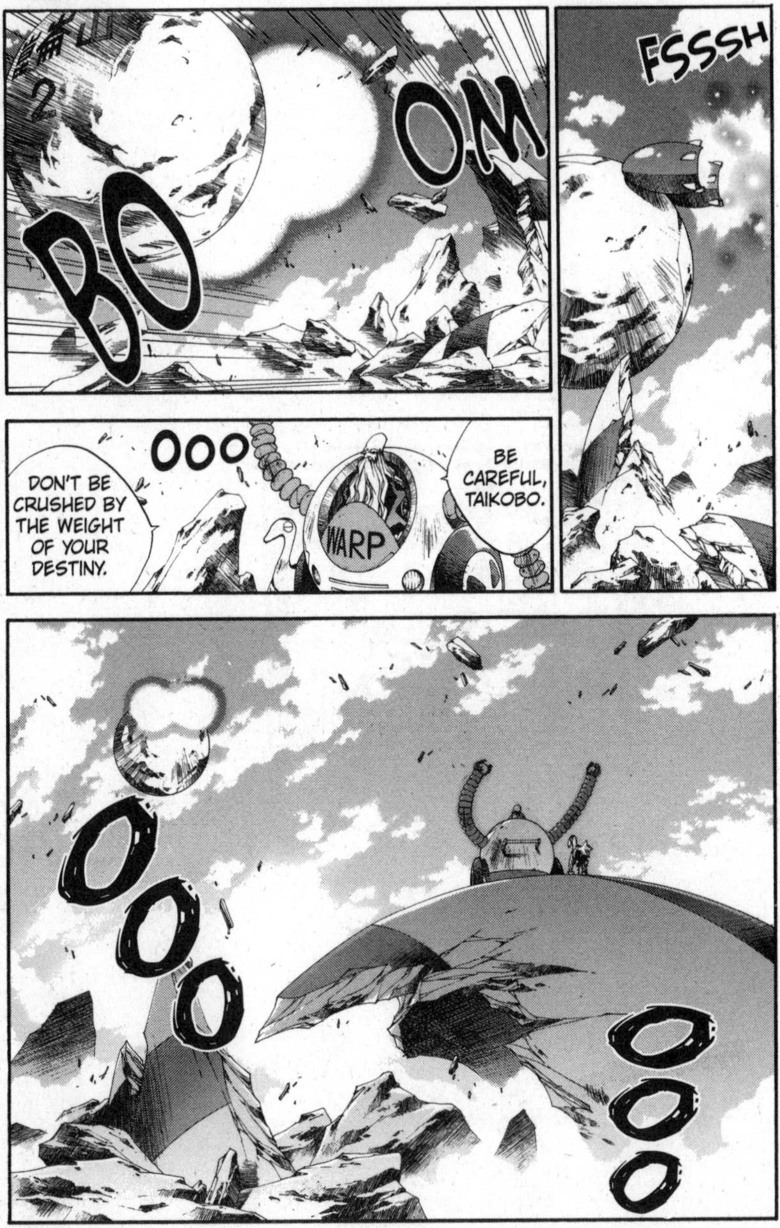
FSSSH
BOOM
BE CAREFUL, TAIKOBO.
DON'T BE CRUSHED BY THE WEIGHT OF YOUR DESTINY.
OOO
WARP
OOOO
OOOO

封神演義

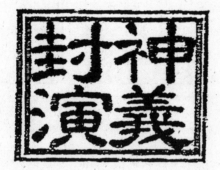

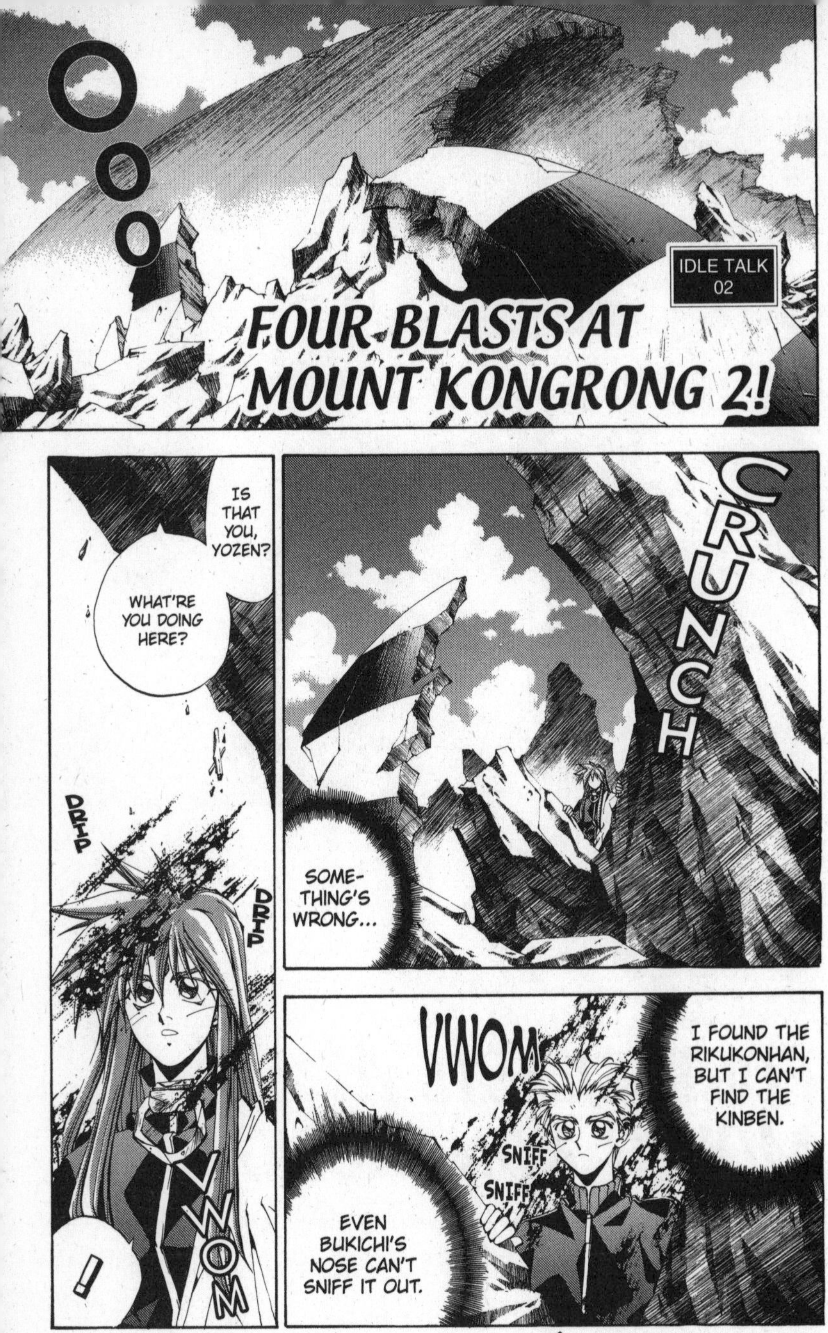
OOO
IDLE TALK 02
FOUR BLASTS AT MOUNT KONGRONG 2!
CRUNCH
SOME-THING'S WRONG...
IS THAT YOU, YOZEN?
WHAT'RE YOU DOING HERE?
DRIP
DRIP
VWOM
I FOUND THE RIKUKONHAN, BUT I CAN'T FIND THE KINBEN.
SNIFF
SNIFF
EVEN BUKICHI'S NOSE CAN'T SNIFF IT OUT.
VWOM
!

↑ NOSE LIKE A DOG

LOOK! IT'S...!

IDLE TALK
02

FOUR BLASTS AT MOUNT KONGRONG 2!

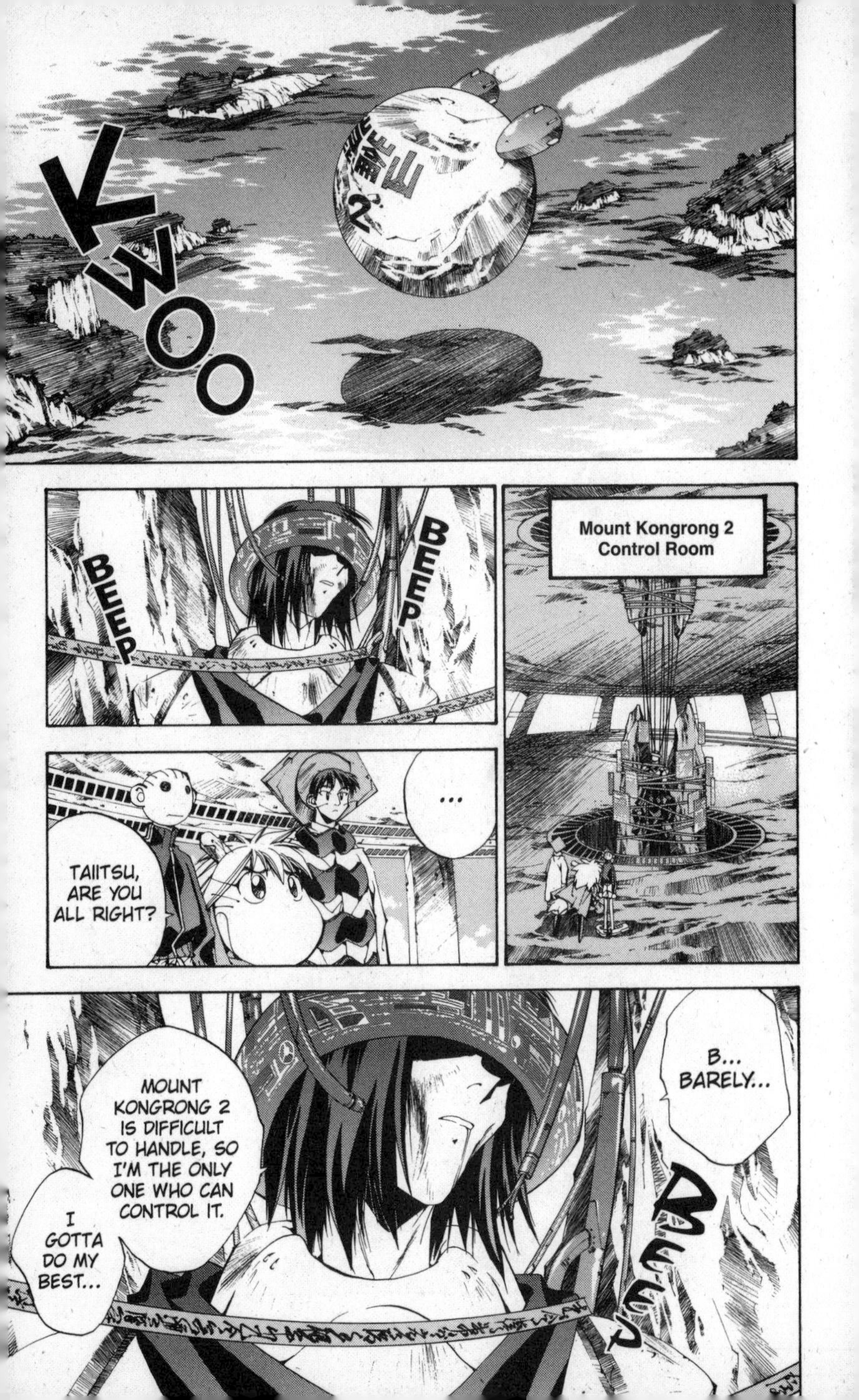
KWOOO
2
Mount Kongrong 2 Control Room
BEEP BEEP
...
TAIITSU, ARE YOU ALL RIGHT?
B... BARELY...
BWEEEN
MOUNT KONGRONG 2 IS DIFFICULT TO HANDLE, SO I'M THE ONLY ONE WHO CAN CONTROL IT.
I GOTTA DO MY BEST...

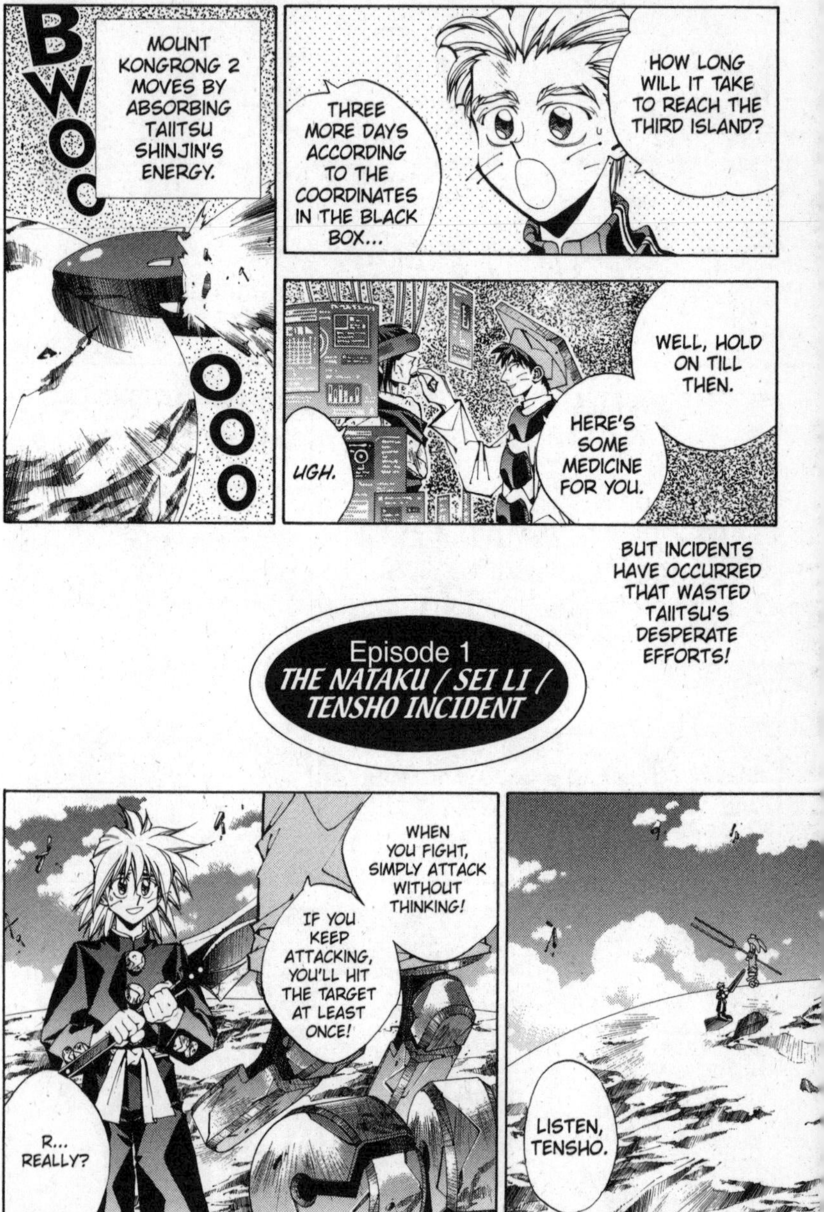
HOW LONG WILL IT TAKE TO REACH THE THIRD ISLAND?
THREE MORE DAYS ACCORDING TO THE COORDINATES IN THE BLACK BOX...
WELL, HOLD ON TILL THEN.
HERE'S SOME MEDICINE FOR YOU.
UGH.
MOUNT KONGRONG 2 MOVES BY ABSORBING TAIITSU SHINJIN'S ENERGY.
BWOOOOOO
BUT INCIDENTS HAVE OCCURRED THAT WASTED TAIITSU'S DESPERATE EFFORTS!
Episode 1
THE NATAKU / SEI LI / TENSHO INCIDENT
LISTEN, TENSHO.
WHEN YOU FIGHT, SIMPLY ATTACK WITHOUT THINKING!
IF YOU KEEP ATTACKING, YOU'LL HIT THE TARGET AT LEAST ONCE!
R... REALLY?

READ THIS WAY

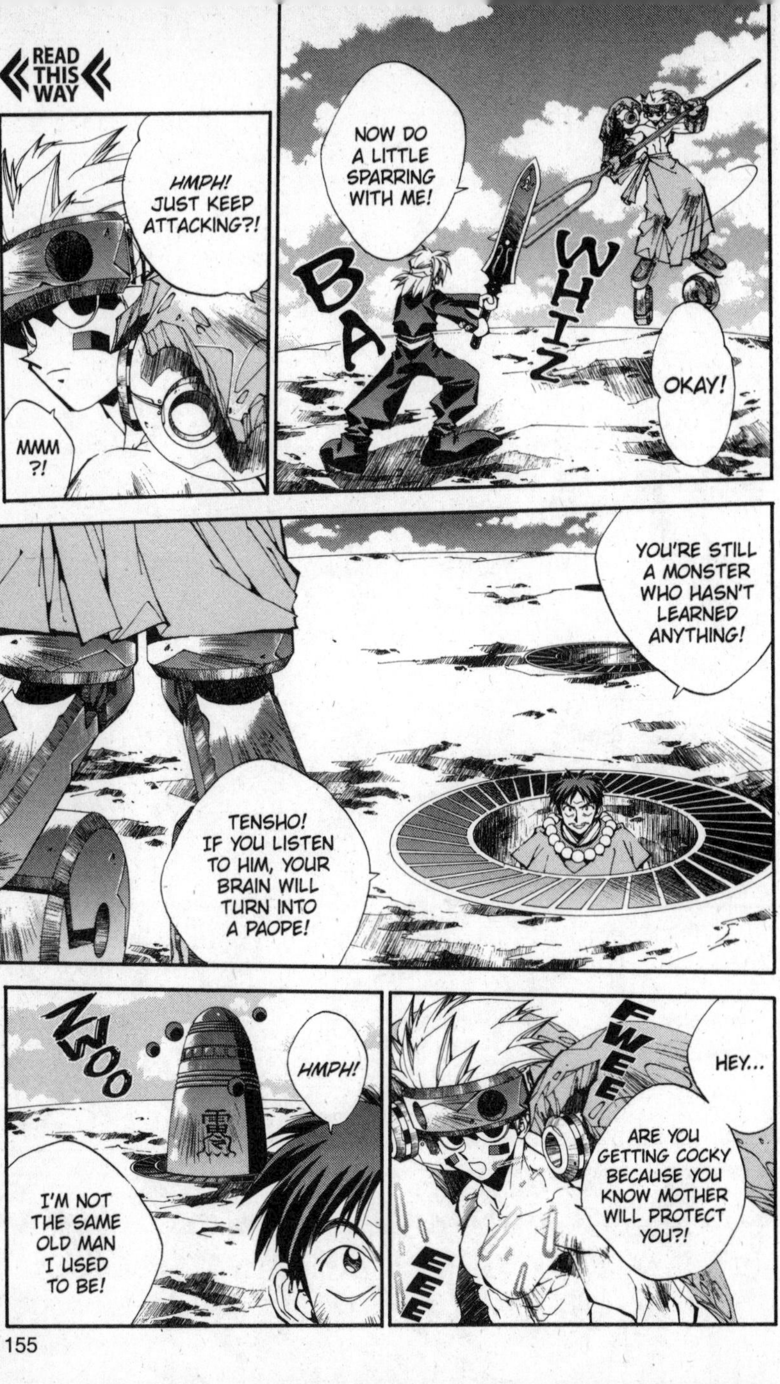

NOW DO A LITTLE SPARRING WITH ME!
BA
WHIZ
OKAY!
HMPH! JUST KEEP ATTACKING?!
MMM ?!
YOU'RE STILL A MONSTER WHO HASN'T LEARNED ANYTHING!
TENSHO! IF YOU LISTEN TO HIM, YOUR BRAIN WILL TURN INTO A PAOPE!
HEY...
FWEE
ARE YOU GETTING COCKY BECAUSE YOU KNOW MOTHER WILL PROTECT YOU?!
EEE
HMPH!
NWOO
I'M NOT THE SAME OLD MAN I USED TO BE!

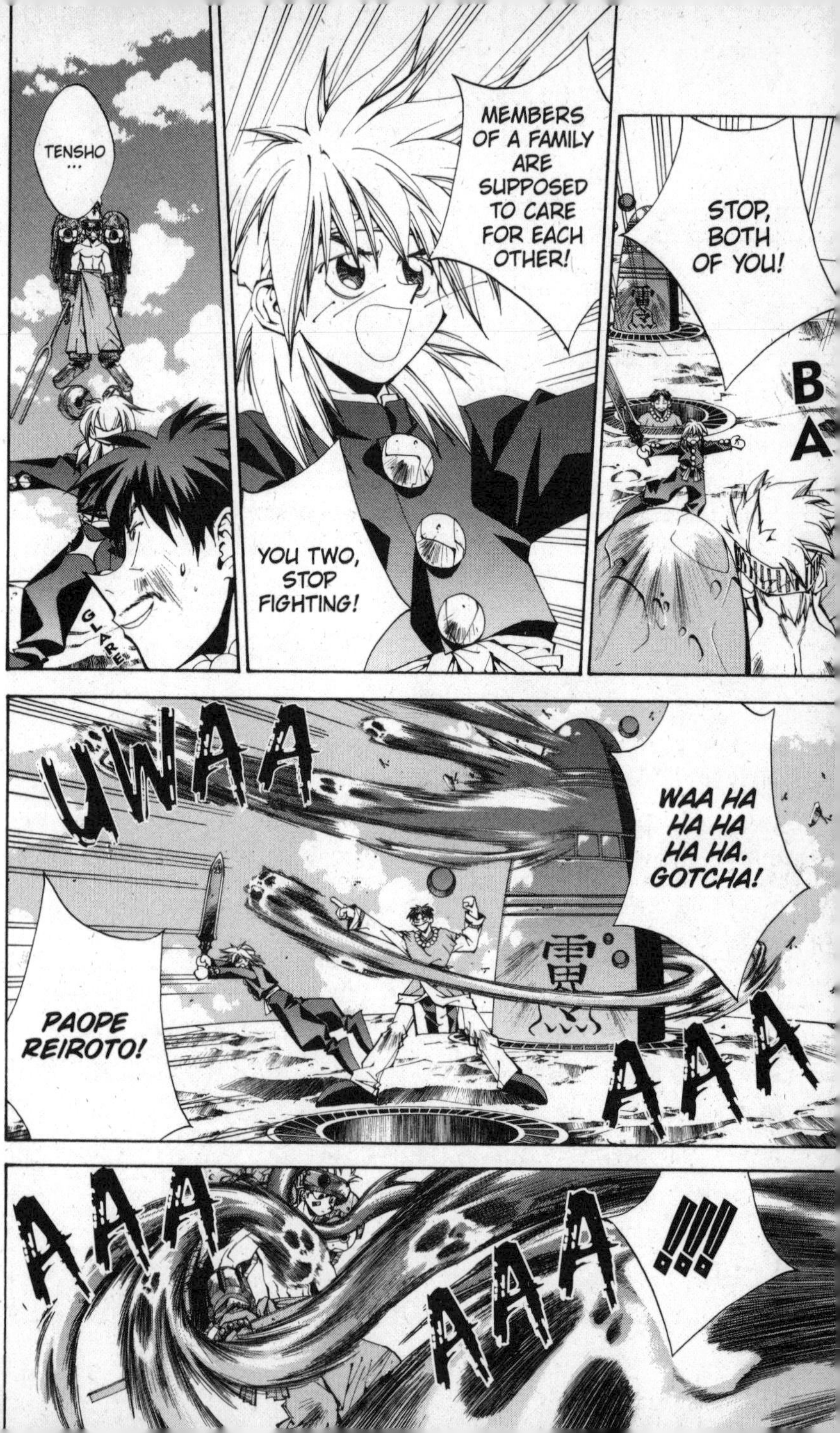
STOP, BOTH OF YOU!
BA
MEMBERS OF A FAMILY ARE SUPPOSED TO CARE FOR EACH OTHER!
YOU TWO, STOP FIGHTING!
TENSHO ...
GLARE
WAA HA HA HA HA HA. GOTCHA!
PAOPE REIROTO!
UWAA
AAA
AAA
AAA!!!!

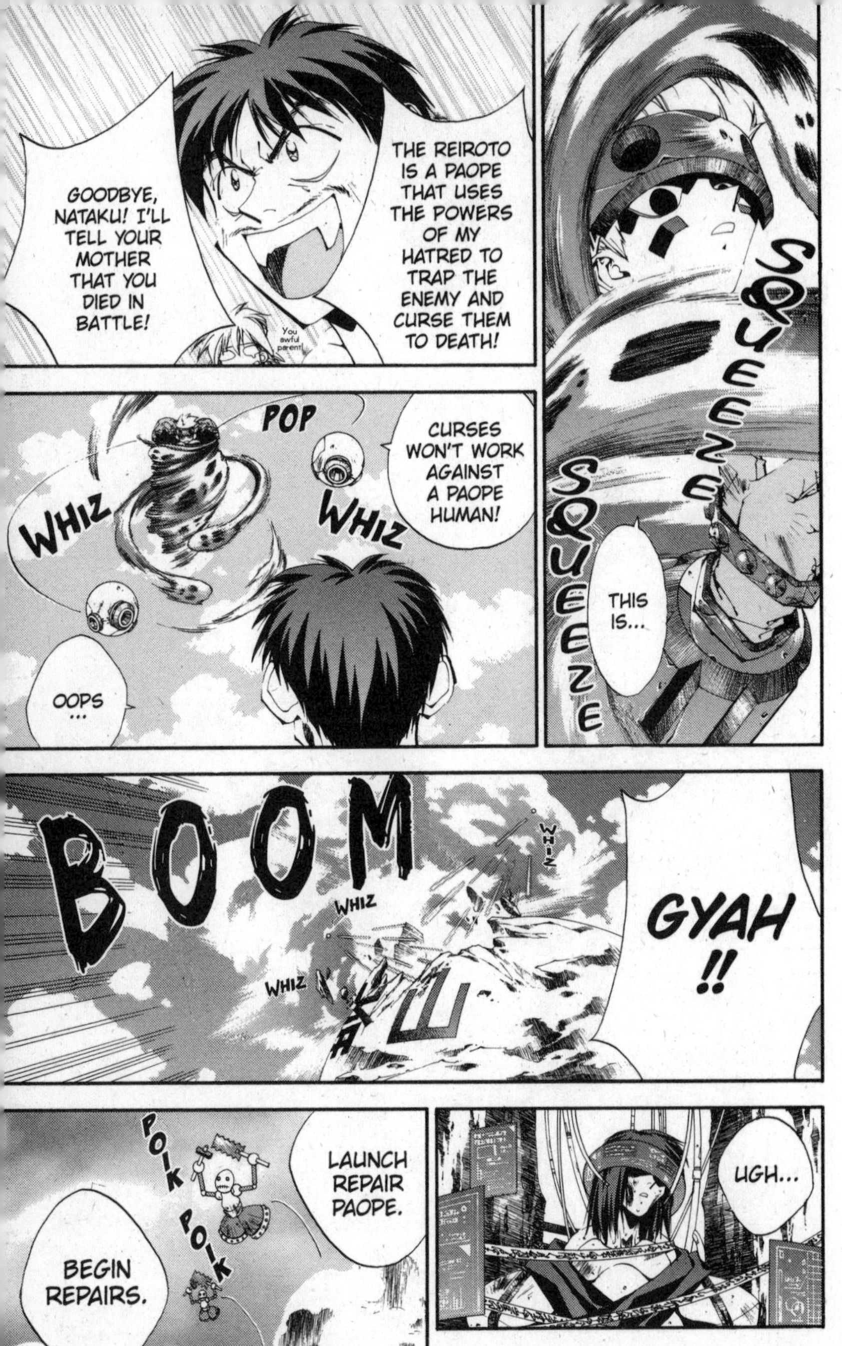

SQUEEZE
SQUEEZE
THIS IS...
GOODBYE, NATAKU! I'LL TELL YOUR MOTHER THAT YOU DIED IN BATTLE!
THE REIROTO IS A PAOPE THAT USES THE POWERS OF MY HATRED TO TRAP THE ENEMY AND CURSE THEM TO DEATH!
You awful parent!
POP
CURSES WON'T WORK AGAINST A PAOPE HUMAN!
WHIZ
WHIZ
OOPS ...
GYAH !!
BOOM
WHIZ
WHIZ
WHIZ
UGH...
LAUNCH REPAIR PAOPE.
POIK POIK
BEGIN REPAIRS.

Episode 2

THE BIRDS, REVISITED

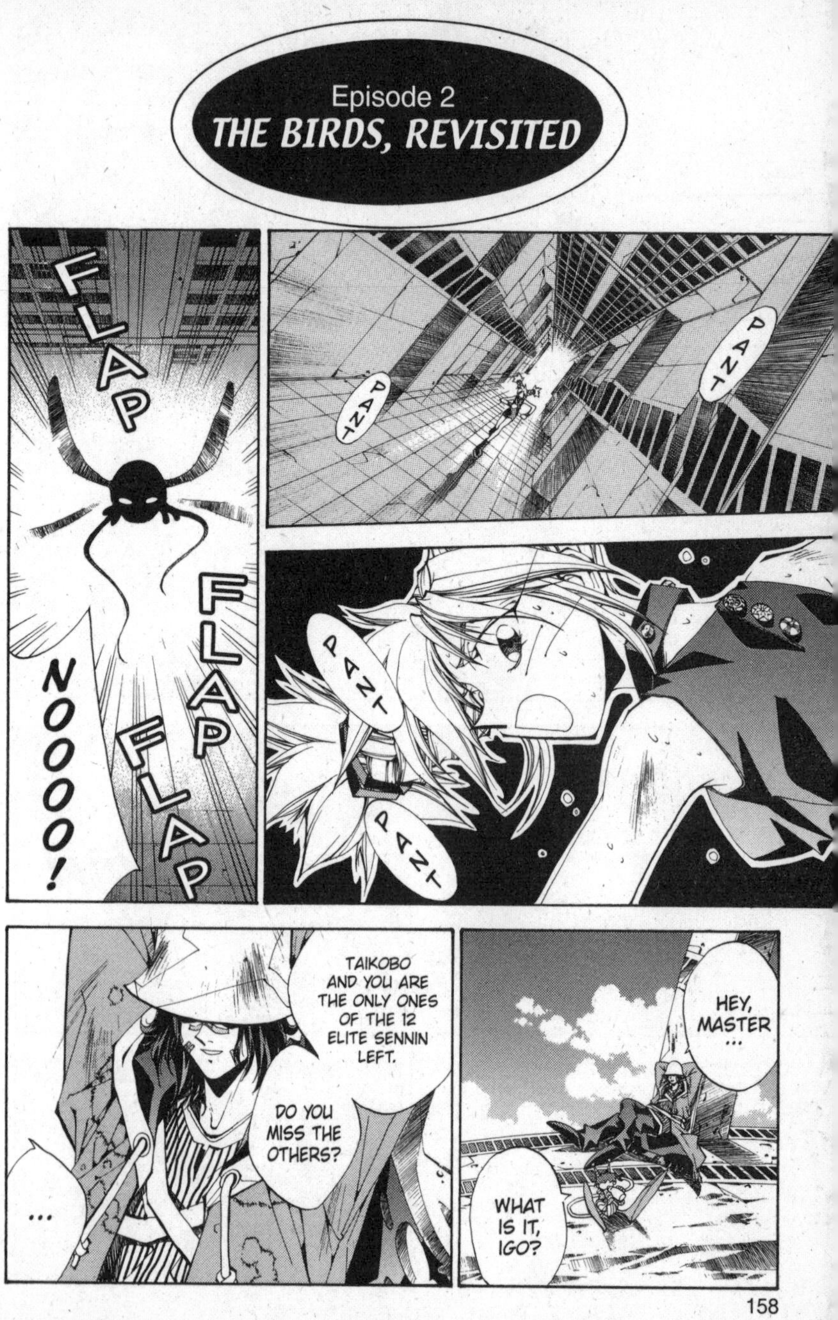
PANT
PANT
PANT
PANT
FLAP
FLAP
FLAP
FLAP
NOOOOO!
HEY, MASTER...
WHAT IS IT, IGO?
TAIKOBO AND YOU ARE THE ONLY ONES OF THE 12 ELITE SENNIN LEFT.
DO YOU MISS THE OTHERS?
...

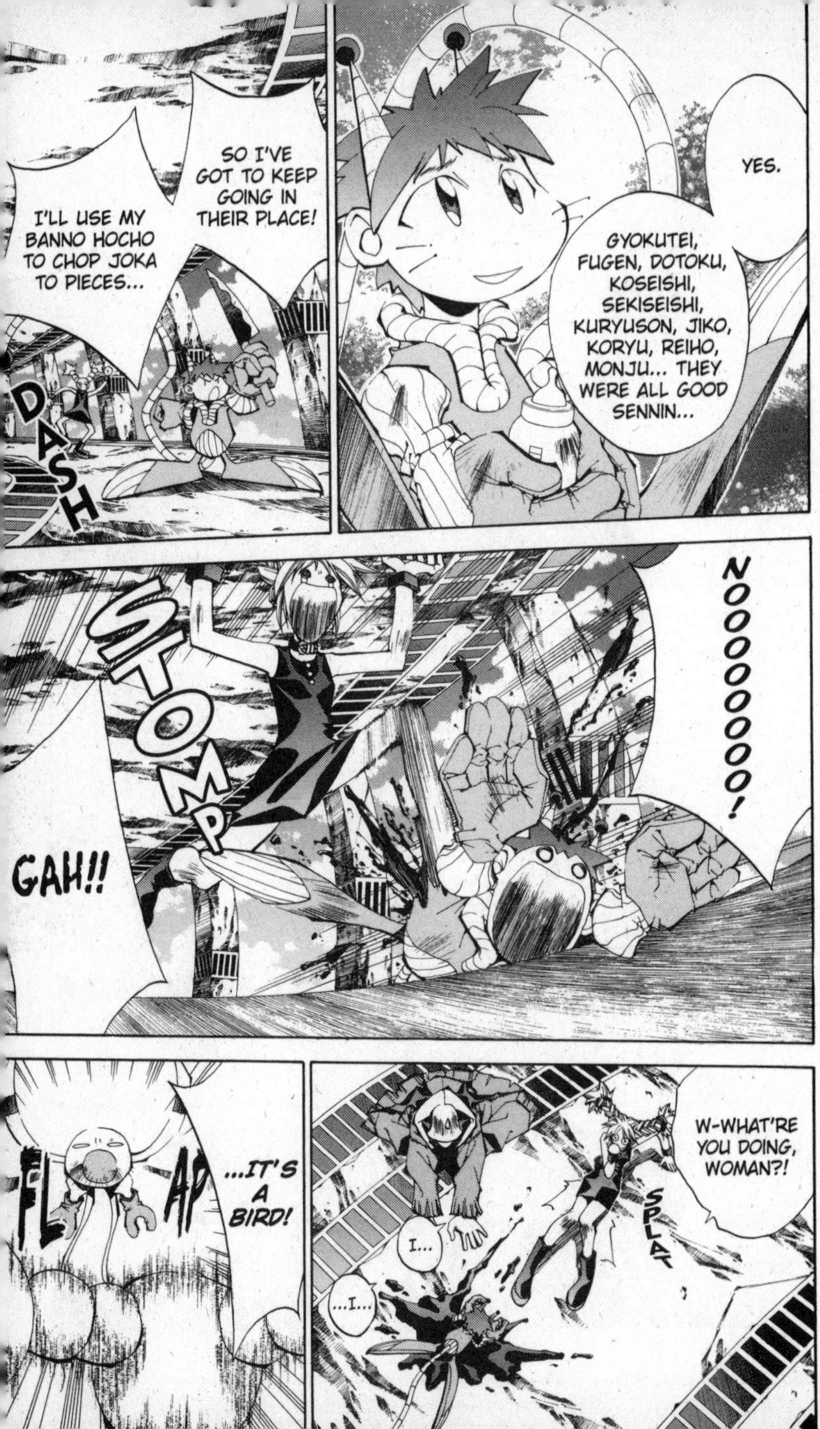
YES.
GYOKUTEI, FUGEN, DOTOKU, KOSEISHI, SEKISEISHI, KURYUSON, JIKO, KORYU, REIHO, MONJU... THEY WERE ALL GOOD SENNIN...
SO I'VE GOT TO KEEP GOING IN THEIR PLACE!
I'LL USE MY BANNO HOCHO TO CHOP JOKA TO PIECES...
DASH
NOOOOOOOOO!
STOMP
GAH!!
W-WHAT'RE YOU DOING, WOMAN?!
SPLAT
I...
...I...
...IT'S A BIRD!
FLAP

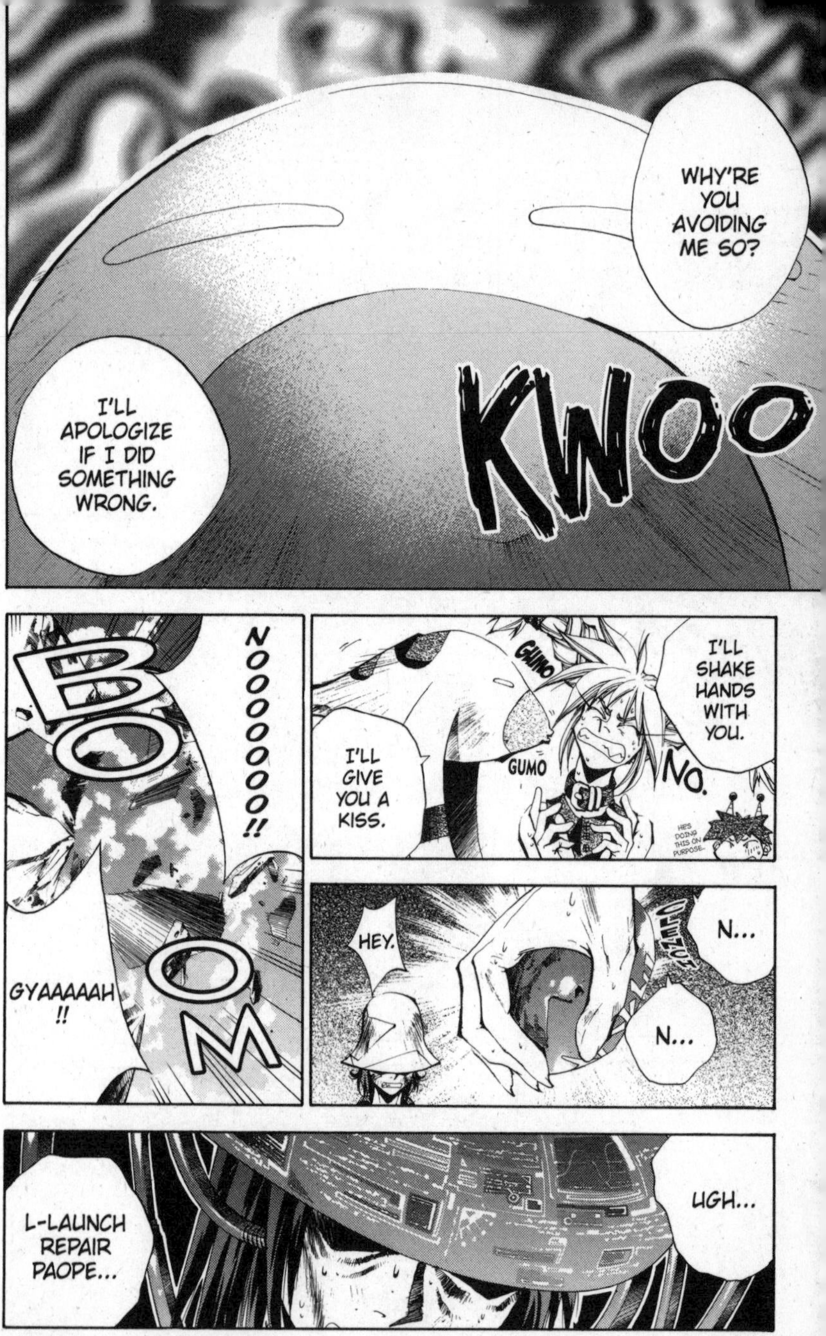
WHY'RE YOU AVOIDING ME SO?
KWOO
I'LL APOLOGIZE IF I DID SOMETHING WRONG.
I'LL SHAKE HANDS WITH YOU.
GUMO
GUMO
NO.
HE'S DOING THIS ON PURPOSE...
I'LL GIVE YOU A KISS.
N...
N...
HEY.
NOOOOOOOO!!
BOOM
GYAAAAAH!!
UGH...
L-LAUNCH REPAIR PAOPE...

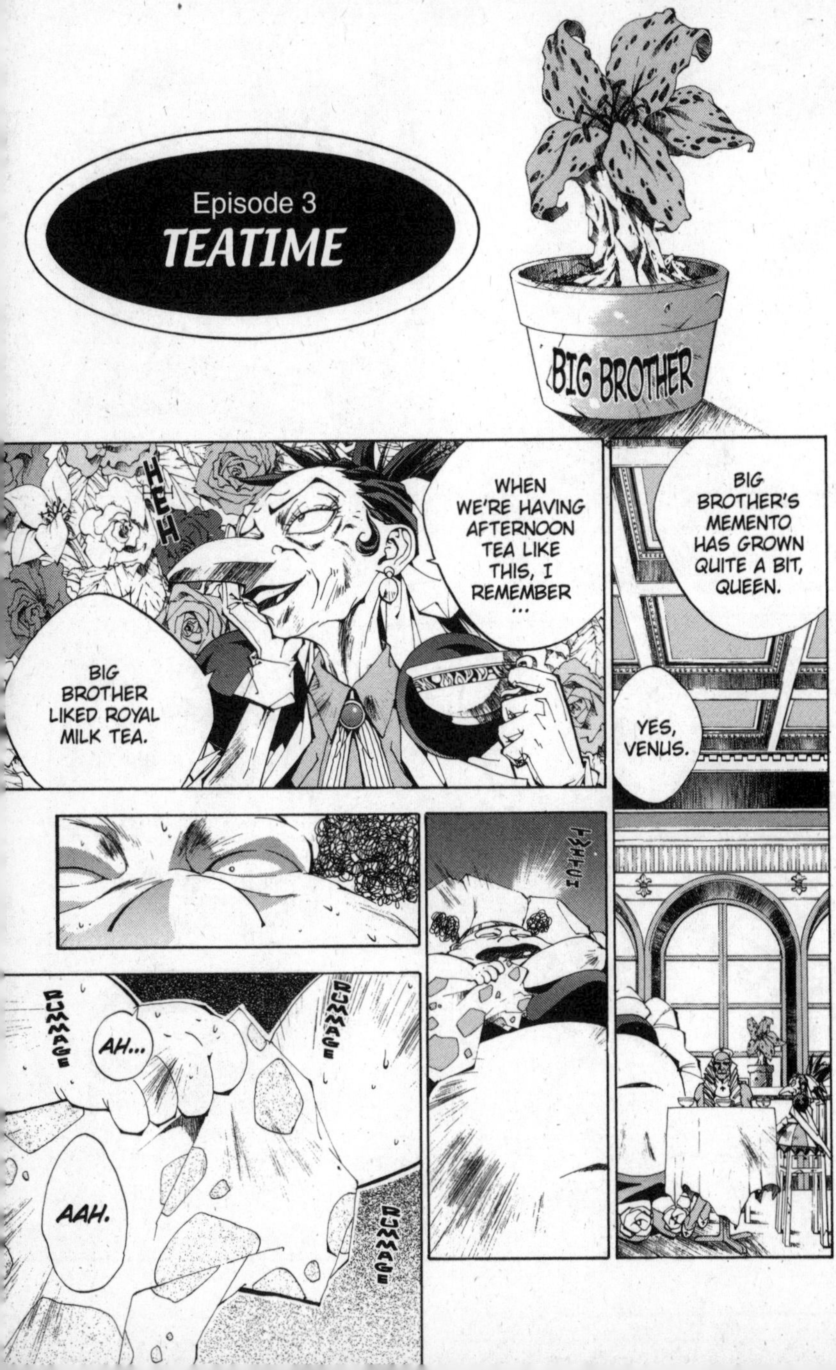
Episode 3
TEATIME
BIG BROTHER
BIG BROTHER'S MEMENTO HAS GROWN QUITE A BIT, QUEEN.
YES, VENUS.
WHEN WE'RE HAVING AFTERNOON TEA LIKE THIS, I REMEMBER ...
HEH
BIG BROTHER LIKED ROYAL MILK TEA.
TWITCH
RUMMAGE
AH...
RUMMAGE
AAH.
RUMMAGE

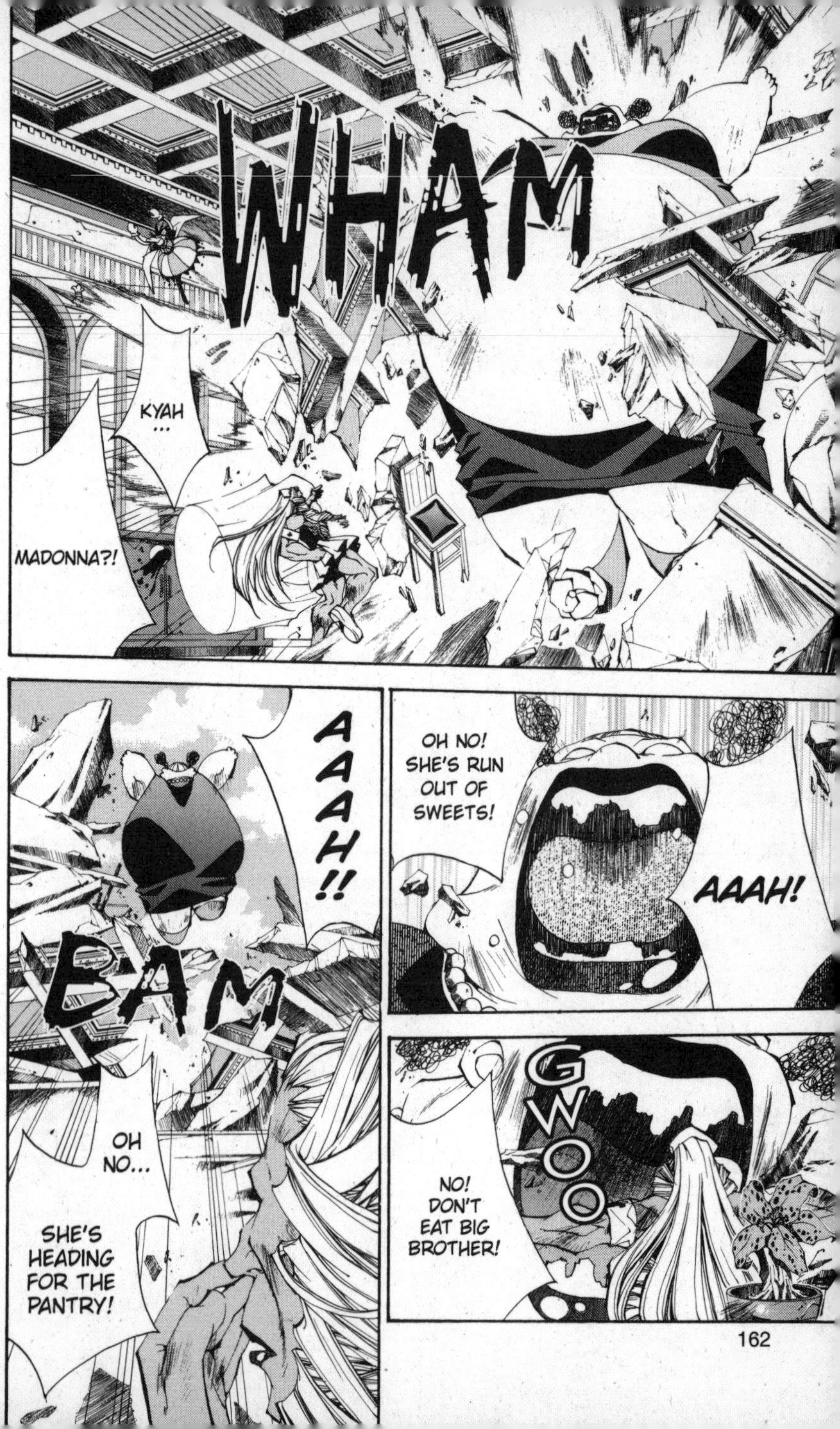
WHAM
KYAH ...
MADONNA?!
OH NO! SHE'S RUN OUT OF SWEETS!
AAAH!
GWOO
NO! DON'T EAT BIG BROTHER!
AAAAH!!
BAM
OH NO...
SHE'S HEADING FOR THE PANTRY!

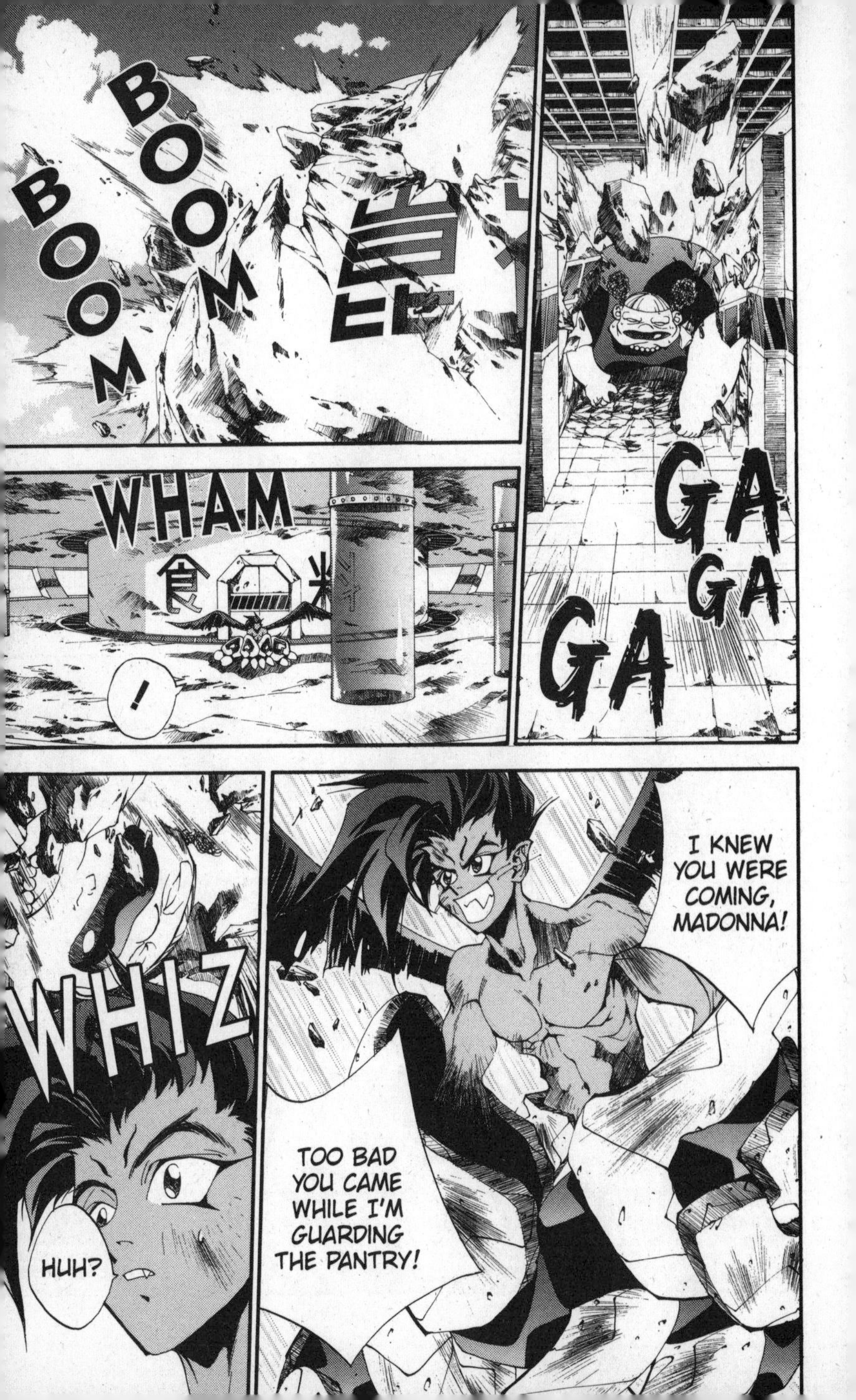
BOOOM
BOOOM
GA GA GA
WHAM
!
WHIZ
HUH?
I KNEW YOU WERE COMING, MADONNA!
TOO BAD YOU CAME WHILE I'M GUARDING THE PANTRY!

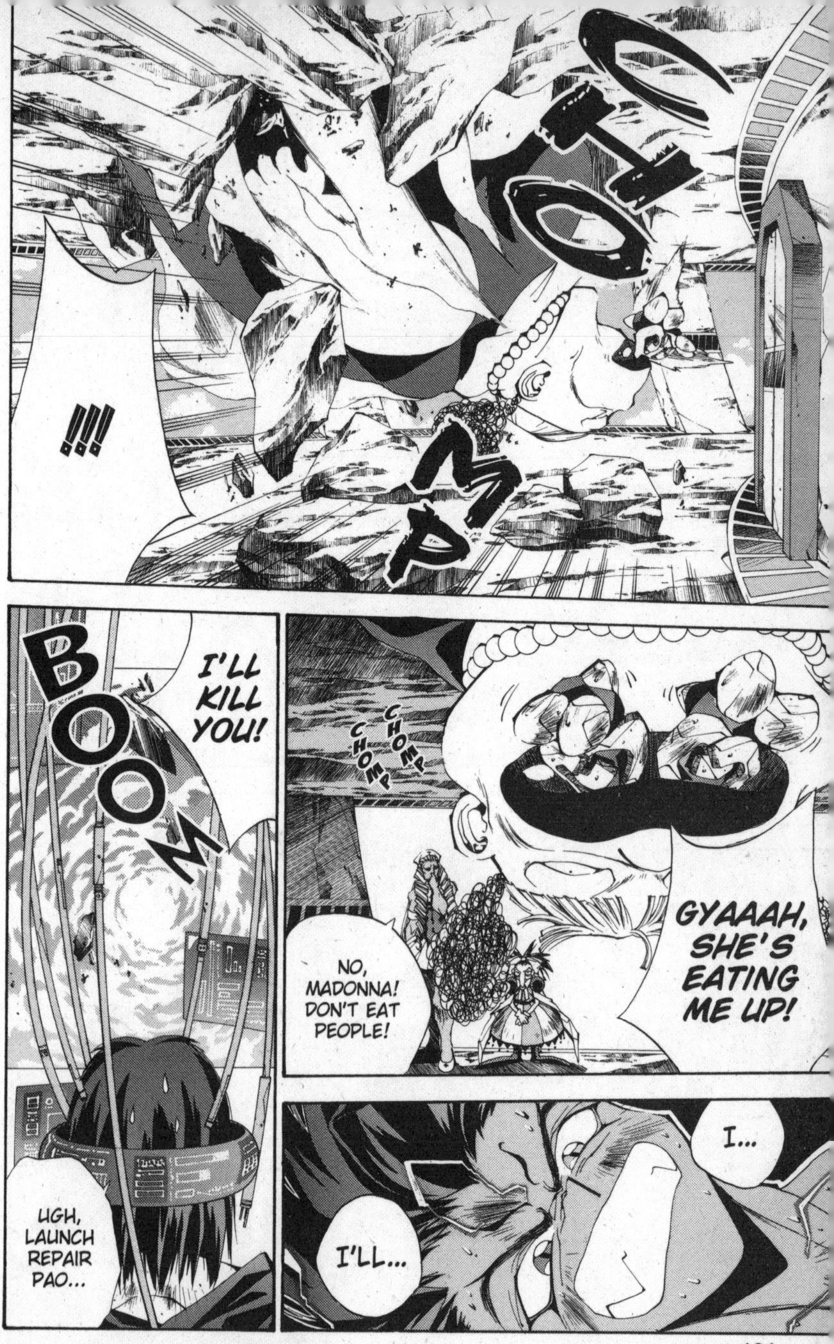
CHOMP
!!!
GYAAAH, SHE'S EATING ME UP!
CHOMP CHOMP
NO, MADONNA! DON'T EAT PEOPLE!
I'LL KILL YOU!
BOOM
I...
I'LL...
UGH, LAUNCH REPAIR PAO...

READ THIS WAY

Last Episode
THE MUMMY

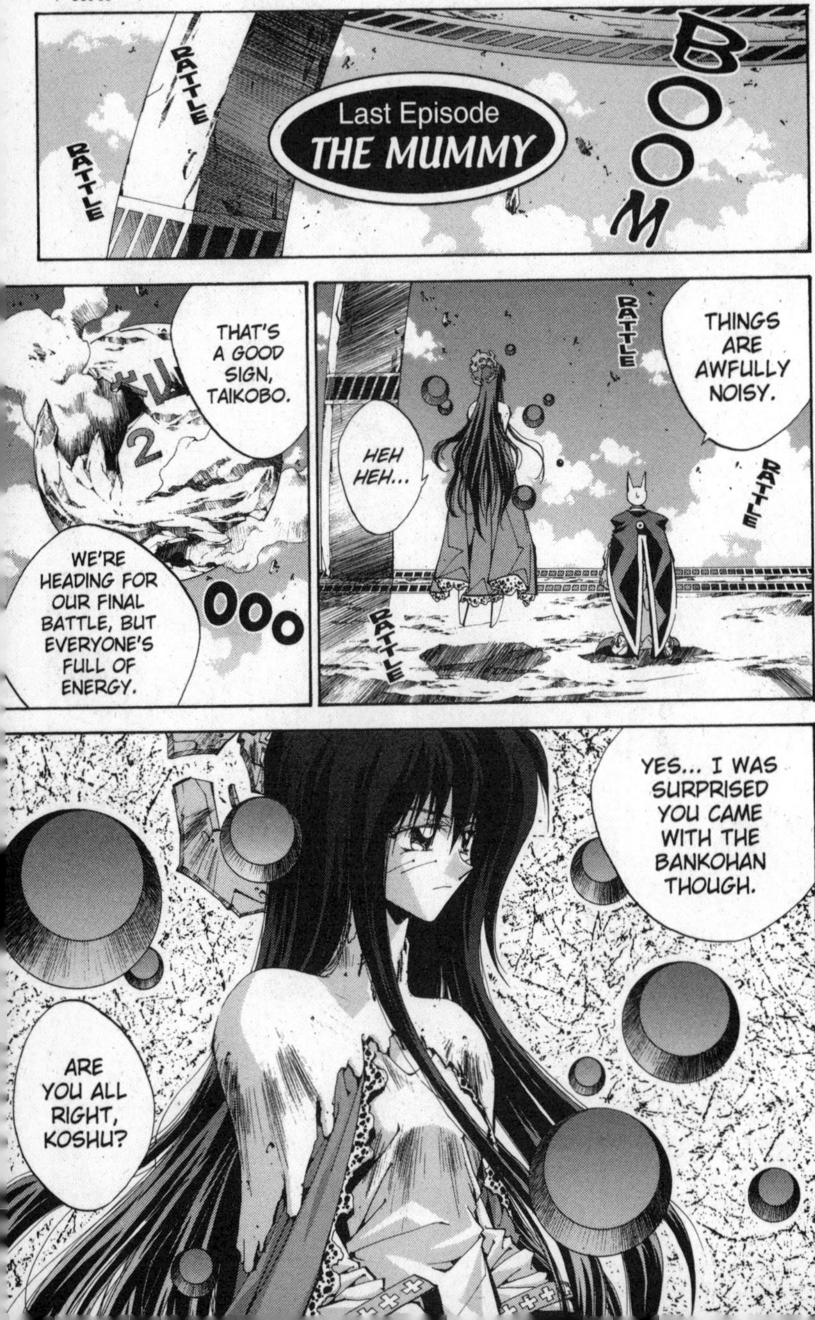
BOOM
RATTLE
RATTLE
Last Episode
THE MUMMY
RATTLE
THINGS ARE AWFULLY NOISY.
HEH HEH...
RATTLE
RATTLE
THAT'S A GOOD SIGN, TAIKOBO.
WE'RE HEADING FOR OUR FINAL BATTLE, BUT EVERYONE'S FULL OF ENERGY.
OOO
YES... I WAS SURPRISED YOU CAME WITH THE BANKOHAN THOUGH.
ARE YOU ALL RIGHT, KOSHU?

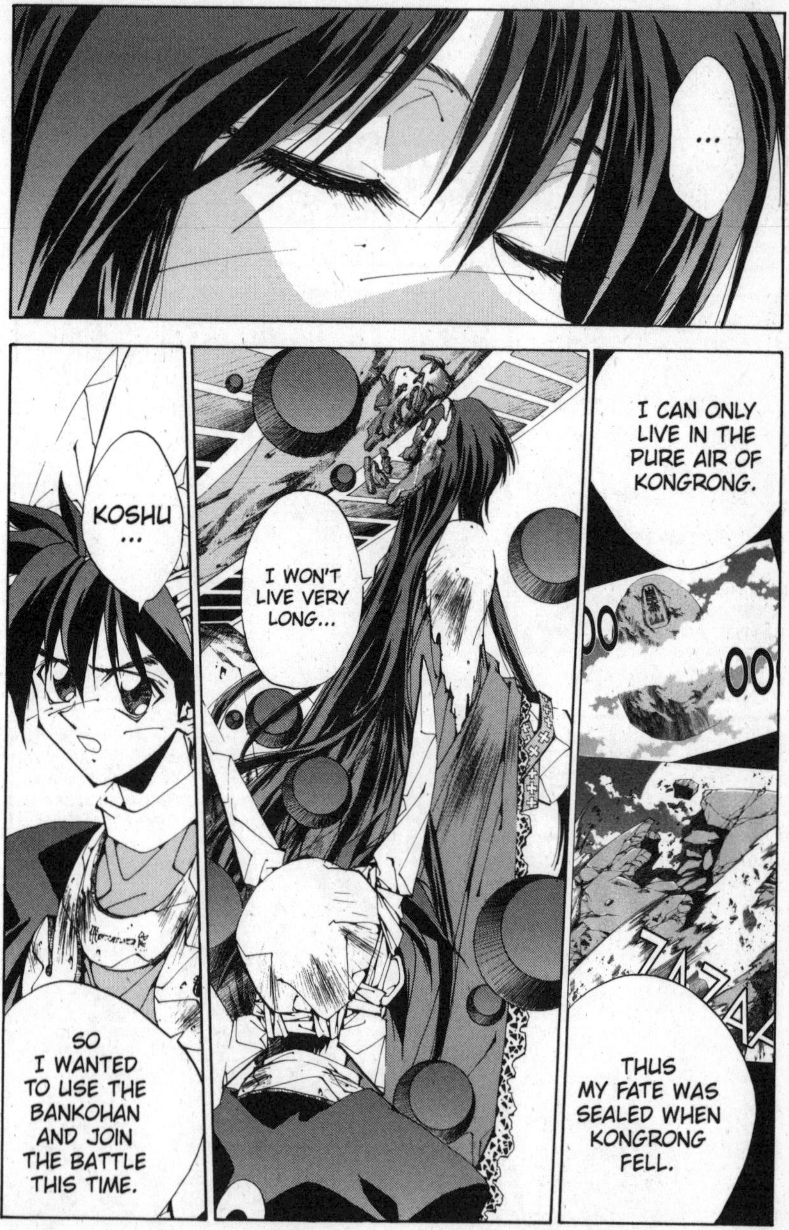
...
I CAN ONLY LIVE IN THE PURE AIR OF KONGRONG.
THUS MY FATE WAS SEALED WHEN KONGRONG FELL.
I WON'T LIVE VERY LONG...
KOSHU ...
SO I WANTED TO USE THE BANKOHAN AND JOIN THE BATTLE THIS TIME.

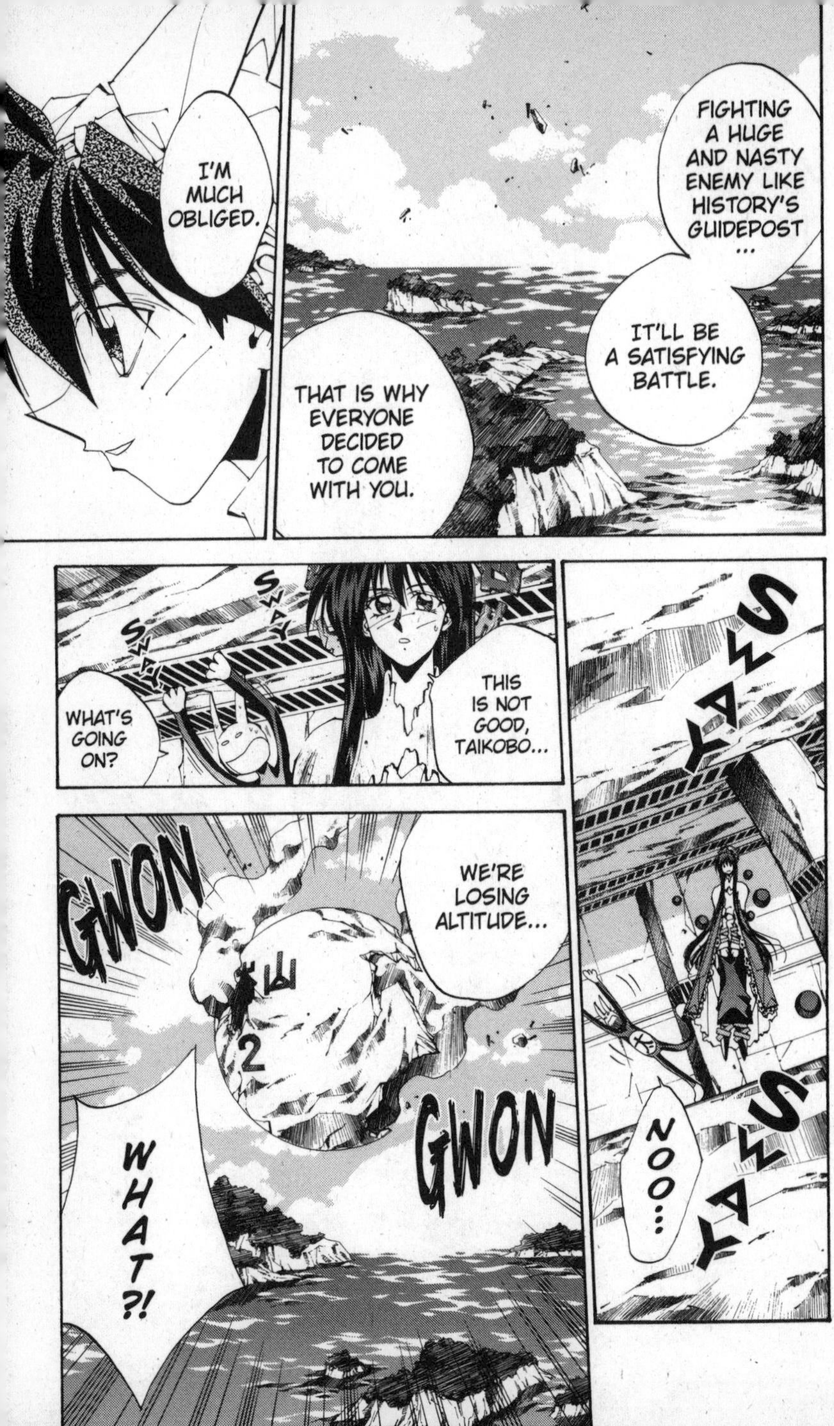

FIGHTING A HUGE AND NASTY ENEMY LIKE HISTORY'S GUIDEPOST...
IT'LL BE A SATISFYING BATTLE.
THAT IS WHY EVERYONE DECIDED TO COME WITH YOU.
I'M MUCH OBLIGED.
SWAY
SWAY
NOO...
SWAY
SWAY
THIS IS NOT GOOD, TAIKOBO...
WHAT'S GOING ON?
WE'RE LOSING ALTITUDE...
GWON
GWON
WHAT?!

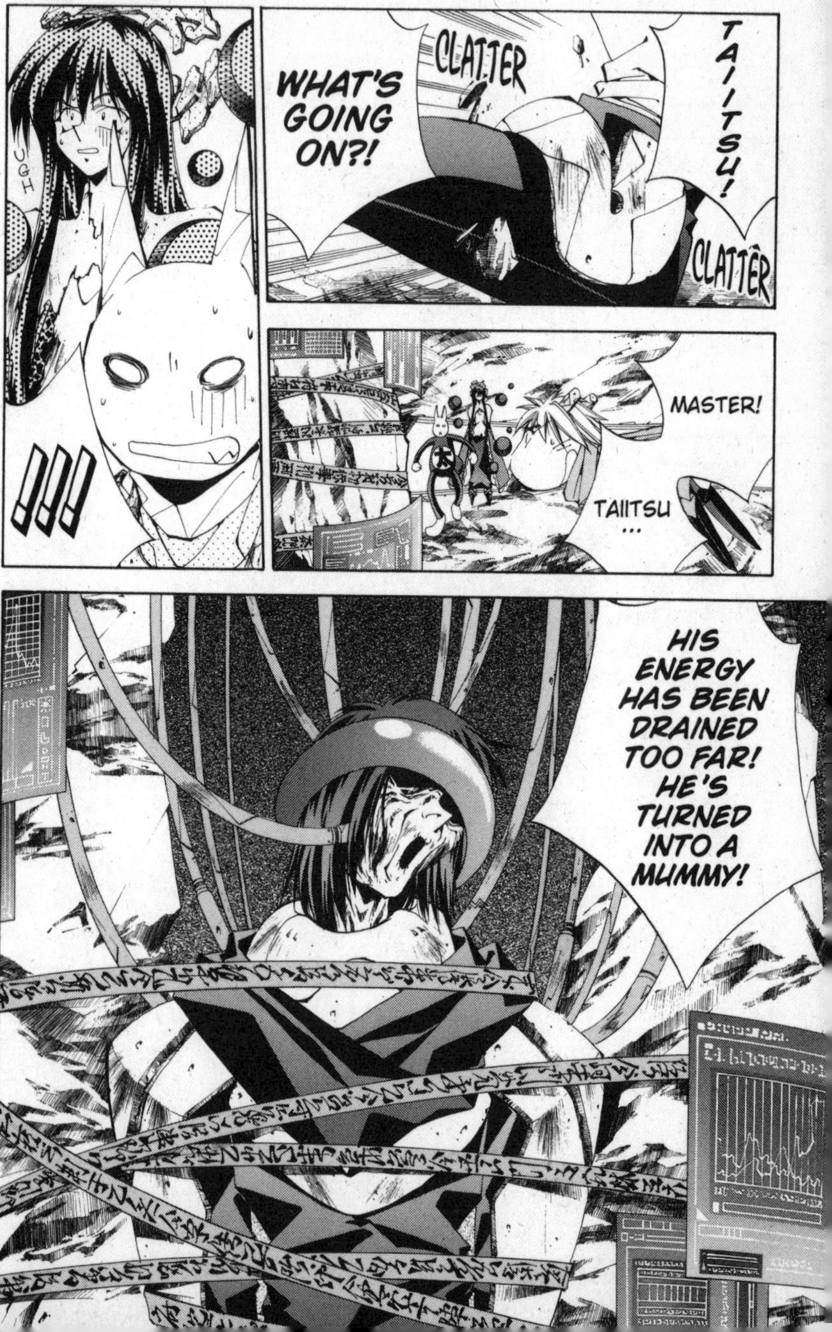
TAIITSU!
CLATTER
WHAT'S GOING ON?!
CLATTER
UGH
!!!
MASTER!
TAIITSU ...
HIS ENERGY HAS BEEN DRAINED TOO FAR! HE'S TURNED INTO A MUMMY!

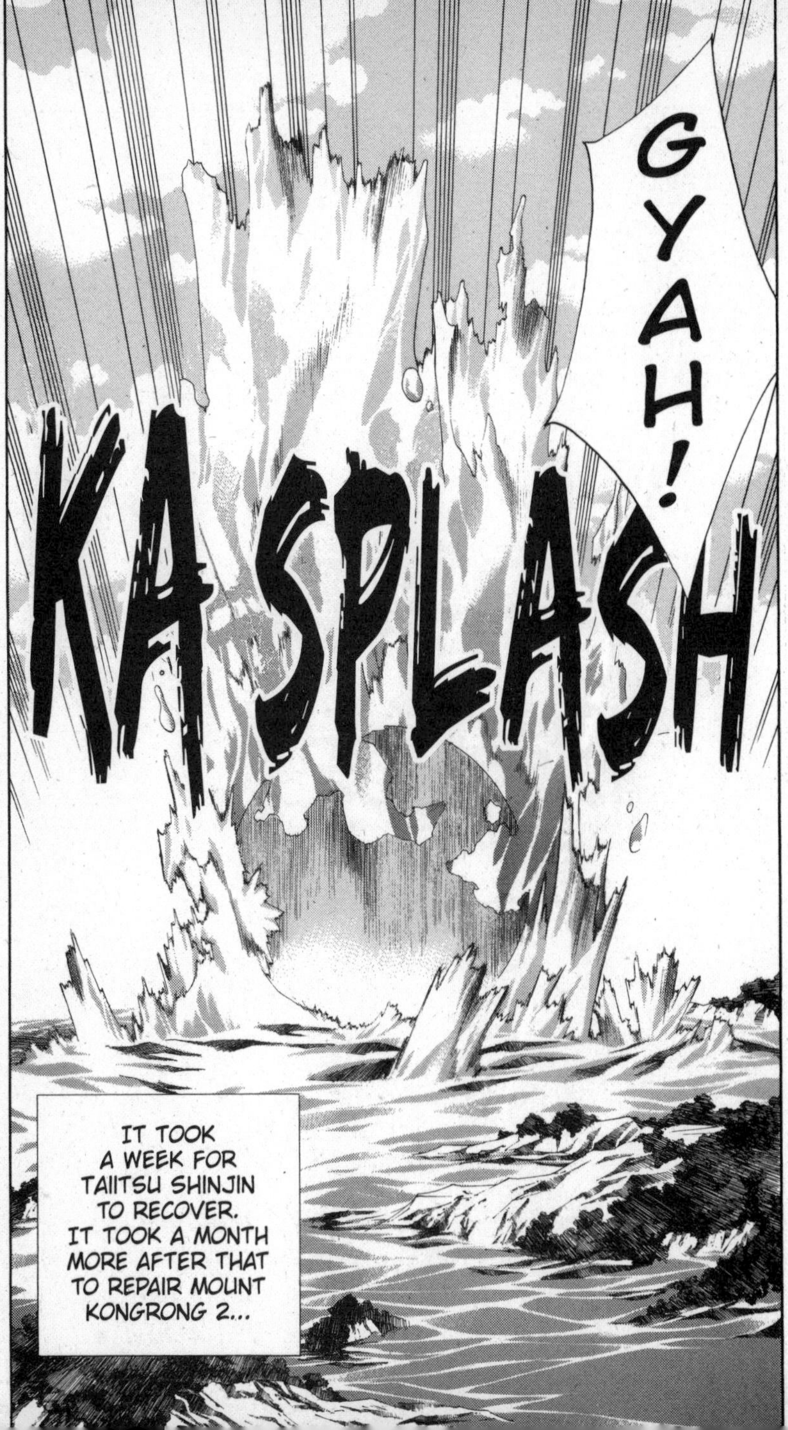
GYAH!
KASPLASH
IT TOOK A WEEK FOR TAIITSU SHINJIN TO RECOVER. IT TOOK A MONTH MORE AFTER THAT TO REPAIR MOUNT KONGRONG 2...

封神演義

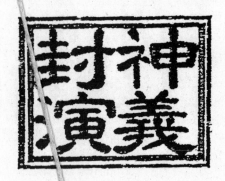

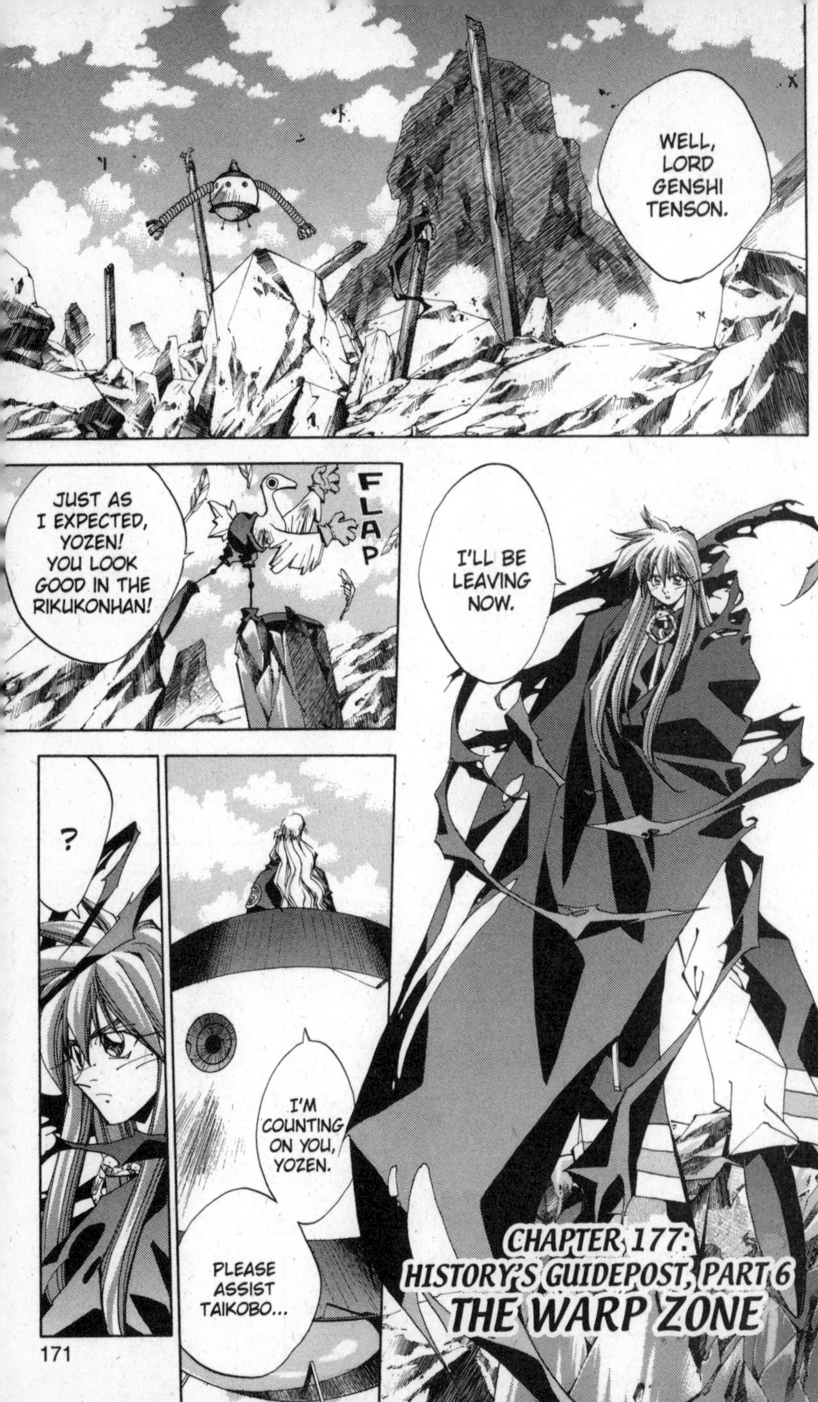
WELL, LORD GENSHI TENSON.
I'LL BE LEAVING NOW.
FLAP
JUST AS I EXPECTED, YOZEN! YOU LOOK GOOD IN THE RIKUKONHAN!
?
I'M COUNTING ON YOU, YOZEN.
PLEASE ASSIST TAIKOBO...
CHAPTER 177:
HISTORY'S GUIDEPOST, PART 6
THE WARP ZONE

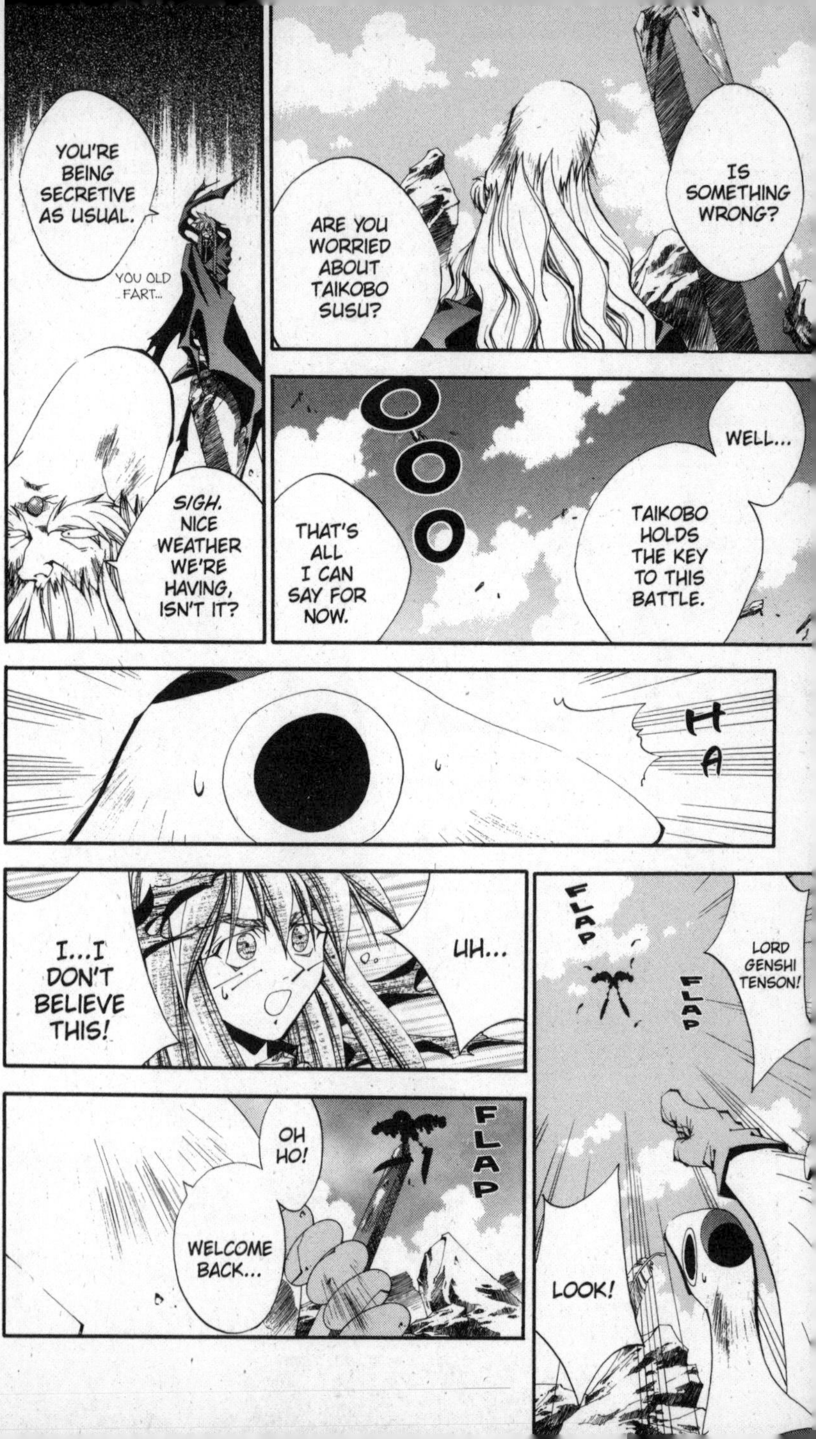
IS SOMETHING WRONG?
ARE YOU WORRIED ABOUT TAIKOBO SUSU?
YOU'RE BEING SECRETIVE AS USUAL.
YOU OLD FART...
WELL...
TAIKOBO HOLDS THE KEY TO THIS BATTLE.
THAT'S ALL I CAN SAY FOR NOW.
OOO
SIGH. NICE WEATHER WE'RE HAVING, ISN'T IT?
HA
LORD GENSHI TENSON!
FLAP
FLAP
LOOK!
UH...
I...I DON'T BELIEVE THIS!
FLAP
OH HO!
WELCOME BACK...

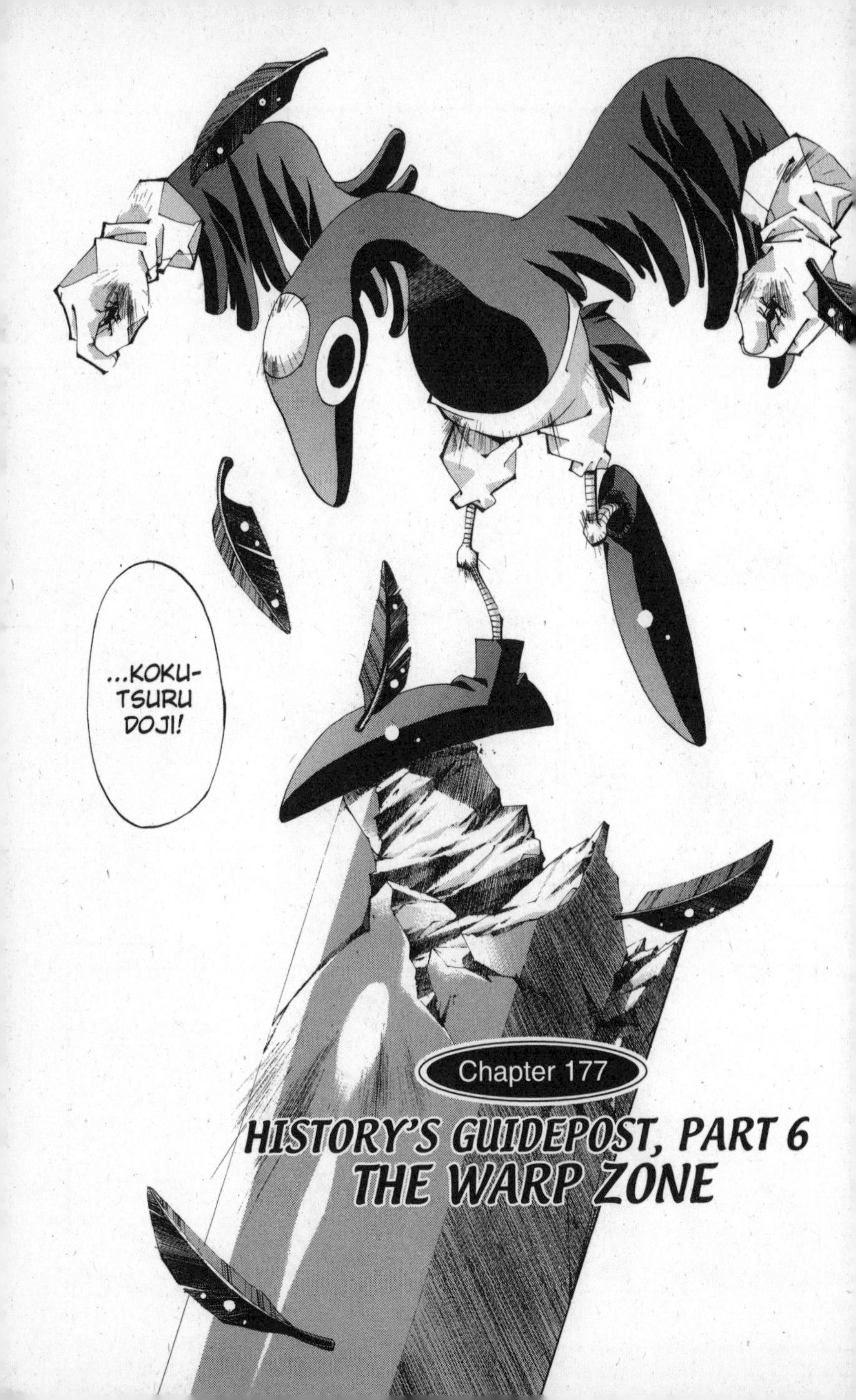
...KOKU-TSURU DOJI!
Chapter 177
HISTORY'S GUIDEPOST, PART 6
THE WARP ZONE

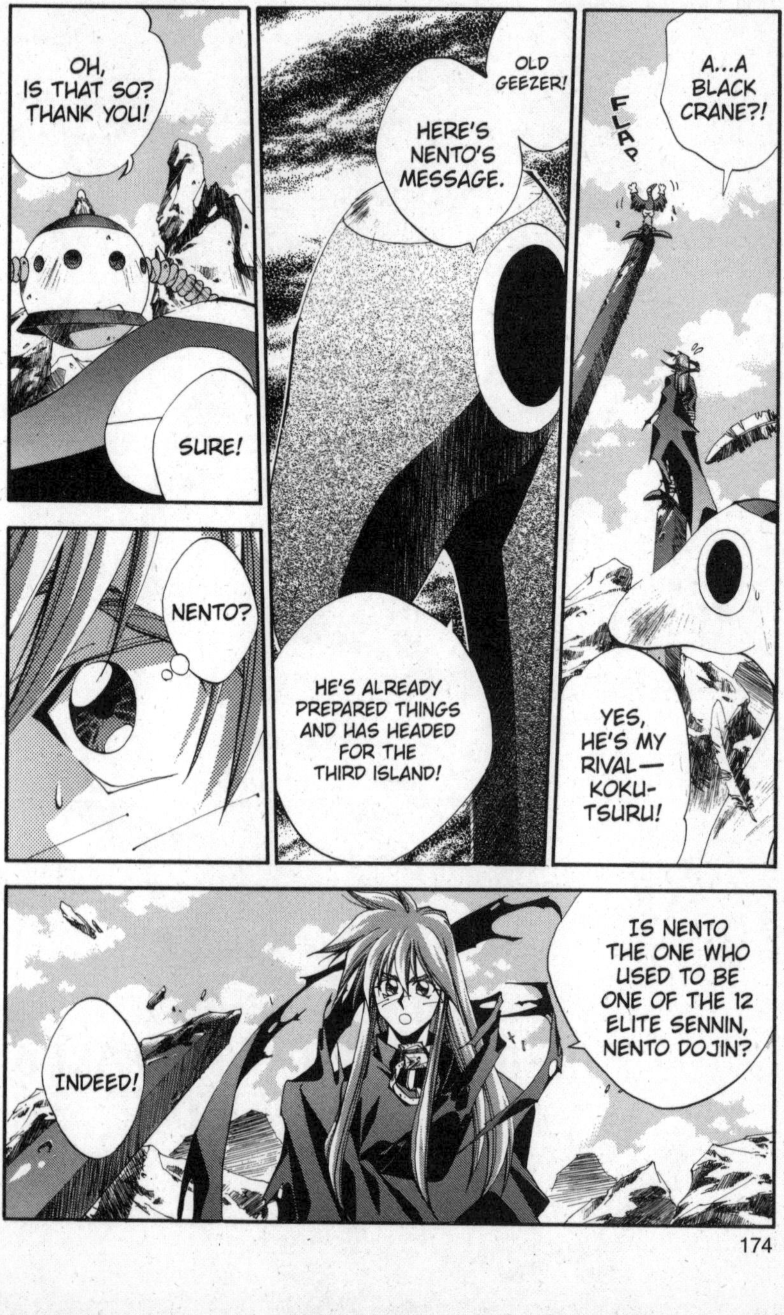
A...A BLACK CRANE?!
FLAP
YES, HE'S MY RIVAL—KOKU-TSURU!
OLD GEEZER!
HERE'S NENTO'S MESSAGE.
HE'S ALREADY PREPARED THINGS AND HAS HEADED FOR THE THIRD ISLAND!
OH, IS THAT SO? THANK YOU!
SURE!
NENTO?
IS NENTO THE ONE WHO USED TO BE ONE OF THE 12 ELITE SENNIN, NENTO DOJIN?
INDEED!

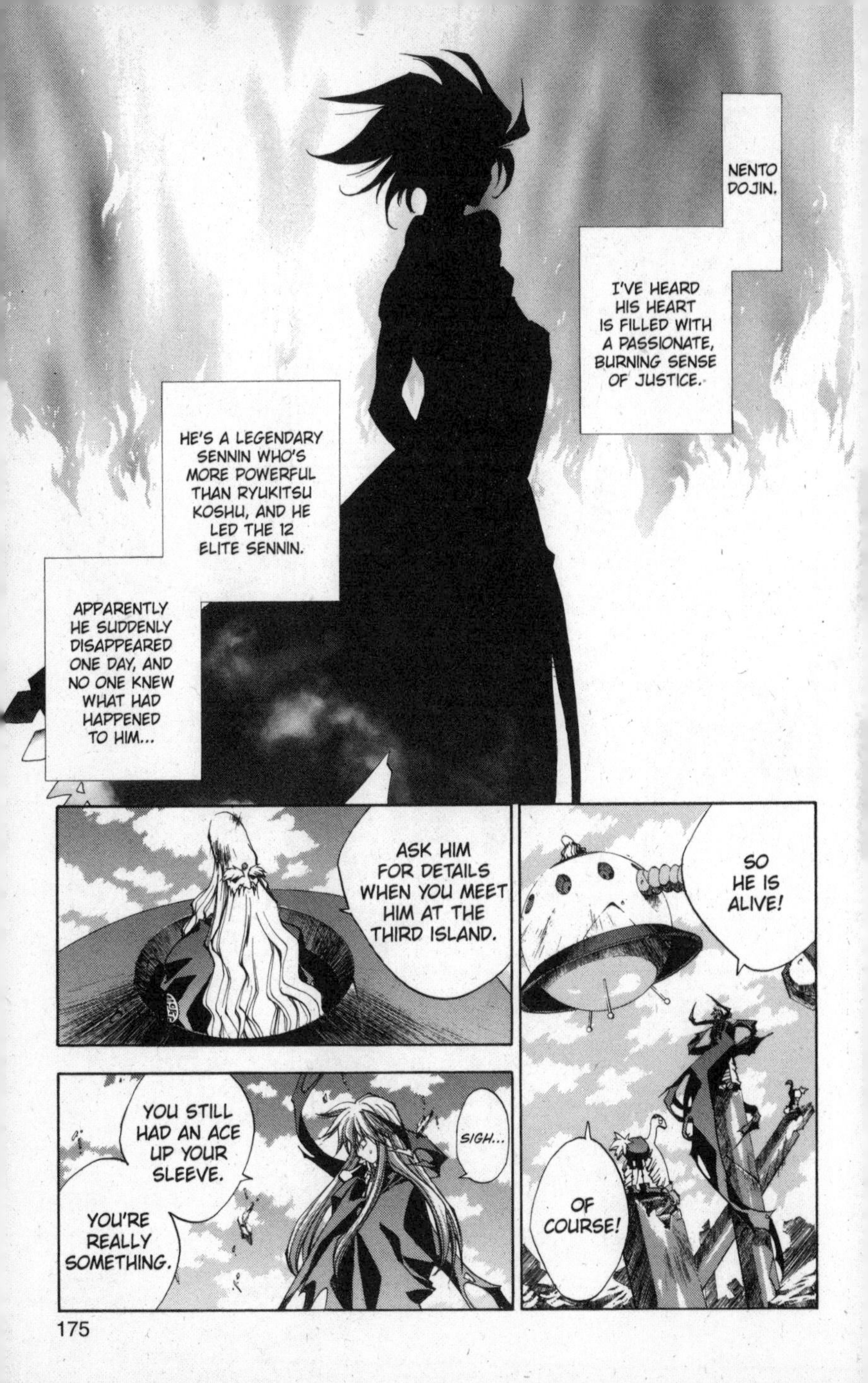
NENTO DOJIN.
I'VE HEARD HIS HEART IS FILLED WITH A PASSIONATE, BURNING SENSE OF JUSTICE.
HE'S A LEGENDARY SENNIN WHO'S MORE POWERFUL THAN RYUKITSU KOSHU, AND HE LED THE 12 ELITE SENNIN.
APPARENTLY HE SUDDENLY DISAPPEARED ONE DAY, AND NO ONE KNEW WHAT HAD HAPPENED TO HIM...
ASK HIM FOR DETAILS WHEN YOU MEET HIM AT THE THIRD ISLAND.
SO HE IS ALIVE!
OF COURSE!
SIGH...
YOU STILL HAD AN ACE UP YOUR SLEEVE.
YOU'RE REALLY SOMETHING.

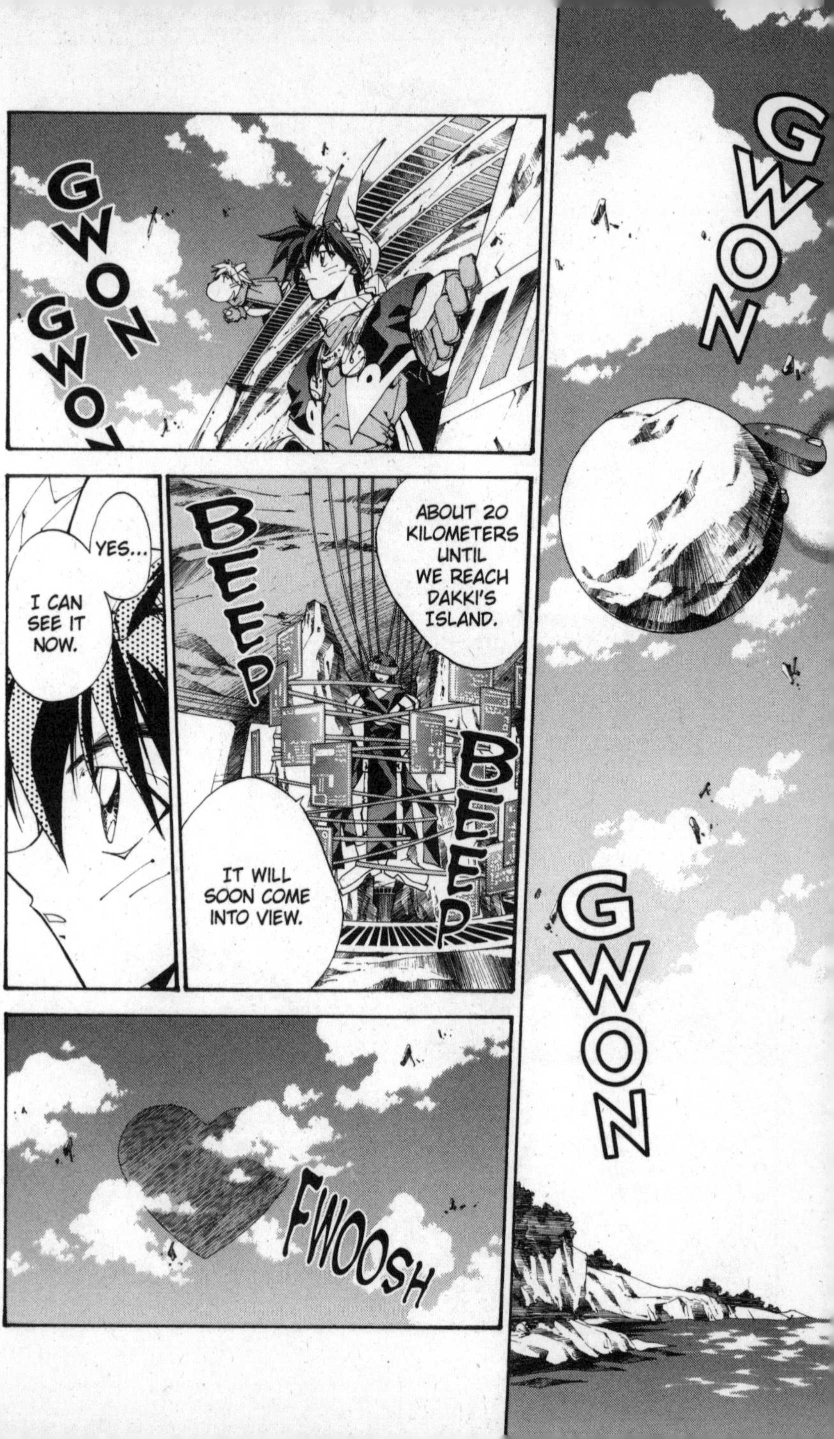
GWON
GWON
GWON
GWON
GWON
ABOUT 20 KILOMETERS UNTIL WE REACH DAKKI'S ISLAND.
BEEP
BEEP
IT WILL SOON COME INTO VIEW.
YES...
I CAN SEE IT NOW.
FWOOSH

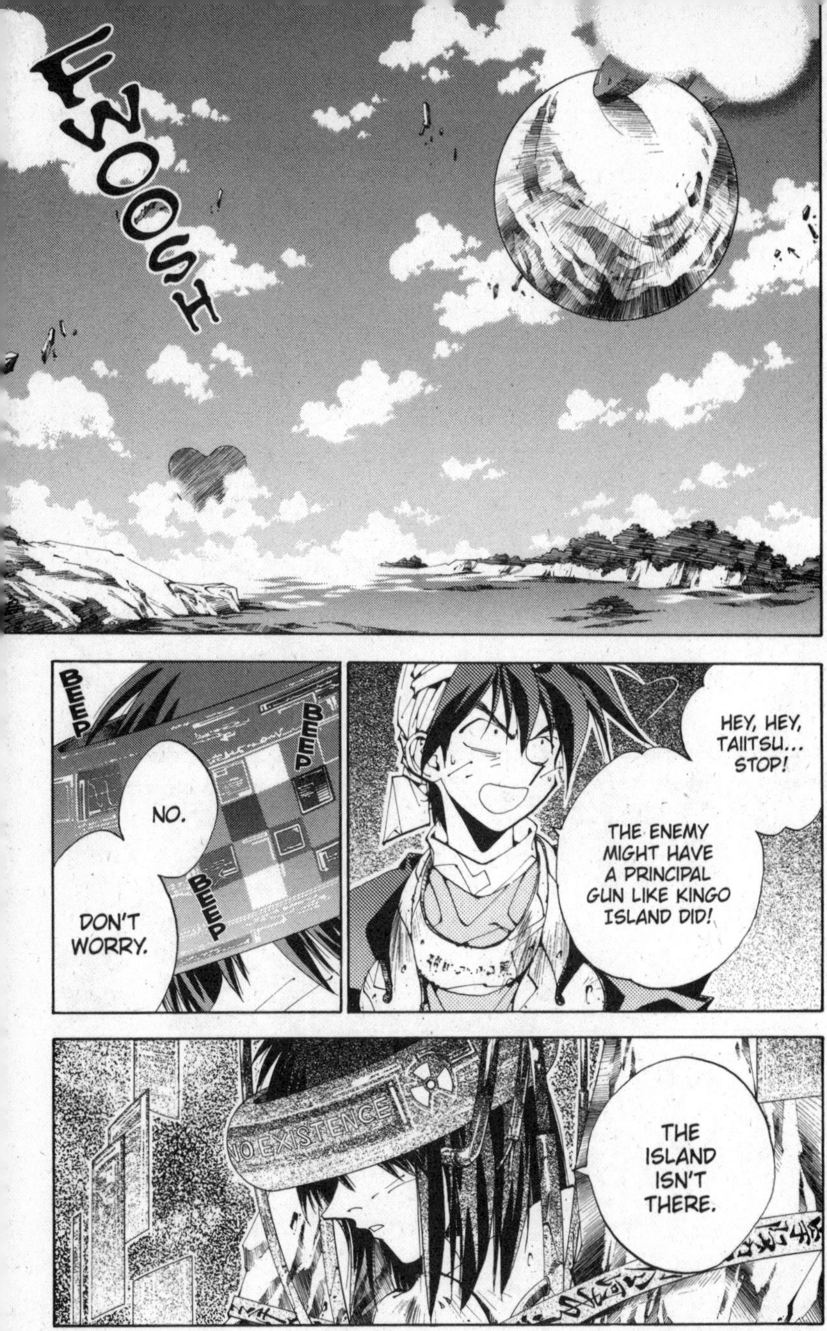
FWOOSH
HEY, HEY, TAIITSU... STOP!
THE ENEMY MIGHT HAVE A PRINCIPAL GUN LIKE KINGO ISLAND DID!
BEEP
BEEP
BEEP
NO.
DON'T WORRY.
THE ISLAND ISN'T THERE.
NO EXISTENCE

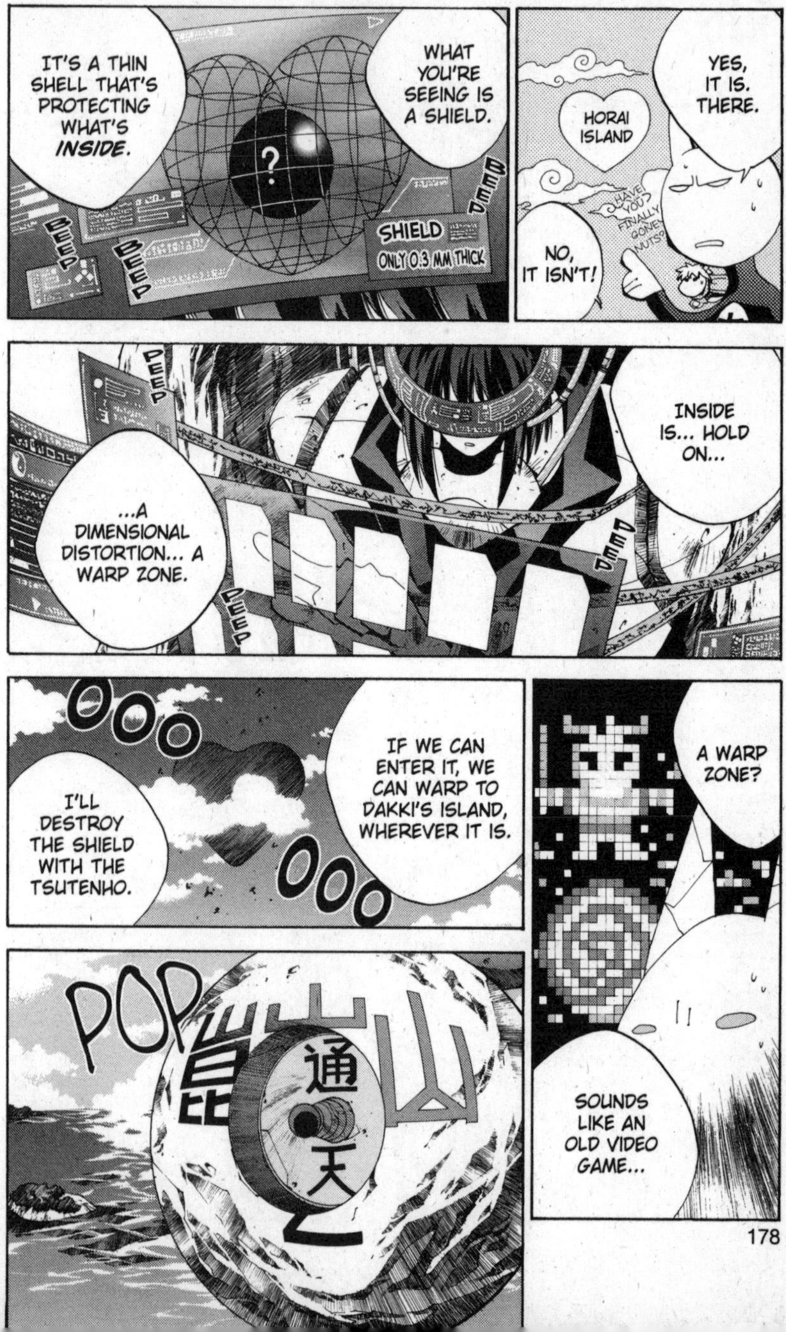
YES, IT IS. THERE.
HORAI ISLAND
HAVE YOU FINALLY GONE NUTS?
NO, IT ISN'T!
WHAT YOU'RE SEEING IS A SHIELD.
IT'S A THIN SHELL THAT'S PROTECTING WHAT'S *INSIDE*.
BEEP
BEEP
BEEP
SHIELD
ONLY 0.3 MM THICK
INSIDE IS... HOLD ON...
...A DIMENSIONAL DISTORTION... A WARP ZONE.
PEEP
PEEP
PEEP
A WARP ZONE?
SOUNDS LIKE AN OLD VIDEO GAME...
IF WE CAN ENTER IT, WE CAN WARP TO DAKKI'S ISLAND, WHEREVER IT IS.
I'LL DESTROY THE SHIELD WITH THE TSUTENHO.
OOO
OOO
POP
通天

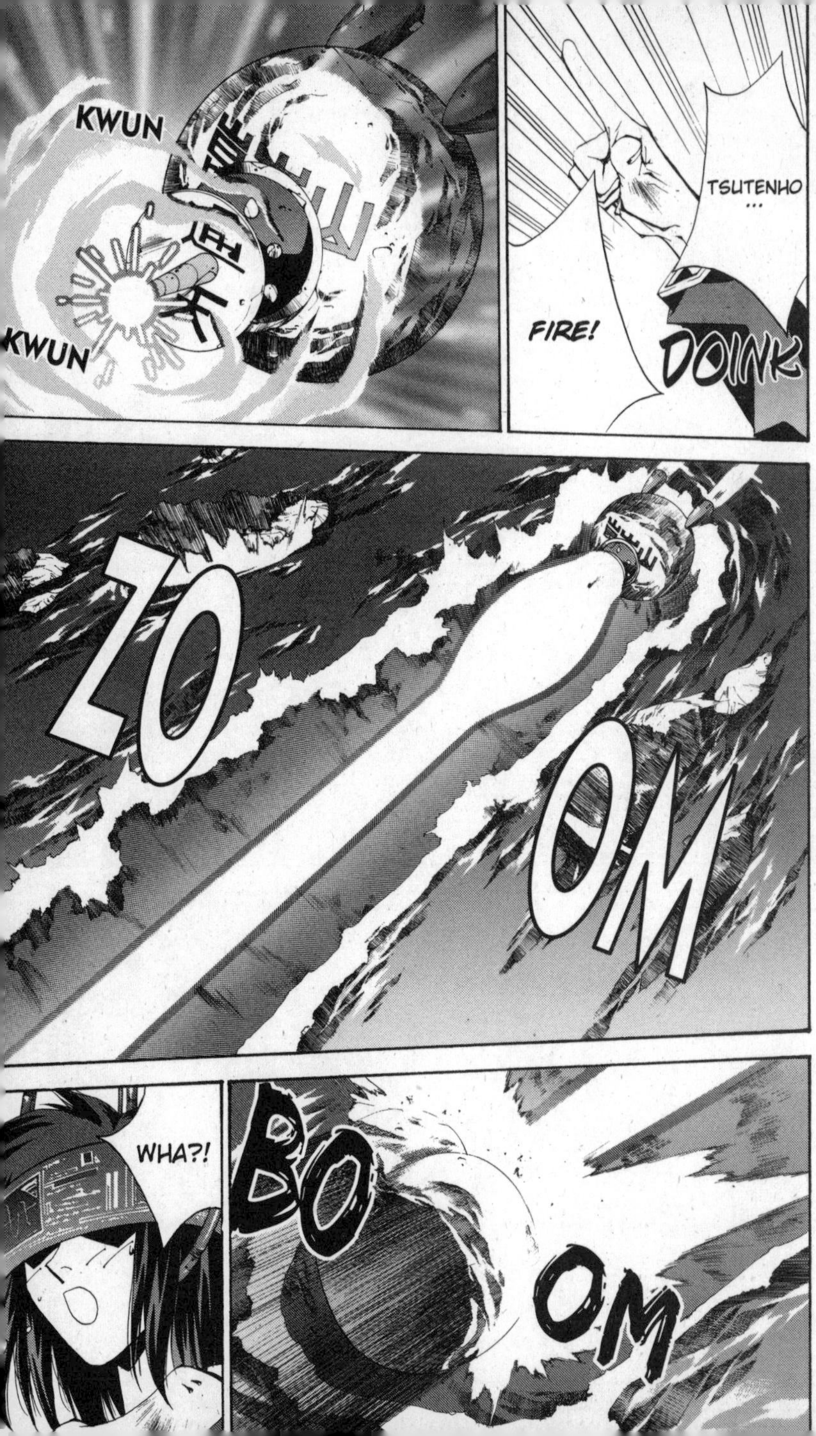
TSUTENHO ...
FIRE!
DOINK
KWUN
KWUN
ZOOM
BOOM
WHA?!

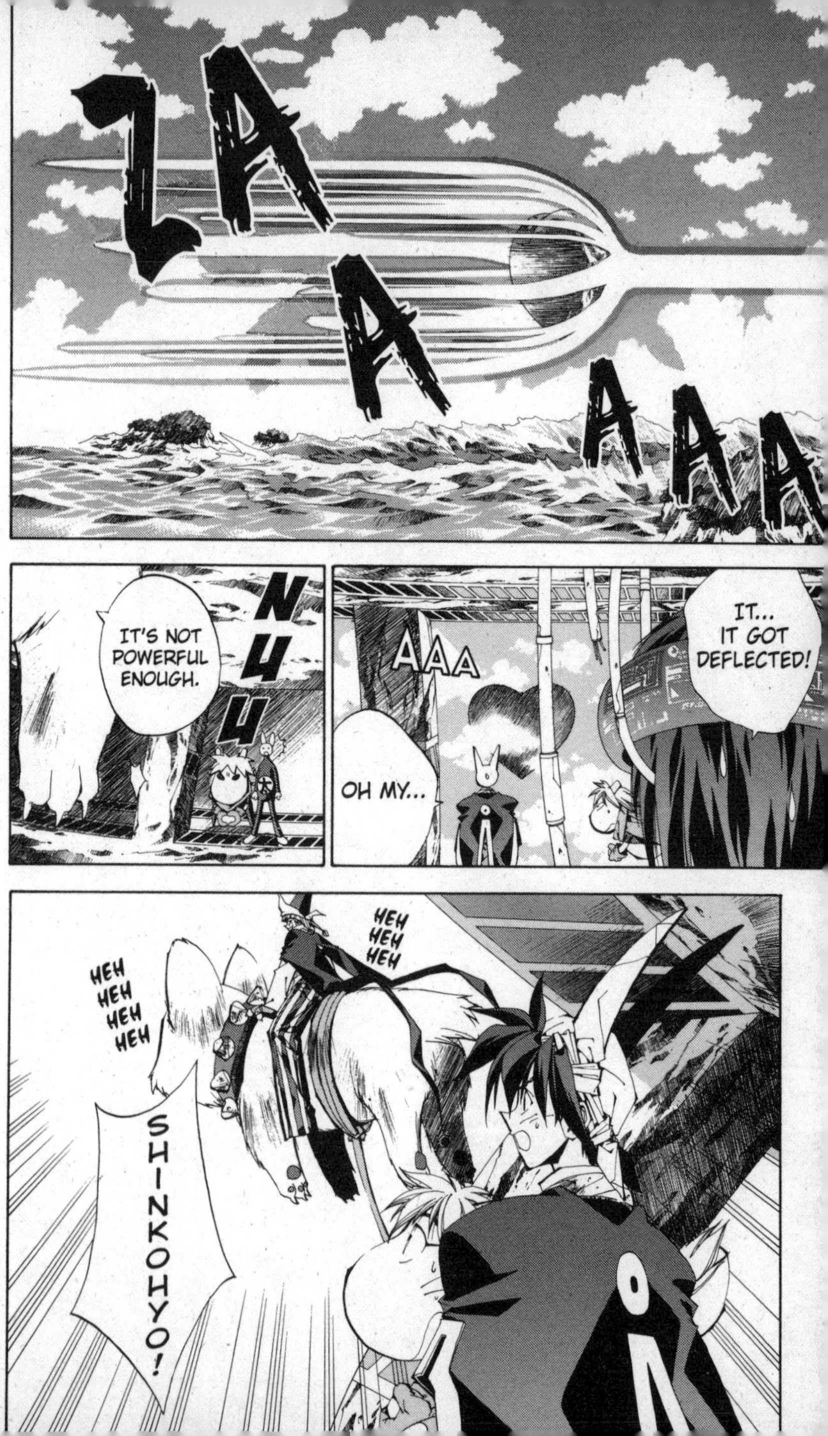
ZAAAAAA
IT... IT GOT DEFLECTED!
AAA
OH MY...
NUUU
IT'S NOT POWERFUL ENOUGH.
HEH HEH HEH
HEH HEH HEH HEH
SHINKOHYO!

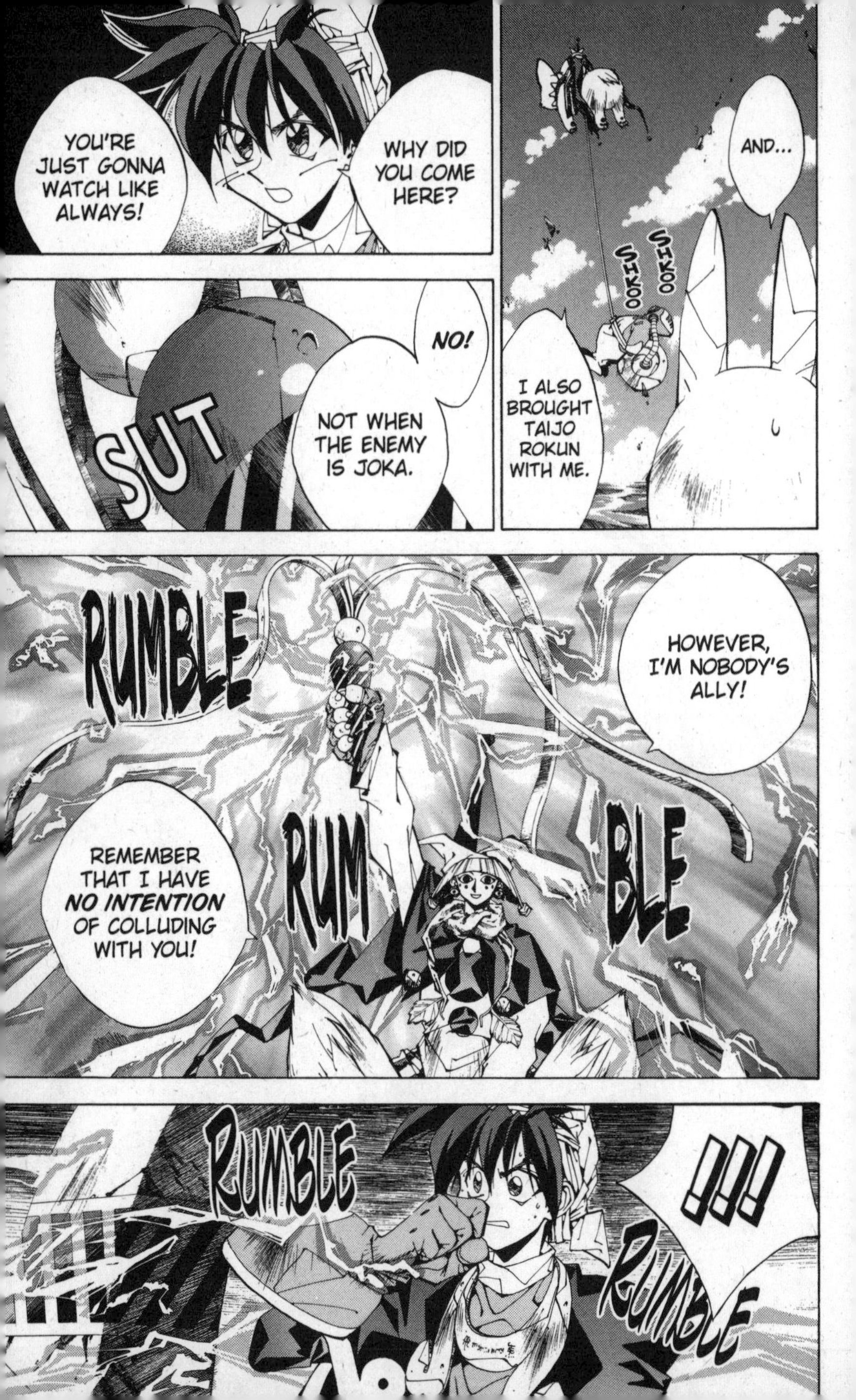
AND...
SHKOO
SHKOO
I ALSO BROUGHT TAIJO ROKUN WITH ME.
WHY DID YOU COME HERE?
YOU'RE JUST GONNA WATCH LIKE ALWAYS!
NO!
NOT WHEN THE ENEMY IS JOKA.
SUT
RUMBLE
HOWEVER, I'M NOBODY'S ALLY!
REMEMBER THAT I HAVE *NO INTENTION* OF COLLUDING WITH YOU!
RUMBLE
RUMBLE
!!!
RUMBLE

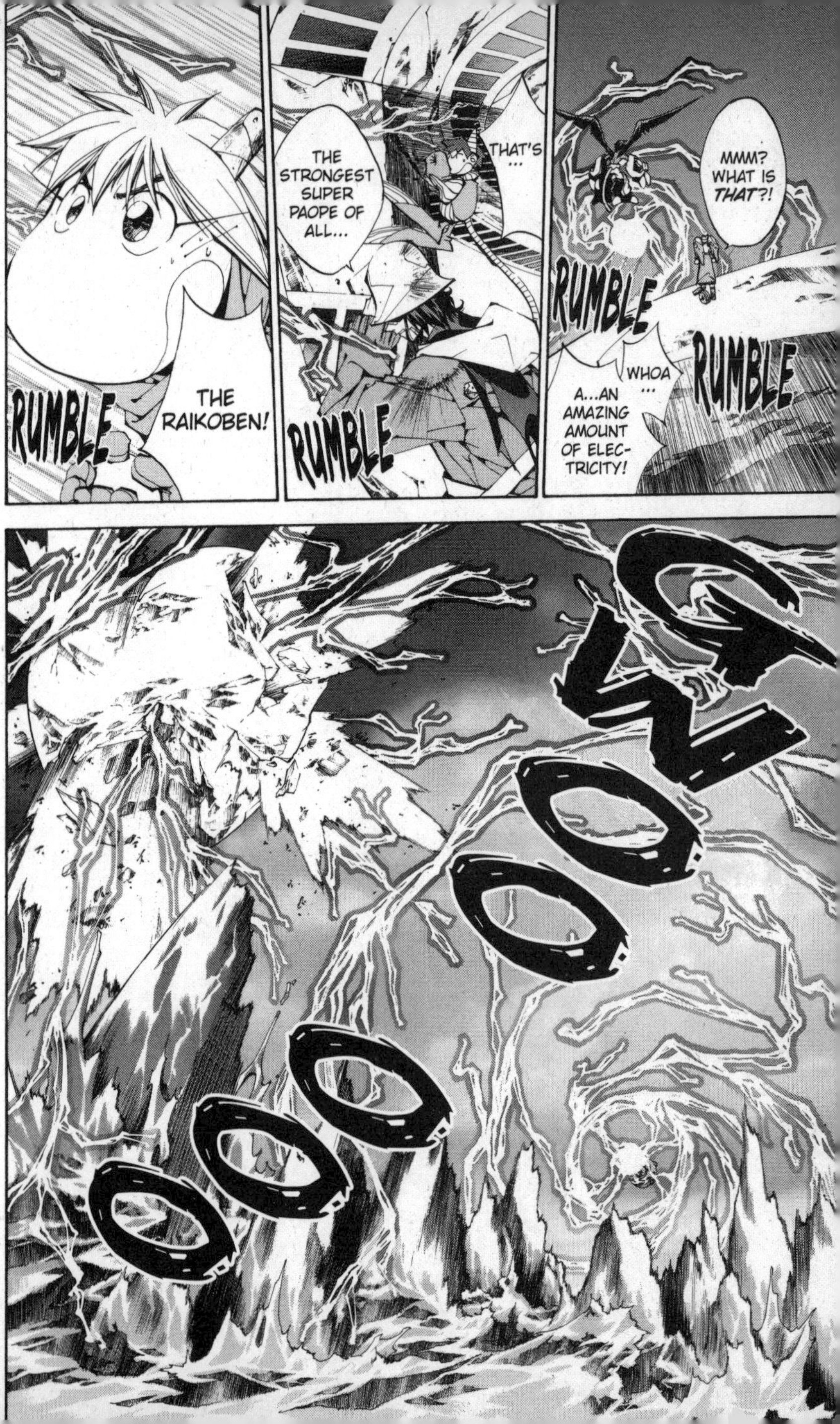
MMM? WHAT IS THAT?!
RUMBLE
RUMBLE
WHOA...
A...AN AMAZING AMOUNT OF ELEC-TRICITY!
THAT'S ...
THE STRONGEST SUPER PAOPE OF ALL...
RUMBLE
THE RAIKOBEN!
RUMBLE

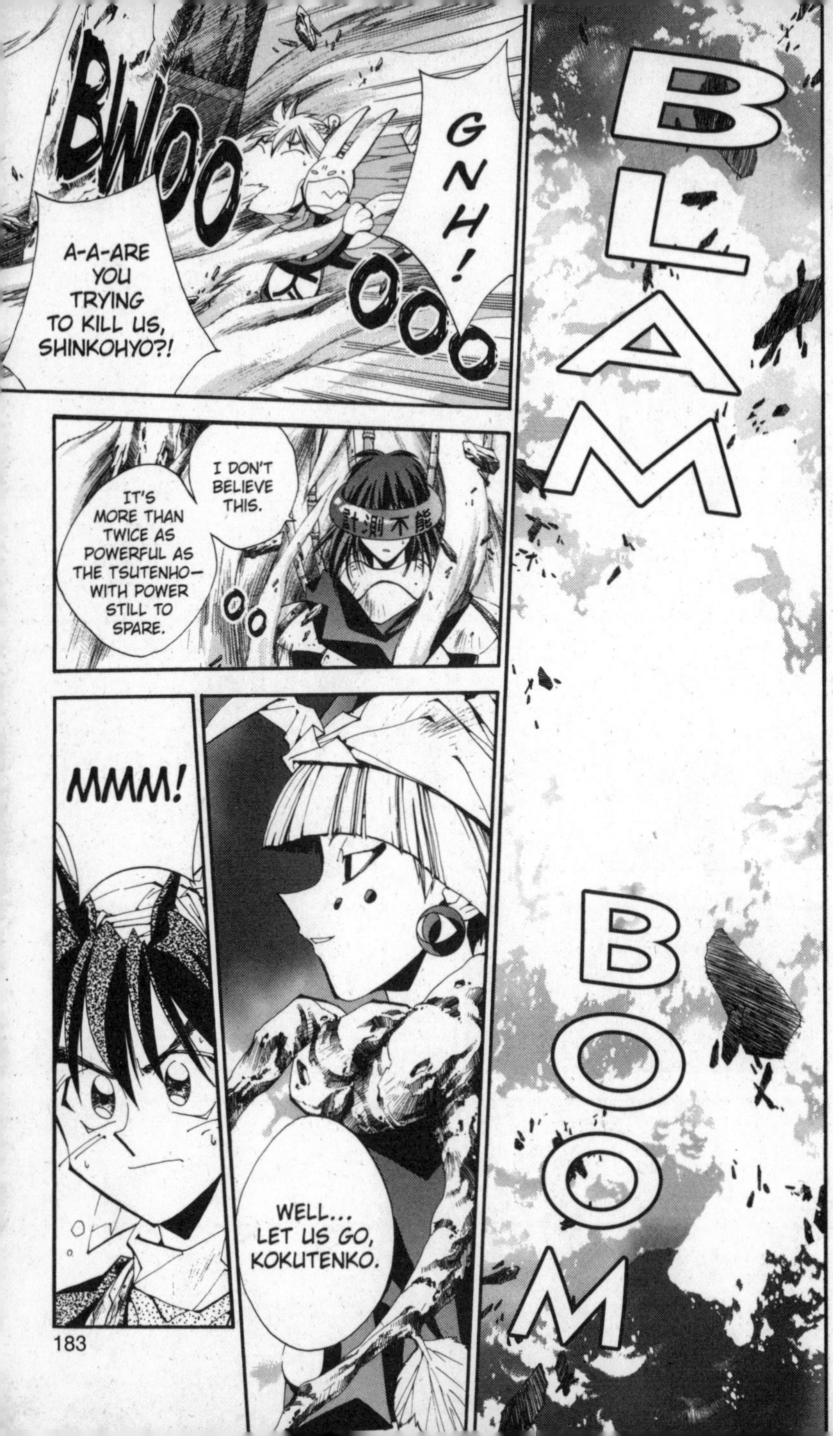
BLAM
BOOM
GNH!
BWOOOOOOOOO
A-A-ARE YOU TRYING TO KILL US, SHINKOHYO?!
I DON'T BELIEVE THIS.
IT'S MORE THAN TWICE AS POWERFUL AS THE TSUTENHO—WITH POWER STILL TO SPARE.
計測不能
WELL... LET US GO, KOKUTENKO.
MMM!

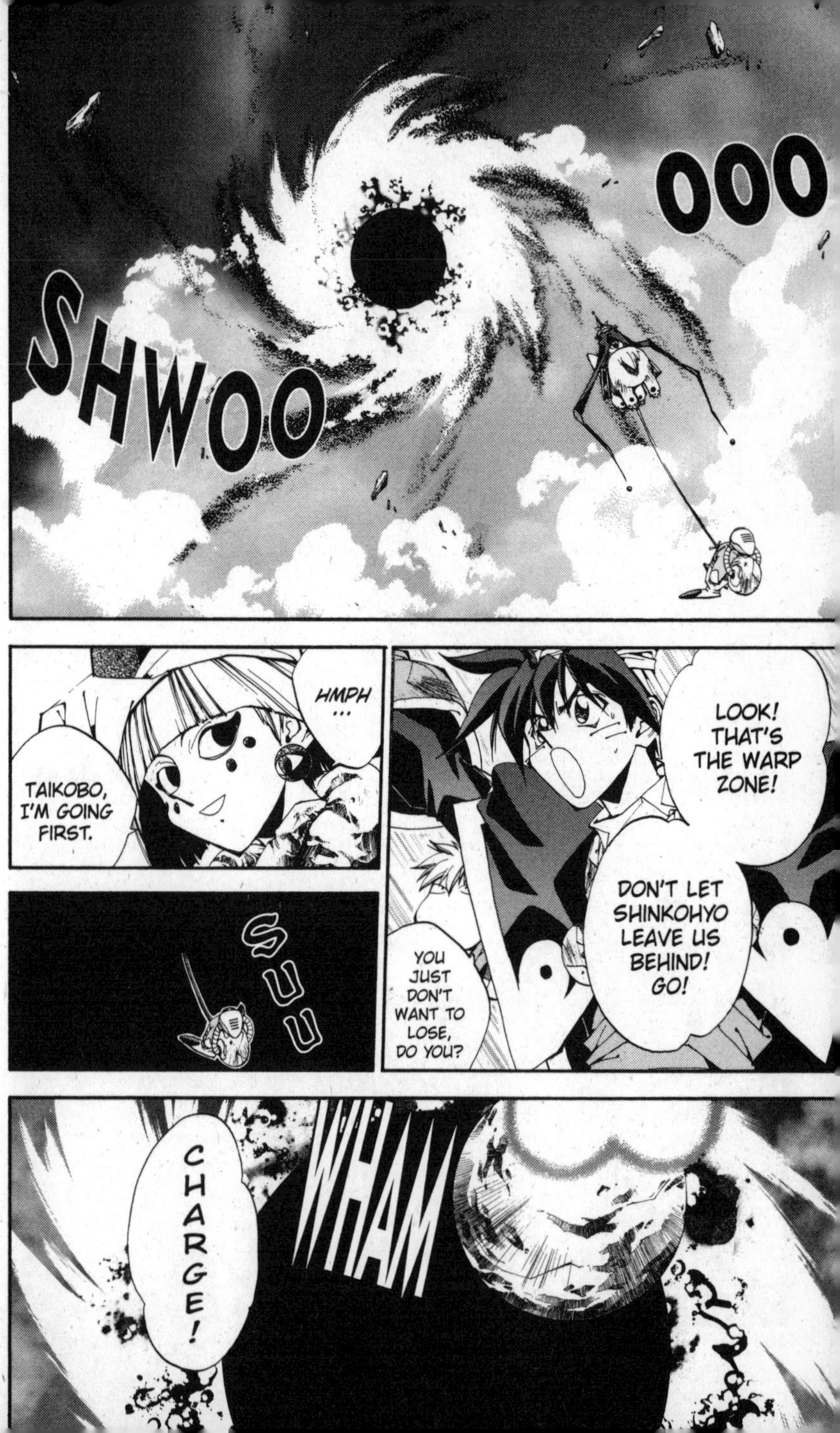
OOO
SHWOO
LOOK! THAT'S THE WARP ZONE!
DON'T LET SHINKOHYO LEAVE US BEHIND! GO!
YOU JUST DON'T WANT TO LOSE, DO YOU?
HMPH ...
TAIKOBO, I'M GOING FIRST.
SUUU
WHAM
CHARGE!

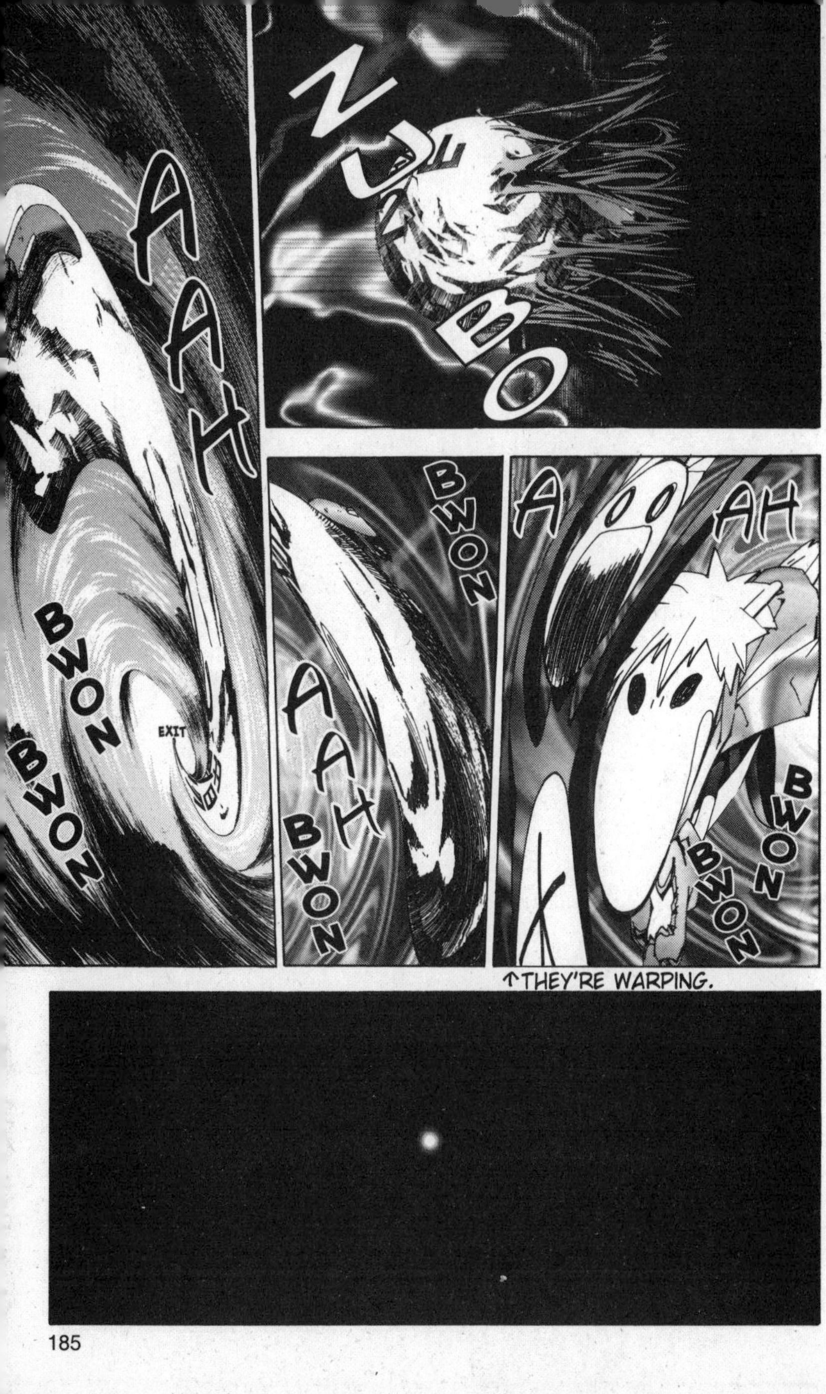
NUBO
AAAH
BWON BWON
EXIT
AH
A
BWON BWON
BWON
AAAH
BWON BWON
A
AH
BWON BWON
BWON BWON
↑THEY'RE WARPING.

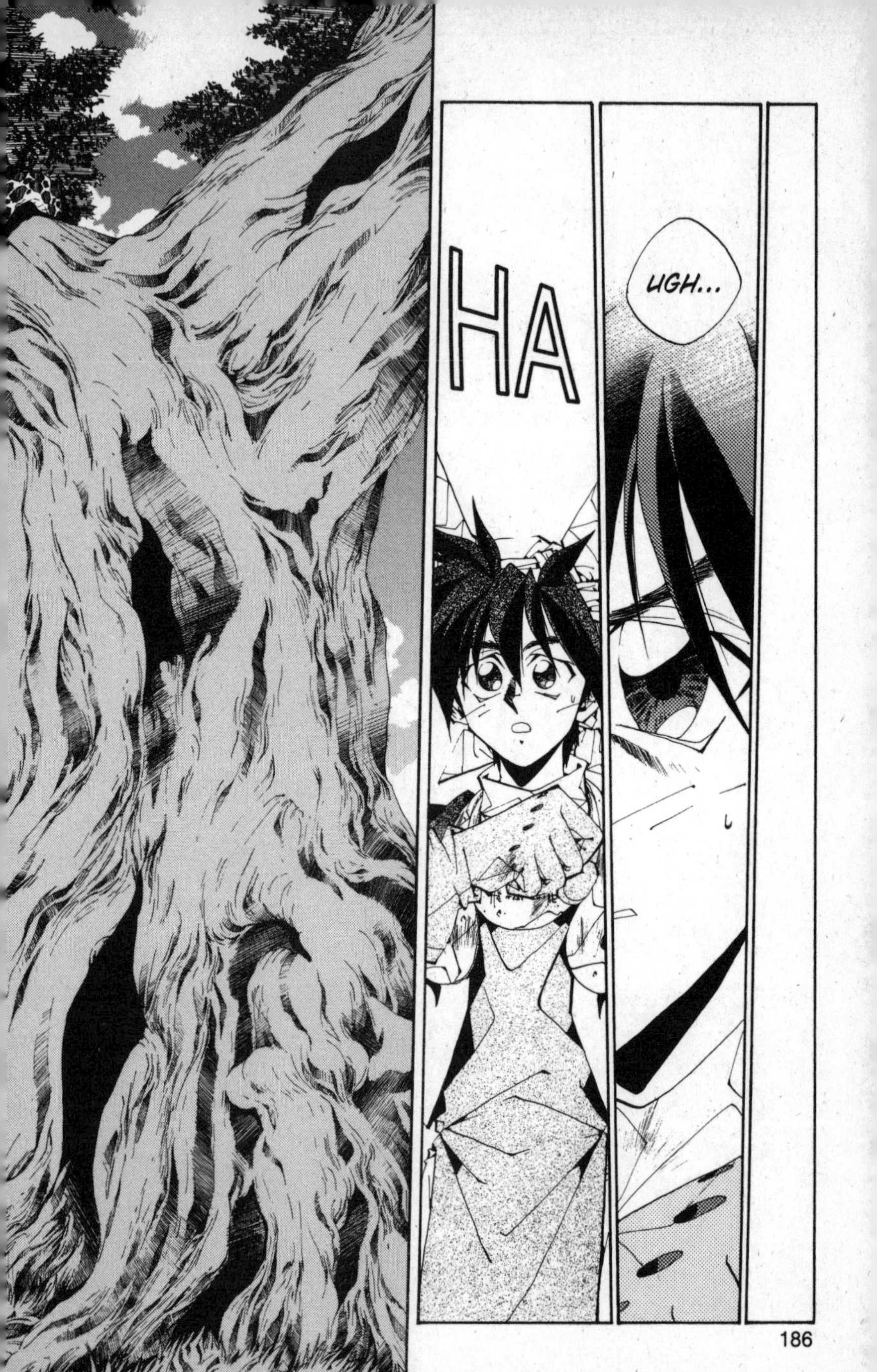
HA
UGH...

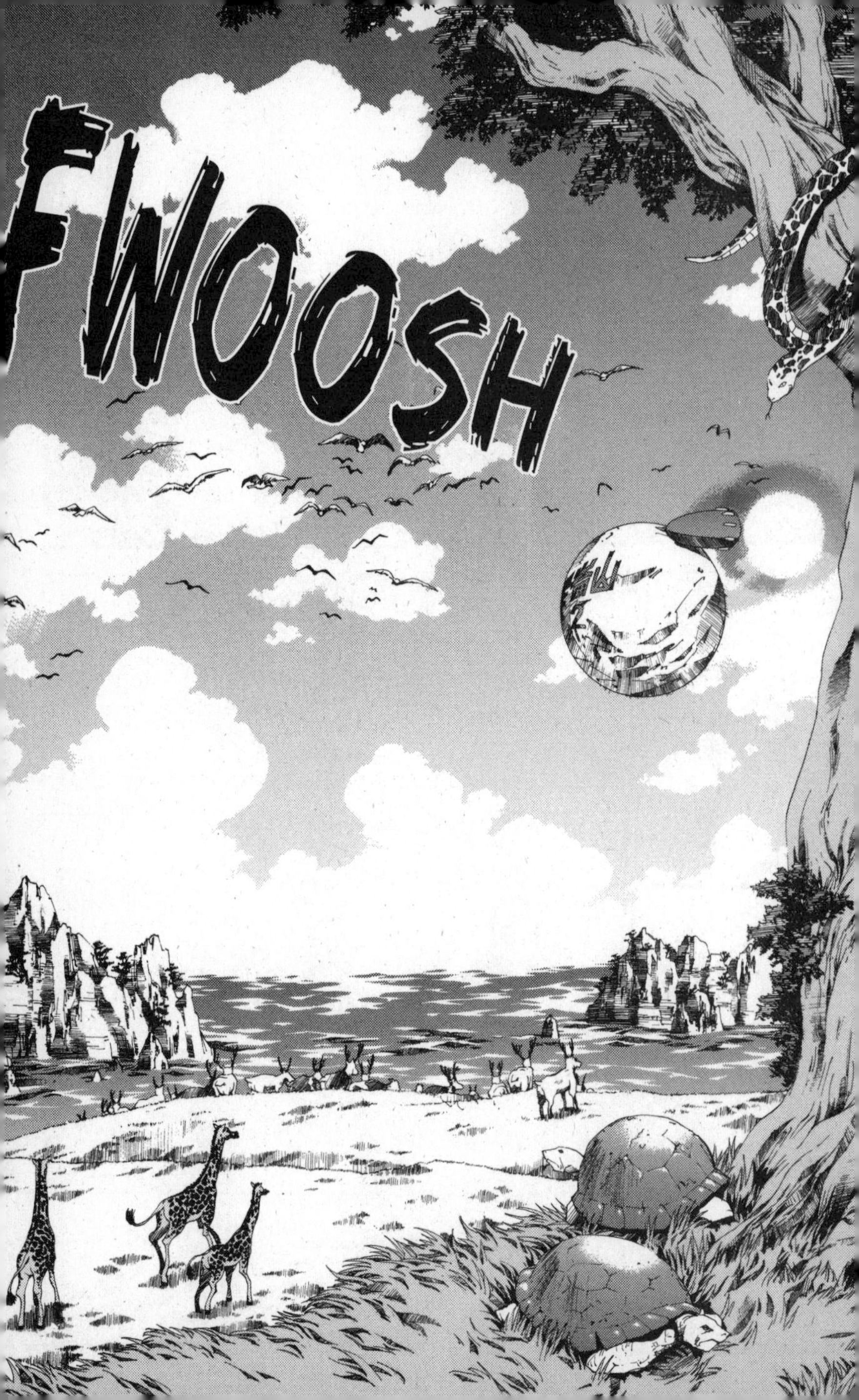
FWOOSH

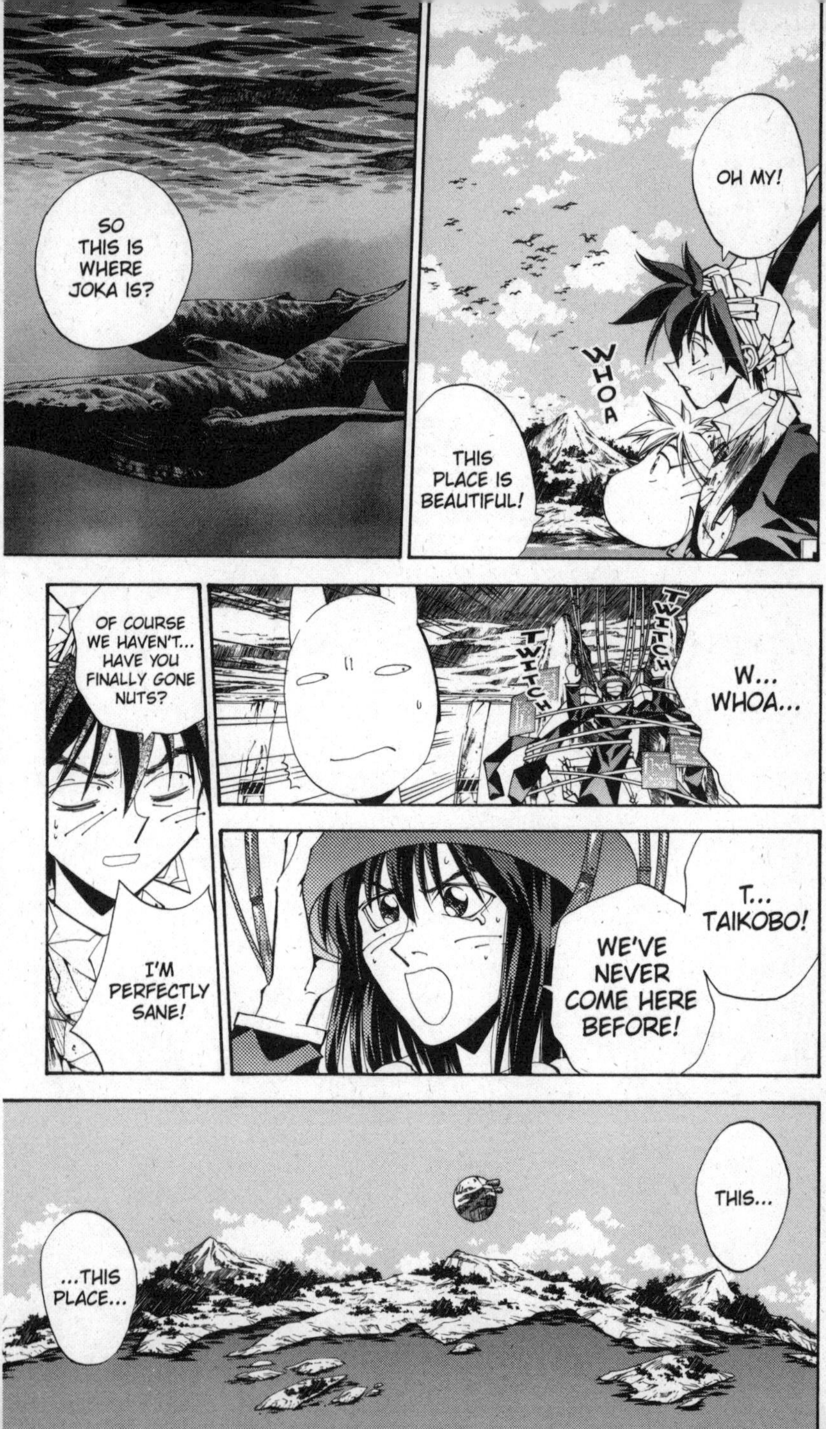
OH MY!
WHOA
THIS PLACE IS BEAUTIFUL!
SO THIS IS WHERE JOKA IS?
TWITCH
TWITCH
W... WHOA...
OF COURSE WE HAVEN'T... HAVE YOU FINALLY GONE NUTS?
T... TAIKOBO!
WE'VE NEVER COME HERE BEFORE!
I'M PERFECTLY SANE!
THIS...
...THIS PLACE...

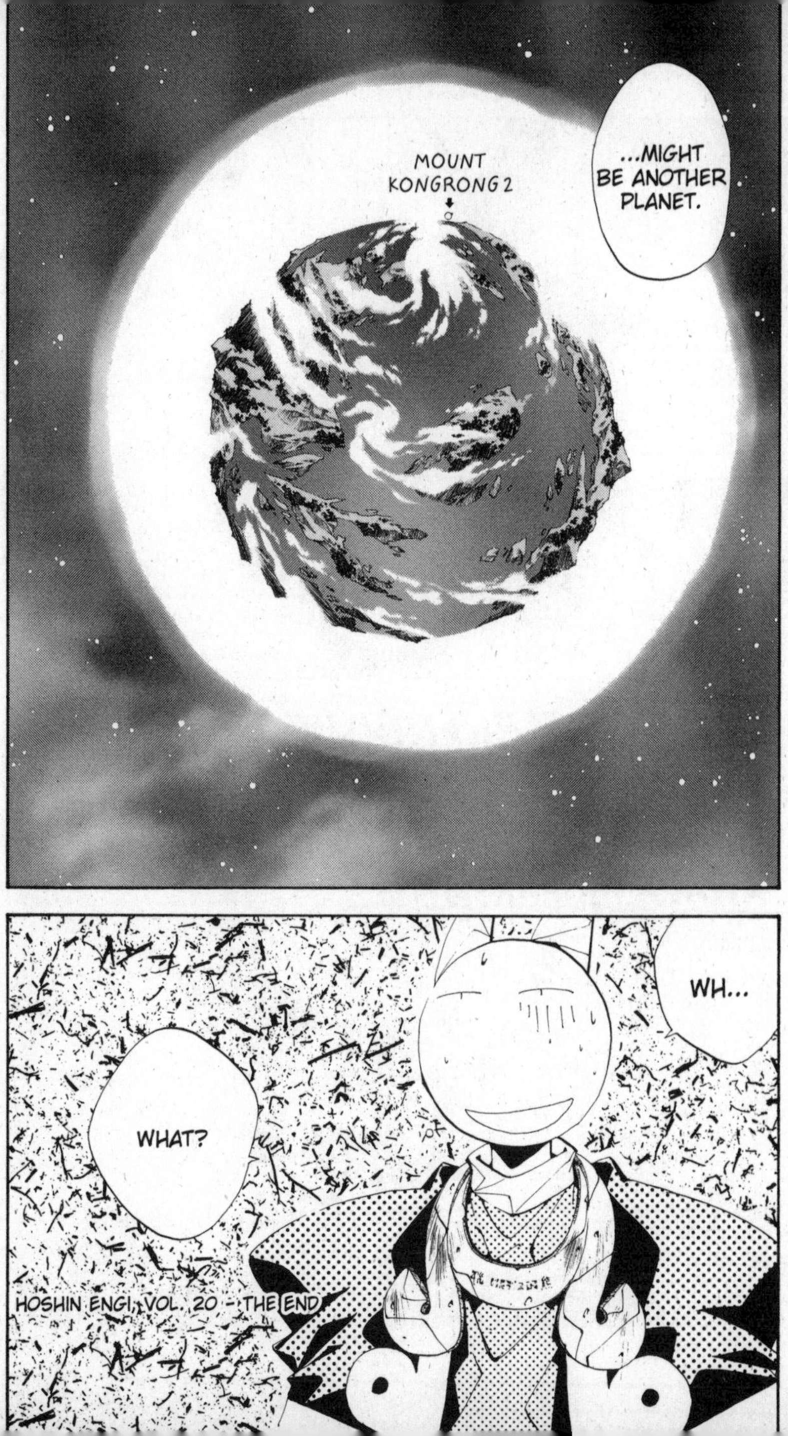
...MIGHT BE ANOTHER PLANET.
MOUNT KONGRONG 2
WH...
WHAT?
HOSHIN ENGI, VOL. 20 - THE END

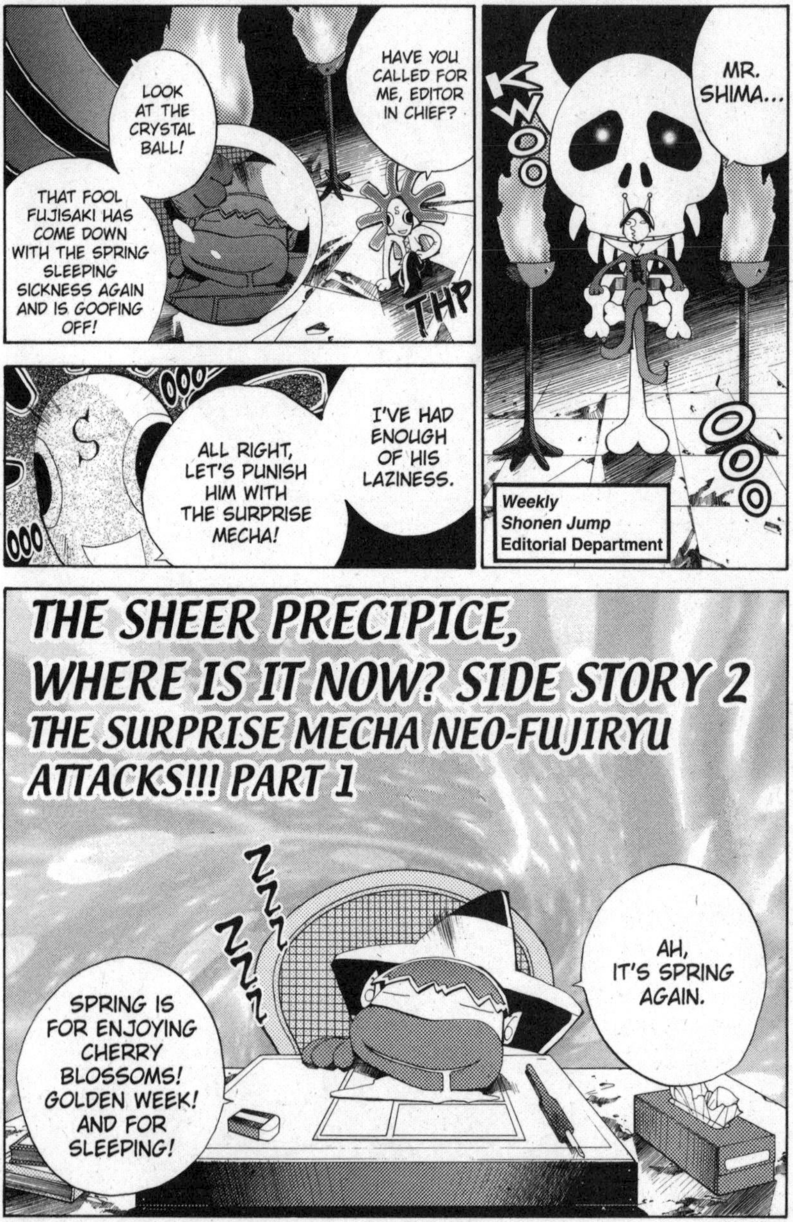
Weekly Shonen Jump Editorial Department
KWOO
OOO
MR. SHIMA...
HAVE YOU CALLED FOR ME, EDITOR IN CHIEF?
THP
LOOK AT THE CRYSTAL BALL!
THAT FOOL FUJISAKI HAS COME DOWN WITH THE SPRING SLEEPING SICKNESS AGAIN AND IS GOOFING OFF!
I'VE HAD ENOUGH OF HIS LAZINESS.
ALL RIGHT, LET'S PUNISH HIM WITH THE SURPRISE MECHA!
OOO
OOO
THE SHEER PRECIPICE, WHERE IS IT NOW? SIDE STORY 2
THE SURPRISE MECHA NEO-FUJIRYU ATTACKS!!! PART 1
AH, IT'S SPRING AGAIN.
ZZZ
ZZZ
SPRING IS FOR ENJOYING CHERRY BLOSSOMS! GOLDEN WEEK! AND FOR SLEEPING!

READ THIS WAY

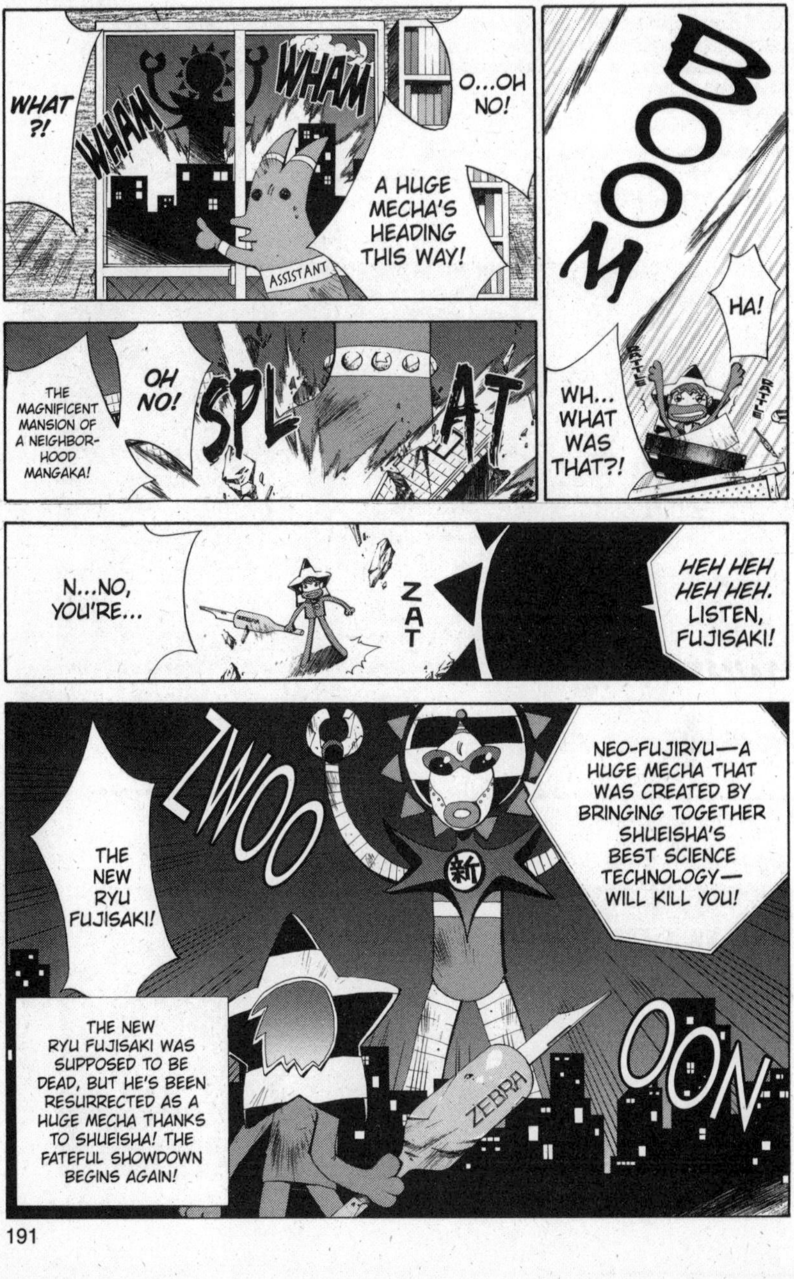

BOOM
HA!
RATTLE
RATTLE
WH... WHAT WAS THAT?!
WHAM
O...OH NO!
A HUGE MECHA'S HEADING THIS WAY!
WHAM
WHAT ?!
ASSISTANT
SPLAT
OH NO!
THE MAGNIFICENT MANSION OF A NEIGHBOR-HOOD MANGAKA!
HEH HEH HEH HEH. LISTEN, FUJISAKI!
ZAT
N...NO, YOU'RE...
NEO-FUJIRYU—A HUGE MECHA THAT WAS CREATED BY BRINGING TOGETHER SHUEISHA'S BEST SCIENCE TECHNOLOGY—WILL KILL YOU!
ZWOOOON
THE NEW RYU FUJISAKI!
新
ZEBRA
THE NEW RYU FUJISAKI WAS SUPPOSED TO BE DEAD, BUT HE'S BEEN RESURRECTED AS A HUGE MECHA THANKS TO SHUEISHA! THE FATEFUL SHOWDOWN BEGINS AGAIN!

Hoshin Engi: The Rank File!

You'll find as you read *Hoshin Engi* that there are titles and ranks that you are probably unfamiliar with. While it may seem confusing, there is an order to the madness that is pulled from ancient Chinese mythology, Japanese culture, other manga and, of course, the incredible mind of *Hoshin Engi* creator Ryu Fujisaki.

Where we think it will help, we give you a hint in the margin on the page the name appears. But in addition, here's a quick primer on the titles you'll find in *Hoshin Engi* and what they mean:

Japanese	Title	Job Description
武成王	Buseio	Chief commanding officer
宰相	Saisho	Premier
太師	Taishi	The king's advisor/tutor
大金剛	Dai Kongo	Great vassals
軍師	Gunshi	Military tactician
大諸侯	Daishoko	Great feudal lord
東伯侯	Tohakuko	Lord of the east region
西伯侯	Seihakuko	Lord of the west region
北伯侯	Hokuhakuko	Lord of the north region
南伯侯	Nanhakuko	Lord of the south region

Hoshin Engi: The Immortal File

Also, you'll probably find the hierarchy of the Sennin, Sendo and Doshi somewhat complicated. Here, we spell it out the easiest way possible!

Japanese	Title	Description
道士	Doshi	Someone training to become Sennin
仙道	Sendo	Used to describe both Sennin and Doshi
仙人	Sennin	Those who have mastered the way. Once you "go Sennin" you are forever changed.
妖孽	Yogetsu	A Yosei who can transform into a human
妖怪仙人	Yokai Sennin	A Sennin whose original form is not human
妖精	Yosei	An animal or object exposed to moonlight and sunlight for more than 1,000 years

Hoshin Engi: The Magical File

Paope (宝貝) are powerful magical items used by Sennin and Doshi. Sometimes they look like regular objects, like a veil or hat. These are just a few of the magical items, both paope and otherwise, that you'll encounter in *Hoshin Engi*!

Japanese	Magic	Description
打神鞭	Dashinben	Known as the God-Striking Whip, Taikobo's paope manipulates the air and wind.
霊獣	Reiju	A magical flying beast that Sennin and Doshi use for transportation and support. Taikobo's reiju is his pal Supu.
五光石	Gokoseki	A rock that changes the face of whomever it strikes into a "weirdly erotic-looking" face.
莫邪の宝剣	Bakuya no Hoken	Tenka's weapon, a light saber.
蒼巾力士	Sokin Rikishi	Kingo's version of the Kokin Rikishi.
通天砲	Tsutenho	Kingo Island's principal gun.
太極符印	Taikyoku Fuin	A paope that can manipulate physical objects on the elemental level.
仙桃エキス	Sento Extract	A medicine made from sento that helps restore your physical strength.
降魔杵	Gomasho	A mallet-like paope that becomes heavy the moment it hits the enemy. Can change shape as well.
究極黄河陣	Kyukyoku Kogajin	A dimension controlled by the Unsho Sisters. Enemies trapped in the dimension become as weak as insects.
エナジードレイン	Energy Drain	Adults of the Supu clan have the power to drain away paope energy and render the paope useless.
怠惰スーツ	Lazy Suit	An environmentally controlled protection suit that allows Taijo Rokun to sleep undisturbed for years.
玲瓏塔	Reiroto	A paope that uses the power of the wielder's grudge to trap the enemy and curse them to death.
補修宝貝	Repair Paope	A special paope that Taiitsu uses to repair Mount Kongrong 2.

Coming Next Volume:
History's Guidepost, Part 1

Taikobo and his allies arrive at the mysterious island of Horai,
where they are presented a challenge: seven of Taikobo's team
against seven of his nemesis Dakki's minions in single combat.
Will Taikobo's battle-weary comrades be able to prevail?

AVAILABLE DECEMBER 2010!

Read Any Good Books Lately?

Hoshin Engi is based on *Fengshen Yanji* (*The Creation of the Gods*, written in the 1500s by Xu Zhonglin), one of China's four classic fantastical novels of adventure, magic and mystery. The other three are *Saiyuki* (*Journey to the West* by Cheng'en Wu, late 1500s), *Sangokushi Engi* (*Romance of the Three Kingdoms* by Guanzhong Luo) and *Shui Hu Zhuan* (*Outlaws of the Marsh* by Shi Nai'an, mid-1500s).

Want to read these books? You can! They're all still in print, more than 500 years later!

These books are North American in-print editions only.

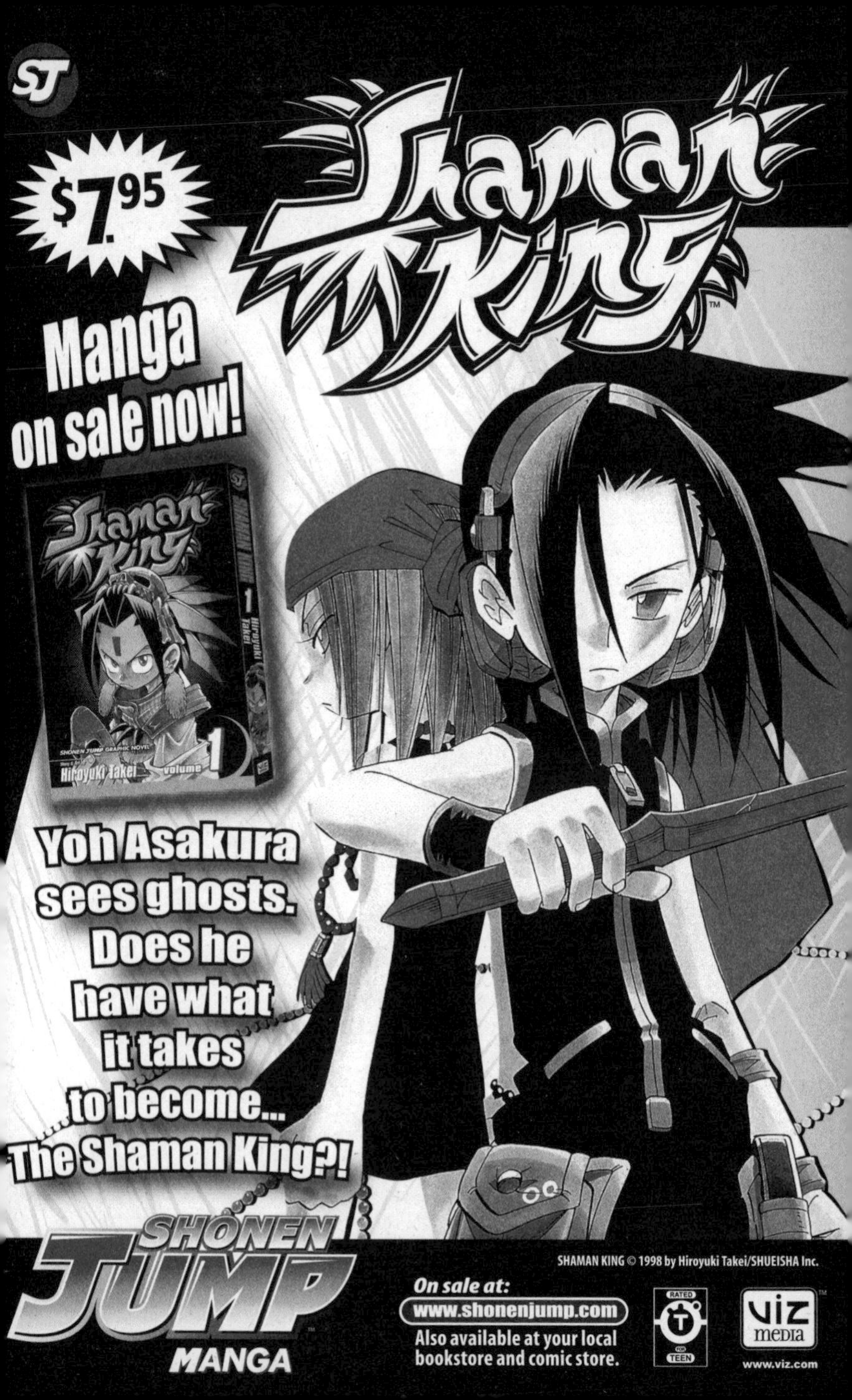
SJ
$7.95
Shaman King™
Manga on sale now!
Shaman King
1
Hiroyuki Takei
SHONEN JUMP GRAPHIC NOVEL
volume 1
Yoh Asakura sees ghosts. Does he have what it takes to become... The Shaman King?!
SHONEN JUMP MANGA
SHAMAN KING © 1998 by Hiroyuki Takei/SHUEISHA Inc.
On sale at:
www.shonenjump.com
Also available at your local bookstore and comic store.
RATED T FOR TEEN
VIZ media
www.viz.com

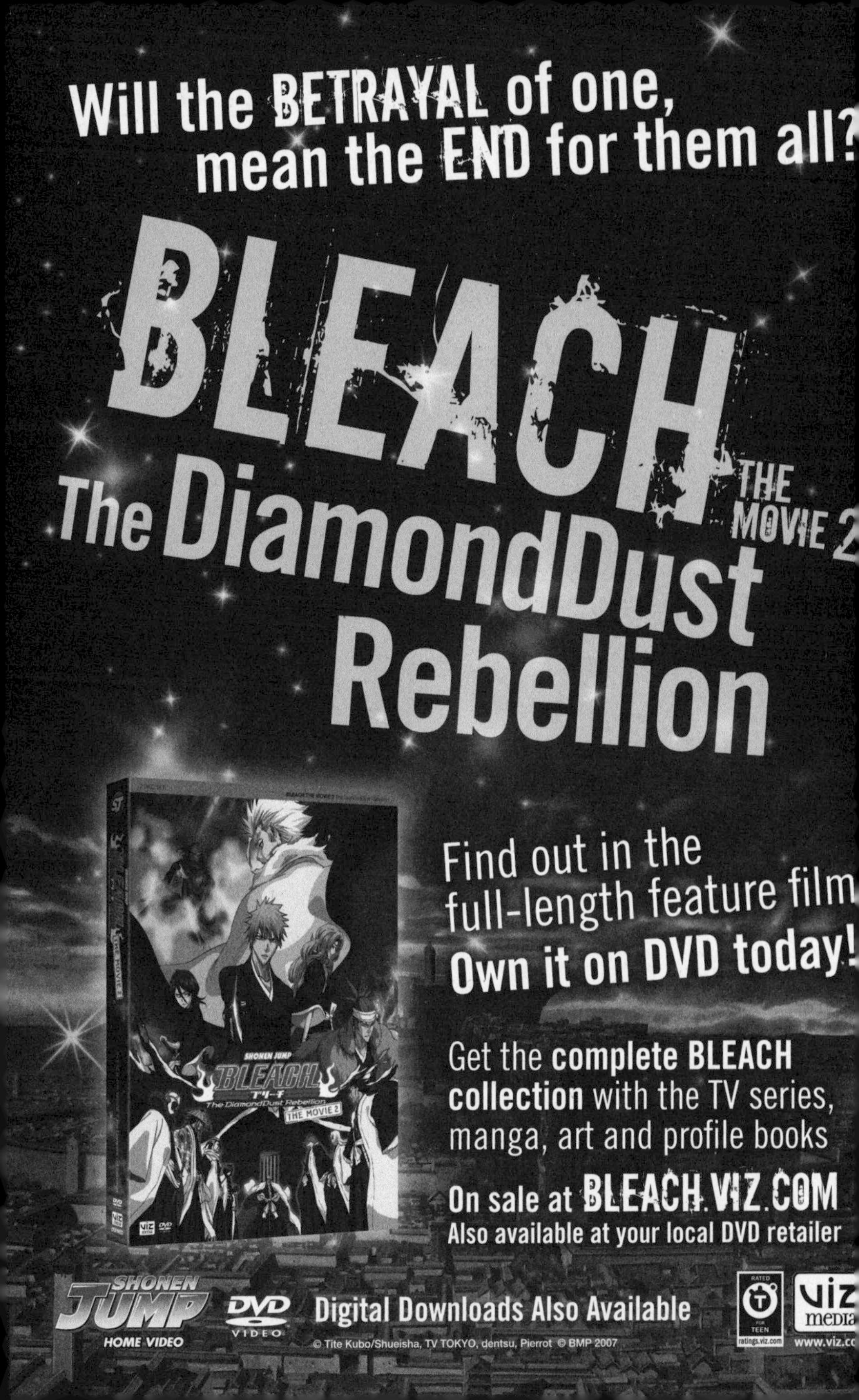
Will the BETRAYAL of one,
mean the END for them all?
BLEACH THE MOVIE 2
The DiamondDust Rebellion
SHONEN JUMP
BLEACH
ブリーチ
The DiamondDust Rebellion
THE MOVIE 2
Find out in the
full-length feature film
Own it on DVD today!
Get the complete BLEACH
collection with the TV series,
manga, art and profile books
On sale at BLEACH.VIZ.COM
Also available at your local DVD retailer
SHONEN JUMP HOME VIDEO
DVD VIDEO
Digital Downloads Also Available
© Tite Kubo/Shueisha, TV TOKYO, dentsu, Pierrot © BMP 2007
RATED T FOR TEEN ratings.viz.com
viz media
www.viz.co

THE WORLD'S MOST POPULAR MANGA

STORY AND ART BY
TITE KUBO

STORY AND ART BY
EIICHIRO ODA

STORY AND ART BY
HIROYUKI ASADA

JUMP INTO THE ACTION BY TELLING US WHAT YOU LOVE (AND WHAT YOU DON'T)

LET YOUR VOICE BE HEARD!

SHONENJUMP.VIZ.COM/MANGASURVEY

HELP US MAKE MORE OF THE WORLD'S MOST POPULAR MANGA!

www.viz.com